Parapsychology in
the Twenty-First Century

Parapsychology in the Twenty-First Century

Essays on the Future of Psychical Research

Edited by
MICHAEL A. THALBOURNE *and*
LANCE STORM

with a foreword by Brian D. Josephson

McFarland & Company, Inc., Publishers
Jefferson, North Carolina, and London

Library of Congress Cataloguing-in-Publication Data

Parapsychology in the twenty-first century : essays on the future of psychical research / edited by Michael A. Thalbourne and Lance Storm ; with a foreword by Brian D. Josephson.
    p.   cm.
    Includes bibliographical references and index.

    ISBN-13: 978-0-7864-1938-8
    softcover : 50# alkaline paper ♾

    1. Parapsychology — Research — Methodology.
I. Thalbourne, Michael A., 1955–   II. Storm, Lance, 1958–
BF1040.5.P36   2005
130'.9'051101 — dc22   2004024775

British Library cataloguing data are available

On the cover: foreground image ©2004 Brand X Pictures; background ©2004 PhotoSpin

Manufactured in the United States of America

McFarland & Company, Inc., Publishers
  Box 611, Jefferson, North Carolina 28640
  www.mcfarlandpub.com

To John Beloff

Contents

SECTION IV. SOCIOLOGICAL AND PHENOMENOLOGICAL ISSUES

Foreword

Brian D. Josephson

Trinity College, Cambridge, is an institution with a strong tradition of interest in the subject of parapsychology: most of the founding members of the Society for Psychical Research were fellows of Trinity, while the most recent past president of the Society, Professor Bernard Carr, is a past fellow of the college. It was there that I was introduced to the subject by George Owen, at the time a colleague of mine. Later, having moved in the meantime to Toronto, Owen invited me to a conference he was organizing on the subject of psychokinesis (i.e., the paranormal influence of mind on matter). I attended the conference, which included lectures as well as convincing demonstrations of psychokinesis.

Having first-hand contact with the ideas and the phenomena meant that I did not fall into the trap of simply dismissing paranormal claims out of hand, as many scientists do, and this contact led to my continuing interest in the field. Over the years, observational techniques have greatly improved, now being carried out in ways responding to the methodological criticisms of the past. These improvements have in no way made the results go away, as has happened with certain claims made by various sciences in the past, indicating that the phenomena are genuine rather than artifactual.

By rights, parapsychology should by now have become a conventional scientific field of research, and yet parapsychology's claims are still not generally accepted. Just as was the case with Alfred Wegener's hypothesis of continental drift,* there is great resistance to acceptance despite the strength of the evidence in favor of them. Wegener proposed his drift hypothesis in order to explain remarkable and otherwise inexplicable observations: the close fit of the contours of the South American and African continents; coincidences in the fossil record in the corresponding

*For a good summary of the history, see http://pubs.usgs.gov/publications/text/historical. html.

1

coastal areas; and the existence of coal deposits containing fossils of tropical plants in Antarctica. In the absence of any explanation for the very large forces that would be needed to move the continents in the way proposed, this compelling body of evidence did not sway the scientific community, though after Wegener's death, further evidence led to a gradual change in opinion and ultimate acceptance of his ideas.

The fact that so many scientists are not swayed by the evidence for the paranormal — the situation parapsychology finds itself in today — just as continental drift did in the past, is not primarily a matter of science. Emotions are involved also, a facet of scientific praxis not commonly acknowledged. Michel Schiff put it well in the introduction to his book *The Memory of Water*: "'Homeopathic dilutions' and 'memory of water' are two expressions capable of turning a peaceful and intelligent person into a violently irrational one."

On the parapsychology front, my daring to mention telepathy in a contribution commissioned by the UK Royal Mail as part of a brochure accompanying its Nobel Centenary stamp collection produced similar responses from scientists responding to requests for comments from the science correspondent of *The Observer*, such as that I had "hoodwinked [Royal Mail] into supporting ideas that are complete nonsense," that "a lot of [US scientists] would be very angry" if the US Post Office did something similar, and that a few Nobel laureates "go off the rails" after getting their prize.

The reader may be thinking that just possibly in this case the critics might be quite right, even though in the case of continental drift time proved the general skeptical response to have been seriously mistaken. My response to this suggestion, which is not a priori unreasonable, is just to say "feel the quality" of the arguments of the critical ones. It is a kind of hobby of mine to review books by "experts" who denounce beliefs such as a belief in telepathy. It is an interesting challenge in such cases to see how fervent belief is led astray from proper argument, that, for example, what the jacket of such a book calls a "devastating critique" of the paranormal turns out to be nothing of the kind, or one again that each of "twelve reasons to remain doubtful about the existence of psi" (from a recently published debate about the subject) turn out to be rather poor reasons. The skeptics are uncomfortable about ideas such as telepathy, and unfortunately being uncomfortable is not an ideal condition to be in when trying to do science.

Science is not about being comfortable. It is about acting rationally, in accordance with the procedures for determining the truth that have been established over the course of time by scientists. The capacity to be self-critical is one of the key necessities for good science, and I welcome this book, authored by a collection of experts in the field. It seems to me that it involves genuine science in a way that the output of the debunkers typically does not. I believe that those already familiar with the subject, as well as those unfamiliar with it, will find much of interest in it.

Preface

Michael A. Thalbourne and Lance Storm

Rational or irrational, the turn of the century, and in our case the turn of the millennium, causes many of us to take stock of what we have learned, and to look ahead with hope at the future. Like all human endeavors, parapsychology — the science of the paranormal — has entered the twenty-first century. To help us examine the future of psychical research at this juncture, we have solicited the learned opinions of 14 parapsychological authors, and offered our own as well. We also recognize the erudite views of Nobel prize–winning physicist Professor Brian D. Josephson, who wrote our Foreword.

Overall, the advantage in a book like this is that it does not present the overarching viewpoint of a single author. Instead, through the wide-ranging interests and expertise of its contributors, it is representative of the field in general.

The main purpose of the book is to explore future directions of parapsychology, though reports of the current status of the field were considered crucial to the overall feel of the book. *Parapsychology in the Twenty-First Century* is unlike a number of books on parapsychology currently available because it does not focus exclusively on past and present achievements, but is oriented towards the future of parapsychology.

Readers might like to know that we have gathered in authors from all over the world. We could never have hoped to get truly comprehensive, or even adequate, coverage of the field had we done otherwise. Parapsychology is an international affair; accordingly, this book is cosmopolitan, in the sense that its approach is not only broad-based, but also multi-ethnic. By that we mean the techniques, protocols, and theories discussed herein have transcended language barriers. Although the book is written in English, it includes contributors whose native tongues are French, German, and Dutch.

Perhaps most importantly, we cross the gender divide, and by so doing, recognize the theoretical and experimental contributions of three outstanding women in the field, each of whom deserves special mention: Christine Hardy, Pamela Rae Heath, and Fiona Steinkamp.

Because the contributors have focused on their areas of expertise, readers can explore research in specific areas of paranormal studies, such as altered states of consciousness (Adrian Parker), meta-analysis (Fiona Steinkamp), and brain function (Vernon M. Neppe and John Palmer). New and innovative approaches to psi are covered, such as Suitbert Ertel's ball-drawing experiment, Michael A. Thalbourne's theory of "psychopraxia," and numerous recommendations for psi researchers (Stanley Krippner and Gerd H. Hövelmann).

The book also includes important chapters on sociological and phenomenological issues from Robin Wooffitt, James McClenon, Pamela Rae Heath, and Lance Storm. A number of other highly skilled and highly regarded professionals have made contributions to the book, including Dean Radin, Robert L. Morris, William Braud, and Christine Hardy.

Altogether, *Parapsychology in the Twenty-First Century* represents psychical research at the razor's edge of scientific investigation. We intend this book for academics and laypersons alike.

On a more personal note, we extend our sincerest thanks to our 15 contributors for their time and dedication to this project.

Section I

GENERAL ISSUES

1

What's Ahead?

*Dean Radin**

In this chapter, Dr. Dean Radin looks back in time to Henry
Sidgwick's lament about the nonacceptance of psi, to the possibly illegal misappropriation of the Thomas Welton Stanford
Fellowship in Psychical Research, and the misrepresentation
of results from it, and links all this to possible futures for psi,
some rather frightening. He opines that psi will eventually be
accepted and assimilated in science and elsewhere, despite
current opposition to it. (Editors)

Imagine a future in which psi phenomena are studied in every major
university without controversy, and where we see rates of progress in this
domain similar to those observed in other scientific disciplines. It is tempting to imagine that such a world will arise because of an overwhelming
mass of experimental data, perhaps combined with an astonishingly successful new theory. Someone will publish this data and theory in a major
professional journal, and then the scientific press will report, "Well, I guess
all those obstinate skeptics were wrong. But of course *we* knew you were
on the right track all along."

Back in the real world, we know that science does not work this way.
The scientific enterprise consists of far more than data and theory. Equally
important is the social context in which science is embedded. This social

*This chapter is a revision of the author's Presidential Address to the Parapsychologi-
cal Association on August 5, 1999, at Stanford University.

context determines to a very large extent not the nature of truth (as best as we can discern it), but what is *allowed* to be studied. Academic taboos and the sociology of science have extensive literatures, but we can easily understand the power of social context without delving into the scholarly literature.

A Phish Tale

Once upon a time we all lived in a dry, desert land far from the ocean. Everyone in this land knows that salty water is poisonous, so all sober-minded intellectuals are taught to dismiss tales about creatures living in the salt-filled ocean as preposterous fantasies promoted by the naïve and the fraudulent.

Unfortunately, in spite of what everyone knows, the stories persist. And not just as historical legends, but as contemporary sightings. We are puzzled by the paradox between what everyone knows to be so, and what people keep reporting, so we decide to see for ourselves if the stories are true. After a long journey, we reach the ocean at the edge of the desert. After carefully watching the surface of the water for a while, we are amazed to find that sometimes creatures do indeed spontaneously jump out of the water. We are motivated to investigate in more detail, so we craft a crude net to try to grab some of those ocean creatures.

After much trial and error, and fending off armchair critics on the shore who have nothing better to do than laugh at our efforts, we are lucky enough to catch a few creatures we will call "phish." We don't catch them every time, and they often slip away from our grasp, but we do catch phish often enough to confirm that what everyone knows is actually incorrect: some creatures *do* live in salty water. With our heads spinning with wonder and delight, we bring these phish home to show to our colleagues.

The end of this story is all too predictable. Even with phish at hand, our discovery does not fit in with accepted wisdom. Since everyone knows that phish tales are mere children's stories, any evidence we offer is guaranteed to be perceived as insufficient, flawed, or fraudulent. It simply does not matter how good our phishing skills and nets are, or how many phish we catch, or how long the legends have persisted.

So how do we break out of this frustrating situation? Three things must occur. First, more solid evidence must be provided; we need robust phish that we can put on display in a petting zoo on the White House lawn. Second, persuasive theories and models must be proposed and tests that explain the existence of phish must be conducted. And third, pressure must be applied to soften powerful societal and scientific prejudices about the existence of salt-water creatures in general.

Returning now to psi phenomena, is there any reason to believe that the world is moving in directions that will eventually accommodate psi research in new and more comfortable ways? I believe the answer is yes, partially because of the excellent work engaged in by researchers in this field, and because science in general is quickly expanding into domains thought impossible just a few decades ago. And more fundamentally yes, because truth is not necessarily that which is easily demonstrable. Instead, truth is that which is *inescapable*. Because it is inescapable, history tells us with high certainty that if psi is real — and I believe the data inform us that it is— then science will eventually and invariably transition psi from the frontier to the mainstream.

When that happens, will the Parapsychological Association serve any purpose? When might such a transition take place? And what will the rest of science look like then? While no one knows yet, I do think it is important to try to visualize that future, because otherwise we are guaranteed to trip upon it accidentally rather than help influence what actually occurs. To help ground my speculations, I will begin by discussing some history.

The Past

Over a century ago, on July 17, 1882, in London, England, Henry Sidgwick was the first president of the Society for Psychical Research (SPR). Sidgwick was a Cambridge professor of ethics and a prominent moral philosopher. The occasion was the first Presidential Address to the SPR. To show how much some things have remained the same, here is what Sidgwick said at that very first meeting:

> It is a scandal that the dispute as to the reality of [thought transference] should still be going on, that so many competent witnesses should have declared their belief in them, that so many others should be profoundly interested in having the question determined, and yet that the educated world, as a body, should still be simply in the attitude of incredulity [Sidgwick 1883, p. 8].

> Scientific incredulity has been so long in growing, and has so many and so strong roots, that we shall only kill it, if we are able to kill it at all ... by burying it alive under a heap of facts. ... [We] should not wrangle too much with incredulous outsiders about the conclusiveness of any one [study], but trust to the mass of evidence for conviction. ... We must drive the objector into the position of being forced either to

admit the phenomena as inexplicable, at least by him [*sic*], or to accuse the investigators either of lying or cheating or of a blindness or forgetfulness incompatible with any intellectual condition except absolute idiocy..." [Sidgwick 1883, p. 12].

Sidgwick then concluded, "I am glad to say that [an acceptable level of evidence] ... has been satisfactorily attained in the investigation of thought-reading ..." (Sidgwick 1883, p. 12). He said this in 1882, and yet it is still commonplace today to see papers published questioning the very existence of telepathy. In my opinion, when considering the compound evidence for telepathy, starting with the earliest experiments on thought-reading in the 1880s, combined with the ESP card tests of the 1930s to 1960s, the dream telepathy studies of the 1960s and 1970s, and the ganzfeld studies from the 1970s through the present, this body of evidence is so overwhelming by any reasonable scientific standard that to continue to entertain the null hypothesis that *nothing* interesting is going on is, to borrow a phrase from Sidgwick, a case of "absolute idiocy."

However, it also points out that unlike Sidgwick's suggested strategy, we cannot expect to bury skepticism alive under a heap of facts, because we have been building mountains of facts for some time and many scientists still remain unconvinced. Instead, skepticism is won over as with any other uncomfortable but true idea, like those who vigorously opposed relativity theory or continental drift: because skeptics die out, and because persuasive explanations are developed, and because the world catches up to the idea.

A Second Cautionary Tale

I will now jump 30 years, to 1911, and discuss a cautionary tale that teaches us another lesson. It is a tale of how somewhere, something went terribly wrong. The research behind this story was documented by Fred Dommeyer, a professor of philosophy at San Jose State, who was also a lifelong student of parapsychology (Dommeyer 1975).

Thomas Welton Stanford was born in 1832, one of eight children. His older brother, Leland Stanford, founded Stanford University, which was named after his son, Leland Stanford Jr. Leland Jr. tragically died as a teenager after contracting typhoid fever. Thomas Welton Stanford was a lifelong fan of spiritualism. In 1911, Thomas Stanford gave £20,000 (about $50,000 at the time) "to a fund which shall be known as the 'Psychic Fund'" (Dommeyer 1975, p. 178).

This fund was to be used "exclusively and wholly for the investigation and advancement of the knowledge of psychic phenomena and the occult sciences ..." (Dommeyer 1975, p. 179). The Board of Directors of Stanford University immediately agreed to use this gift for these purposes, as the university was not yet rich enough to turn down such a princely sum. About 20 years later, Thomas Stanford died, and his will left an additional $526,000 (worth about $6 million in 2003 dollars) to a special endowment which "shall forever be kept intact, ... wholly and exclusively ... to the general advancement or development of psychical or psychological science" (Dommeyer 1975, p. 180). It was clear from Stanford's enthusiasm for spiritualism and his original gift that he meant psychic research in the parapsychological sense, and not psychology in the modern academic sense.

The first Thomas Welton Stanford Psychical Research fellow at Stanford University was a man named John Edgar Coover. He held the chair from 1912 to 1937. After Coover, no one was ever permanently appointed to this research fellowship again. Most of Coover's psychic research was reported in one book published in 1917 (one wonders what he was doing for the next 20 years to honor Thomas Welton Stanford's bequest). Coover reported in his book that he found completely negative results. In particular, he said he found no evidence for telepathy because the results of his tests "did not exceed the chosen chance limit" (Dommeyer 1975, p. 185).

This sounds pretty bad, and on the surface it provides a plausible reason for why Stanford University let this fellowship descend into obscurity. That is, until you learn that Coover's definition of a "chosen chance limit" was a p-value of 2×10^{-5}. Coover's actual telepathy tests resulted in a two-tailed p-value of 0.006, a highly significant result by today's standards. And yet, he claimed that this result was insufficient to provide evidence for telepathy (Coover, 1917).

What motivated Coover to dismiss what we would accept today as a solidly significant result? One would think that something as interesting as telepathy would have prompted Coover to immediately escalate his research. He had the financial endowment, the deep personal interest of a major benefactor, the personnel, and the facilities. So what went wrong?

What went wrong was that instead of taking this incredible opportunity, a case of absolute idiocy intervened. When Coover retired in 1937, the president of Stanford University, Ray Lyman Wilbur, along with the chairman of the Psychology Department at the time, jointly decided to redefine the purpose of the Psychical Research Fellowship. Now it was to include not only the study of mediumistic phenomena, telepathy and clairvoyance, but also hypnosis, subliminal perception, and "research with electrical potentials of the central nervous system" (Dommeyer 1975)—

that is, what we would today call the neurosciences. These are all perfectly fine topics of study, but the redefinition of "psychical research" was so broad that it effectively defeated the purpose of Thomas Stanford's endowment.

As far as we know, no attorneys were ever consulted about the legality of changing the definition of this endowment, which raises the possibility that this was an illegal appropriation of a rather substantial sum. I am sure that Stanford's president and the Psychology Department chairman believed they were acting in good faith, but what caused them to imagine that this was the right thing to do?

Before I answer, I might mention that by a curious twist of fate, the research fellow appointed immediately after John Edgar Coover was a man named John L. Kennedy.* At the end of his two-year appointment Kennedy reported no significant results. A few years later, in 1942, Charles Stuart was appointed to the chair for two years. He reported several statistically significant studies. And yet 20 years later, in 1962, Robert Lamar, science editor for the Stanford News Service, issued a report on the status of psychical research at Stanford. He wrote:

> The most comprehensive work done under this endowment was probably that of Dr. John Edgar Coover. His findings were all negative. Some of the first fellows, particularly Dr. John Kennedy, checked many of the claims of the well known Dr. Rhine of Duke University, but was unable to verify any of them. When this had continued for a number of years, [the president of the university] asked that a man trained by Dr. Rhine be appointed as a fellow. This was done — Dr. Charles Stuart was the man, and he was given a completely free hand. Dr. Stuart *had to admit failure* in verifying the Rhine material" [Dommeyer 1975, p. 195, emphasis added].

By examining Stuart's original results, we now know that this official pronouncement from Stanford University was flatly false. What caused the Stanford News Service to make such an egregious mistake, and why did Stanford President Ray Wilbur defeat Thomas Stanford's endowment with a stroke of his pen? Well, the answer is not secret. Psychical research touches raw emotional nerves among some in academia, so any quasirational opportunity to "run it out of town" is always used. Unfortunately, this cautionary tale is not unique to Stanford. As we are well aware, social pressure (especially in academic circles) is just as strong today as it was in Henry Sidgwick's time, 117 years ago.

The quasicoincidence is that J. Edgar Hoover was the director of the U.S. Federal Bureau of Investigation when John F. Kennedy was president of the United States.

The moral of the Stanford Psychical Research Fellowship story is that even virtuous, honest and ethical people can and will rationalize that appropriating funds against the wishes of a benefactor is perfectly acceptable (even if illegal). It is acceptable because the social climate dictates what "everyone knows" to be true. In this particular case, everyone (within small academic circles) *knew* that Thomas Stanford's endowment would have been wasted on a lost cause, or worse, it might tarnish the reputation of the university. Thus, because university administrators fear embarrassment more than they fear death, funds specifically donated for psychical research magically vanished with a stroke of the pen. (Sadly, an almost identical tale can be told about a similar endowment at Harvard University.)

Now, keeping in mind the incredible power of academic taboos, which have slowly but steadily diminished over the course of the twentieth century, let us shift gears and glimpse into the future.

The Future

My optimistic guess is that a future historian might dub the first few decades of the twenty-first century the "Era of Para-Integration." By this I mean that new views of time and causality in physics, and the adoption of modern physics into the biological sciences, will begin to make some aspects of parapsychology much more palatable to the mainstream. In addition, distant healing research within the context of alternative medicine will continue to grow in importance, driven largely by the failure of allopathic medicine to effectively deal with many chronic diseases. DMILS ("direct mental interactions with living systems") experiments will take on a new, pragmatic immediacy that will significantly and effectively challenge dogmatic skepticism. And the softening of academic taboos against consciousness studies will continue. These accelerating trends are already plainly evident at the dawn of the twenty-first century.

By the 2050s, I suspect that parapsychology will no longer exist, at least not as it had existed in the nineteenth and twentieth centuries. I believe that the course of science and society are heading precisely in the direction that will accommodate psi not as impossible, or as implausible, or even as anomalous, but as normal and expected. After all, psi experiences are not new. They are as ancient as human history, predating science by thousands of years. It is only the social context of the last 200 or 300 years that have cast these effects into the anomalous fringe. The primary impetus that will spark this shift is the growing recognition that the fabric of the physical universe, as described by physics, is precisely the sort of "interconnected infrastructure" required to support psi experiences.

The year 2050 is only a few generations from now (the article that the present chapter is based on was originally written in 1999). That seems awfully soon for such a dramatic transition to take place, but on the other hand, by 2050 parapsychology will have 200 years of cumulative data in hand, a scientific worldview likely to be astoundingly different from what we know today, and a social context that may be fantastically different. The implication is that because science is strongly influenced by social context, if the world becomes too radically different from what we know today, then even my best, educated guesses will undoubtedly be far off the mark (Harman, 1976).

For example, what if we had asked James Watt, the inventor of the steam engine: "What's that thing good for?" Watt might have speculated that it could help cut wood faster, which might lead to building more structures. But he would have been astonished to learn that his invention changed the course of world history by sparking the Industrial Revolution. Nor could Madame Curie have possibly imagined that her work with radium would have led to the creation of weapons that still threaten to extinguish the entire world. Nor could Charles Babbage have possibly imagined that his analytical engine would have made the authors of instructions that control the modern version of his machine (the computer) the wealthiest people on the entire planet.

Those discoveries and inventions dramatically changed the world. But psi is more than a scientific curiosity. It is also a powerful idea that challenges basic epistemological and ontological assumptions, so guessing its consequences is like someone with tunnel vision attempting to navigate through a dynamically changing hall of mirrors. Nevertheless, some day, some future society is going to have to deal with a much better understanding of psi than we have today, and that is the world that intrigues me.

Future historians might look back upon the world beyond the year 2050 and dub it "the age of reconciliation between science and religion," or "the age of the reenchantment of science," or "the age of the technology of spirituality," or perhaps, "the age of the birth of collective consciousness." You will notice that the concept of psi does not appear in these "ages." That is because I think by the time the world has comfortably accommodated psi, it will not be thought of in today's terms at all. Notice also that these ages freely mix the ideas of spirituality, science and technology, which I think is inevitable.

Some less optimistic future possibilities include "the age of ontological crisis," "the age of reactionary backlash," "the age of depressing chaos," and "the age of absolute idiocy." These depressing scenarios may arise because of the inviolate Law of Unintended Consequences. To spin just one possible scenario, imagine that a rogue team of scientists developed a designer drug that stimulated superpsychic abilities. Anyone who took this drug would gain veridical psychic information, under full intentional control. This drug could be synthesized fairly easily, and it had no adverse physical side-effects.

To avoid overwhelming a person with too much psychic information (like wearing too loud a hearing aid), the scientists find a way to limit psi spatial perception to a radius of about 100 yards and temporal perception to about 100 minutes in the future (or past). So far, no one outside the research team knows about this drug, so the team discusses what to do with their new invention. They debate a long list of options, then with rash idealism they put this drug in all the world's water supplies, hoping to end violence, crime and greed by causing everyone to feel everyone else's pain, thus creating a race of superempathic, compassionate beings.

Unfortunately, what actually happens is that very quickly no one can stand to be within 100 yards or 100 minutes of anyone else. Society becomes paralyzed because everyone knows what is about to happen in the short term, and emotional pain radiating from a minority of poor souls is amplified and echoed a thousandfold through the newly empathic majority. As a result, no one is willing to do anything anymore. But societal paralysis is unacceptable, so necessity adapts it into a totalitarian regime that strictly enforces 100-yard and 100-minute "personal space zones." Legions of "psi cops" carefully monitor the compulsory time and space schedules, and act ruthlessly when compliance is lax.

The very wealthy can afford huge houses to accommodate the new space rules, and they do not have to work so they have less stringent time constraints. But the masses are forced to suffer each others' misery even more intensely than before, and they are forced to do things that they know (in some cases) are not going to work out. So a mass collective consciousness quickly jells and the populace wipes out the wealthy in a bloody revolution. There are many possible scenarios like this, and I am afraid that most of them end up destabilizing the existing world fairly quickly.

Perhaps the biggest challenge that psi presents to future society is the realization that what we think of as objective and subjective may not be so different after all. This creates a very serious challenge that threatens the very foundations of modern civilization. Blurred psychic boundaries endanger personal egos, jeopardize the social egos of patriotism and nationalism, imperil the concepts of foundational personal intention and responsibility within the criminal justice system, and terrorize the vast machinery of secrecy and privacy.

These issues are so deeply engrained into the structure of society that any challenge to them must be violently rejected. Thus a case can be made that even the *possibility* of strongly functioning psi will be energetically (albeit unconsciously) opposed by society. Those individuals with especially aggressive tendencies, desperately seeking approval from society, will gladly become self-appointed defenders of the faith. History is rife with examples of how the Zeitgeist unfailingly manifests callous brutes to carry out "its" plans. If such a reactionary scenario comes to pass, then the Parapsychological Association will be around for a very, very long time, always on the fringe, and always struggling in the same way that caused Henry Sigdwick to grumble in the nineteenth century.

When Mind and Matter Blur

Let us examine this issue of subjective and objective a little deeper. Let us say we ask Albert, a modern scientist, to take a ribbon and tie it together to make a circle. On the inside of the ribbon Albert is asked to write down mind-like things and on the outside he will write down matter-like things. Like most people, he writes words like "experience," "consciousness," and "subjective" on the inside and "matter," "physics" and "objective" on the outside. The gulf between psyche and physics on this ribbon is complete. There is no way to connect across Albert's forbidden zone.

Now we ask Betty, a sensitive psychic, to do the same task. Betty's thoughts are a mixture of hers and the thoughts of others. Betty can perceive what is happening on the other side of the world, and sometimes her moods disrupt the operation of electrical equipment. Not surprisingly, Betty has trouble deciding what concepts to write on the inside of her ribbon, because her psyche and the rest of the physical world are not so clearly distinct.

But we insist. So Betty thinks a while and then she takes the ribbon, gives it a single twist, and ties it into a circle. On the inside of the circle she writes "psyche" and on the outside she writes "physics." What Betty has done, of course, is to create a Moebius strip, a circle with only one side. From a distance, Betty's circle looks just like Albert's, but topologically they are radically different. Albert's act of distinction between inside and outside ensured that mind and matter would never meet. But Betty's creative twist guaranteed that despite appearances, mind and matter were actually identical.

The laboratory evidence from parapsychology suggests that the world is more like Betty's Moebius strip than Albert's closed circle. The implication is that some things certainly appear to be mind-like, and others matter-like, but such distinctions are really mere appearances. It all sounds like mysticism déjà vu, but this time the conclusion is based on empirical evidence rather than anecdotal reports.

A world in which what goes on inside our head literally manifests in the outer world sounds like a horrifically unstable existence. And indeed, this recognition has spawned numerous famous stories, including works like *The Tempest*, by William Shakespeare, the movie *Forbidden Planet*, and the novel *Sphere*, by Michael Crichton. Such stories suggest that fluid realities that can be manipulated by our out-of-control unconscious minds would destroy us all very quickly. And so perhaps society at large really does act as a sort of "reality governor," preventing us from learning too much about psi, or about any radical ideas, too quickly.

Conclusion

In closing, the past teaches us that scientific resistance to psi is far more than an intellectual disagreement. Psi is an idea that challenges tightly held ideological assumptions, and as a result promotion of the idea stimulates the scientific immune system into high gear. Only with repeated educational vaccinations will the social immune system learn that the idea of psi is not necessarily dangerous (although the widespread application of psi itself might be, as discussed). The present has revealed that science is changing rapidly. Surprising new discoveries are now measured in months, not decades. That is good news for eventual acceptance of the psi idea, because by comparison to other wild ideas, it makes psi seem less outlandish.

Finally, the future beckons us with visions of competing worlds: creative societies that are radically different from those we know today, some of which are wonderful and others disastrous, and neoconservative societies that vigorously block evolutionary advances, including psi, out of fear of the known and unknown. Ultimately, I trust that evolutionary necessities will force us past short-term myopic fears, so that, regardless of whether the psi-friendly future arises during the twenty-first or the thirty-first century, I do believe it will come to pass.

REFERENCES

Coover, J. E. (1917). *Experiments in psychical research at Leland Stanford Junior University.* Stanford, CA: Stanford University.

Dommeyer, F. C. (1975). Psychical research at Stanford University. *Journal of Parapsychology* **39** 3: 173–205.

Harman, W. (1976). The societal implications and social impact of psi phenomena. In Morris, J. D., W. G. Roll, and R. L. Morris, (Eds.) *Research in Parapsychology 1975* (pp. 225–242). Metuchen, NJ: Scarecrow, 1976.

Radin, D. I. (1997). *The conscious universe.* San Francisco: HarperEdge.

Sidgwick, H. (1883). President's Address. *Proceedings of the Society for Psychical Research* **1**, 7–12, London: Trübner.

2

Parapsychology in the Twenty-First Century

Robert L. Morris

Professor Robert L. Morris picks up where Dr. Dean Radin left off by introducing the reader to 10 basic problems that he believes will be faced by parapsychologists in the coming decades. These same problems may resurface throughout the twenty-first century. Rather than give our own synopsis of his chapter, the reader may launch straight into it, and let Professor Morris give his own explanations of, and solutions to, these problems. (Editors*)

Thirteen years ago, the author (Morris 1990–1991) identified 10 areas of potential difficulties facing parapsychology as it approached the last decade of the twentieth century:

1. Parapsychology is linked to problematic metaphysical origins.
2. Parapsychology is linked with concepts that have been exploited and misused in the past.
3. Parapsychology can be easily linked with delusional systems.
4. Parapsychology threatens the tidiness of our scientific methodology.
5. Parapsychology forces us to look at some theoretical concepts that science has found problematic in the past.

*The editors thank the Journal of Parapsychology *for granting permission to reprint this article.

6. Parapsychology threatens fixed beliefs about how the world works.
7. Parapsychology's most obvious potential research projects often raise ethical issues.
8. Parapsychology involves the study of complex, open systems.
9. Parapsychology has difficulty in generating and testing theory-based hypotheses.
10. Parapsychology has often been labeled a pseudo-science by philosophers and sociologists of science.

The current paper revisits each of these 10 areas in the light of events during the intervening years, and offers six strategies for parapsychology to adopt as it enters the twenty-first century:

1. We need to evaluate more completely what we have learned.
2. We need to learn more from our negative results.
3. We should focus on measures that have a good track record in terms of effect sizes and consistency.
4. We need to break down the divisions between "skeptic" and "researcher."
5. As we attract more interest from experts in other areas, we need to integrate more effectively with them and their expertise.
6. We need as individuals and as groups to be more effective at interacting with the media.

What might the future hold for us, or rather, what could the future hold for us if we are adequately proactive? Arbitrary temporal divisions such as millennia always provide a convenient excuse for planning. In fact, at the beginning of this decade I published an editorial essay in the *European Journal of Parapsychology* entitled "Parapsychology in the 1990s: Addressing the Challenge" (Morris 1990–91). It discussed several problematic aspects of parapsychology and how we at the Koestler Chair were planning to deal with them. I will start by summarizing them, followed by commentary, as by some criteria we have had some successes during the past decade. We have had 13 people complete Ph.D.s specializing in parapsychology and there are now related parapsychology units at several additional British universities: Hertfordshire; Coventry; Liverpool Hope; and University College, Northampton, all have programs started by former Edinburgh students, in addition to the University of the South Pacific, in Fiji. Each of these universities is encouraging the development of potential centers of excellence in parapsychology or anomalistic psychology. In fact there are two staff at Liverpool Hope and three at University College, Northampton, with strong parapsychology backgrounds, with Deborah Delanoy recently appointed a professor of psychology at UCN. Several additional British universities also have active parapsychology research. It is increasingly seen as a legitimate topic for academic research. Several more universities include the topic in coursework and recently I was honored to serve as president of the Psychology Section of the British Association for the Advancement of Science. A new Open University textbook (Hayes 1999) devotes half a chapter (17 pages) to parapsychology. The point is that we appear to be regarded as doing something worthwhile by our own academic peers who know us well, for example, those in Britain.

At the start of the 1990s, my essay identified 10 problematic aspects of parapsychology which I felt needed to be addressed if our field is to advance. It then presented strategies which we hoped to use in addressing each of them. The first six are conceptual, the last four linked more with methodological issues.

Problem 1: Parapsychology Is Linked to Problematic Metaphysical Origins

One of the problems parapsychology faces, is that it is generally identified with the spiritualist aspects of psychical research, in which it had its roots, and with occultism, with which it is indirectly associated; the public tends to regard parapsychology as an attempt to use the tools of science to prove the existence of a nonphysical soul, or to prove that we all have special occult powers. Parapsychologists are seen as people who have already made up their minds, who are now attempting to use the tools of science to persuade others that parapsychologists' view of the world is correct (e.g., Alcock 1987). Thus we acquire enemies that we haven't earned and don't deserve. Some are from a neoreductionist, rationalist, secular humanist tradition, perhaps exemplified by many of the formal skeptical groups that now also have organizations in most major countries (Hansen 1992).

Others come from more orthodox religious traditions, readily linking parapsychology with its heterodox metaphysical precursors (e.g., Linday 1972; Logan 1988). Both views are fed by the present-day linkages that the practitioners of various current spiritualist, occult, New Age traditions often make with parapsychology. The findings of psychical research and parapsychology are frequently cited in support of various beliefs and practices of these traditions, and often incorporated in a host of bogus claims as evidence for their scientific validation.

How did we attempt to deal with this problem? According to the terms of the Koestler bequest, parapsychology is taken to mean, "the scientific study of paranormal phenomena, in particular the capacity attributed to some individuals to interact with their environments by means other than the recognized sensory and motor channels." This definition makes no metaphysical presumptions.

We take a bottom-up approach, oriented toward building a more complete understanding of the phenomena, experiences, and experimental data that suggest that psi exists. It is not wedded to a specific theoretical approach, but is data-driven, seeking to develop models that will, we hope, come to link our empirical data with the various partly developed theoretical systems that currently exist. In turn, such systems may eventually enable a firmer linkage with some of the main metaphysical questions that fostered the origins of psychical research (e.g., Gauld 1968), but such links will only form gradually, in good time. That linkage, once made, may serve to confirm, modify, or completely disconfirm.

Problem 2: Parapsychology Is Linked with Concepts That Have Been Exploited and Misused in the Past

A central tenet of parapsychology is that we humans (and perhaps animals as well) appear to have access to certain mental abilities above and beyond those presently acknowledged by orthodox bodies of scientific knowledge. Unfortunately, special mental powers are surprisingly easy to fake (e.g., Morris 1986) and have been incorporated into exploitative practices both by individual frauds, who seek financial, personal or political gains, and by fraudulent groups such as religious cults, whose leaders "demonstrate" special powers to validate the cult's philosophy and practices (e.g., Keene 1979; Mills 1979). If a particular anomalous event does not readily admit to an orthodox explanation, then those wishing to be regarded as good scientists have long since learned that it is safe to label the event a likely fraud, albeit a clever one. Such assertions may be a safety net for the researcher's (or commentator's) reputation, but, unless a viable fraudulent scenario is offered, these attitudes do little to advance our understanding.

We attempt to confront this problem directly by studying the techniques of exploitation (Wiseman and Morris 1995a) and their social context (Lamont 1999), to build as detailed an understanding of them as possible. This information can then be used both to design and conduct better research on claimants of the sort that may be involved in public exploitation, and to help people who may have been exploited in the past, or are currently at risk (Wiseman and Morris 1995b). There are several aspects to this investigation as it is conducted at Edinburgh:

1. Understanding physical effects and their means of production.*
2. Understanding mental effects and the strategies for manifesting them.†
3. Understanding the roles the observer may play.
4. Developing models for the social context of the claim and its negotiated acceptance in the interactions among claimants and their evaluations.
5. The evaluation of written or audiovisual archival material bearing on claims.
6. Understanding the techniques of the verbal reading.
7. Understanding pseudopsychics as confidence artists and the techniques they employ to inspire such confidence in their legitimacy.
8. Developing models for the overall psychosocial context of such exploitation.
9. Developing a general model of deception.

Problem 3: Parapsychology Can Be Easily Linked with Delusional Systems

The possibility that we ourselves may have special mental powers, or may be influenced by the special powers of others, can lead us to develop problematic belief systems about how we interact with the world around us. Many counselors and mental health specialists find the existence of parapsychology very inconvenient.§ To the extent that we succeed in verifying the existence of psychic ability, even to a limited extent, we appear to give credence to dysfunctional beliefs. If people are confused about their own mental activities, and know of parapsychology's positive findings, they can readily form beliefs based on some of the more exaggerated or speculative interpretations of psychic functioning. The task of the mental health specialist who accepts our evidence as valid can be made still more complicated by the need to tease out the legitimate from the bogus psychic events that their clients may present. In 1989, the Parapsychology

---

Note that the author here distinguishes between physical and mental events, and thus seems to subscribe to the philosophical doctrine of dualism. Materialistic and idealistic alternatives are possible.

†*See footnote above.*

§*Note the strong link between paranormal belief and schizotypy which has not yet been resolved (cf. Thalbourne 1994).*

Foundation devoted an entire conference to these topics (Coly & McMahan 1993).

We are addressing this responsibility in both general and specific ways. The deception work described earlier includes the study of self-deception. The models we are developing are useful for describing human error, and can be readily linked with models from other areas, such as social attribution theory and human factors research in industry and technology. At a more specific level, we are working to build concrete links to the public and professional communities, pacing ourselves as best we can, bearing in mind our limited resources.

Although we are just in the very early stages, we are beginning to relate our work to existing models of mental dysfunction, including delusion formation, that have been developed within the psychiatric and clinical psychology communities (such as Oltmanns and Maher 1988; Bentall 1990), and it is our hope to contribute productive, fresh insights into these areas. Such contributions may involve helping counselors assess the likelihood of genuine psychic functioning in their clients. If the likelihood is high, counselors need to know how to help their clients deal with the possibility that the client will occasionally have experiences about which we know very little at present.

Finally, we need to help counselors assess the likelihood that they themselves may be using psychic functioning, intentionally or unintentionally, in the process of providing therapy. This may show up in interactions between therapist and client, as many have argued; or in the process of achieving clinical insight itself (Ehrenwald 1955; Eisenbud 1970).

Problem 4: Parapsychology Threatens the Tidiness of Our Scientific Methodology

If scientists in various disciplines take seriously the possibility of an indefinite set of additional means by which organisms are capable of interacting with their environments, then they would see that much of their experimental methodology appears to need modification and improvement. Sciences that study organisms generally need to control the range of influences between organism and environment (including investigators and experimenters) that transpire during the course of an investigation. Otherwise, interpretation of their results is rendered uncertain, due to the possibility of unmonitored, unwanted environmental influences. Some scientists feel that the apparent absence of detectable psi in their (nonpsi) experiments counts as evidence against psi's existence (e.g., Gregory 1986).

At the same time they are likely to have some emotional resistance to the idea of developing psychic functioning in the public as a whole, because that would make the business of conducting controlled scientific experiments extremely problematic.

One specific way we are attempting to deal with these issues is to apply the general concept of systems theory to our work: to regard spontaneous cases, field investigations and experimental studies as complex systems, themselves part of larger systems and yet having many subsystems themselves as well (e.g., Morris 1999).

By its nature, parapsychology compels us to regard individual researchers, as well as larger segments of the research community, to be part of the overall system in which our work is done. This can be seen both in dealing with experimenter effects (e.g., Palmer 1997; Schmeidler 1997) and in coming to grips with the nature of replication attempts (e.g., Morris 1980).

A systems approach may help us understand why psychic functioning isn't more manifest in nonpsi experimental studies. Psi-liberal systems models would posit that psi functioning may be present in such studies but not detected, especially by researchers not oriented toward looking for it. Psi-conservative systems models would posit that psi functioning occurs relatively rarely, because sufficient convergence of psi-conducive factors would rarely occur; when they did, their effects would tend to be discarded as bad data or anomalies to be ignored, if they were non-recurrent (Morris 1981).

Problem 5: Parapsychology Forces Us to Look at Some Theoretical Concepts That Science Has Found Problematic in the Past

By its very nature, parapsychology focuses on the nature of consciousness and experience, through its involvement with imagery, a variety of altered states, volitional mentation and so on. The last includes both free-choice behavior in the apparent absence of biasing information, as done in restricted-choice ESP tests, and conation or striving as is done in PK tests. Volition is also intimately involved in any attempt to distinguish between spontaneous, unintended events in daily life, versus deliberate attempts to "be psychic" by the research participant or professional psychic (Morris 1993).

Because these topics have been difficult to conceptualize and research experimentally in the past, little is known about them. It is only relatively recently that experiential topics such as imagery have become actively researched. Volition has largely disappeared, replaced by motivation and, in a handful of studies, simple intentional acts (but see Kuhl and Beckmann 1994, for an example of its partial reemergence).

Much of our work explores aspects of consciousness as they relate to psychic functioning; our efforts thus may contribute to our general understanding of these elements of experience and how to study them. Imagery, in visual as well as other modalities, is an important part of several lines of research. An additional area of exploration is in the area of volitional mentation, and we are currently incorporating the research of Kuhl and associates into our own studies.

It seems evident to us that parapsychology should not be seen as problematic for psychology and psychobiology just because it compels us to reexamine concepts, such as consciousness and volition, that have been difficult and perplexing in the past. Instead, we should strive to be seen as colleagues, offering additional avenues for pursuing such questions. After all, part of the public's seeming indifference or antagonism to psychology may well stem from its reluctance to address the many aspects of human experience that are truly of most interest to the lay community.

Problem 6: Parapsychology Threatens
Fixed Beliefs About How the World Works

By suggesting that we may interact with our environments through some unspecified new means, parapsychology threatens to reintroduce uncertainty for those who have come to espouse very specific worldviews. For those holding a reductionist, materialistic, secular humanist interpretation of the world, we appear to raise the possibility of some sort of direct nonphysical influence, perhaps even a spiritual one, of the sort advocated by various religions and held in disdain by many proponents of traditional science. Some critics have clearly sought in their writings to identify parapsychologists as researchers in search of the soul (e.g. Alcock 1987).

On the other hand, many theologians are also troubled by parapsychology and its implications. Some regard us as secularizing sacred experiences, as raising the possibility that religious experiences, including supplicatory prayer, visions, ecstasy, and so on, will all be explainable as a combination of known psychobiology plus some additional mental force that is not necessarily spiritual in nature. As a result, such people hope we will fail or, if their faith is quite firm, they know we will fail and regard us as temporarily dangerously misleading. Of course, some of them assume that we will succeed in verifying their own view and are thus more friendly, regarding us as buttressing their own arguments. This latter group is often disappointed to learn that we ourselves still debate the meaning of our results. Finally, of course, are those religious advocates who regard us as at best profaning the sacred, or at worst promoting the work of Satan (Lindsay 1970).

As noted earlier, we do not ally ourselves with any specific metaphysical view or theoretical system, and prefer a bottom-up approach. Although we don't completely ignore metaphysical concerns, we do maintain that none of the present worldviews seems acceptable as it is; some modification is inevitably needed. It seems important to reaffirm that parapsychologists as a group are not engaged in some major spiritual quest, just as we are not dedicated to debunking spiritual interpretations. Secular humanism, on the other hand, can itself be seen as a major world religion in many respects, with its own set of metaphysical positions and rituals (Hansen 1992). As with other religions, we neither support nor disavow its main tenets.

Problem 7: Parapsychology's Most Obvious Potential Research Projects Often Raise Ethical Issues

Much of parapsychological research as currently done seems bland and not to the point. If we take as our starting point the patterns that seem to run throughout the most striking spontaneous cases, we should be doing much more of our ESP research with participants in altered states of consciousness, including some fairly extreme ones; our target material should be highly arousing, emphasizing strong emotions and realistic emotional environments for agents; and our entire experimental milieu should be consistent with the first two points. Our PK research should follow analogous patterns, involving circumstances of strong need for our agents, and target material dramatically relevant to those needs. Many of our studies should involve strongly emotionally charged situations, with outcomes that are truly important for our participants and perhaps even dangerous. But such circumstances may raise strong ethical concerns for the physical and psychological well-being of our participants, researchers as well as subjects. Procedures for altering states may have side effects, both during the study and outside the experimental situation.

Many metaphysical and spiritual development traditions offer specific warnings about the use and misuse of psychic ability, and caution that participants who are not sufficiently spiritually advanced should not embark upon the path of psychic development (Mishlove 1988). Another set of ethical issues arises when working with claimants who may be motivated to cheat or exploit connections with respected researchers. Such researchers need to ensure that any procedures in a study are sufficiently fraud-proof that a claimant who attempts fraud will not succeed and will, ideally, be detected. This is necessary both to prevent or at least minimize fraud as well as to protect both the researcher's reputation and the reputation of any successful claimant (Morris 1987).

We are working to develop research procedures that will allow us to explore unusual experiences that have strong, meaningful messages and also allow us to explore potential psychic training procedures (e.g., Delanoy et al. 1999). At Edinburgh this process starts in our initial participant recruitment stage; we recruit through word of mouth, courses and lectures, as well as through screening the various people who contact us. Each candidate is sent a participant information form, which helps us to identify those who are clearly goats, have had mental difficulty with psi in the past, are uncomfortable with the notion of exploring internal events or displaying psychic functioning, or would be otherwise unsuitable for a scientific study. Researchers needing participants can select potential candidates based on their responses, contact them, explain the study to them, and let them decide whether or not to participate.

In the experimental settings themselves, we try to spend extra time so that we get to know our participants, their preferences, how they are reacting to their participation, and so on, and can take this into account in our interactions with them, (see Delanoy 1997, for good examples of this).

There are additional ethical issues that need to be considered, by different labs in their own ways. It is important to have research procedures that are adequately safeguarded, to enable researchers to feel positive regarding successes without becoming concerned about whether good results are simply indicators of fraud or a flaw in design (e.g., Dalton et al. 1996). The participant also deserves to be protected, by having the procedures sufficiently well controlled that any legitimate successes cannot be easily dismissed (Wiseman & Morris 1995b).

Problem 8: Parapsychology Involves
the Study of Complex, Open Systems

It seems appropriate to regard parapsychology settings, be they the natural settings of spontaneous cases or the controlled environment of experiments, as complex, open systems. A system is a set of interactive parts; an open system is a system whose boundaries of influence cannot be precisely delineated.

In parapsychology, our studies become more artificial and sterile as we try to simplify and close off the systems under scrutiny, and it is difficult, if not impossible, to place the researchers guaranteeably outside the system of study. Such considerations can be especially germane when attempting to evaluate the importance of a failed replication attempt.

We are still proceeding gradually in this area, because it represents a more complex, and in some respects a less precise way of doing research. The usual strategies of controlled experimentation, with independent and dependent variables, may often be quite inappropriate. We may need to focus more on strategies for evaluating the output of definable psi conducive systems, foregoing at least at the start the systematic exploration of specific causal linkages. This is especially true of studies done in other cultures, or in evaluating training techniques or individual claimants with idiosyncratic procedures, and so on so long as we do not then attempt to treat the outcomes of such studies as though they were in fact controlled studies, for example, by prematurely inferring causation.

Problem 9: Parapsychology Has Difficulty in Generating and Testing Theory-Based Hypotheses

Largely as a consequence of the above factors, parapsychology has not been able to reach a strong consensus about its domain of enquiry: the range of phenomena, of genuine events and experiences it is studying. As a result, it has been unable to specify with any precision the range and strength of phenomena that any theoretical system is obliged to explain. This makes theory construction difficult. Need we account for macro-PK phenomena, or can we settle for explaining information-based effects, disturbances in randomicity of large sets of events? Must we explain ghosts, poltergeists, reincarnation, and the healing power of crystals? Also, as a result in part of the factors discussed in earlier sections, we have had difficulty in producing any psi phenomena under adequately controlled conditions consistently enough to allow for effective systematic hypothesis testing.

There are several aspects to the problem of improving the construction and testing of theory in parapsychology. First, it is important to define our domain of inquiry. Ultimately, we all strive towards a "theory of everything," but to arrive at that stage we must first do business in more manageable areas of enquiry (Atmanspacher 1999).

Second, we need to generate more complete descriptions of the phenomena that do seem genuinely parapsychological. Clarification is also needed of the patterns of experimental findings that have shown up with reasonable consistency under adequately controlled conditions. We are now in a much better position to do this than ever before, thanks to recent advances in meta-analysis techniques (Utts 1991).

Once we have a picture of the patterns in our data, we can: (a) compare them with existing models as well as existing theoretical systems, where those systems are sufficiently refined to generate predictions; and (b) develop new models based on the patterns observed. Such new models can then be compared with existing theoretical systems, and can be tested by new data.

A colleague once noted how boring it was to read original research reports that simply looked for evidence of psychic ability, but that made no attempt to test any hypothesis derived from theoretical considerations. This observation is important, because far too much research has been done in a theoretical vacuum, aimed solely at obtaining evidence of psychic functioning, to persuade oneself and others that it actually exists. It is equally boring, however, to read a study based on elegant theory-driven hypothesis testing, incorporating a clever research design, that pays so little attention to previous successful psi testing techniques that it nevertheless obtains so little evidence for any psychic functioning whatever, that we learn nothing at all about the theory in question. An effective research program incorporates research procedures likely to produce effect sizes sufficiently strong that serious testing of models, of theory-driven hypotheses, can be done.

Problem 10: Parapsychology Has Often Been Labeled a Pseudoscience by Philosophers and Sociologists of Science

This problem stems in part from the other problems, and is addressed in the same ways. However, it can have advantages as well as disadvantages. As students of science have attempted to separate science and pseudoscience, good and bad science, they have proposed demarcation criteria to distinguish them. Such criteria can be helpful to us, as indicators of the criteria by which we may be able to judge our own progress. Some criteria may be misapplied to academic parapsychology, the result of misinformation about us, in which case we have become aware of a misconception that needs to be corrected. Often this may be a matter of distinguishing in the public eye between serious parapsychological research and frivolous or exploitative occult practitioners. Other criteria may have some partial validity, such that awareness of them provides us with useful guidelines for where we need improvement, how we can best proceed beyond being a protoscience (Morris 1987).

The above statements are all drawn fairly directly from the essay, noted at the beginning, although considerably condensed and minus the descriptions of our specific lines of research and practices specifically designed to address these problems. Looking back, there is little that I would now regard as incorrect although much is incomplete and most of it has gone unaccomplished. Our general bottom-up approach appears to have served us well, as has the emphasis on "what is not psychic but looks like it," including work on deception by self and others and belief formation and maintenance. It is evident that much more must be done in the way of model construction and testing but that those activities need to be tied in intimately to methods of observation; measurement theory and measurement are inevitably linked and must also be taken into account. Biases cannot be avoided, but we could be better at recognizing and acknowledging them. In general we must develop richer means of observation, description and measurement, and should avail ourselves more of the expertise that already exists in the physical, biological and social sciences. Regardless of whether we are doing field or lab-based studies, we still have major ethical issues to solve, if we have any hope at all of doing ecologically valid research. If we are to apply a systems approach to our work, we must learn much more about how to think in terms of complicated, open systems; otherwise we will never come to grips with experimenter effects, replicability issues and the apparently elusive nature of psi itself.

Some Strategies for the Future

Regarding the issues raised above, some progress has been made, within our own unit and in many other locations as well of course. Nothing that has been said or is about to be said is original to myself; it all emerges from considerations of the rich phenomena and experiences we study. However I would like to conclude with a few comments about some additional strategies that might be useful to us in the twenty-first century.

1. We need to evaluate more completely what we have already learned. It seems clear that the formal techniques of meta-analysis currently in

use have considerable potential if deployed intelligently. But they are still evolving and can be misused. There is less consensus about their use than we might hope, and the techniques of formal meta-analysis still need to be refined. Many of the same issues of replicability that affect experimental studies also can affect meta-analysis (see Utts 1991 and the ensuing commentaries for a discussion of many of these issues). We need to be at the cutting edge of meta-analysis research itself if it is to become a useful tool. This has been so painfully evident in the recent debates over meta-analytic practice in evaluating the ganzfeld data (Milton 1999; Milton & Wiseman 1999, 2002; Schmeidler & Edge 1999; Storm & Ertel 2001, 2002). Used well, they can help us extract richer patterns from our databases. Used poorly, they can induce both false positive and false negative inferences. Unfortunately, most of our databases are very small compared to those in other disciplines in which meta-analyses have become more successful.

2. We need to learn more from our negative results. Much of what we now appear to know is how not to conduct research. We should examine those procedures which have very small effect sizes and identify their common characteristics so that we can learn what we can from them and stop attempting to use them as measures of psi. Numbers were largely abandoned as targets a long time ago because of the non-random responses they tended to elicit (Rhine 1935/1973). Recent meta-analyses seem to indicate that group testing, especially large-scale public testing, produces very weak effects if any (Honorton & Ferrari 1989; Milton 1994). Should we not then avoid using such methods in formal research unless we have very good reason to retain them?

3. We should focus on measures that have a good track record in terms of effect sizes and consistency, and work to improve them so that they can serve as useful tools for theory evaluation. Often we publish studies which devise new measures and attempt to use them in process-oriented research without presenting any justification for the measurement used. It would seem best to do extensive pretesting on any new measures, before treating them as though they were both valid and reliable. Method development can be informed by theory and observation. Naïve methods do no great service to theories and models if used to test them. Other disciplines make better use of exploratory research and do not feel the same need to report each exploratory session in the literature. Such sessions can be (and generally are) designated in advance and not presented in the literature. This is one of the main issues raised by Milton and Wiseman (1999) in their recent meta-analyses.

4. We need to break down the divisions between "skeptic" and "researcher."

Regardless of our views, most if not all of us have a tendency to critique any research we dislike, until we find flaws, and minimally critique research having outcomes we prefer. The playing field needs to be leveled; some very poor methodology has appeared in print when the outcomes have been agreeable to editors. Given the extensive monitoring of our own research, it seems very appropriate to monitor as well the research and writings of members of the formal skeptical community. Just as we may have much to learn from informed, intelligent criticism, so do they, as certain of them increasingly acknowledge. With time, divisions may break down rather than become exaggerated, and we can all go on with our work. Ideally, of course, serious researchers always should be prepared to adopt a skeptical stance toward their own research and that which appears confirmatory.

5. As we attract more interest from experts in other areas, we need to integrate more effectively with them and their expertise, by consulting with them, working in teams, and making sure that our own research is not seen as less than competent by their standards. We should also offer aspects of our own expertise as they relate to others' work. This benefits all concerned in many ways and enriches our own research literature as well as allowing us to contribute to theirs.

6. One way or another, we need as individuals and as groups to be more effective at interacting with the media. Otherwise, in today's world, our entire field is judged on the output of a select few who may or may not be representative. It is also judged on the output of the counteradvocacy groups who actively raise money through the promise that it will be used in part to combat media coverage favorable to psi and "other pseudosciences"; yet there is no provision for "policing the police."

Although they are general, as strategies, the tactics for implementing them are often specific to the individual. I am more optimistic now than ever before that in the years to come we can practice an integrative parapsychology rather than the divisive one we have often had in the past. And of course before long the term parapsychology will naturally evolve into at least one, and probably several, more precise terms, as we develop the knowledge to inform that evolution.

REFERENCES

Alcock, J. E. (1987). Parapsychology: Science of the anomalous or a search for the soul? *Behavioural and Brain Sciences* **10**, 553–565.

Atmanspacher, H. (1999). Replication and meta-analysis in parapsychology. *Statistical Science* **6**, 363–382.

Bentall, R., ed. (1990). *Reconstructing schizophrenia.* New York: Routledge.

Coly, L., and J. McMahon, eds. (1993). *Proceedings of an international conference: Psi and clinical practice.* New York: Parapsychology Foundation Inc.

Dalton, K. S., R. L. Morris, D. L. Delanoy, D. I. Radin, R. Taylor, and R. Wiseman (1996). Security measures in an automated ganzfeld system. *Journal of Parapsychology* **60**, 129–148.

Delanoy, D. L. (1997). Important psi conductive practices and issues: Impressions from six parapsychological laboratories. *European Journal of Parapsychology* **13**, 63–70.

Delanoy, D. L., R. L. Morris, and C. Watt (1999). A study of free response ESP performance and mental training techniques. *Journal of the American Society for Psychical Research* **93**, 204–221.

Ehrenewald, J. (1955). *New dimensions of deep analysis.* New York: Grune and Stratton.

Eisenbud, J. (1955). *Psi and psychoanalysis.* New York: Grune and Stratton.

Gauld, A. (1968). *The founders of psychical research.* London: Routledge & Kegan Paul.

Gregory, R. J. (1986). *Odd perceptions.* New York: Methuen.

Hansen, G. P. (1992). CSICOP and the skeptics: An overview. *Journal of the American Society of Psychical Research* **86**, 19–64.

Hayes, N. (1999). *Foundations of psychology: An introductory text.* London: Nelson.

Honorton, C., and D. Ferrari (1989). "Future telling": A meta-analysis of forced choice precognition experiments, 1935–1987. *Journal of Parapsychology* **53**, 281–308.

Keene, M. L. (1976). *The psychic mafia.* New York: Dell.

Kuhl, J., and J. Beckmann (1994). *Volition and personality: Action versus state orientation.* Seattle: Hogrefe & Huber.

Lamont, P. (1999). How convincing is the evidence for D. D. Home? *Proceedings of Presented Papers: The Parapsychological Association 42nd Annual Conference,* 166–179.

Lindsay, H. (1972). *Satan is alive and well on planet earth.* Grand Rapids: Zondervan.

Logan, K. (1988). *Paganism and the occult.* Eastbourne: Kingsway.

Mills, J. (1979). *Six years with God.* New York: A & W Publications.

Milton, J. (1994). Mass ESP: A meta-analysis of mass-media recruitment ESP studies. *Proceedings of Presented Papers: The Parapsychological Association 37th Annual Convention,* 284–292.

Milton, J. (1999). Should ganzfeld research continue to be crucial in the search for a replicable psi effect? Part 1. Discussions paper and introduction to an electronic mail discussion. *Journal of Parapsychology* **63**, 309–334.

Milton, J., and R. Wiseman (1999). Does psi exist? Lack of replication of an anomalous process of information transfer. *Psychological Bulletin* **125**, 387–391.

_____, _____. (2002). A response to Storm & Ertel (2002). *Journal of Parapsychology* **66**, 183–185.

Mishlove, J. (1988). *Psi development systems.* New York: Ballantine Books.

Morris, R. L. (1980). Some comments on the assessment of parapsychological studies: a review of *The Psychology of the Psychic* by David Marks and Richard Kammann. *Journal of American Society Psychical Research* 74, 425–443.

_____. (1981). Developing "extreme case" causal models for synchronistic phenomena. B. Shapin & L. Coly, eds., *Concepts and theories of parapsychology* (pp. 80–90). New York: Parapsychology Foundation.

_____. (1986). What psi is not: The necessity for experiments. In Edge et al., *Foundations of parapsychology* (pp. 78–110). London: Routledge & Kegan Paul.

_____. (1987a). Minimizing subject fraud in parapsychology laboratories. *European Journal of Parapsychology* 6, 137–149.

_____. (1987b). Parapsychology and the demarcation problem. *Inquiry* 30, 241–251.

_____. (1990-1991). Parapsychology in the 1990's: Addressing the challenge. *European Journal of Parapsychology* 8, 1–26.

_____. (1993). Psi research and the concept of volition. In L. Coly & B. Shapin, eds., *Psi research methodology: A re-examination.* (pp. 255–273). New York: Parapsychology Foundation Inc.

_____. (1999). Experimental systems in mind-matter research. *Journal of Scientific Exploration* 13, 561–578.

Oltmans, T., and B. Maher, eds. (1988). *Delusional beliefs.* New York: Wiley-Interscience.

Palmer, J. (1997). The challenge of experimenter psi. *European Journal of Parapsychology* 13, 110–125.

Rhine, J. B. (1973). *Extra-sensory perception* (Rev. Ed). Boston: Bruce Humphries. (Originally published 1935).

Schmeidler, G. R. (1997). Psi-conducive experimenters and psi-permissive ones. *European Journal of Parapsychology* 13, 83–94.

Schmeidler, G. R., and H. Edge (1999). Should ganzfeld research continue to be crucial in the search for a replicable psi effect? Part II. Edited ganzfeld debate. *Journal of Parapsychology* 63, 335–388.

Storm, L., and S. Ertel (2001). Does psi exist? Comments on Milton and Wiseman's (1999) meta-analysis of ganzfeld research. *Psychological Bulletin* 127, 424–433.

_____, _____. (2002). The ganzfeld debate continued: A response to Milton and Wiseman (2001). *Journal of Parapsychology* 66, 73–82.

Thalbourne, M. A. (1994). Belief in the paranormal and its relationship to schizophrenia-relevant variables: A confirmatory study. *British Journal of Clinical Psychology* 33, 78–80.

Utts, J. (1991). Replication and meta-analysis in parapsychology. *Statistical Science* 6, 363–382.

Wiseman, R. and Morris, R. L. (1995a). Recalling pseudo-psychic demonstrations. *British Journal of Psychology* 86, 113–126.

_____, _____. (1995b). *Guidelines for testing psychic claimants.* University of Hertfordshire Press: Hatfield.

3

The Farther Reaches of Psi Research: Future Choices and Possibilities

William Braud

> Dr. Braud opens the doors to a range of possible future research, including astrology, synchronicity, magic, out-of-body experiences, near-death experiences, altered states of consciousness, mystical experience, etc. Researchers are advised to increase their awareness of "fads" in parapsychology, such as meta-analysis and ganzfeld, and carefully assess their conclusions and assumptions. For example, Dr. Braud asks if ganzfeld procedure really facilitates psi; if receptive psi is an information transfer process; and whether parapsychologists' research designs consider everyday life situations. Dr. Braud's solution to these and other questions give parapsychologists some future choices and possibilities. (Editors)

Over four decades ago, an article describing a Symposium on the Future of Parapsychology appeared in the *International Journal of Parapsychology* (Amadau et al. 1962). The article summarized responses to questionnaires that had been submitted to 29 authorities. The participants in this "symposium" included the following luminaries of psi research and related disciplines: Robert Amadau (France), C. I. Ducasse (U.S.), Jule Eisenbud (U.S.), Eileen I. Garrett (U.S.), Alfred Goldsmith (U.S.), Hornell Hart (U.S.), Rosalind Heywood (Great Britain), Sir George Joy (Great Britain), C. G. Jung (Switzerland), G. W. Lambert (Great Britain), Henry Margenau (U.S.), C. A. Meier (Switzerland), C. W. K. Mundle (Great Britain), Gardner Murphy (U.S.), Carroll B. Nash (U.S.), Fraser Nicol (U.S.), Arthur T. Oram (Great Britain), Humphry Osmond (Canada — Great Britain), Joseph Rush (U.S.), J. B. Rhine (U.S.), W. H. Salter (Great Britain), Gertrude Schmeidler (U.S.), Emilio Servadio (Italy), Ian Stevenson (U.S.), Robert Sommer (Canada), Robert van de Castle (U.S.), Gerda Walther (Germany), René Warcollier (France), and Rhea White (U.S.). The 29 participants had been asked to respond to the following 10 questions:

1. How do you define parapsychology?
2. Which areas of research, in your opinion, should be classified as belonging within parapsychology and which do not?
3. Do you anticipate that future research would emphasize quantitative or qualitative work?
4. Do you believe that accomplishment of a repeatable experiment is essential to strengthen the position of parapsychological studies within the scientific community?
5. Have you any comments on recent criticisms employed in parapsychological studies?
6. Do you believe that certain qualitative researches may be quantified in order to achieve wider acceptance?
7. In the qualitative area, where do you foresee the greatest potential for future research progress— spontaneous phenomena, crisis telepathy, survival studies, out-of-the-body experiences, or any other?
8. Do you feel that during the past decade, parapsychology has become more widely accepted among scientists in other areas?
9. Have you any comments regarding the psychological significance of certain psychic phenomena?
10. Have you any comments regarding the special psychological conditions that seem to favor or reduce the likelihood of an occurrence of psychic phenomena?

I cite this information in order to indicate the types of issues that were felt to be most important at that time. It would be of interest to ask those same questions, today, to a panel of experts and compare their answers with those of four decades ago. It also would be interesting to examine the accuracy of the predictions of that earlier panel. These are not my aims in this present chapter. I will, however, cite some of the content of this earlier "survey" in connection with some of the observations I will be making.

In this chapter, I make three sets of suggestions for the future development of psi research. The first is that our subject matter and our discipline might be situated in a larger, more general context than that in which it currently resides. The second is that it would be fruitful for us to revisit many of our research designs, findings, conclusions, and assumptions in order to examine these more deeply and thoughtfully and, possibly, to reconceptualize some of these. In the third set of suggestions, I present ways in which psi research might be extended and expanded in the years to come.

Toward a Larger Contextualization of Our Work

The domain of contemporary psi research is relatively narrow. When psi research formally began — in the guise of psychical research, in the early 1880s — its researchers, such as F. W. H. Myers, were addressing a wide range of interesting and unusual experiences and phenomena that were not yet well-understood. The investigated topics included disintegrations of personality, genius, sleep, hypnotism, sensory automatisms, phantasms of the dead and of the living, sensory and motor automatisms, trance, possession, ecstasy, various manifestations of the unconscious (the *subliminal self*), as well as phenomena of thought-transference, clairvoyance, Reichenbach's observations and theories, hauntings, physical and mental mediumship, and other types of psychical experiences. Gradually, many of these phenomena were incorporated into the subject of matter of psychology proper, no longer were considered paranormal, and eventually were excluded from the ambit of psychical research. This gradual exclusion of former subject matter meant that psychical research — as it metamorphosed into parapsychology and then into psi research — became increasingly limited in its coverage: it became concerned more and more with less and less. Today, psi research restricts itself almost exclusively to the "big four" phenomena of telepathy, clairvoyance, precognition, and psychokinesis, with an occasional nod toward survival and afterlife topics. Along with this topical limitation has come a narrowing of its favored research methods, a privileging of contrived quantitative correlational and experimental studies, and a deemphasis of qualitative studies of naturally occurring experiences and phenomena. A British colleague once quipped that, in psi research today, "ESP" might appropriately stand for "*extinction of spontaneous phenomena.*"

The already narrow range of studied phenomena — telepathy, clairvoyance, precognition, and psychokinesis — suffered further restriction as an increasingly small number of variations of each of these received serious attention. Thus, telepathy — which originally referred to instances of distant feeling (literally, distant suffering) — came to be represented by the guessing of specific shapes on Zener cards and, later, by the specific content of pictorial targets. Clairvoyance became nearly synonymous with the guessing of the order of concealed cards and with remote viewing of natural and artificial sites. Precognition and psychokinesis became increasingly identified, respectively, with the foreknowledge and influence of the outputs of electronic random event generators (REGs, also known as random number generators, or RNGs). Even the variations of the variations have been increasingly restricted — nearly all target events and response protocols are visual in nature, with other sense modalities virtually ignored. Additionally, the means of investigating each of these narrow processes have themselves become correspondingly narrow. Not very long ago, I was distressed to find an announcement of the program for a professional parapsychological convention so worded that it appeared that the entire conference was to be devoted to a large number of new ganzfeld and RNG studies.

Admittedly, there are occasional exceptions to the generalizations made above — now and then a new topic or research technique makes an appearance. However, my characterization of a general trend toward a decreasing range and variety of studied phenomena seems to be an accurate one.

I suggest that our field can profit from an expansion of its subject matter and from a larger contextualization of what is studied in psi research. Others have made similar recommendations. John Beloff (1978) urged psi researchers not to preclude unusual phenomena that seem to fall outside of the traditional psi domain and suggested that we be willing to explore anomalous processes other than those that fit securely within the well-known "big four" psi categories. John Palmer (1980) suggested that it might be useful for psi researchers to include additional "correspondence" phenomena (such as those found in astrology, synchronicity studies, and in the magical tradition) to those that we already study intensively. Susan Blackmore (1985, 1988) often has recommended that we expand parapsychology to include unusual mental phenomena such as out-of-body experiences, near-death experiences, lucid dreams, mystical experiences, and altered states of consciousness that suggest other "planes" of mental functioning — even when these are not accompanied by ostensible or veridical forms of the "big four." A recent compendium of relatively unfamiliar experiences — the *Varieties of Anomalous Experience* volume edited by Etzel Cardeña, Steven Lynn, and Stanley Krippner (2000) —

follows in a similar direction by including experiences such as hallucinations, synaesthesia, lucid dreaming, out-of-body experiences, alien abduc-
tion experiences, near-death experiences, anomalous healing experiences,
and mystical experiences along with its treatment of the more familiar
parapsychological topics. I think these extensions are commendable. The
term "anomalous," however, is unfortunate in that it suggests that these
various experiences are not normal or natural.

The *psi-mediated instrumental response* (PMIR) and *conformance
behavior* theories of Rex Stanford (1978, 1990) and the *psychopraxia* theory of Michael Thalbourne (e.g., see Chapter 8; and Storm & Thalbourne,
2000) are additional instances of models in which psi, as we conventionally conceive it, is only one manifestation of more general processes
through which intended aims or events that fulfill or correspond with
needs or dispositions come about, both endogenously and exogenously.
These models open their doors to include psychological processes that
ordinarily would not be considered legitimate topics for parapsychological consideration — processes such as meaningful coincidences; insight;
creative problem-solving; creativity in general; memory; and various
attentional, intentional, and volitional acts and mind-body interactions.

Michael Thalbourne's construct of transliminality provides still
another way in which the subject matter of psi research can be extended
(e.g., see Sanders, Thalbourne, & Delin 2000). The transliminality construct — which harks back to Myers' (1903) similar construct of *subliminal consciousness* and the *subliminal self*— includes psychic functioning as
one among several related processes in which one accesses ordinarily inaccessible "unconscious" materials; the construct later was extended to cover
susceptibility to and awareness of an unusually large volume of subliminal, supraliminal, and external inputs (Thalbourne, Bartemucci, Delin,
Fox, & Nofi 1997). This umbrella construct brings together a great variety of related processes such as psi functioning, paranormal beliefs, magical ideation, manic-like experience, depressive experience, creativity,
mystical experience, fantasy-proneness, absorption, hyperaesthesia, and
schizotypy.

Rhea White (1997) has gone, perhaps, further than anyone in urging
psi researchers to broaden their investigatory interests to include, as proper
subject matter, not only the familiar forms of psychic functioning, but
also other kinds of exceptional human experiences (EHEs), including mystical and unitive experiences, encounter experiences, unusual death-related
experiences, peak experiences, exceptional human performance or feats
experiences, healing experiences, desolation or nadir experiences, and dissociative experiences— even when these exceptional experiences do not

include what we ordinarily consider to be "paranormal" content or accompaniments. In White's view, EHEs constitute the larger context, within which conventionally recognized psi phenomena are only one of many classes of unusual experiences that may share important features. By studying these seemingly diverse experiences in connection with one another, we may learn much more about them and about their essential qualities than would be possible were we to continue to study them only in isolation.

In the 1962 survey mentioned above, respondents were asked which areas of research should be classified as belonging within parapsychology. J. B. Rhine's answer is representative of the views of many investigators, both then and today: "The subject's experience of environmental influences through ESP on one hand, and his action upon the environment through psychokinesis on the other" (Amadau et al. 1962, p. 8). This response is telling, in two ways. First, it emphasizes interactions with the external environment; there is no mention of more exclusively internal events or interactions. Second, this response specifies particular, alternative forms of *knowing* and of *doing*; it does not address particular or alternative forms of *being* nor *changes in one's mode of being*. In its future growth, psi research might be expanded to address more fully ways in which its studied phenomena may interact with or influence their experiencers' ways of being in the world — and this would include issues of self schema, identity, and worldview, as well as possible transformative changes in these areas.

Mention of alternative modes of knowing, doing (influence), and being suggests the relevance of the growing field of *transpersonal studies* as an appropriate larger contextual frame for parapsychological research. Transpersonal studies recognize ways in which identity, development, modes of knowing, modes of influencing, and other human potentials can extend and expand beyond those that are present in our typical, egoic mode of functioning. There is a recognition of what William James (1902/1985, p. 508) termed a *More*, and that there are intimations of such a More in each of these areas of our nature and functioning. Elsewhere (Braud 2001), I have elaborated, in detail, many interfaces of parapsychological, transpersonal, and consciousness phenomena.

Considering transpersonal studies to be a suitable larger rubric in which to situate our psi studies, in the future, carries with it an additional and important benefit — it would motivate us to move beyond our concerns chiefly with the individual and with her or his conscious, egoic functioning to the larger unconscious, nonegoic, social, global, ecological, and spiritual contexts in which we are embedded. Such a contextual expansion would allow us to address more adequately the larger meanings and impacts of the paranormal experiences and events that we study. Situating our work in a larger context can permit us not only to study a wider range of topics, but also to learn much more about the interrelationships among these topics and about the range of processes, persons, and larger social groupings upon which our studied experiences may have important interactions and impacts.

It has been suggested that "professionalism" means "disciplinary autonomy" and that "a field of study (or any line of work) is a profession when its practitioners are answerable for the content of their work only to fellow practitioners" (Menand 2002, p. 100). In our discipline of psi research, I think we have been "answerable" to a too-narrow range of persons—both in terms of those we might serve and those to whom we might look for inspiration and useful ideas. Expanding our discipline could have beneficial consequences, in both of these respects.

Taking Stock of Our Findings: Consolidation, Integration, and Reconceptualization

Of course, it is important for us to continue to collect new data, in the future. It is equally important, however, for us to examine more carefully the data we already have accumulated, the conclusions we have reached, and the often unexamined assumptions that might be guiding our work. In these future consolidation, integration, and reconceptualization endeavors, the following guidelines can assist us.

Increased Awareness of Fads and Wariness of Too-Limited Time Frames

Too often, our discipline seems to be driven, excessively, by the latest new thing. In an important and delightful book, *The Psychology of Science: A Reconnaissance*, Abraham Maslow—one of the founders of both humanistic psychology and transpersonal psychology—included his now-familiar aphorism: "I suppose it is tempting, if the only tool you have is a hammer, to treat everything as if it were a nail" (Maslow 1966, p. 15–16). The history of psi research has sometimes seemed to me to be a succession of hammers—each one promising to be the golden tool that will, at last, allow us to achieve the elusive goals of replicability of our findings and scientific acceptance of our discipline and our conclusions, and each one eventually failing to fulfill its promise, being discarded, and replaced by the next shiny new hammer in the never ending series. Members of the

Hammer Hall of Fame have included well-attested and multiple witnessed spontaneous occurrences, carefully orchestrated sittings with mental and physical mediums, Zener card guessing, dream telepathy experiments, animal psi experiments, RNG experiments, remote viewing tests, and ganzfeld sessions. Three hammers *du jour* that now feature prominently in psi research include the techniques of meta-analysis, direct mental interactions with living systems (DMILS) research, and presentiment research. I suspect these, too, shall pass ... and be replaced by still other hammers.

I mention this because if one is aware of this cyclical flow of discovery, enthusiasm, popularity, decline, and replacement of various research approaches, one will be less likely to become overly attached to any one of these, and less likely to invest any given approach, experiment, or outcome with too much importance or significance — less likely to see the world of psi exclusively through filters tinted by a particular tool, no matter how popular or faddish that tool might be. Such awareness and nonattachment, in turn, can facilitate freedom to explore other topics or the same topic in other ways — ways that would not be as possible were one to remain in the thrall of a currently privileged approach.

Along with a narrowness associated with allegiance to a limited range of research methods or topics comes another form of narrowness — a tendency to restrict our attention to a too-limited time window, in reviewing what is known about our subject. This is but another aspect of a pervasive syndrome of overvaluing the latest new thing. It always has struck me as curious that we, along with a majority of natural scientists, tend to behave as though knowledge has an expiration date — that findings and thoughts older than five years or so tend to be discounted as no longer valid or applicable. This tendency is evidenced by the time frames typically covered in our literature reviews and in the methods and evidence that we emphasize in our work and writings. Although progress undoubtedly has been made in some areas (chiefly in terms of technology), there are many instances in which early psi-related thinking and work rival, and sometimes even surpass, more recent efforts. It seems unwise for us to ignore or disdain important findings merely because they were published some time ago. In some cases, modern workers may not even be aware of the existence of relevant early work; such ignorance is an insult to the practice of good scholarship.

Space limitations allow me to mention only a sampling of cases that illustrate the relevance of early work.

- The Patanjali Yoga Sutras present a sophisticated system of psychophysiological exercises that fostered the psychospiritual development of the practitioner. Aspects of these exercises were claimed to facilitate certain *siddhis* (powers) akin to those that modern psi researchers would like to cultivate in their research participants. The sutras present an early anticipation of the much later models of "noise reduction" advocated by Honorton (1977) and Braud (1978).

- Gustav Theodor Fechner (1801–1887) is well known for his ground-breaking work in the area of psychophysics. Less well known is a series of seven books that were much more philosophical and speculative: *Das Büchlein vom Leben nach dem Tode* [*The Little Book of Life After Death*] (1836), *Nanna oder das Seelenleben der Pflanzen* [*Nanna or the Mental Life of Plants*] (1848), *Zend-Avesta oder über die Dinge des Himmels und des Jenseits* [*Zend-Avesta or Concerning the Things of Heaven and the Hereafter*] (1851), *Professor Schleiden und der Mond* [*Professor Schleiden and the Moon*] (1856), *Über die Seelenfrage* [*Concerning the Question of the Soul*] (1861), *Die drei Motive und Gründe des Glaubens* [*The Three Motives and Grounds of Beliefs*] (1863), *Die Tagesansicht gegenüber der Nachtansicht* [*The Daylight View as Opposed to the Night View*] (1879). In these works he presented ideas concerning mind-body interrelationships, consciousness, life after death, the possibility that consciousness might be mediated by alternative structures, and the idea of a "large" or nonlocal body — each of which resembles modern thoughts about such topics. He also presented a clear anticipation of the more recent Gaia hypothesis.
- In terms of scrupulous care, thoroughness of investigation, and thoughtful presentation of research on spontaneous cases, the work of the founders and early members of the [British] Society for Psychical Research — as exemplified in, for example, Myers' *Human Personality and Its Survival of Bodily Death* (1903) and Gurney, Myers, and Podmore's *Phantasms of the Living* (1886) — remains unrivaled to this day.
- In the early 1970s there was much interest in the possible connections of "right versus left hemispheric functioning" and psi. Building on the work of Hughling Jackson, F. W. H. Myers (1903) and William James (1890) had suggested similar connections in their turn-of-the-century writings.
- In the writings of Carl du Prel (1889) one finds clear descriptions of state-dependent memory and other processes of great relevance to psi research.
- In the 1980s, Rupert Sheldrake advanced his ideas about the laws of nature as habits; very similar thoughts had already been put forward by Charles Sanders Peirce — the American philosopher, polymath, associate of William James, and one of the founders of pragmatism — in a series of papers published in *The Monist* (e.g., see Peirce 1891).

- In an early and eloquent statement, the British social critic and writer Edward Carpenter (1912) suggested that by "dying" to our thinking selves, in a manner made possible by meditation and related techniques, we might gain access to a larger self, with its increased nonlocal interconnections that could allow the types of awarenesses that we now call "psychic."
- In the late 1980s, W. G. Roll (1988) developed his notions of the "long body" and its role in psychical phenomena. The idea of the "large body" had been presented by Henri Bergson in 1935, and had been part of the worldview of indigenous American Indians long before then. A similar notion appeared in the work of Fechner, mentioned above. The *long body* is an Iroquois notion; it includes not only the individual but other people, places, and things that are important to the individual and the group (see Aanstoos 1986). Henri Bergson (1935) advanced his concept of *our large body*, which he conceived as co-extensive with our consciousness, comprising all that we perceive, reaching even to the stars. This view aligns itself well with the concept of *Mind at Large*, also found in Bergson, as well as in many subscribers to the perennial philosophy, throughout the ages.
- Evelyn Underhill, in her classic book on *Mysticism*, in 1911, presented thoughts on the importance of reducing sensory distractions in order to access higher knowing that are virtually indistinguishable from the noise-reduction models of psi optimization proposed in the mid–1970s by Charles Honorton and William Braud.
- Leonid Vasiliev's (1963) work on remote mental influences, conducted in the 1920s and 1930s, rivals similar contemporary work in its creativity, care, sophistication, and positive results.
- In his descriptions of *turbulent systems* — isolated macroscopic systems with non-unique futures— in an early paper in the *International Journal of Parapsychology*, David Davies (1966) anticipated the importance of qualities of indeterminacy, randomness, and lability, which were later to be emphasized as important qualities of systems susceptible to psychokinetic influence.

In the future, more thorough scholarship and a greater honoring of the thoughts of earlier contributors might uncover important clues to psi functioning that otherwise might be lost, and a greater attention to the past might hasten future advances and prevent the redundant reinventions of many intellectual "wheels."

Alfred North Whitehead (1929) once suggested that the European philosophical tradition consisted of a series of footnotes to Plato. It may not be inappropriate to suggest that many of the more recent works within the traditions of philosophy, psychology, and psychical research are, similarly, often pale shadows of the incisiveness and depth of thought of our predecessors. The quality and depth of the work of earlier contributions may be attributable to greater aptitude, more thoroughgoing education and training, stronger motivation and passion, and — perhaps—fewer distractions on the part of these earlier scholars. In any case, in my view, we might benefit greatly from attending as much to these rich, early statements as we do to their more modern — but, sadly, often more superficial — simulacra.

More Careful Assessment of
Our Conclusions and Assumptions

Our future psi research can be assisted by deeper and more thoughtful analyses of our conclusions, generalizations, and assumptions. Here are a few areas to which greater attention might be directed.

Do "psi-favorable test conditions" such as ganzfeld procedures really facilitate psi? Certainly, psi hitting does appear to occur frequently and well during such procedures. Whether psi occurs significantly more frequently or significantly more accurately under these conditions is not at all clear — due to the typical absence of appropriate contrast or control conditions with which these ostensible psi-facilitators could be compared. Further, it is not yet clear to what extent any psi manifested in such conditions might be attributable to psi-enhancing properties of the conditions themselves or to various sampling, demand characteristics, or experimenter effects. In addressing this issue, much more trenchant analyses seem to be in order, rather than taking it for granted that these conditions actually facilitate psi rather than simply provide occasions for psi to occur at a more usual rate. It is fortunate that, lately, at least some investigators are beginning to include the necessary contrast and control conditions that provide baseline estimates of psi expectations in the absence of the ostensible facilitators; however, a much greater number of such controlled studies are needed.

Is psi really independent of distance? Although such a claim is made extremely often, its validity is not yet clear. What can safely be concluded is that psi can occur at various distances and often at great distances. Sufficient experimentation and sufficiently profound thinking have not yet occurred which could justify the conclusion of distance-independence of psi functioning. The difficulty of reaching a valid conclusion about this issue revolves around a number of complexities. First, we have no really good measure of the intensity or likelihood of a given psi occurrence. So, to say that psi happens well at various distances does not necessarily mean that the resultant psi had equal "strength," acuity, accuracy, or likelihood at those distances. Second, there may be a mathematical curve relating psi to distance, but tests conducted thus far may not have explored appropriate distances in which the curve is not reasonably flat — i.e., we may have inadvertently been exploring extents of space that are too small or too large to show a distance-related gradient effect. The curve relating psi magnitude to distance may not be a simple inverse square function, throughout all parts of the distance range. Third, there may be something akin to an automatic gain control in our organisms that tends to amplify weak psi "signals" and attenuate strong psi signals, resulting in an artifactual appearance of signals of equal strength, when, in fact, there may be great differences (perhaps distance-dependent) in the strength of the "arriving signals" themselves. Fourth, as long as the relevant experimental personnel are aware of the distances being tested, there is the possibility of conscious or unconscious differences in effort or belief, at the different tested distances, that could influence obtained results. Adequate tests of the influence of physical distance should be done using multiple blind protocols, so that possible psychological modulators and confounds might be eliminated or at least minimized. Such experiments have rarely been done. In fact, the only such work of which I am aware is that of Karlis Osis (e.g., Osis, Turner, & Carlson 1971). Interestingly, in these well-controlled studies, Osis did find indications of a decline in psi scoring rate with increasing distance. Osis and others have also reviewed large bodies of other evidence that indicated possible psi scoring declines with distance. Fifth, if psi interactions are minimally constrained by time, then it becomes difficult to distinguish real-time psi at a distance from later or earlier psi at closer range, when the target events and percipients may have been closer together before the actual experiments or during checking. It is important to recognize that arguments similar to these, marshaled in connection with distance dependence or independence, also may apply to considerations of whether psi is time-independent, as is typically claimed. I always have been struck by the curious need to honor the importance of time (observing real-time occurrences, for purposes of determining veridical correspondences) in order to explore space-independence, and the need to honor space, in order to explore time independence of psi. In the future, more thoughtfully and creatively designed studies will be necessary to address adequately the issues of psi's temporal and spatial independence or dependence.

Is system susceptibility to psychokinetic influence related to physical randomness or perceived (psychological) randomness (variability)? It appears to be assumed or concluded without question that physical randomness or indeterminateness is a facilitating factor for psychokinesis. In virtually all experimental situations, however, a target's physical randomness is confounded by its perceived randomness—or, better, by its perceived variability. It may be that what seems to be a physical effect may, in fact, be an artifact of participants' (and investigators') increased confidence or expectation for change in target systems associated with random as opposed to static behavior. Incisive studies could be designed, in which these two factors could be artificially dissociated, in order to learn which might more adequately account for obtained PK effects.

Do our commonly-used research designs address the functions that psi might ordinarily serve in everyday life situations? In laboratory studies of psi, the presence of psi is indicated by veridical evidence, and veridical evidence nearly always is indicated by formal correspondences between target content and percipient responses—correspondences of shape, color, name, formal associations and similarity, and so on. Are there any cases of spontaneous psi in which the participants describe, primarily, shapes, sizes, and orientations? Rather, is it not the case that, in everyday life instances, situations are described, particular persons are identified, and so on? Are we witnessing, here, a serious mismatch of how psi normally operates and how we expect it to accommodate itself to our artificial laboratory protocols? In the future, might there be creative ways of designing and exploring experimental tests that more closely approximate psi's everyday functioning? Gardner Murphy touched on this issue, briefly, in a passage in an essay on Frederic Myers and Myers' concept of the subliminal self and of the spectrum of different levels of the psyche (Murphy 1971):

> Now what kind of personality manifestations would we be concerned with at the highest levels of this analysis? We would be concerned with meaningful *communication* from person to person whenever the message is deep and significant: A message regarding values, regarding ideas, regarding aspects of human living which are most precious. That is what we should be able to communicate through these subliminal strata of our personality. For the ordinary tasks of daily living, it may be sufficient to work with simple, conscious symbolism. But if one is in need of communicating something vastly significant and broadly human, it may require the use of all the levels at once, so to speak. It may require a telepathic message which is more than a telepathic message [Murphy 1971, pp. 138–139].

Virtually all contemporary research on receptive psi (telepathy, clairvoyance, and precognition) is founded on the assumption that psi is essentially an information transference process. Hence, we emphasize, almost exclusively, the nature of the information that seems to be conveyed in psi interactions—examining, chiefly, formal correspondences of the *content* of psi-mediated messages. What if, however, the actual informational content of the psi experience is not paramount, but is only an incidental accompaniment of a more essential function of calling attention to certain persons or situation, serving as an indicator of distress or need, providing a preparatory signal, or providing indications of interconnection or relationship with certain persons or situations? It may be that the specific content of psi-mediated "message" is not as important as the fact that there is a message; that there is a particular source of the message; that certain subtle, yet profound, connections exist. Perhaps specific content is simply an incidental, ready-at-hand, or convincing way to convey the more general meanings to which I have just alluded. Stated somewhat differently, psi might simply be a dramatizing lesson-provider, and the lesson may be more important than the particular (incidental) informational content employed to provide the main lesson. If this is indeed the case, more attention — in future research —could be directed to identifying and exploring the additional functions that psi might serve, and "lessons" it might provide for those who participate in its occurrences, apart from the specific information that might be used in readily serving those functions and in providing more general lessons. This possible lesson-offering function of psi is not unrelated to the notion of the *mythopoetic function of the unconscious* (a term apparently coined by F. W. H. Myers; Theodore Flournoy called the process, poetically, "romances of the subliminal imagination"), in which unconscious processes continually and autonomously construct stories, fictions, and myths, which are dramatized in the form of dreams and other productions (see Ellenberger 1970; Flournoy 1900; Myers 1903). Here, psi correspondences, the selection of targets, and even psi itself may be subtle and impressive mythopoetic productions.

It is commonly assumed that, in receptive psi, the true "target" is the actual, concrete target instance at hand. Hence, veridicality is assessed by carefully noting clear and precise correspondences between a percipient's protocol utterances and drawings and the physical details of the specific content of some target event. What if, however, the true target in receptive psi is not the specific, concrete, particularly actualized target, but a more generic form of which the particular target is but one instance? What if psi taps into the more abstract forms, "ideas," potentials, possibilities, or "archetypes" of which particular targets happen to be only one of many possible instantiations? Such psi access to a more general form, template, or model could account for at least some of what hitherto have been called "misses." This issue is a large one, albeit one that might be explored fruitfully in future psi research. Such research would have to expand to include correspondences that are more relevant to shared meaning — and perhaps other qualities (see below) — than to formal correspondences alone.

Another assumption which has been guiding our research is that alphanumerical targets are much more difficult to psychically access than are more nonverbal target properties such as shapes, forms, textures, colors, and so on. Although there are intimations that this might be true, there is no strong, direct empirical support for such an assumption or conclusion. Perhaps there have been so few successful "readings" of left-hemispheric-type targets not because such tasks have been tried repeatedly and have consistently failed, but rather because such attempts are extremely few and have not been given fair or adequate tests. There have, indeed, been cases in which there have occurred accurate readings of psi target information. Could we be finding much evidence for psychic access of forms, colors, and other right-hemispheric-type qualities because these are chiefly what we have been looking for and emphasizing in our research — both to ourselves and to our research participants? Could such findings be instances of self-fulfilling prophecies and selective attention on the part of investigators and participants alike?

Psi-favorable conditions — typically, particular states of consciousness — usually are inferred from the presence of some ostensibly state-inducing procedure. For example, the ganzfeld procedure is assumed to produce certain changes in the percipient. As many have remarked through the years — particularly Charles Tart, in his perennial admonitions — it is unwise simply to assume that a state has been altered merely by noting the presence of some ostensible induction procedure. It is much more useful actually to assess the influence of the induction procedure — i.e., to provide a *manipulation check*. Much of the variability in obtained psi results, in connection with state production aims, might be attributable to variations in the extent to which induction techniques actually are effective in yielding the aimed-for state changes. More direct measures of state changes — using both subjective and objective accompaniments indicators — could be employed in future research into psi-favorable and psi-antagonistic conditions.

Among those psi researchers who are interested in survival and afterlife research, an assumption or conclusion is often made — either explicitly or implicitly — that if an out-of-body or near-death experience occurs in this life, such experiences might continue after death. Such a view is neither logically nor empirically justified. It must be remembered that those experiences occur in living beings, and it may be that life is a necessary condition for their occurrence or maintenance. Their occurrence in the living is *consistent* with a hypothesis that they may also occur after death, but the latter is only a hypothesis and not a guaranteed conclusion or legitimate inference from their presence in the living.

Related to the above is a view — prominent among advocates of survival of bodily death — that out-of-body, near-death, and psi experiences in general, as these occur in the living, demand a conclusion that physical substrates cannot explain and are not required for these phenomena, and that, therefore, these phenomena make plausible the survival of consciousness and certain aspects of human personality following the death of the body. I agree that these psi-related phenomena are *consistent* with such a view. However, in the future, we might consider the alternative interpretation that these and other psi-related phenomena may be operations or properties of *emergent* processes or structures that have their basis in the living physical brain and body, and arise from these, but might continue to depend upon the latter and might cease functioning and existing when the foundation from which they emerged disintegrates, with death. Emergence does not imply independence from the foundations or components of what emerges, nor does emergence imply persistence in the absence of substrate.

Possible Future Extensions and Expansions

I offer the following suggestions of ways in which psi research might be extended and expanded in the future. Such expansions would enrich our discipline, allow us to contextualize our studies more fully, and allow our work to become more meaningful to a greater range of persons and groups.

We can expand the *content* of psi research by including important processes that we have neglected and by identifying gaps in our current understanding of psi functioning. We can extend our investigations beyond the usual "big four" processes of telepathy, clairvoyance, precognition, and psychokinesis. Including some of the related processes mentioned in the "Larger Contextualization" section of this chapter (see above) would be one way of doing this. This would involve inviting other experiences — exceptional human experiences, nonordinary and transcendent experiences — into our investigatory ambit. We might also consider some of the large number of nonordinary experiences identified by Stanislav Grof (1972, 1975, 1985, 1988) for possible inclusion.

We can expand the *aims* of our research efforts. Currently, most of our research is devoted, directly or indirectly, to establishing evidence for the existence, in as "pure" a form as possible, of the processes of telepathy, clairvoyance, precognition, and psychokinesis. A second emphasized aim of our work is to understand better the processes through which these abilities operate. To these two aims, we could add a third aim of exploring the life impacts of experiences and the meanings and interpretations that people attribute to their experiences, whether or not their experiences have demonstrated veridical aspects. To participants and to the public, impacts, meanings, and interpretations are of great interest — even more so than are evidential proofs and posited mechanisms. The addition of this third aim also could allow us to address potential practical applications and implications of our work far better than we are presently doing.

Within the traditional realms of our research, we could entertain additional choices and innovative approaches to our more familiar subject matter. In the area of receptive psi, we could devote more attention to nonvisual targets and target events. Rather than deliberately rule out meaning in our targets (as, for example, Ed May and his co-workers have done, albeit for good reason, in their studies of the information and information change qualities of targets; see May, Spottiswoode, & James 1994), we could add more meaningful elements to our target events and to our experiments in general. This should enhance their relevance to our research participants and could add useful motivational, need-relevant components to our studies. (The Gardner Murphy passage that was quoted in an earlier section of this chapter also has relevance here.) Rather than restrict our PK targets to random electronic and mechanical devices, we could extend our target events to include not only biological systems, but also psychological, social, cultural, and even planetary processes and events. Not only would such studies provide information about the possible range and limits of psi influence, but they also would open up new areas for potential practical applications.

In future studies, we could enlarge our conceptualization of psi's major function. Virtually all of our work has been guided by the (often unstated) assumption that psi operates chiefly in ways that are redundant with sensory processing. Thus, we study how well psi can duplicate vision (in becoming aware of the visual forms, colors, and other qualities of targets) and the other conventional senses. However, we have excellent senses for accessing such information. Why would nature have developed a psi process that merely duplicates already excellent sensory functioning? Might psi operate, more effectively, in areas that are not so readily accessible by our regular senses? Perhaps an important function of psi is to provide knowledge of qualities of the world that are not immediately evident to the senses. Such *nonevident* qualities would include relationships in which various objects, events, or persons are embedded; the past histories and possible future trajectories of present objects and events; associative networks of which particular objects or events are but nodes; instances that are parts of the same whole; meanings; and potentials. This accessing of latent or implicit tendencies or potentials that are not yet available to the senses calls to mind a definition of *intuition* once provided by Carl Jung: "the perception of the possibilities inherent in a situation" (1960, p. 141). *Nonevident psi* might account for at least some interesting "misses" that have occurred or might occur in our experiments— instances in which several participants might psychically perceive subtle qualities of target events that are "incorrect" with respect to their sensory referents, but might, nonetheless, be discernable with some degree of consensus among similarly and properly prepared psychic observers. I have elaborated this idea of nonevident psi elsewhere (Braud 1982). Is there such a thing as *psychic space*, and can it, its dimensions, or its contents be discerned directly? Can our conscious awareness itself be a measuring instrument or a *psychoassay* for events and influences for which no other detectors presently exist? In the future, we could develop creative research designs and approaches that might allow us to learn about other realms in which psi might be more active, more accurate, and more at home. In exploring such areas, challenges involving the validity and trustworthiness of these observations and knowings would be great, but not insurmountable. Two specific methods might serve us well in exploring nonevident psi. One of these is to conduct very thoughtful and probing phenomenological studies of persons' subjective experiences upon confronting a given ESP target; by identifying a greater range of experiences, including bodily and other "preconceptual" experiences, and by noting possible commonalities of such experiences— especially those that are present in many percipient reports but are not obviously related to the formal properties of the target — across percipients. Another promising method could be the use of the *projective differential* technique developed by Peter Raynolds (1997) and his co-workers. This technique assesses persons' reactions to rapidly presented pairs of abstract images as a way of measuring holistic and intuitive responses to a wide range of objects, persons, situations, or concepts, and it can provide both quantitative and qualitative assessments of subtle, nonevident qualities and meanings, as well as indications of the degree to which these might be shared by the research participants.

We can devote more attention to possible experimenter effects— both conventional and psi-mediated — and also to possible effects of *place*. As far as I know, there has not yet been any systematic study of the possible role of the *location* at which our studies are conducted. Certainly, our study outcomes can be influenced, both directly and indirectly, by conventional physical characteristics of the testing location — for example, the geomagnetic ambiance of the locale, or even (as Spottiswoode's 1997 local sidereal time work has suggested) the test site's cosmic situation or orientation — as well as more subtle qualities of place. Some of the latter, no doubt, still await discovery and exploration.

It should be possible, in the future, to integrate our studied phenomena more fully with other processes. For example, there are great resemblances between direct intentional influences (psychokinetic influences) and what has been called *himmah* and *empowered imagination*. Henry Corbin (1972, 1981) has elaborated Ibn al-'Arabî's description of *himmah* — a kind of transfigured or empowered imaginal process or creative imagination, through which it becomes possible to directly perceive subtle or spiritual realities and to endow products of one's imagination and intention with a form of external reality, capable of being perceived by others. Jess Hollenback (1996) has described *enthymesis* or empowered imagination, with properties identical to those of *himmah*. In these systems of thought, ordinary imagination may remain "local" in what it may know and accomplish. However, a special form of concentrated, empowered, transformed, or dynamized imagination can know and act veridically and nonlocally. There are, of course, many other descriptions of processes in various esoteric, spiritual, and wisdom traditions that bear close resemblances to the processes studied in psi research. Being aware of these and what is known about these could help advance our own knowledge of the similar phenomena that we study. To deny such similarities and to privilege our own studies as somehow more objective and valid are indicators not only of poor scholarship and limited inquiry, but of hubris, on our part, as well.

The foregoing considerations prompt the suggestion that we employ much more inclusive inquiry approaches in our future work. Psi researchers often behave as though the only useful approach for learning about psi is to mimic the methods of natural science. I believe that such an attitude and approach is unnecessarily narrow and limiting. Whereas much may be learned about science through this approach, we can learn even more by augmenting this strategy with additions from the human sciences; from psychological investigations (as opposed to purely cognitive or behavioral ones); from the findings and thoughts of various esoteric, spiritual, and wisdom traditions; from philosophy; from history and other humanities, and from the arts. In the case of psi, as in the case of all other areas of human experience, we can learn much from these diverse areas. Not only can this expand and enrich our store of knowledge and wisdom regarding psi, but it also can foster more meaningful dialog with those in other disciplines and with the public at large — for whom the languages and observations of these "nonscientific" areas are often more accessible and more meaningful to their lives than those of science. Thus, I suggest a future investigatory stance of *science plus* rather than *science only*. Perhaps, rather than continuing to be framed as "parapsychology," our field might be broadened and reframed as "paranormal studies"?

In a previous section of this chapter, I suggested transpersonal studies as a possible larger framework for our studies. Building on the prior "three forces" of psychology (behavioristic, psychoanalytical, and humanistic approaches), the "fourth force" of transpersonal psychology included the valuable contributions of all of these, but added an emphasis on a *More*—beyond the personal or egoic processes that had been the major subject matter of the first three forces— and, especially, how experiences of that *More* (more ways of knowing, doing, and being) influenced one's expanded sense of identity and one's values. In some cases, the resultant changes may be sufficiently persistent, pervasive, and profound studies to be considered transformative. In the future, psi researchers, too, might concern themselves, to a greater degree, with the possible impacts of psi-related experiences upon the sense of identity, the values, the worldview, and the possible transformative changes of those who have these psychic and other exceptional experiences.

The "elusive" nature of psi has been much discussed (e.g., Kasahara 1993; Kennedy 2001). Some have suggested that a fear of psi might account for at least part of this elusiveness (e.g., Braud 1985; Tart 1984 — see, also, Grossman 2002, for related considerations). If this is so, then any tactics that might reduce such fear could help reduce the inhibition of psi. In the future, two research approaches might help reduce fear of psi. One of these would be projects specially designed to explore the limits of psi, and — more specifically — how psi might be attenuated or *blocked*. If persons could become more confident in their ability to reduce unwanted instances of psi, this could free them from fears of being overwhelmed, or influenced in unwanted ways, by psi. Such empowerment could, in turn, reduce psi-related anxieties and concerns. Another fear-reducing approach would be to encourage studies that focus on *positive practical applications* of psi. Increased awareness of, and direct experiences of, positive psi impacts could help counter apprehensions about possible negative influences.

In addition to exploring possible limits of psi, in the future, psi researchers might explore more extensively and more boldly the range of events and systems that might be psychically influenced. If physical randomness is, indeed, an important factor in determining the susceptibility of various "target events" to possible psychic influence, there are numerous physical processes in nature that could be so explored. Thus far, psychokinesis investigators have limited their target events almost exclusively to bouncing dice and deliberately constructed REGs. There exist much more dramatic, larger scale, natural target systems that possess random and chaotic characteristics that could be explored for susceptibility to direct mental influence. These include wind currents, weather phenomena, ionospherically mediated radio transmissions, and even sunspot activity, other solar emission phenomena, and cosmic rays. There already have been a handful of preliminary studies of psi influences upon weather and weather-related processes (e.g., Barker 1979; Castillejo 1973; Chauvin 1988; Cox 1958, 1962a, 1962b, 1978; Nelson 1997; Schmeidler 1973), and these have yielded provocative results. Such investigations could continue and could be extended to some of the other labile natural systems just mentioned.

In various societal contexts, persons or groups who are insecure or feel threatened about their acceptance or position may try to emphasize their own feelings of worth and enhance their own value by distancing themselves from other persons or groups whom they perceive as being below them in some hierarchy of acceptance. By playing down the qualities and accomplishments of those "others," their own status is relatively elevated — at least in their own eyes. This dynamic may contribute, in part, to the disdain that psychology — whose own status as a science sometimes is questioned — often shows toward parapsychology and other novel areas of study. Unfortunately, establishment parapsychology sometimes displays this same pattern in its attitude toward novel findings within its own areas of interest and, especially, toward workers who are viewed as not having the requisite credentials and not belonging to the professional parapsychological ingroup. Specific instances of this dynamic can be seen in the devaluing of the work of "amateurs," "New Age practitioners," popularizers, and advocates of various esoteric traditions. I hope future psi researchers can be more open to novel principles and discoveries in many areas, including those just mentioned, rather than being closed to contributions of these "others" due to feelings of defensiveness. These potential outsider contributions, of course, should be carefully evaluated through thoughtful consideration and critical thinking, but not subjected to a blanket rejection or neglect, on the basis of their sources.

Perhaps the most important and most effective future emphasis for our psi studies is one in which all of us become much more intimate and familiar with our subject matter. We can do this by becoming more attentive to psi experiences that may occur in our own lives, and learn more about these from a first-person perspective (e.g., see Braud 1994). We also can devote greater attention to more thoroughly *preparing ourselves* in ways that might allow psi experiences to visit us more often. For such preparation, we can find useful advice in our accumulated psi studies, findings, and theories, and also in various spiritual, wisdom, and esoteric traditions in which psi and psi-like processes are recognized and are honored for the important roles they may play in our lives, well-being, growth, and development.

REFERENCES

Aanstoos, C. M. (1986). Psi and the phenomenology of the long body. *Theta* 13/14, 49–51.

Amadau, R., et al. (1962). Symposium: The future of parapsychology. *International Journal of Parapsychology* 4, 5–26.

Barker, D. R. (1979). Psi phenomena in Tibetan culture. In W. G. Roll, ed., *Research in parapsychology 1978* (pp. 52–54). Metuchen, NJ: Scarecrow Press.

Beloff, J. (1978). The limits of parapsychology. *European Journal of Parapsychology* 2, 291–303.

Bergson, H. (1935). *The two sources of morality and religion.* New York: Henry Holt.

Blackmore, S. (1985). Unrepeatability: Parapsychology's only finding. In B. Shapin and L. Coly, eds., *The Repeatability Problem in Parapsychology* (pp. 183–206). New York: Parapsychology Foundation.

_____. (1988). Do we need a new psychical research? *Journal of the Society for Psychical Research* 55, 49–59.

Braud, W. G. (1978). Psi conducive conditions: Explorations and interpretations. In B. Shapin and L. Coly, eds., *Psi and states of awareness* (pp. 1–41). New York: Parapsychology Foundation.

_____. (1985). The two faces of psi: Psi revealed and psi obscured. In B. Shapin and L. Coly, eds., *The repeatability problem in parapsychology* (pp. 150–182). New York: Parapsychology Foundation.

_____. (1982). Nonevident psi. *Parapsychology Review* 13, 16–18.

_____. (1994). Honoring our natural experiences. *Journal of the American Society for Psychical Research* 88, 293–308.

_____. (2001, May). *Non-ordinary and transcendent experiences: Transpersonal aspects of consciousness.* Paper presented at the Fourth Consilience Conference, "Towards A Consilient Model of Knowing: Consciousness and the Participatory Worldview," of The Graduate Institute, The Standing Conference for Educational Research, Yale University, New Haven, CT. Available at http://integral-inquiry.com/cybrary.html#nonordinary.

Cardeña, E., S. J. Lynn, and S. Krippner, eds. (2000). *Varieties of anomalous experience: Examining the scientific evidence.* Washington, DC: American Psychological Association.

Carpenter, E. (1912). *The drama of life and death: A study of human evolution and transfiguration*. London: George Allen.

Castillejo, I. C. de (1973). The rainmaker ideal. In *Knowing women* (pp. 131–147). New York: Putnam.

Chauvin, R. (1988). "Built upon water" psychokinesis and water cooling: An exploratory study. *Journal of the Society for Psychical Research* 55, 10–15.

Corbin, H. (1972). *Mundus imaginalis*, or the imaginary and the imaginal. *Spring*, 1972, 1–19.

_____. (1981). *Creative imagination in the Sufism of Ibn 'Arabi* (R. Manheim, trans.). Princeton, NJ: Princeton/Bollingen.

Cox, W. E. (1958). *Is nature ever amenable to psi control?* Unpublished manuscript, Institute for Parapsychology, Foundation for Research on the Nature of Man, Durham, NC.

_____. (1962a). Can wishing affect the weather? In I. J. Good, ed., *The scientist speculates* (pp. 172–173). New York: Basic Books.

_____. (1962b). The PK placement of falling water. *Journal of Parapsychology* 26, 266.

_____. (1978). The psychokinetic placement of water bubbles: Confirmation of a blind-target automated procedure. *Journal of Parapsychology* 43, 44. (Abstract)

Davies, D. (1966). The physics of macroscopic systems with non-unique features. *International Journal of Parapsychology* 8, 417–444.

Du Prel, C. (1889). *The philosophy of mysticism* (2 vols., C. C. Massey, trans.). London: George Redway.

Ellenberger, H. (1970). *The discovery of the unconscious: The history and evolution of dynamic psychiatry*. New York: Basic Books.

Flournoy, T. (1900). *From India to the planet Mars: A study of a case of somnambulism with glossalalia*. New York: Harper.

Grof, S. (1972). Varieties of transpersonal experiences: Observations from LSD psychotherapy. *Journal of Transpersonal Psychology* 4, 45–80.

_____. (1975). *Realms of the human unconscious: Observations from LSD research*. New York: Viking.

_____. (1985). *Beyond the brain: Birth, death, and transcendence in psychotherapy*. Albany, NY: State University of New York Press.

_____. (1988). *The adventure of self-discovery: I. Dimensions of consciousness, II. New perspectives in psychotherapy*. Albany, NY: State University of New York Press.

Grossman, N. (2002). Who's afraid of life after death? *Journal of Near-Death Studies* 21, 5–24.

Gurney, E., F. W. H. Myers and F. Podmore (1886). *Phantasms of the living* (2 vols.) London: Trubner.

Hollenback, J. B. (1996). *Mysticism: Experience, response, and empowerment*. University Park, PA: Pennsylvania State University Press.

Honorton, C. (1977). Psi and internal attention states. In B. Wolman, ed., *Handbook of parapsychology* (pp. 435–472). New York: Van Nostrand Reinhold.

James, W. (1890). *The principles of psychology* (2 vols.). New York: Henry Holt.

_____. (1985). *The varieties of religious experience.* New York: Penguin Classics. (Original work published 1902)

Jung, C. G. (1960). The structure and dynamics of the psyche. In *Collected works* (vol. 8). Princeton: Princeton University Press. (First German edition, 1926–1958)

Kasahara, T., ed. (1993). *The elusiveness problem of psi.* Tokyo: Shunjusha Press (in Japanese).

Kennedy, J. E. (2001). Why is psi so elusive? A review and proposed model. *Journal of Parapsychology* 65, 219–246.

Maslow, A. H. (1966). *The psychology of science: A reconnaissance.* New York: Harper & Row.

May, E. C., S. J. P. Spottiswoode and C. L. James (1994). Shannon entropy: A possible intrinsic target property. *Journal of Parapsychology* 58, 384–401.

Menand, L. (2002). *The metaphysical club: A story of ideas in America.* New York: Farrar Straus and Giroux.

Murphy, G. (1971). Frederic Myers and the subliminal self. *Journal of the American Society for Psychical Research* 65, 130–143.

Myers, F. W. H. (1903) *Human personality and its survival of bodily death* (2 vols.). London: Longmans, Green.

Nelson, R. D. (1997). Wishing for good weather: A natural experiment in group consciousness. *Journal of Scientific Exploration* 11, 47–58.

Osis, K., M. E. Turner Jr., and M. L. Carlson (1971). ESP over distance: Research on the ESP channel. *Journal of the American Society for Psychical Research* 65, 245–288.

Palmer, J. (1980). Parapsychology as a probabilistic science: Facing the implications. In W. Roll, ed., *Research in Parapsychology 1979* (pp. 189–215). Metuchen, NJ: Scarecrow Press.

Peirce, C. S. (1891, January). The architecture of theories. *The Monist,* 161–176. [Reprinted as Peirce, C. S. (1955). *The architecture of theories.* In J. Buchler, ed., *The philosophical writings of Peirce.* New York: Dover.]

Raynolds, P. A. (1997). On taming the evaluation monster: Toward holistic assessments of transformational training effects. *Simulation and Gaming: An International Journal of Theory, Practice and Research* 28, 286–316.

Roll, W. G. (1988). Memory and the long body. *Proceedings of Presented Papers: The Parapsychological Association 31st Annual Convention,* 291–307.

Sanders, R. E., M. A. Thalbourne and P. S. Delin (2000). Transliminality and the telepathic transmission of emotional states: An exploratory study. *Journal of the American Society for Psychical Research* 94, 1–24.

Schmeidler, G. R. (1973). PK effects upon continuously recorded temperature. *Journal of the American Society for Psychical Research* 67, 325–340.

Sheldrake, R. (1988). *The presence of the past: Morphic resonance and the habits of nature.* New York: Times Books.

Stanford, R. G. (1978). Toward reinterpreting psi events. *Journal of the American Society for Psychical Research* 72, 197–214.

Stanford, R. G. (1990). An experimentally testable model for spontaneous psi events: A review of related evidence and concepts from parapsychology and other sciences. In S. Krippner, ed., *Advances in parapsychological research 6* (pp. 54–167). Jefferson, NC: McFarland.

Storm, L., and M. A. Thalbourne (2000). A paradigm shift away from the ESP-PK dichotomy: The theory of psychopraxia. *Journal of Parapsychology* **64**, 279–300.

Tart, C. T. (1984). Acknowledging and dealing with the fear of psi. *Journal of the American Society for Psychical Research* **80**, 133–173.

Thalbourne, M. A., L. Bartemucci, P. S. Delin, B. Fox, and O. Nofi (1997). Transliminality: Its nature and correlates. *Journal of the American Society for Psychical Research* **91**, 305–331.

Underhill, E. (1911). *Mysticism: A study in the nature and development of man's spiritual consciousness.* London: Methuen.

Vasiliev, L. L. (1963). *Experiments in mental suggestion.* London: Institute for the Study of Mental Images. (English translation)

White, R. A. (1997). Dissociation, narrative, and exceptional human experience. In S. Krippner and S. Powers, eds., *Broken images, broken selves: Dissociative narratives in clinical practice* (pp. 88–121). Washington, DC: Brunner-Mazel.

Whitehead, A. N. (1929). *Process and reality.* New York: Macmillan.

Section II

EXPERIMENTAL ISSUES

Psi and Altered States of Consciousness

Adrian Parker*

In this chapter Dr. Parker relates the topic of altered states of consciousness to the subject of psi, dealing first with an illustrative case study and then with hypnosis, dreams, and the ganzfeld. With regard to the latter, he describes in detail the so-called Real-Time Digital Ganzfeld Technique (RTDGT). His conclusion throughout is that altered states are psi-conducive by giving access to the Cognitive Unconscious. He argues cogently for the RTDGT to become widely available to researchers. (Editors)

Some of the most remarkable successes in the history of parapsychology have been made by two women — a young Norwegian, Hermione Ramsden, and her close English friend, Clarissa Miles. In these ESP experiments, Miss Ramsden took the role of the receiver and recorded, at a prearranged time her impressions of what her friend Miss Miles, the sender, happened to be doing at various locations of which Miss Ramsden had no knowledge. These locations could be in London or Belgium or the north of France, and although the targets themselves were not formally chosen at random, they were hardly predictable, since they often depended on

*The author wishes to thank the Institut für Grenzgebiete der Psychologie, Freiburg, and the Bial Foundation, Portugal, for support during the writing of this chapter.

what seemed to be fortuitous events. Both the sender and receiver recorded their impressions on postcards and sent them to each other so that the postmarks would verify the dates.

Some of the trials in their first experiments were very accurate. During the first trial, the sender, Miss Miles, sat at the fireside and concentrated on the word Sphinx, and Miss Ramsden correctly described how her friend was sitting and finished with "There is some word with the letter S." Clarissa tried again to send the same image of Sphinx for the second trial and Hermione finally responded with "Luxor in Egypt." On the fourth trial, apparently oblivious to the task in hand, Clarissa was "busy writing a letter to a Polish friend" when Hermione wrote on her card "You were not thinking of me but were reading a letter in a sort of half German writing." On trial 7, the sender wrote only "spectacles" as the target on her postcard and the receiver likewise wrote "spectacles— this was the only thought that came to me"; it is unlikely to be a lucky guess because Miss Miles did not wear spectacles. Then on trial 10, the sender wrote "hands" and "drew hands in charcoal" and the receiver wrote "Little black hand was the most vivid impression." Later sessions were more focused on the remote viewing of the surroundings the sender found herself in at the agreed time. Here again there were some striking successes, but there were also many failures. The apparent failures can perhaps teach us more than the successes since sometimes these impressions were surprisingly correct about experiences that were not intentionally meant to be transferred but with which the sender was preoccupied at the time or later during the day.

A questionnaire was given to the above participants putting to them many of the questions similar or identical to those in widely used psychological test scales such as the Transliminality Scale (Thalbourne 2002) and the Anomalous Experiences Inventory (Kumar & Pekala 2001). Results showed that both participants were artistically inclined, and Hermione Ramsden in particular had vivid hypnagogic (sleep onset) and hypnopompic (sleep awakening) experiences to which many of her successes seemed to relate. Clarissa Miles was on the other hand a strong visualizer or even could be said to have a "fantasy prone personality" (Wilson & Barber 1983) in the sense of the absorptive power of her fantasy (often, as it seemed to be in this case, a positive characteristic of creative persons).

Both participants had experienced several times "a sense of presence" and even on occasion seen apparitions. Clarissa had psychic experiences since her childhood, and sometimes apparent psychokinetic effects in the forms of raps occurred during the course of telepathy. This suggested that psi (telepathy, clairvoyance and psychokinetic effects) is a unitary phenomenon. Perhaps the most outstanding clue to their success was the importance that Hermione attributed to sleep-onset (hypnagogic) images and to a "soundless voice" as bearers of telepathic impressions.

A further analysis of the replies to the questionnaire also indicated that there would sometimes occur a "deferred reproduction" of the targeted image which later arose into consciousness following "the law of association" of ideas. This observation seemed to be indicative of subconscious states being essentially like conscious ones provided we regard them as having an ongoing active nature. Finally, Hermione Ramsden's own words as to how she made her successes and what they meant, are worth noting and taking seriously:

> I pictured to myself consciousness, the dream consciousness, when all idle thoughts come and go. Leaving impressions which are difficult to distinguish from genuine telepathic messages. Lastly, universal consciousness, which I thought of as a great, calm sea, existing deep, deep down, where all is One. Thoughts of this kind are certainly a great help, although the reason may only be that they help to concentrate the attention. I have sometimes experienced a feeling of having become one with the friends with whom I was experimenting — of seeing with their eyes and hearing with their ears— it lasted only for a mere fraction of a second, but whenever it occurred, the experiment was more than usually successful.

Indeed, in many ways the results of this experimentation are an excellent summary of what currently appears to be known about psi and its relationship to altered states. The methods used by Hermione Ramsden and Clarissa Miles are actually a combination of the two most promising psi-conducive techniques available in contemporary parapsychology. These are *remote viewing,* in which the sender is actively viewing the target while the receiver tries to achieve an inner focus beyond sensory and fantasy images, and the *ganzfeld technique,* which utilizes sleep-onset imagery for incorporating the target material sent by the sender.

Given all this, it may come as a surprise to the reader that the above experimentation was actually carried out in 1905 under the supervision of Sir William Barrett (Miles 1908; Miles & Ramsden 1908–09) and the analysis of the questionnaire was carried out and reported by James Hyslop (1911) where the above quotation is to be found (p. 696). Neither of the ladies were professional mediums but were in fact well-heeled members of the Norwegian and English aristocracy who could travel extensively in Europe where they enjoyed painting their surroundings. This was, of course, ideal for carrying out remote viewing experiments— the type of experiments that would later gain fame many years later through the experiments of the Central Intelligence Agency's Stargate project (Gruber 1999; McMoneagle 2000).

The reader might be then somewhat disillusioned and wonder why a hundred years of research has not taken us further and ask if there is any reason to believe that the next hundred will give us anything more of substance. In reflecting on this, we first need to realize that even given that so many years have passed, proper experimentation in parapsychology has been extremely limited and is calculated to be the equivalent of only two month's research in psychology (Schouten 1998)—enough to establish that there is a phenomenon worth investigating, but barely enough to develop a terminology and methodology for bringing it forth, and this is without thought of the special difficulties that this may entail. Moreover, it should be said that experiments such as those of Ramsden and Miles would never carry much credibility with critics: there were no built-in controls for chance so the correspondences could always be dismissed as mere coincidences or what is currently being called *subjective validation* (sifting through associations until they match)—or in some cases *thought concordance* in that close friends may be said to think of similar things. Finally, it is only by bringing the phenomena into the laboratory that we have a chance of first confirming or discounting claims, and only then moving on to discover something new.

Hypnosis and Dreams

It was the great achievement of the founder of experimental parapsychology, J. B. Rhine at Duke University, to virtually eliminate the above counterhypotheses by introducing statistics in this area in the context of using card-guessing tests. This base level for chance could even be extended to the later blind matching of all the images received to all the target images sent, or against so-called dummy targets, with the aim of seeing if the participant or judge could put the correct image and target together using the information that had apparently been received. With this methodology in place, the aim of research was to use it to capture the phenomena in the laboratory so that their true nature and implications could then be revealed.

Although the attempt during the 1930s and '40s was a valiant one and appeared initially to be successful, the earlier spectacular results with subjects in card-guessing tests were difficult to replicate and seemed to depend crucially on the experimenter and their ability to enthuse their participants. But perhaps the main reason that the Rhine revolution did not succeed was because it may have denaturalized the phenomena in the process of bringing them into the laboratory, taking them out of their natural context and then stripping them of their magical quality. Rhine and his contemporaries regarded ESP as sort of sixth sense or an ability like intelligence or creativity which could manifest in gifted people if one merely motivated them enough.

While there may be some truth in this viewpoint, even Rhine's own observations told not only of the importance of the atmosphere of the laboratory and the expectancy of the experimenter in producing motivation, but also of the crucial role that subtle states of consciousness played. In speaking of his high-scoring subjects, Rhine says:

> Several subjects have described their ESP experiences as involving a state of "detachment," "abstraction," "relaxation," and the like. And it is rather apparent to the objective observer in many of them. Miss Bailey practically goes into a light trance with eyes closed. Pearce seems to me to approximate to being in a light trance after he works steadily for some time. ... Cooper, Zirkle and Miss Turner close their eyes when they do not have to keep them open: Both Linzmayer and Pearce like to look off with "a far away look" much of the time. The former was given to staring out of the window. He preferred this to closing his eyes saying that the images were uncontrolled with the eyes closed. The fact that Miss Ownbey perceives the figures on the back of the cards and on the wall by hallucination, suggests that she, too, has achieved relatively good abstraction from sensory disturbances [Rhine 1934, p. 181].

Given that these observations appeared so obvious, it is rather inconsistent of the Duke University laboratory that virtually no attempt was made to study the effects of hypnosis. Part of the reason was that Rhine was working in the Zeitgeist of behavioral science, and regarded hypnosis, because of its complexity and its association with occultism, as "a return to the jungle of experimentation." There occurred also an unfortunate historical vicissitude in the form of a visit at the time from the leading expert in the hypnosis and psi field, John Björkhem. Björkhem had published extensively on the subject in Sweden concerning his remarkable success in bringing forth phenomena that in many ways seemed to have belonged to nineteenth-century hypnosis (traveling clairvoyance, telepathically induced sleep, apparitional effects) rather than its modern-day variant. But Björkhem, during his visit in 1952, was unable to transcend the cultural and language barriers and had little or no success in hypnotizing American students at Duke's Psychology Department (M. Johnson, personal communication, 2002) or indeed in inspiring Rhine in this matter. Rhine was later (1952) to write: "The general feeling we had at the Duke laboratory was that we did not know what to tell the hypnotized subject to do to increase his powers." In some ways this was a rather strange statement since most researchers on hypnosis would agree all that was needed was the very suggestion of success.

Nevertheless, other experimenters outside of Duke continued to use hypnosis, and with the heated debate during the 1960s concerning whether hypnosis was a form of role playing rather than a trance state, many parapsychological experiments led to the use of sophisticated experimental designs in parapsychology by comparing hypnosis groups with waking control groups in order to assess how much of the success was actually due to expectancy and motivation. What is then the relationship between psi and hypnosis?

The relationship between hypnosis and psi is certainly a historical one dating from Mesmer onwards. However, many of the leading hypnotists in the nineteenth century, such as Liebault, Charcot, Janet, and Wetterstand, all testified that the connection was also a very real one. In fact the major influential hypnotist in Sweden during Björkhem's time was Poul Bjerre who was trained by Otto Wetterstrand, one of the major hypnotists of the nineteenth-century Nancy school (Parker 2003a).

What experimental evidence is there for a true link between the phenomena above and beyond expectancy? Honorton and Krippner (1969) reviewed the studies that had controls for waking expectancies and found nine of the 22 studies had significant differences but sometimes, as well as the psi-hitting effect in getting the target correct, there could be a so-called *psi-missing effect*. In the latter case participants would not just miss, but consistently avoid the target thereby scoring significantly under chance expectancy. In the 1990s the issue attracted the attention of Rex Stanford, one of the most skilled methodologists in modern parapsychology, who used the tools now available (meta-analysis and effect size) to try to extract what might be at the core of this relationship (Stanford & Stein 1994). What was found perhaps was not what was hoped for but was equally interesting. Instead of a clear-cut relationship, the results were very dependent on who the experimenter was, and on the selection of suitable participants: about a third of the 29 studies had four or fewer participants which curtailed any firm conclusions based on statistical analysis. Whatever characteristics that might constitute a suitable participant then remained unknown. Very recently an analysis of the numerous psychological questionnaires that have been used to measure anomalous experiences concluded that trance-like states show a thread of relations tying paranormal experiences to those of dissociation and fantasy proneness.

The ability to dissociate was found to be the strongest predictor of "anomalous and paranormal experiences" whereas hypnotizability was a more moderate predictor (Kumar & Pekala 2001; Pekala & Cardeña 2000). Nevertheless a major problem which bedevils this kind of approach is that so-called anomalous experiences actually include as well as "normal" psychic experiences everything from the belief in fairies to UFOs, thereby showing a more or less total disregard for the fact that psychic experiences are a homogenous group in themselves that have little in common with the all and sundry that anomalous experiences include.

Faced with this fact, one is tempted to concede that Rhine was to a large extent right about hypnosis being "the jungle of experimentation" even if he could be faulted on pragmatic grounds for not using the technique to enhance the scores of suitable subjects. Certainly, what is simply given the label "trance" does appear to be a complex combination of personality and perceptual characteristics. A list of these would include an ability to become fully absorbed in fantasy, to be able to immerse oneself in playing roles, and to be able to dissociate these roles from each other. Hypnosis appears to be also dependent on many external factors such as expectancies about hypnosis and how the situation is defined (Kirsch & Lynn 1995). Perhaps because of this complexity, for many years the issue of psi and hypnosis has been a mute one and the interests of professional parapsychologists and their limited resources simply left the issue unresolved and moved on elsewhere.

There were pointers to the importance of other more easily definable states, in particular the dream state that could easily be defined by the presence of rapid eye movements as the *REM period*. Moreover, telepathic and premonitory dreams were part of folklore and the case studies collected by Rhine's wife and co-worker, Louisa Rhine, showed that ESP is most frequently associated with such dream states rather than with the waking state. Less known but equally important was that ESP during the dream state has more information content (L. Rhine 1962).

These findings formed part of the background for establishing, in 1962, the Maimonides Dream Laboratory, which was one of the most successful parapsychological laboratories: it carried out 12 major projects on dream telepathy and precognition until it closed in 1979 due to lack of funding. Of the 12 major projects, nine were independently statistically significant. The procedure was ingeniously simple. Usually the sender concentrated on a randomly chosen art picture target or went through some form of randomly chosen emotional and sensory experience while the receiver was dreaming (as could be identified from the REMs—the rapid eye movements). The receiver could then be awakened after every dream or REM period in order to give a report of the ongoing dream images and then was allowed to sleep on until the next REM period. The final result was a set of dream records which could be compared to the set of possible targets presented in randomized order with a view to seeing if the dream contents would allow correct matches to be made. This procedure is a standard one known as blind matching. In addition to the dream telepathy studies, two successful precognitive (premonitory) studies were carried out with a gifted psychic, Malcolm Bessent. On this occasion the target experience Bessent was to go through was not actually chosen until the next day (Ullman, Krippner, & Vaughan 1974).

There is one further finding which could easily go unnoticed. One of Honorton's successful ESP participants who performed well in the dream studies and in earlier hypnosis studies was an assistant called Felicia Parise. Being inspired by a film about the Russian psychic Nina Kulagina who on film seemed to be able to perform psychokinesis (PK)— the mental movement of objects— Felicia Parise began herself to experiment and, after several months of training, claimed to be able to move a small bottle simply by willing it to do so. Apparently, Honorton was not easily convinced but observed this and other PK effects on several occasions and all his efforts to detect fraud failed. Finally with the help of a magician-photographer, he was able to film the effect (Honorton, 1993).

Like the Clarissa Miles case, this suggests that ESP and PK abilities may be closely linked in the same individual. This fits well with Michael Thalbourne's concept of *psychopraxia* (see Chapter 8), with its emphasis on one generic psychic ability (psi) as an expression of the influence consciousness can exert on the brain and its environment.

More than 25 years later, the Maimonides work has stood the test of time. Some of the criticisms that earlier had been given lip service were shown to be ill-founded although this did not stop some critics from continuing to cite these (see Child 1985, for a review). A recent analysis of the 450 Maimonides dream-ESP sessions (Radin 1997) using a simple either–or, hit or miss classification, found a 63-percent hit rate when chance would be 50 percent, which is an astronomical result occurring by chance only once in 75 million times. Some critics such as James Alcock have attempted to deal with these findings merely by saying they are non-replicable but even this "let-out" no longer seems tenable. Sherwood (2002) collected 21 attempts at replicating the Maimonides work. There are naturally some weaknesses in the collection: some studies included were not fully reported and many were "conceptual replications" with participants recalling their own dreams on awakening rather than, as was the case in the original Maimonides studies, using the actual dream reports received through awakenings from REM periods. Moreover, what is obvious from Sherwood's analysis is that some experimenters were very successful, others not — a usual finding which no doubt has not escaped the reader, and which is so common that it might be called the first law of parapsychology. Nevertheless, the conclusion seems unequivocal: dream telepathy appears to be a relatively robust and replicable finding.

Even given this success, the problems facing researchers on hypnosis and dreams proved insurmountable: hypnosis was far too complex and itself a controversial phenomenon to offer a royal road to psi, and dream research itself was costly, time-consuming and involved access to a sleep laboratory. What was needed was a simpler and cheaper technique.

The Ganzfeld State

In the face of the pending closure of the Maimonides Laboratory, Charles Honorton and others, including William Braud and myself, began in the mid-'70s to work on less expensive and less cumbersome equipment, which did not require access to a sleep laboratory. This became known as the ganzfeld technique, which can be regarded as a natural evolution from anecdotal claims of ESP in dreams and reports of telepathy during psychotherapeutic contact, as well as more controlled hypnosis and dream research (Figure 4.1).

The common feature, as Honorton described it, is the elimination of "noise" or unwanted sources of stimulation. By "noise" was meant not just external stimulation and sources of distraction but also inner chatter. The objective is to still the mind in order for internal imagery to spontaneously manifest; or, expressed in another way, the brain requires a minimal level of stimulation and in the absence of an external source, it will turn internally for this. Some years earlier Rhea White (1964) had in a classic paper reviewed many of the insights given by participants with outstanding performances of ESP. Interestingly, of the 16 participants in this collection, 10 had also acted as experimenter at some stage. What appeared to be another common feature was they all attributed importance to the ability to still the mind, to avoid guessing strategies, and to allow spontaneous imagery to develop without interference from these sources. In this respect this so-called *psi-conducive state* resembles a Zen-meditative state. The ganzfeld could be said to be a simple means of producing such an apparently psi-conducive state in the laboratory.

The concept of "ganzfeld" (whole field) itself has historical roots in the work of the gestalt psychologists during the 1920s where it was first

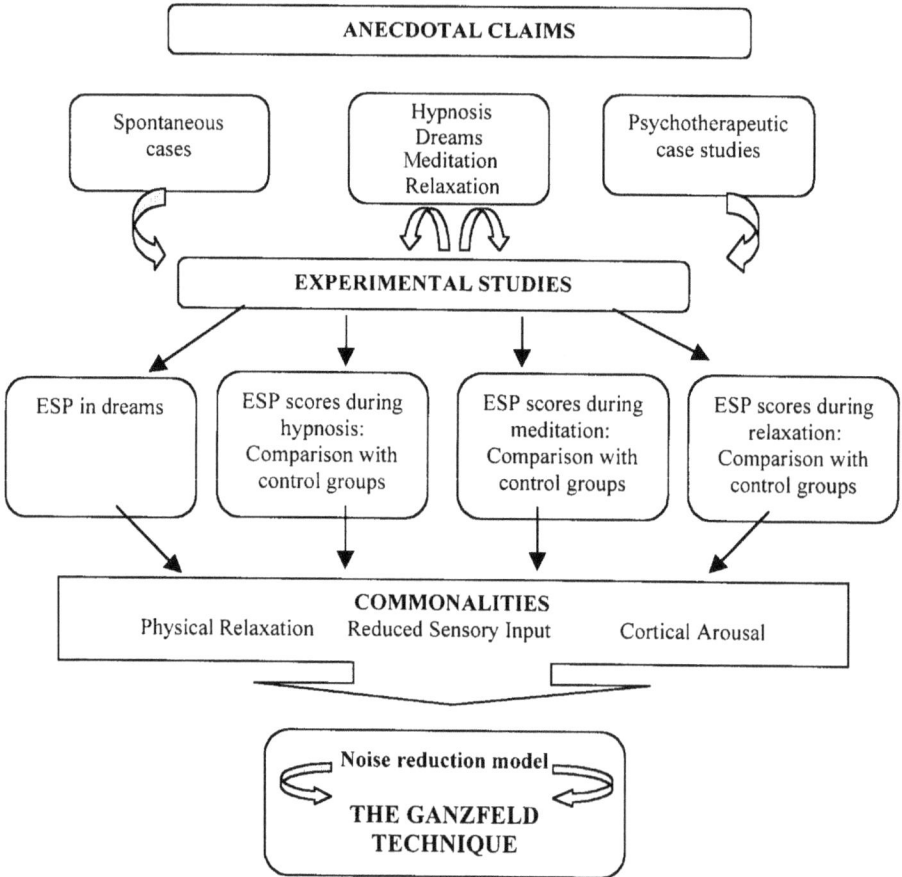

Figure 4.1. The evolution of the ganzfeld (modified from Honorton 1994).

used at the Psychological Institute of Berlin, located then in the Imperial Palace. Participants sat in front of a large white wall of a lecture room that covered their whole field of vision thereby enabling internal images to be projected onto the blank image. Eventually the same effect was achieved by substituting the wall for translucent hemispheres placed over the eyes. A source of uniform auditory stimulation was then added, usually in the form of white noise or the rhythmic sound of sea waves. The publication of Charles Tart's landmark book, *Altered States of Consciousness* (1969), contained a report using the ganzfeld technique in this way, and it was this technique that provided the impetus for myself, and I believe also for Charles Honorton and William Braud, to begin to apply the technique to parapsychological research.

The basic principle here was much the same as with the dream telepathy studies: to incorporate the two most basic "facts" which we know from spontaneous paranormal experiences. We know from these that the receiver is most often in an altered state (or at least in a relaxed state) and the sender is most often in an emotional or even life-threatening crisis (Stevenson 1970). The ganzfeld, with its homogeneous field of visual and auditory stimulation, induces a sleep-onset or hypnagogic-like* state in the receiver. The receiver stays in this state for 30 minutes while giving a verbal report of the images that appear. During this time the sender views a randomly chosen image from sets of emotionally engaging picture slides or films. Afterwards, the task is for the receiver or a judge to identify this film clip from decoy clips (usually three in number) that formed part of the original set of four from which the clip was randomly chosen ($P = 0.25$).

The psi-ganzfeld experiments began in 1964. Despite the fact, as mentioned earlier, that the time passage amounts in practice to less than one or two months of ordinary psychological research, the number of experiments that have now accrued are close to a hundred studies and have been conducted at some dozen different laboratories. From this effort, one might easily expect that there would be a clear answer as to whether or not psi can be produced at will in the laboratory. If we look superficially at all the experimental results, then this certainly does appear to be the case, but then not all the studies were done with the requisite controls against sources of error and it is still possible that the successful studies were merely replicating errors or even in some cases fraud.

To be fair, very few studies were designed with the support of the resources that would have been needed to pay the double bill of being proof-oriented and replication-oriented. Nevertheless, in one of the few examples in psychology of a constructive dialogue between a proponent and a critic, Charles Honorton and the leading critic, Ray Hyman, agreed on a set of guidelines for further research. This meant that Honorton, in the early 1980s, went back to the drawing board and designed a computerized and virtually "fail proof" version of the ganzfeld known as the automated ganzfeld or *autoganzfeld*. He and his immediate colleagues then

---

Although an EEG-monitoring study by Wackermann et al. (2000) claimed that the ganzfeld state was a waking state and did not resemble sleep-onset or the hypnagogic state, the study had several shortcomings: it did not run prior sessions to give participants the opportunity to become adjusted to the discomfort of the EEG electrodes, no relaxation was used, and the sessions were much shorter than standard ganzfeld ones. Certainly many of our participants do give classical hypnagogic imagery and even occasionally fall asleep!

went on to carry out 10 more studies with this autoganzfeld at his Psychophysical Research Laboratory and produced an overall 32-percent hit rate, significantly higher than the chance expectancy of 25 percent (Bem & Honorton 1994). Video film clips were used, which gave a noticeably higher result and were responsible for the overall significance. At the time, critic Hyman could only lamely ask why the original manual slide presentations of the targets no longer produced the same level of success they had done 10 years earlier and why the overall success was now due to the new modern video clips? This is surely not so strange given that every teacher knows that using teaching techniques that were used 10 years ago would be deemed pedagogically ineffective and every therapist knows that new treatments have a limited durability.

It might be thought that the issue was now settled, especially since Bem and Honorton's work was of sufficient merit to be published in a leading psychological journal, *Psychological Bulletin*. However, psychology departments across the world did not rush to install the autoganzfeld and by 1999 only three parapsychology laboratories in the world had used the technique. Worse was to come. Criticism was now being made that perhaps there just might have been some sensory leakage, which might have reached the experimenter, who might then have inadvertently communicated this to the participant. Finally, a hiatus was reached when the next 30 studies were barely significant overall, and had a near zero-effect size (Milton & Wiseman 1999). The controversy dragged on in the journals with the next 10 studies reestablishing the psi-effect. An elegant study reported by Bem, Palmer, and Broughton (2001) gave some reassurance that the effect was a robust one by presenting empirical evidence that the slump had been due to many experimenters, who having tired of straight replications, had tried some rather deviant designs that simply did not pay off. A review of the overall picture of success by Storm and Ertel (2001) also gave a more positive picture.

The Real-Time Digital Ganzfeld

The initial ganzfeld project at Gothenburg University, which began in 1996 and continued for four years, kept to the orthodox standard procedure — except for the first study. Because the Psychology Department had just then moved premises and facilities were limited, the first study had to be run without a set-up that would have allowed the sender to monitor via one-way intercom the ongoing verbal reports of the ganzfeld images being given by the receiver in the ganzfeld state. Although participants in this state can periodically lose contact with the external world, most of them are able to follow the instruction to give an intermittent report of what they are experiencing. This monitoring of the ganzfeld report (or *mentation report* as it is often called) has become a standard feature of the ganzfeld procedure.

The five studies were initially run each with 30 trials and the overall results were highly significant with a scoring rate at 36 percent and if only the four "monitored studies" are included, this reaches a 40-percent hit rate where chance should again be 25 percent (Parker 2000). During one study (Study 3) we asked several of our promising participants to return and be retested. Among these were seven pairs who had made direct hits and four of these succeeded in repeating their success. We were sufficiently encouraged by this to invite, at the end of the project, successful participants from all five series for a further study (Study 6). This was our greatest disappointment. On this occasion, a pure chance result, five hits in 29 trials, was obtained. In retrospect, there are some quite plausible reasons for this: two years had now passed and many of the relationships of those involved had altered or in some cases ended. The same was true from our side where the main experimenter from the earlier studies now had other commitments and was essentially unavailable.

These studies were never intended as final proof of psi but had the purpose of producing a workable procedure from which we could learn something about the process. What was most striking in this respect were the cases where the *content* of the ganzfeld experience would seem to follow the content of film clips, especially when the film scene suddenly changed. For this reason we began to make *real-time recordings*. Real-time recordings meant that we copied the film while it was being shown and fed the sound record of the receiver describing the ongoing ganzfeld imagery onto the sound track of this copy. (In the first few cases, we merely put a second tape recorder into the sender's room and synchronized the receiver's words with the sound being recorded from the film.) For instance, the participant in ganzfeld described being swung around as if on a carousel when the scene in the film clip concerned being swung around in a broken elevator. This could conceivably be a coincidence, but when the elevator crashed at the same point in time as when the receiver said: "Something crashes down with a dunce — a thud," it appeared as if some causal law was at work. In another sequence a subject described an unlikely sequence including a race-car driver, an embankment, a midnight sky, trains, and some kind of insect, all of which were correct and given in real time with the appropriate images in the film. This particular participant was herself a successful experimenter from another laboratory, and as with all our participants, had no access to our video library and therefore no prior knowledge of the target film.

On one single occasion I had myself the opportunity to be a receiver during one session as a receiver-participant. For this session four film clips were chosen which I had not seen and which were presented in random order. The content of these four clips was very different — a snake, a river scene followed by someone being shot, a motorway film, and a scene with a woman dressed as an Arab woman with a scarf around her head. The content was accurately recorded in each case and this enabled all four films to be placed in their correct order. For instance, in the last sequence from Brian Gilbert's (1991) film *Not Without My Daughter*, the sender was seen dressed in Indian or Arab clothes. Although the sender did not usually act out film scenes, on this one occasion she had taken a scarf around her head to act out the scene (Parker, Persson & Haller 2000).

To further ensure that there was causality involved, rather than as is sometimes said an anomalous correspondence between two processes, I decided to see what would happen if an unexpected "intervention" were made in the processes. During a session with one of our most successful participants, unbeknown to her, I asked the sender to leave the room and a close friend of hers to enter. At this point in time she responded with "Where have you been?"—the words unaccountably entering her consciousness. It seemed like we were now repeating the Ramsden and Miles work but documenting the events accurately in real time.

The next stage was to improve the procedure and digitize all these real-time aspects. The real-time digital ganzfeld technique (RTDGT), which to a large extent was the brainchild of Joakim Westerlund, offers several major improvements over the earlier autoganzfeld. Like the auto-ganzfeld, in the digital ganzfeld, the computer randomly selects the target from the video library and the target film clip from the set, and records all choices and outcomes in the procedure.

The distinctive aspect here in digital procedure is that it automatically enables the real-time recording of the mentation report so as to be synchronous with the film clip. This mentation report is also simultaneously replayed with the decoy clips, thus providing the opportunity to use this aspect as an important aid in determining which is the target film-clip and which are the decoys, as shown in Figure 4.2.

But the digital ganzfeld is more than this: it is a portable procedure that should allow the ganzfeld to spread to ordinary psychology departments. It is also a procedure that potentially should teach us something about how psi enters consciousness. With the manual procedure, there were already some indications from the qualitative material that psi in

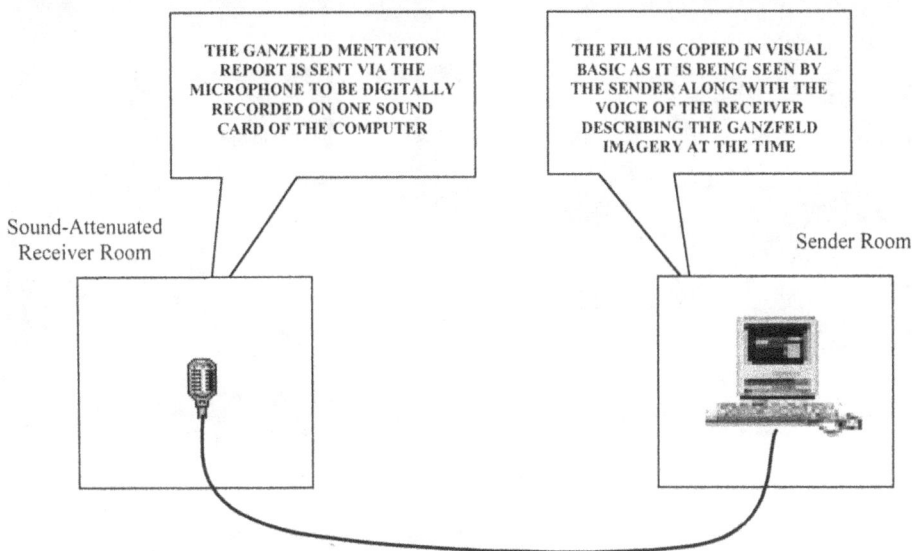

Figure 4.2. The Real-Time Digital Ganzfeld Technique (RTDGT) set-up.

many ways functioned as a sixth sense and following the same associative, gestalt and top-down laws of perception. In other words, if you are groping to see something in the dark, you see outlines and fill these in, not with guesswork, but with expectancies based on previous learning.

After having said that, it would be foolish to believe that all the magic is in the technique. It is clearly important to choose the right kind of emotionally engaging film material and have a relaxing environment for the procedure (see Figure 4.3).

One unexpected, but unfortunately dire, disadvantage of the RTDGT during our first experiments was stress. The programs that were developed for it were very demanding on the memory and graphic display capabilities of the existing available hardware (although this has since improved), which meant there were constant teething problems and several delays before new experiments could be run. To make matters worse a new hard disk finally crashed during the second major study losing much of our data.

The first RTDGT study (Goulding, Westerlund, Parker & Wackermann 2003) involving 128 trials was run during one term with periods of intensive testing. Normally in ganzfeld testing receivers make their own judgments as to which film clip is the target using their own mentation reports. In this case, since we had access to real-time recordings, it was

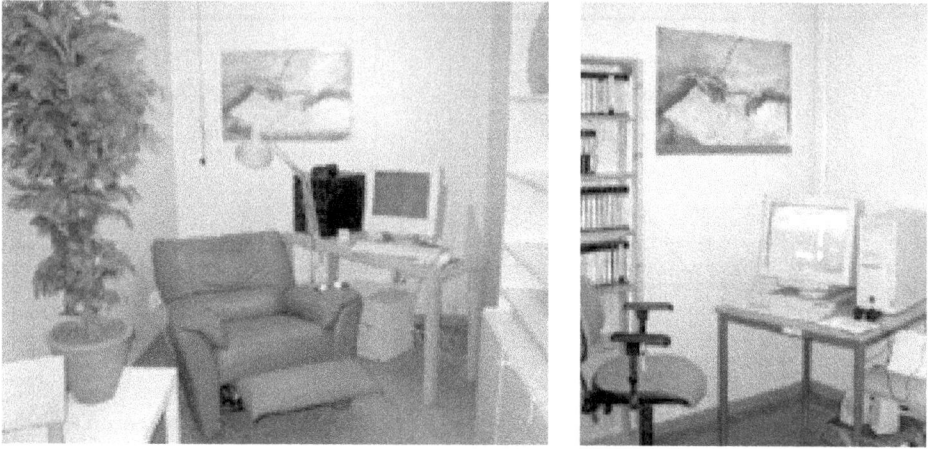

Figure 4.3. Testing rooms

reasoned that an external judge might be able to do better. To systematically go through a comparison of the mentation report with each film is time-consuming. In practice, all the 128 trials (we used two trials—that is, two independently chosen film clips per session) were judged by the external judge, Joakim Westerlund, and exactly half the trials were judged by the receiver as well. The judge's direct hits were close to chance expectancy. However, in this case the receiver's judgments for whatever reason were not only significantly different from the judge's, but by giving a 14-percent hit rate were significantly below chance expectancy, a so-called psi-missing effect.

There may be numerous reasons here why the judge's results were nonsignificant. If the psi-missing was genuine (and the statistics suggest it was), then it could be that the judge, who was able to spend more time making systematic judgments, actually raised the scoring rate from significantly below chance expectancy to chance expectancy. It is often thought that stress in interpersonal aspects can lead to target avoidance — in effect, that which psi-missing implies. Certainly, it was the case here that because of technical breakdowns the experimentation had to be done in record time and with conflicts between us all about the method of evaluating the outcome. Anneli Goulding, who ran all the experiments when she worked alone as an experimenter with receivers who brought their own senders, obtained scores at about the level we have come to expect, 32 percent direct hits. This is significantly higher — actually twice as high as when she worked with her fellow graduate students. We are not sure if this is due to the receivers bringing their own choice of senders with them because this was generally decisive in giving a significantly higher rate (46 percent) compared with when they were paired with a helper, usually a graduate student (19 percent).

As for the possibility that the judge may have raised the scoring from 14 percent to 23 percent by a more albeit time-consuming but more systematic evaluation, the qualitative data from his real-time records gave some impressive hits, as had been the case in the previous experiments (where about one in five or six were qualitatively good hits).

The perplexing aspect was that there were some apparent correspondences to nontarget (decoy) films. The most striking of these was a rather stark suicide scene from Bo Widerberg's (1967) film *Elvira Madigan*. In the lead-up to the tragedy, a young woman dressed in clothes from the turn of the century hunts butterflies in a meadow. The participant said: "a meadow a woman who hunts butterflies. She has a long light dress on. The turn of the century." This was, however, *not* in real time with the film content. The film clip by chance or design turned up again shortly afterwards when Anneli Goulding, the experimenter, asked me to run a session for herself as subject. Ironically, the same apparent anomaly arose, which Ramsden and Miles noticed, that experiences which were not intended as targets but occurred at another time, would appear. Naturally, the question remains, could this be in some way merely a chance occurrence or does it tell us something about the nature of psi?

Other strange occurrences would occur that did not fit into the notion of ESP as an extra, or sixth, sense obeying normal laws. For instance, the judge, Westerlund, when he was about to carry out a judging session sat down, ate some sandwiches and then began playing a game of patience while intending to listen to the mentation tape. On putting on the ganzfeld session tape, he heard the words: "Someone who is eating sandwiches. Playing cards. Is there someone who is playing patience?"

In attributing such events to psi, we are of course widening the "trawling net," but we may need to do this in order to catch the beast that seems to constantly allure us. Obviously these kinds of event are impossible to quantify, but Dr. Westerlund has devised a rough way of evaluating some of the qualitative hits: for this to work only one single utterance is collected from every trial in which there appears to be striking real-time correspondences between the mentation and the film clip. A collection of these one trial per selected sessions then should contain mostly hits. The existing collection he has evaluated is as yet small, but raised his rate from one-quarter to one-third hits.

The second RTDGT study (Parker & Wright 2003) was more successful according to traditional criteria, achieving a hit rate of 33 percent over 74 trials, but using receiver judgments this time (giving an effect size of .17, $p =. 09$). Again stress seemed to be a factor. Previous work (Sondow 1979) indicates that more than one session per day was likely to be unsuccessful. Unfortunately, again because of time pressure, about half the experiment had to be run with more than one session per day, and where there were only single sessions there was a significantly higher scoring rate (45-percent hit rate compared to 19 percent for multiple sessions, $p = .05$).

Clearly much more work is needed, but now we have a technique that can potentially capture the psi process when it happens and relate this not only to other variables in the environment but study what is happening in consciousness and the brain.

Conclusions

We have followed the gradual evolution of a technology, but have we in fact come a step further in dealing with the phenomena? The skeptic might still ask: can we be certain that this is all not due to chance and the need embedded in our consciousness to try always to see meaning in what nevertheless may be merely fortuitous events? There can be no *final* answer to such questions since in some areas it is impossible to define chance. While it is totally unjustified to claim that psi is finally proven, critics who still insist that there is no solid evidence for psi are beginning to sound like Comical Ali, the Iraqi information minister, who continually insisted that there were no US or UK troops in Iraq. What is important is that research moves on by asking new questions. This is, after all, how science works, not with final statements, or proofs, but by formulating working hypotheses about processes.

Despite the evolution of a workable technique, it is important to emphasize that, like psychotherapeutic techniques or laptop presentations, new technologies in parapsychology are mere tools that are totally ineffective without the appropriate skills. This is not to say that successful experimenters are charismatic or even supersociable even if social skills may play a role (White 1976a, 1976b). There is some evidence that the situation is probably even more complicated by the experimenter's own psi-ability (White 1977). Indeed, if we accept psi as a workable hypothesis then why should some experimenters not also have access to this ability? Such considerations are all part of the realization that paranormal phenomena present a problem that is not like any other phenomenon in natural science.

In a 2003 issue of the *Journal of Parapsychology* there are several articles relating to this theme illustrating how widespread this realization is now becoming. One of these, titled "Scientists, shamans, and sages," is the Presidential Address given at the Parapsychological Association where Dr. Mario Vargolis argued that researchers in this field need to accept that there are several roles to play, only one of which is the traditional scientist, whereas another, in giving permission for a miracle to occur, is more akin to that of the shaman or magician. Given that professional magicians, despite their expert knowledge of the psychology of deception and illusion, are strongly predisposed to believe in the paranormal (Hansen 1990; Truzzi 1997) this may not be so far-fetched as it sounds.

In the same issue, a second paper takes up the psychology of the psi-conducive experimenter. According to this investigation (Smith, in press), successful experimenters have not only often had their own psychic experiences, but also believe in their own psychokinetic ability to mentally influence their experiments and surroundings. This confirms earlier work published some years ago indicating that psi-conducive experimenters as a group score successfully as subjects and are overrepresented as psi-conducive subjects (Parker 1976a; Millar 1979). It seems almost heresy to mention this in a scientific review, but one of the most successful ganzfeld studies (Wezelman, Gerding, & Verhoeven 1997) attributed its success to the use of ritual and prayer. Certainly such findings relate well to what Thalbourne has for better or worse coined *psychopraxia* where ESP and PK are aspects of a unitary process (see Chapter 8).

Have we then come further than the insights that Ramsden and Miles left us with? I think we have confirmed and given more precision to some of these:

- The selection of gifted participants is important and in particular the application of such scales as the Transliminality Scale, may enable us to select participants who under the right conditions can demonstrate this ability.
- Psi appears in many of these individuals to be a unitary process. Thalbourne (Chapter 8) has reviewed the evidence for how both ESP and PK experiences appear to occur under phenomenologically similar conditions.
- Psi is largely an unconscious process. The recently developed concept of psychopraxia takes into account the fact that "the self" can have unconscious components.
- Altered states open a door to this unconscious process. One most promising hypothesis which deserves further work concerns the fact that psi occurs during a sudden *shift in state* (Alvarado 1998; Murphy 1966;

Parker 1976b). It is just possible that during this shift, information enters consciousness from sources other than the individual's own memory.

At least one of Ramsden and Miles' insights was before its time. This concerns the unconscious nature of the processes involved. Several psychologists and psychical researchers in the early 1900s such as William James, Frederic Myers, and James Hyslop regarded psi as a transference of information from the unconscious of one individual to the unconscious of another. Myers and James even believed that an individual could have several streams of consciousness, of which the main stream could be unconscious. J. B. Rhine endorsed this view of psi although he did little to enlarge upon this. The reason for this lack of progress was that the concept of the unconscious was for many years totally disowned by mainstream psychology as a disreputable Freudian doctrine. Nevertheless it has become recently reintroduced under the mantle of the *Cognitive Unconscious*. While there is still a debate just as to how "smart or dumb" (Kihlstrom 1987) this cognitive unconscious is, in many respects the unconscious has now come to be regarded as being as much of a mystery as consciousness itself is. It has even been suggested that consciousness has only a retrospective existential function by making sense of everything that happens to us, but that the decisions and ensuing events are largely steered by unconscious motivational and emotional processes (Öhman 1999).

As for access to the unconscious, the concept of *subliminality* was first introduced by the psychical researcher Frederic Myers in order to denote the potential accessibility of unconscious processes to consciousness. Myers, in contrast to Freud, regarded the unconscious as a "gold mine as well as a rubbish heap" and the concept has given rise to two roots which have spread into modern psychology. The first is *transliminality*, which is defined by Thalbourne (2002) to be the "hypothesized tendency for psychological material to cross thresholds into or out of consciousness," (p. 109) and encompasses creative, psychotic-like, and paranormal experiences. The Transliminality Scale has been developed to measure the common core of these experiences.

The second concept is that of *percept-genesis* originating from research at Lund University that describes how our perceptual images are developed under the influence of personality dynamics. By presenting pictures for a fraction of a second and lengthening the exposure time, the way perceptual images develop can actually be studied experimentally (Kragh & Smith 1970). As a test predicting ESP scores, it has not fared well (Haraldsson, Houtkooper, Schneider, & Bäckström 2002), but it is a technique that could be used in combination with the ganzfeld or with the other field that is prominent in parapsychology research relating to perception without awareness: so-called *presentiment studies.*

The experimental design used in presentiment studies was first developed in the early 1980s by Holger Klintman, also at Lund University in Sweden, when it was discovered that participants appeared to be reacting to the interference that future stimulus slides would have before they were actually shown (Klintman 1983, 1984). Since then parapsychologists have used this design to study physiological responses to pictures with a strong emotional content compared with neutral pictures. In the case of erotic and violent slides, there appears to be a bodily reaction before the slides were seen (Radin 1997) although it might be the case that a culmination of excitement in anticipating what is to come explains at least some of the effect seen. Such results do, however, fit rather well with a theory which is gaining popularity in modern psychology: Antonio Damasio has succeeded in reinstating a theory originally formulated by William James, that bodily emotional reactions come first and then feelings follow along afterwards or as he puts it "the brain is the captive audience of the body." Ongoing research suggests that some individuals are more sensitive than others to these bodily cues, or so-called somatic markers, and this naturally offers an area of rapprochement with perception without awareness and presentiment studies since it may be these individuals who do well in both psi and perception-without-awareness tasks.*

Even if progress in it has taken a hundred years for psychology and parapsychology even to begin to deal with this common heritage of unconscious and paranormal experiences, there would nonetheless appear to be some genuinely new insights. Some of these concern the real difficulties that impair the progress in this field into psi and altered states. These are:

* The existence of experimenter effects.
• Psi can go in two directions: psi-missing and psi-hitting.
• There appears to be a form of elusiveness as a fundamental characteristic of the phenomenon.

These findings have led to a new question, which scarcely could have been conceived by our Victorian predecessors, or even during the time of

An area of related interest concerns a method of bodily learning developed by the successor in Sweden to John Björkhem, Lars-Eric Unestähl. Dr. Unestähl has found that novice athletes and musicians can dramatically attain a high level of skills if they are subjected to the lengthy viewing of the performances of elite members of their group. This is reminiscent of the Felicia Parise case related earlier. By collecting several convincing video documentations with elite psi performers, Dr. Unestähl and I would like to see if this method can be used by participants in psi tests.

Rhine, and it concerns the very nature of psi. The question that emerges: Is psi merely a little understood form of *communication*, a sixth sense in the form of extrasensory perception and an exteriorized motor activity as in psychokinesis, or (based on anecdotal evidence), is it a form of *connectiveness* that is a sort of psychic web whose connections are determined by meaning and personal relevance rather than normal space-time relations?

This is obviously highly speculative but if we aim to answer this question, we need to study high-quality psi and not just small statistical aberrations. I believe the RTDGT offers this possibility, but in the long run it may be counterproductive to continue to try to strip psi of its magical heritage and study it as a simple ability to be controlled. If the earlier findings mentioned above are taken seriously, we should do as modern psychology does now in dealing with the placebo effect — seek not to eliminate the experimenter effect, but to harness its potential. Indeed, some professional magicians would make plausible psi-experimenters even if professional parapsychologists should retain control of the ethical and security aspects of experimentation.* It seems entirely appropriate to resort to using some form of "magic" in order to capture psi as it happens.

Given this claim, the way will open to learn something fundamentally new about the phenomena and as such the nature of mind, which is the true quest of parapsychology. The greatest hindrance to future research is no longer the replication problem, but the need to produce theories that relate to mainstream psychology. To be able to study the phenomenon under at least semicontrolled conditions without denaturalizing it, and then to relate this knowledge to neuroscience, is the challenge of parapsychology in the twenty-first century.

REFERENCES

Alvarado, C. (1998). ESP and altered states of consciousness: An overview of conceptual and research trends. *Journal of Parapsychology* 62, 27–64.

Bem, D. and C. Honorton (1994). Does psi exist? Replicable evidence of an anomalous process of information transfer. *Psychological Bulletin* 115, 4–18.

Bem, D., J. Palmer, and R. Broughton (2001). Updating the ganzfeld database: A victim of its own success? *Journal of Parapsychology* 65, 207–218.

*Just as the division between skeptics and parapsychologists is a false one, the division between magicians and parapsychologists is also a fleeting one. Some parapsychologists, such as James Alcock, Loyd Auerbach, Daryl Bem, George Hansen, Arthur Hastings, Peter Lamont, Russell Targ, the late Marcello Truzzi, and Richard Wiseman, are or were skilled as magicians, and others such as Robert Morris and myself have a working knowledge of the methods.

Child, I. L. (1985). Psychology and anomalous observations. *American Psychologist* **40**, 1219–1230.

Goulding, A., J. Westerlund, A. Parker, and J. Wackermann (2003). A real-time digital ganzfeld study. To be submitted.

Gruber, E. (1999). *Psychic wars: Parapsychology in espionage and beyond.* London: Blandford.

Hansen, G. (1990). Magicians who endorsed psychic phenomena. *The Linking Ring, International Brotherhood of Magicians.*

Haraldsson, E., J. M. Houtkooper, R. Schneider, and M. Bäckström (2002). Perceptual defensiveness and ESP performance. *Journal of Parapsychology* **66**, 249–270.

Honorton, C. (1993). A moving experience. *Journal of the American Society for Psychical Research* **87**, 329–340.

Honorton, C., and S. Krippner (1969), Hypnosis and ESP performance: A review of the experimental literature. *Journal of the American Society for Psychical Research* **63**, 214–252.

Hyslop, J. (1911). Experiments and experiences in telepathy by Miss Miles, Miss Ramsden and Miss Statkowski. *Proceedings of the American Society for Psychical Research* **5**, 673–753.

Kihlstrom, J. F. (1987). The cognitive unconscious. *Science* **237**, 1445–1452.

Kirsch, I., and S. J. Lynn (1995). The altered state of hypnosis. *American Psychologist* **50**, 846–858.

Klintman, H. (1983) Is there a paranormal precognitive influence in certain types of perceptual sequences? Part 1. *European Journal of Parapsychology* **5**, 19–49.

_____. (1984) Is there a paranormal precognitive influence in certain types of perceptual sequences? Part 2. *European Journal of Parapsychology* **5**, 125–140.

Kragh, U., and G. J. Smith (1970). *Percept-genetic analysis.* Lund: Gleerups.

Kumar, V. K., and R. Pekala (2001). Relation of hypnosis-specific attitudes and behaviors to paranormal beliefs and experiences. In J. Houran and R. Lange, eds., *Hauntings and poltergeists: Multidisciplinary perspectives.* (pp. 260–279). Jefferson, NC: McFarland.

McMoneagle, J. (2000). *Remote viewing secrets: A handbook.* Charlottesville, VA: Hampton Roads.

Miles, C. (1908). Experiments in thought transference. *Journal of the Society for Psychical Research* **13**, 243–262.

Miles, C., and H. Ramsden (1908–09). Experiments in thought transference. *Proceedings of the Society for Psychical Research* **21**, 60–69.

Millar, B. (1979). The distribution of psi. *European Journal of Parapsychology* **3**, 78–110.

Milton, J., and R. Wiseman (1999), Does psi exist? Lack of replication of an anomalous process of information transfer. *Psychological Bulletin* **125**, 387–391.

Murphy, G. (1966). Research in creativeness: What can it tell us about extra-sensory perception? *Journal of the American Society for Psychical Research* **60**, 8–22.

Öhman, A. (1999). Distinguishing unconscious emotional processes: Methodological considerations and theoretical implications. In T. Dalgleish and M. Power, eds., *Handbook of cognition and emotion.* London: John Wiley.

Parker, A. (1976a), Parapsychologists' personality and psi in relation to the experimenter effect. *Research in Parapsychology 1976* (pp. 107–109). Metuchen, NJ: Scarecrow Press.

_____. (1976b). *States of mind.* New York: Taplinger.

_____. (2000). A review of the Ganzfeld work at Gothenburg University. *Journal of the Society for Psychical Research* 64,1–15.

_____. (2003), Hypnosis and paranormal experiences: Is there more than a historical connection? *Abstracts of Papers at 1st Nordic Hypnosis Congress,* Oslo.

Parker, A., and T. Wright (2003). Experimentation with the real-time digital ganzfeld. Paper presented at the *27th International Conference of the Society for Psychical Research.*

Parker, A., A. Persson, and A. Haller (2000). Using qualitative Ganzfeld research for theory development: Top-down processes in psi-mediation. *Journal of the Society for Psychical Research* 64, 65–81.

Pekala, R. J., and E. Cardeña (2000). Methodological issues in the study of altered states and anomalous experiences. In E. Cardeña, J. Lynn, and S. Krippner, eds., *Varieties of anomalous experience.* (pp. 47–82). Washington, DC: American Psychological Association.

Radin, D. (1997). *The conscious universe.* New York: HarperCollins.

Rhine, L. E. (1962). Psychological processes in ESP experiences. Part II. Dreams. *Journal of Parapsychology* 27, 172–199.

Rhine, J. B. (1934/1964). *Extrasensory perception.* Boston: Bruce Humphries.

_____. (1952). Hypnosis and ESP. In L. Lecron, ed., *Experimental hypnosis.* New York: Macmillan.

Schouten, S. (1998). "Are we making progress?" In L. Coly and J. McMahon, eds., *Psi research methodology: A re-examination. Proceedings of an International Conference* (pp. 295–322). New York: Parapsychology Foundation.

Sherwood, S. J. (2002). ESP during sleep: Sweet dreams or a nightmare. Invited paper presented at *45th Annual Convention, Parapsychological Association,* Paris.

Smith, M. (in press). The psychology of the psi-conducive experimenter: Personality, attitudes towards psi, and personal experience. *Journal of Parapsychology.*

Sondow, N. (1979). Effects of associations and feedback on psi in the Ganzfeld: Is there more than meets the judge's eye? *Journal of Society of the American Society for Psychical Research* 73, 123–143.

Stanford, R. G., and A. G. Stein (1994). A meta-analysis of ESP studies contrasting hypnosis and a comparison condition. *Journal of Parapsychology* 58, 235–269.

Stevenson, I, (1970). *Telepathic impressions: A review and report of 35 new cases.* Charlottesville, VA: University of Virginia Press.

Storm L., and S. Ertel (2001). Does psi exist? Comments on Milton and Wiseman's (1999) meta-analysis of ganzfeld research. *Psychological Bulletin* 127, 424–433.

Tart, C. (1969). *Altered states of consciousness.* New York: Anchor.

Thalbourne, M. A. (2002). In defense of transliminality: A response to Goulding and Parker. *European Journal of Parapsychology* 17, 109–113.

Truzzi, M. (1997). Reflections on the sociology and social psychology of conjurors and their relations with psychical research. In S. Krippner, ed., *Advances in parapsychological research* (pp. 231–271). Jefferson, NC: McFarland.

Ullman, M., S. Krippner, and A. Vaughan (1974). *Dream telepathy.* Baltimore: Penguin Books.

Wackermann, J., P. Pütz, S. Büchl, I. Strauch, and D. Lehmann (2000). A comparison of Ganzfeld and hypnagogic state in terms of electrophysiological measures and subjective experience. Abstracts of the Parapsychological Association 44 Convention, *Journal of Parapsychology* **64**, 254–255.

Wezelman, R., H. Gerding, I. Verhoeven (1997). Eigensender ganzfeld psi: An experiment in practical philosophy. *European Journal of Parapsychology* **13**, 28–39

White, R. A. (1964). A comparison of old and new methods of responding to targets in ESP research. *Journal of the American Society for Psychical Research* **58**, 21–26.

_____. (1976a). The influence of persons other than the experimenter on the subject's scores in psi experiments. *Journal of the American Society for Psychical Research* **69**, 133–166.

_____. (1976b). The limits of experimenter influence on psi test results: Can any be set? *Journal of the American Society for Psychical Research* **70**, 335–369.

_____. (1977). The influence of the experimenter motivation, attitudes and methods of handling subjects in psi test results. In. B. B. Wolman, ed., Handbook *of Parapsychology* (pp. 273–301). New York: Van Nostrand Reinhold.

Wilson, S. C., and T. X. Barber (1983) The fantasy-prone personality: Implications for understanding imagery, hypnosis, and parapsychological phenomena. In *Imagery, Current Theory, Research, and Application* (pp. 340–387). New York: John Wiley and Sons.

5

The Ball Drawing Test: Psi from Untrodden Ground[*]

Suitbert Ertel

German parapsychologist Professor Suitbert Ertel has designed and implemented the novel ball drawing test. The following chapter is the only technical chapter in this book, but we include it here because it describes a procedure that yields a comparatively moderate effect size with a lot less effort on the part of experimenters and participants than most psi experiments to date. Since participants test themselves at home, Professor Ertel believes the ball drawing test adds ecological validity to psi testing — an aspect of paranormal experimentation that has been largely ignored in parapsychology, and a methodological consideration that should be made in future experimental design. Interested readers can refer to the more technical issues concerning the ball drawing test in the chapter's appendix. (Editors)

A Deplorable State of the Art

John Beloff (1993) wrote: "What, then, might the future hold for parapsychology? The vanguard of experimental parapsychology may reach a

*Based on a paper presented at the 43rd Annual Convention of the Parapsychological Association in Freiburg, Germany, August 17–20, 2000.

pitch where the effects become so reliable that it is no longer possible to ignore them without incurring a charge of being scientifically illiterate or incurably prejudiced" (p. 228). At the moment, however, parapsychological experiments are encumbered with problems, which are widely deplored. First, *there is too much effort-expenditure.* Paranormal phenomena may not come to the fore without considerable effort from both participant and experimenter. For example, experiments on telepathic influence with dreamers allow for merely one single trial per subject per night. One remote viewing performance requires roughly five hours; each ganzfeld trial, two hours. That is, experimental techniques commonly used in ESP research today are time-consuming. Multiple-choice procedures such as card guessing and other low-cost procedures, favored in earlier years, would allow for, say, three trials per minute. But having come under continued attack by skeptical opponents, and due to monotony effects for participants (next point), they have been largely abandoned.

Second, *lack of motivation.* Participants are bored and demotivated by psi tests — in particular, multiple-choice tasks. Experimenters generally try to compensate for such dissatisfaction by creating the right social ambience. They know too well that "better ESP results [are obtained by experimenters who] provide a warm, supportive, and caring atmosphere for their participants" (Broughton 1991, p. 134). Broughton adds: "I have always regarded subject motivation as one of, if not the, chief problems facing parapsychologists looking for psi abilities among the general population" (p. 189). But it is doubtful whether an experimenter's smiling and offering a cup of coffee is sufficiently effective.

Third, *psi-effects are too small.* In general, psi-effects produced in laboratories are tiny. Even ganzfeld results (e.g., those from 30 studies meta-analyzed by Milton & Wiseman 1999) may shrink to near nonsignificance after biased scrutiny, and even then, arduous defense is necessary to save those small gains (see Storm & Ertel 2001). Psi effects obtained from random event generators (REG) are extremely small (0.05 percent on average, 0.5 percent with exceptionally gifted participants). And while Princeton Engineering Anomalies Research (PEAR) researchers using REGs have obtained convincing levels of significance ($p = .0001$) for PK effects from 33 participants, it still took 1,000 man-hours to reach the same level of success (estimate based on information by Jahn & Dunne 1999).

Fourth, *effects tend to decline.* Psi effects are said to decline, as a rule, and therefore are hard to replicate so that skeptics tend to doubt their existence altogether — Haraldsson et al. (2002) note: "The persistent difficulty in coming up with experimental findings with an acceptable degree of replicability has remained the most important serious criticism of parapsychology" (p. 249). One of the largest replication experiments ever conducted in the field, using PEAR's REG design in three laboratories, failed (Jahn et al. 2000). A comprehensive review of the decline effect — the "most consistent finding [of parapsychological research]" (Palmer 1978) — is provided by Boesch and Wallach (unpublished).

Fifth, *good results are dubious.* Large psi effects are likely to raise suspicion of bias or fraud. This has bothered psi experimenters ever since Rhine's early days. Those attempting to improve experimental methods in order to produce increased effect sizes may encounter disbelief and dismissal, even within the psi research community itself. Fear of suspicion of fraud has hitherto led to increasingly stricter safeguards, tighter controls, and computer automatization — all of which may inhibit psi-conducive conditions.

Sixth, *lack of process orientation.* Experimenters, while spending much effort on proof-oriented research, tend to forego process-oriented studies of psi under varying conditions. Results from such studies are needed, however, to gain theoretical groundwork on which an ultimate acceptance of psi-phenomena is dependent.

In what follows, an account is given of a new psi-measuring technique, the ball drawing test, which might help mitigate these problems or even solve them. The idea arose in 1996 when I was still rather ignorant — fortunately so in hindsight — regarding conventional parapsychological methods. The test was designed ad hoc to meet the demand of a client who urged me to test and thereby acknowledge her extrasensory power. We conducted 3,000 trials. The test did not show that she had such power. Did she really lack psi power, or had I tinkered with an invalid test? Another reason I pursued this idea was that my students wanted me to provide an ESP demonstration in class.

The Ball Drawing Task

The Standard Procedure*

Participants are handed an opaque bag containing 50 table tennis balls on which the numbers 1 to 5 are written, each number on 10 balls. A participant's trial consists of shaking the bag, blind-drawing a ball from

*Another test design requires two bags from which participants draw balls with their right and left hand simultaneously. An increased complexity of this condition entails additional methodological advantages. An account of research results obtained from the two-bags procedure will be published separately.

the bag and putting the ball back. On each trial, the number is guessed in advance and recorded. The number on the ball that is subsequently drawn is also recorded. Participants are instructed individually — they are shown how to shake the bag, how to draw the balls, etc. They are told that when the test is done and the data analyzed, they will receive individual feedback. If their score exceeds chance significantly, they would be invited to participate in additional experiments under controlled conditions. The participants take the material home, where they perform six runs of 60 trials each at self-selected times. The total testing time for 6 × 60 = 360 trials, spread over a week, amounts to 1.5 hours. Participants whose hit rate exceeds expectancy by roughly 30 percent or more are invited to participate in follow-up studies.*

Participants

The first sample consisted of seven students taking a course on "anomalistics" in 1997. Since four of them showed exceptional psi-hitting (perhaps a self-selected sample of psi-gifted students) their results will not be included in the standardization sample which consists of unselected participants: five successive cohorts of first-year psychology students took part in this test under identical conditions (57 in 1998; 38 in 1999; 56 in 2000; 36 in 2001; 44 in 2002). In total, 231 students (192 females, 39 males) were tested using the standard procedure just described. Some students were tested subsequently under alternative conditions. Participants were granted credit points for their study records, and they were paid for additional participation in the lab. Occasional experiments were also conducted with other volunteers (mostly nonstudents). Results of only two of them (K.G. and T.K.), who drew balls under my observation, will also be referred to in this chapter.

Data Analysis

How large must hit rates be so as to become statistically significant? The mean chance expectancy for one run, consisting of 60 trials, is 12 hits because with five numbers among which participants guess one number 60/5 = 12 hits will be drawn on average anyway. Significance levels were determined using the Binomial test.† For example, 18 hits from one run is significant ($p = .038$, one-sided), 20 hits very significant ($p = .008$). The significance value, however, does not tell us whether hit rates are large or

---

*Instructions and photographs of the material are accessible via www.suitbertertel. net.

†Rosenthal and Rubin's (1989) Z-test which had been used first seems to suffer from an as yet uncorrected error (D. B. Rubin, personal communication).

small — a measure of *effect size* is also needed. The simplest measure is the *percentage-of-hit surplus*. With, say, 18 hits, a participant's surplus is six hits which is 50 percent above expectancy, because $^{6}/_{12}$ = 0.5, multiplied by 100 = 50 percent. With 24 hits the surplus is 100 percent and so forth.* A participant's average hit-rate of 14.17 across six runs (one test series), which is 18 percent surplus, is significant; an average of 15.0 hits, which is 25 percent surplus, is very significant.

Another more practical effect size measure was used based on an interesting rationale developed by Nelson (1994), which incorporates effort expenditure as a criterion. His formula has been modified so that a participant's psi ability can be expressed in man-hours (hours and minutes), which are required, on average, to accumulate deviations from chance until the benchmark of significance (p = .05) is reached. For example, C.G., the most psi-gifted student participant that I tested, reached the .05-benchmark on average in two minutes. The time needed for 60 trials at "slow speed" is 20 minutes, so C.G. drew 60/20 = three balls per minute, or six balls in two minutes. Instead of hitting the predicted number only 1.2 times on average across six trials (chance expectancy), she hit them 2.8 times on average. Participants with moderate psi-giftedness may reach the benchmark in one to two hours, and those without any psi-ability may not reach the .05-benchmark even if they kept on drawing balls *ad infinitum*.

Does the Ball Drawing Test Tap Psi?

Hit-rates and Effect Sizes

For all 231 students, the average hit-rate deviation is 9.0 percent above mean chance expectancy (*MCE*), which is extremely significant (Z = 12.07, $p<10^{-15}$).† The overall effect size was weak (*ES* = .04). Figure 5.1 shows per-

---

*The percentage-of-hit surplus *is a common-sense effect size measure compared to more technical effect size measures (e.g., Rosenthal's π, Cohen's h, or z/√n). Since hit probabilities for ball test variations have been kept constant (one in five balls correct by chance — i.e., 0.20), no problem arises with comparing hit surpluses among different experimental conditions. Results from Zener card guessing (where MCE is also 0.20) may be compared using this scale.*

†*In 1997, seven students in an advanced course on anomalistics, who were excluded from this study, obtained a 41.2-percent surplus in 224 runs (13,440 trials). Four of them were high hitters (surpluses 110.2 percent, 107 percent, 50.0 percent, 27.3 percent), two had chance results (1.6 percent, 0.5 percent), one showed significant psi-missing (-8.3 percent). The students' total including the seven course participants (138 students in all) obtained 14.1 percent surplus.*

cent deviations of hit rates from chance as well as Z- and p-values for five successive student cohorts separately. Hit rates of the two first cohorts are almost equal, and two succeeding cohorts dropped off slightly, which looked as if a decline effect would follow. But the fifth cohort regained and even surpassed numerically the first cohort's level.*

The 231 students reached the $p = .05$ benchmark on average with 3.12 man-hours of effort. This is much less than what an unselected REG-sample of PEAR participants yield who spent about 132 hours to reach the $p = .05$ level (Dunne & Jahn 1992; see Figure 5.2). For the PEAR studies, the work of one experimenter per participant is shown in Figure 5.2. Even ganzfeld research, where two participants and two experimenters are involved, an equal gains investment will require roughly 12 times the effort of the ball drawing participants (i.e., 105 hours, based on Bem & Honorton 1994, see Figure 5.2).

High scorers (i.e., those obtaining at least 33.3-percent hit rates above MCE) did not work long hours to obtain the 5-percent significance benchmark. M.L. (#25), who is the last among 25 best scorers, reached the benchmark in 41 minutes (See Table 5.1, column 6). C.G. at the top of the rank order (#1) made it in record time (two minutes), as mentioned above.

Table 5.1 shows hit surpluses (column 5), Z-deviations (column 7) and associated significance values (column 8) of the 25 best hitters, which is 10.8 percent of the total of 231 students. Column 9 indicates for 11 participants whether or not they were also successful when tested under controlled conditions. The results may remind readers of early Duke findings: "[A]mong Rhine's immediate entourage, there were in all some eight 'high-scorers' (...[reaching], say, 7, 8, or even 9 hits over a large number of runs)" (Beloff, 1993, p.136) — a 40-percent, 60-percent, or even 80-percent hit surplus based on a 0.2 hit probability, which also applies to the ball test. Rhine's successes are often regarded as peaks of the golden years of experimental psi research which have never come back. But Table 5.1 shows 17 participants with hit surpluses above 40 percent, and three participants

*The ball test's total of 9 percent surplus seems to be roughly representative for an unselected student population, at least for psychology beginners. An overall result from Rhine's ESP studies at Duke University makes an interesting comparison: Nabours (1943) provides two numbers (which were "authoritatively stated"), one based on 907,030 trials which yielded a 7.2-percent hit surplus (0.2 was MCE as for the ball test). Another 220,455 "more accurately conducted trials" yielded a 4.6-percent surplus. Note that a large proportion of high-hitters contributed to this data, because experimenters tended to prolong test series with successful participants in the first place. Results from additional ball tests with selected high-hitters have not been included in the 138-subject database.

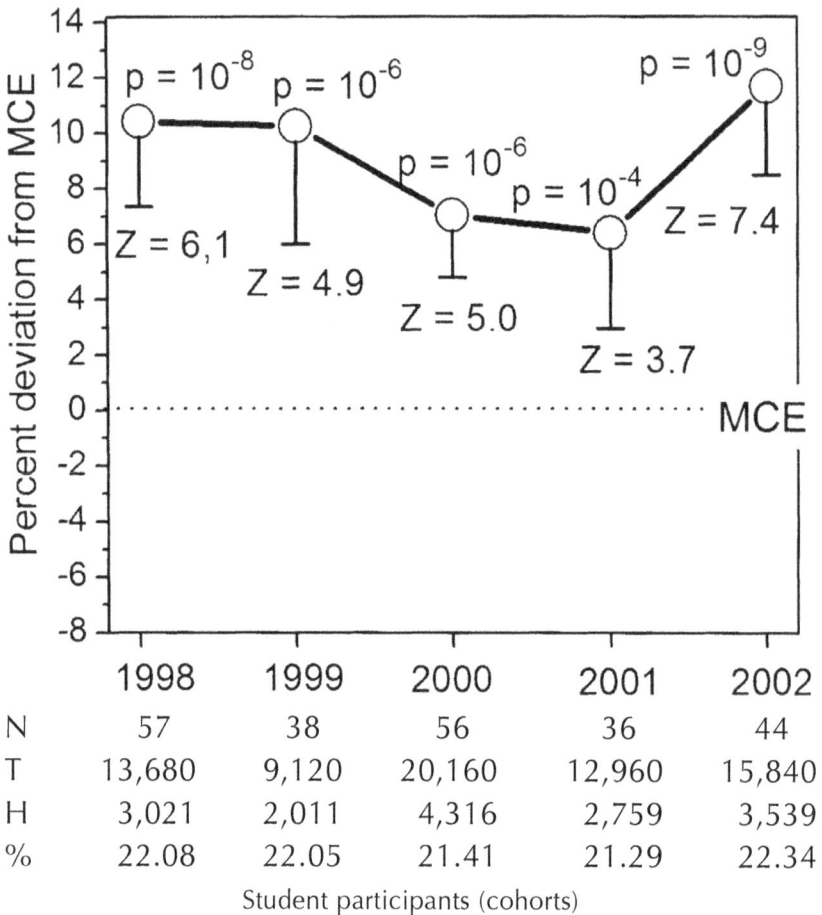

	1998	1999	2000	2001	2002
N	57	38	56	36	44
T	13,680	9,120	20,160	12,960	15,840
H	3,021	2,011	4,316	2,759	3,539
%	22.08	22.05	21.41	21.29	22.34

Student participants (cohorts)

Figure 5.1. Hit rates by percent deviations from mean chance expectancy (*MCE*) for five cohorts of student beginners at the Georg-Elias-Müller Institute of Psychology, Göttingen (Total: 231). p-values and Z-values are shown. Error bars indicate confidence limits for $p = .95$ (Newcombe, 1998). N = number of participants, T = number of trials, H = number of hits, % = percent hits, expectancy = 20%.

exceeded Rhine's best hitters (his best participant actually obtained 98-percent surplus).*

    It should be noted that, in terms of effect size *ES*, which captures psi manifestation without looking at workload, the overall result of the ball test for unselected student samples lies within the range of earlier values.

---

*Stars among ESP subjects (card guessing) at Duke in early times were Adam J. Linzmayer — hit surplus 98 percent in 21,247 trials, according to Beloff (1993, p.136) or 34.6

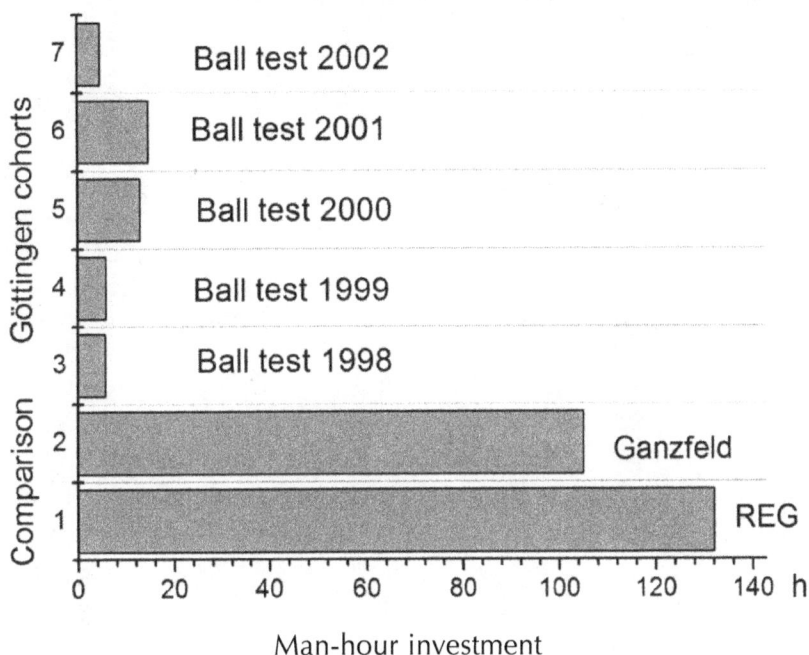

Figure 5.2. Effect size based on man-hours for five cohorts of Göttingen students (unselected participants), compared with man-hours for typical ganzfeld and REG experiments. Benchmark criterion: Man-hours needed to achieve significance ($p = .05$).

Among 11 projects in various domains, nine of which were listed in Storm and Thalbourne (2000) and one additional domain (Radin 1997), the ball test's effect size takes the middle position 6 when *ES* values are ranked (see Table 5.2).

Table 5.2 also shows that an average trial of multiple choice tasks and of other short-trial tests in general (card guessing, dice tossing etc.), done

percent(?) in 1,500 trials according to Broughton (1991, p. 68; numbers provided in the literature are all transformed to the percent surplus scale); Hubert Pearce— 98 percent in 1,850 trials, according to Broughton, Beloff, and Carpenter (1977, p. 211); Basil Shackleton— 35 percent in 4,000 trials (this and the remaining numbers are based on Carpenter (1977, p. 209f); Charles E. Stuart— 30 percent in 1,300 trials); Gloria Stewart— 27 percent in 37,100 trials. One famous subject of M. Ryzl (Prague) was Pavel Stepanek— 33 percent in 42,598 trials. The latter value, originally based on an experiment with p = .05 MCE, has been transformed using Rosenthal and Rubin's (1989) π formula. The largest hit surplus that I found in the literature was obtained by a "young female subject" of B. F. Ries (1937). Her surplus was purported to amount to an exceptional 264.8 percent, in 1,850 trials, according to Carpenter (p. 209).

Table 5.1. Average hits per run (expected 12 hits with probability *P* = 0.20) for individual high hitters (column 2) reaching p = .001 (col. 8) in the ball test (360 draws).

1 #	2 Name of participant	3 # of runs	4 Hits per run	5 Hit surplus %	6 Time (mins.) to reach p = .05 benchmark	7 Z	8 p	9 Control Sign
1	C.G.	*	2,775	131.25	2	10.1	< 10-15	
2	B.F.	**	2,522	110.17	3	24.1	< 10-15	
3	K.H.	**	2,488	107.33	3	23.5	< 10-15	+
4	C.K.		2,200	83.33	6	7.8	< 10-14	+
5	S.K.		2,167	80.58	7	7.6	< 10-13	−
6	S.B.		2,017	68.08	8	6.4	10-10	+
7	S.T.		2,000	66.67	8	6.3	10-9	+
8	E.PG.		1,950	62.50	9	5.9	10-8	+
9	N.L.W.		1,950	62.50	9	5.9	10-8	−
10	G.R.		1,900	58.33	11	5.5	10-7	−
11	O.R.	*	1,900	58.33	11	4.4	10-5	
12	F.L.		1,850	54.17	12	5.1	10-6	
13	T.M.	*	1,825	52.08	13	4.0	.00004	−
14	G.G.	**	1,800	50.00	15	10.9	< 10-15	+
15	S.K.	*	1,775	47.92	17	3.6	.0001	
16	U.F.	*	1,700	41.67	23	3.2	.0008	
17	C.C.		1,683	40.25	23	3.8	.0001	
18	K.B.	*	1,675	39.58	24	3.0	.001	
19	A.W.	*	1,675	39.58	24	3.0	.001	
20	A.J.	*	1,675	39.58	24	3.0	.001	+
21	C.O.		1,667	38.92	24	3.6	.0001	
22	R.K.B.	*	1,650	37.50	25	2.8	.002	
23	S. H.	*	1,625	35.42	30	2.7	.004	
24	A.D. J.		1,617	34.75	31	3.2	.0006	
25	M.I.	*	1,600	33.33	41	2.5	.006	

Note: Effect size is indicated by hit surplus as percent deviation from expectancy (col. 5) and by the time needed to reach the benchmark of p = .05 (col. 6). The number of runs differs (col. 3), but hits per run (col. 4) are comparable. Z values (col. 7) and p (col. 8) are dependent on (3). Hit surpluses by ball drawing tests under lab control were significant (+) or not significant (−) (col. 9)
*Screening test results based on 4 runs (240 trials)
**Based on 32 runs (1,920 trials)
All other results are based on 6 runs (360 trials)

Table 5.2. Effect size (ES) of ball test results (position 6)
and ES-values obtained in other domains of experimental psi research
(Source: Storm & Thalbourne 2002 [ST], Radin 1997 [R])

#	Source 2	Domain	Source 1	Mean ES
01	R	Telepathic dream studies	Ullman & Krippner (1970)	.260
02	ST	DMILS (biological psychokinesis)	Braud & Schlitz (1991)	.178[a]
03	ST	Free Response (GESP) — Remote Viewing	Milton (1998)	.170
04	ST	Ganzfeld	Storm & Ertel (2001)	.154
05	ST	Autoganzfeld	Storm & Ertel (2001)	.117
06	n/a	Forced choice: Ball test (5 cohorts)	Ertel (this chapter)	.046[b, c]
07	ST	Forced choice: Precognition	Honorton & Ferrari (1989)	.012
08	ST	Forced choice: Precognition	Steinkamp et al. (1998)	.010
09	ST	Clairvoyance	Steinkamp et al. (1998)	.009
10	ST	Dice throwing	Radin & Ferrari (1991)	.003[d]
11	ST	RNG (random number generator)	Radin & Nelson (1989)	.0003

[a]Storm & Thalbourne's (2002) published entry .42 is erroneous (L. Storm, personal communication, May 16, 2003; ES recalculated by L. Storm)
[b]Mean ES = .073 including the 7-student sample of 1997
[c]Mean ES = .209 for 15 subjects tested under control condition after being selected as high hitters under alone-at-home conditions (11 of which belonged to students cohorts)
[d]Dice tossing ES = .024 if Radin's (1997, p. 134) numbers are used

"within a few breaths," does not elicit as much psi as an average trial of long-trial tests (free response, ganzfeld, etc.) where one trial takes hours. Within its own domain, however (i. e., multiple choice), the ball test's *ES* exceeds that of traditional tests by a factor of four using unselected samples, and by a factor of 20 using samples of "alone-at-home" participants tested subsequently under controlled conditions (see Note c, Table 5.2). The supposable reason for the ball test's success within its domain, i.e., the nature of the task and psi-conducive conditions, will be discussed below. But caution is needed — are the remarkable successes of Table 5.1 participants due to fraudulent contributions?

Hit Rates Under Controlled Conditions

One of the reasons for asking participants to draw balls at home without controls was the conjecture that a person's home atmosphere might be particularly psi-conducive while hit probabilities are likely to be diminished under lab surveillance. This has indeed been confirmed for individual cases. Column 9 of Table 5.1 shows that four of 11 participants, tested under lab control, did not reach a significant hit surplus. Or did these four, while drawing balls at home, tamper with their records?

Observations with students who did reach a significant surplus under controlled conditions might help explain why some fellow students failed. K.H.'s record (#03) is particularly informative. After a period of exceptional hit excess at home I invited her to draw balls in my office, under video control. She was worried and first suggested she do one run as a pretest in my office, without video. Her hit rate dropped dramatically from an average of roughly 100 percent above *MCE* to only 15 percent. She was upset because, as she said, I might now suspect that her home results were tampered with. Her disappointment lasted for six months, after which she resumed doing the ball tests at home. Her record across 16 runs showed excellent hit rates as before (see Figure 5.3, runs #1 to #16). So I dared invite her again to draw balls for eight sessions under my control, this time foregoing the frightening video camera. She complied, and the results are shown in Figure 5.3 (runs #17 to #24). (In the meantime, I made videos of other high-hitters).

It can be seen that K.H.'s hit rate dropped considerably when she did her first run in my office. Subsequently her scores recovered gradually, eventually approaching her home test level (note that runs in Figure 5.3 were done using a two-bags procedure; hit counts in that case are taken from simultaneous left and right draws, *MCE* = 24 hits). The total of K.H.'s surplus above *MCE* across eight runs under controlled conditions was extremely significant ($Z = 8.0$, $p < 10^{-15}$).

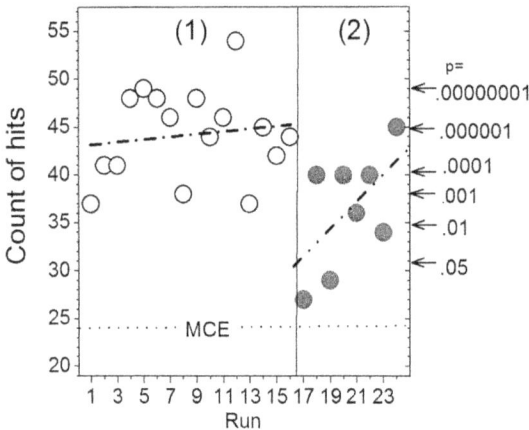

° Home condition (subject alone)
• Laboratory condition (control by experimenter

Figure 5.3. Percent deviation from *MCE* of K.H. under home (1) and laboratory (2) conditions. Significance levels (near the right vertical) refer to individual runs of the two-bags procedure with 2 × 60 draws (60 left-hand and 60 right-hand); *MCE* is 24 hits in this case.

The results of Figure 5.3 are noteworthy for three reasons. First, under controlled conditions, K.H. could not juggle the record as she might have done alone at home. Her highly significant hit excess in the experimenter's office must be considered genuine. Second, since K.H. proved that she was able to reach above chance levels under controlled conditions, it is unreasonable to suspect that her home results were tampered with. Finally, the results also show that laboratory controls can have deleterious effects on psi-talented participants. Changing home to lab conditions caused K.H.'s scores to drop initially even though, after two years of ball drawing experiments, she was familiar with the experimenter's business. If K.H. had been tested in a conventional way (i.e., under controlled conditions from the very beginning), her exceptional psi talent might not have been discovered.*

Unlike K.H., performances for four participants did not recover from their initial declines (Table 5.1, column 9). Do we have to assume that they juggled their home records? Not necessarily, because they might have reacted like K.H. For some reason or other they might have needed more than eight runs of exercise to regain a leisurely attitude as experienced at home.

One exceptionally surprising and comforting observation was made with ball test taking participants in my office. Two of those seven students with *positive* ball test results under controlled conditions surpassed their own home hit-rates considerably. Hit rates of A.J. (#20) and S.T. (#7) dropped initially, as was the case with K.H., and they increased thereafter. But unlike K.H., their hit rates jumped up enormously, outdoing by far their home levels. A.J., after four initial lab runs yielding hit rates near *MCE*, reached 143 percent across four subsequent runs (her home level never surpassed 40 percent). S.T., making 66.6 percent hit surplus at home, showed — after two initial lab runs with hit-rates near *MCE*— an unexpected upsurge up to 220 percent (!), on average, the level of which did not decline across five additional runs under controlled conditions.

To sum up, hit rates tend to change by replacing home with lab conditions, some changes being plausible, due to the participant's initial and understandable fear of failure. As long as hit rates recover with continued testing, we can rule out suspicion that their home results had been tampered with (e.g., recall K.H.'s performances). Another kind of change occurred under controlled conditions— an excessive hit increase, which is *implausible*, but such cases are even more at odds with the suspicion that high-hitters at home are data jugglers (viz., A.J. and S.T.). Consequently, lab results without hit surpluses, as observed with four participants, persisting across eight runs, while home results were highly significant, should be evaluated with caution. Social components of psi testing conditions might be responsible for inhibiting — or enhancing — hit-rates in unexpected and drastic ways.

Common experimental investigations in psi laboratories are done with unselected student participants, often for only one session, and participants rarely meet experimenters who can create a friendly atmosphere within a few minutes.

Social Conditions Affecting Hit Scores —
The Factor of Cooperation

Aside from control, cooperation had considerable impact on hit rates. In 1998, in Tamil Nadu, India, I met a highly psi-gifted boy — 16 years old — K.G., who drew balls under my observation with average hit rates of 112 percent above *MCE*. At one point during test sessions I wanted to know whether K.G. was also able to guess the numbers that I, the experimenter, would draw from the bag. More than 50 runs that I had completed earlier on my own had yielded chance results. I hoped K.G.'s "psi power field" would improve my poor record.

For three successive runs of 60 trials each, K.G. guessed the numbers and I drew the balls. I obtained only six, eight, and eight hits (12 are expected per run). A highly significant psi-missing effect had ensued ($p = .01$, two-tailed). After changing roles, when I guessed the numbers that K.G. would draw (four runs) — he hit them 25, 21, 19, and 21 times — his hit score (79 percent surplus, $p = 10^{-9}$) was almost as large as under ordinary conditions (i.e., when he guessed and drew numbers while I merely recorded them).

Another surprising observation with cooperating participants was made some time later. Two psychology students, B.F. and O.M., diploma candidates under my supervision, and in close relationship to each other (later they married), completed 32 ball drawing runs individually under home conditions. O.M. did not deviate from *MCE* at all, while B.F.'s hit scores were, on average, 110 percent above *MCE* (# 2 in Table 5.1).

I then instructed the couple to draw balls together, O.M. guessed numbers while B.F. drew the balls, and vice versa. My own experience with K.G. led me to expect that interaction effects might emerge, even though possibly not exactly the same that I had observed with K.G.. Since lovers generally want to reduce too much discrepancy between themselves, B.F.'s hit score might decline to some extent while O.M.'s hit score might increase.

The results (see Figure 5.4) confirmed this expectation only in a very broad sense. O.M.'s scores, at mere chance level without his partner, did not increase. His hit rate declined with her assistance to a significant psi-missing level — just as *my* scores had been brought down by K.G. B.F.'s hit scores, excellent when she drew balls alone, did not merely decrease to some extent — rather they went down dramatically. They actually joined O.M.'s psi-missing level in a way which experimenter and participants themselves had not expected. The couple was concerned about their continuous misses. B.F. reported that she eventually avoided immediate feedback. She drew the balls and showed them to O.M. without looking at them while O.M. recorded the numbers in silence.

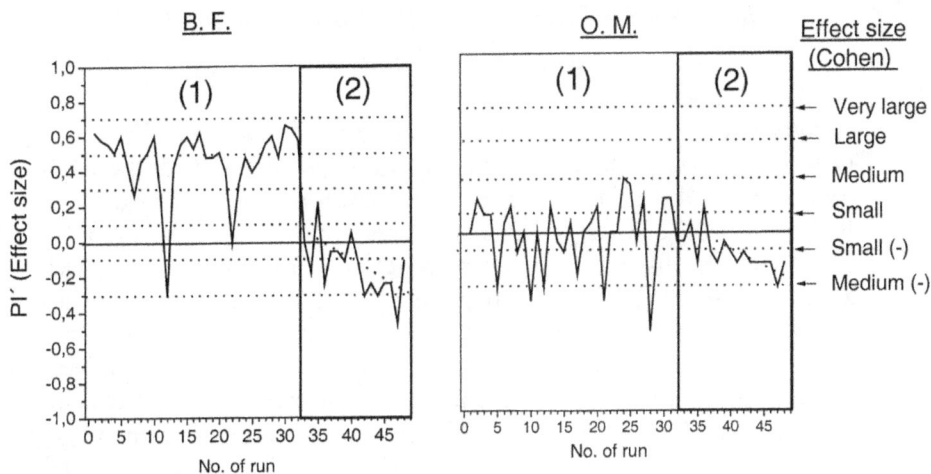

Figure 5.4(a), *left:* Percent deviations from *MCE* for B.F. drawing balls alone: (1) 32 runs, and in interaction (2) 16 subsequent runs. Significance levels refer to individual runs. Figure 5.4(b), *right:* Percent deviations from *MCE* for O.M. drawing balls alone: (1) 32 runs, and in interaction (2) 16 subsequent runs. Significance levels refer to individual runs.

These observations suggest two general conclusions. First, even seemingly psi-unsusceptible participants (e.g., O.M. and myself) might deviate from chance, even in an unwanted direction, while being assisted by psi-gifted persons. Second, ball drawing results of high-scorers may decline conspicuously due to the cooperation of low-scorers (as with B.F.), but not necessarily (as with K.G.).

All this might prompt a more general supposition: psi effects seem to be susceptible to varying social conditions. They may appear or disappear; they may increase dramatically or change from hitting to missing. No other experimental manipulation showed hit score variance to such an extent: prescribing numbers that should be drawn instead of letting participants guess at will, using colors instead of numbers, using two bags from which balls are drawn with both hands instead of using one bag, drawing balls after meditation instead of under ordinary mental conditions, etc., (results will be published elsewhere)—all this did not affect hit scores as powerfully as did the attendance of controlling or cooperating people. As far as my knowledge goes, such observations have not been made previously; they should be pursued as a promising new avenue for process-oriented investigations.

Psychometric Properties of the Ball Drawing Test: Validity and Reliability

As a newcomer to psi research, I am fond of applying mainstream-patterned standards. It seems to me that the deplorable state of the art in psi research is due to the fact that it lacks appropriate measuring devices. Basic measuring devices, agreed upon by researchers, are indispensable in every scientific discipline. But even though most psi researchers are well aware of individual differences regarding paranormal ability, just as they are aware of individual differences regarding (say) intelligence, I do not see them pursuing psychometric goals. Nothing exists that might compare, for example, with the development of tests for intelligence assessment. Key words like "test," "assessment," "reliability," "validity," are missing in Wolman's (1977) *Handbook of parapsychology*, as well as in Radin's (1997) comprehensive *Conscious universe*, and other survey books. Not much seems to have changed.

Validity

I did not set out, in the beginning, to develop a psychometric program of my own, but after six years of ball test studies I find myself encompassed by a considerable amount of data that seems suitable, psychometrically, for evaluation. (Note that the validity issue is also addressed in Appendix 5.A.) Do ball test results achieved by participants at home really reflect psi ability, or rather, do they reflect dishonesty, or merely some intricate way of applying one's sensory and mnemonic capacities (see Appendix 5.A)? The ball test's *construct validity* is addressed here. Does this test measure what it is purported to measure, or are the results due to some artifact? In psychometric contexts, all hotly debated questions about fraud, sensory leakage and the like are methodological questions that give rise to subsequent steps in research, which is business as usual in test development programs. Particular construct-fitting features for a test purported to measure psi power are the above-mentioned "earmarks of psi." The occurrence of good misses, significance but in an unwanted direction, and the like (see Appendix 5.A), add a lot to the construct validity of such a test, but more research on the validity of the ball test is desirable:

• The ball test would meet requirements of *concurrent validity*, if people reporting frequent spontaneous psi experiences (precognitive dreams, poltergeist experience, telepathic contact, dissociative experiences and the like) were to obtain higher hit rates in this test than people without anomalous experiences in their life records.

- The ball test would meet requirements of *convergent validity*, if hits from drawing balls correlate sufficiently with hits from card guessing or dice tossing, or with DMILS reactions (e.g., telepathic influence on another person's skin conductance), or with remote viewing successes (perceiving a target located distantly in space), and so forth.
- Requirements of *discriminant validity* would be met if ball test results do *not* correlate with conjurer performance (most secondary effects in the ball test are probably beyond any conjurer's awareness) and with questionnaire or other measures of inclination to deceive and manipulate people, ignoring ethical norms (e.g., Machiavellianism).
- The ball test would have *predictive validity* in naturalistic settings if high-hitters in the ball test generally experience longer runs of good luck (or longer runs of bad luck, due to psi-missing reversals) at casino-like games than low-hitters, or if they were likely to have better intuitions in everyday life situations than low-hitters (canceling a flight that ends in disaster). They might even be more successful at attempts at humanitarian paranormal application like mental healing.

First results of studies addressing concurrent and convergent validity aspects of the ball test are encouraging (to be published elsewhere).*

Reliability

The reliability issue in parapsychological studies ranks equally highly with the validity issue. Strangely, researchers have neglected it continuously despite (i) early awareness of the problem (Schmeidler 1964), (ii) disappointing reviews (Palmer 1977, p. 176*ff*), and (iii) occasional warnings later (Blackmore et al. 1980; Boller & Boesch 2000; Timm 1982). Whenever reliability indices of ESP tasks have been obtained, they were extremely low. Note Palmer's comment: "I would estimate the average reliability [of ESP scores] to be in the low-positive range, in the neighborhood of +0.30" (1977, p. 176).

The ball test's reliability has been investigated as follows: a split-half correlation was determined by using hit scores for runs #1, #3, and #5,

Examples of concurrent validity: six ball test high-hitters A.J., G.K., K.H., S.B., T.K., and I.K., whose average hit surplus was 84 percent, were also tested using a Zener card guessing procedure. The experimenter turned cards over face down without looking at them. Participant behind a screen guessed each card as it was turned over. The hit surplus total for the card-guessing test was also very significant, but much less conspicuous (16.7 percent). Two other subjects, A.O. and S.E., both without any success with ball drawing, failed, as expected, with Zener cards.

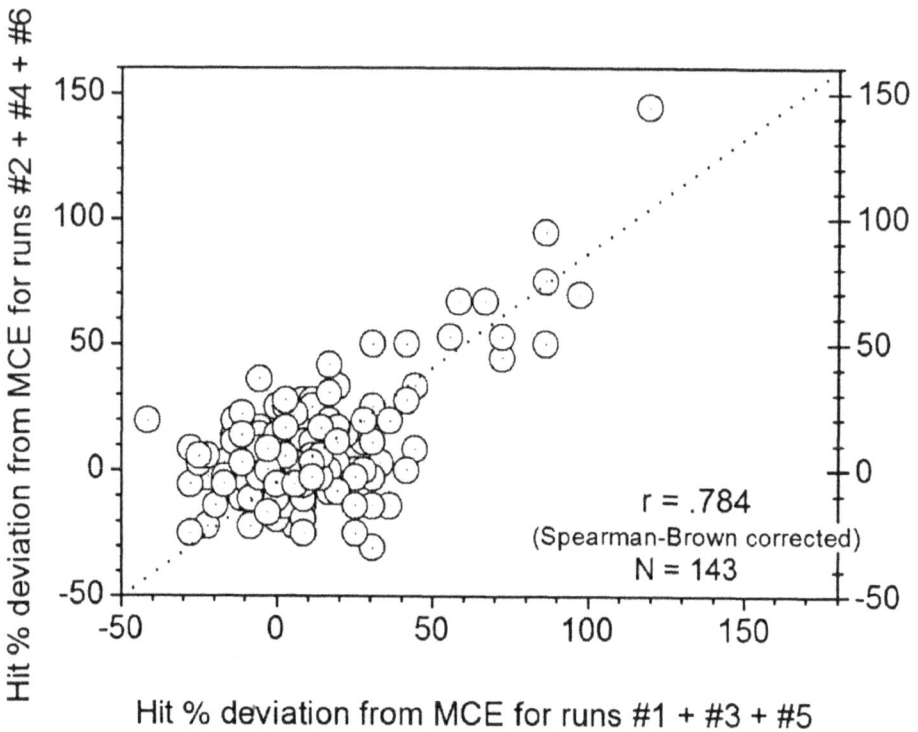

Figure 5.5. Scatter plot of individual percent deviations ($N = 143$) for the first three (X-axis) and the second three (Y-axis) of six runs of the standard test series. The split-half correlation indicates degree of reliability.

combined (variable X), and runs #2, #4, and #6, combined (variable Y), each half consisting of 180 trials ($N = 143$).* The correlation (Spearman-Brown corrected) amounts to $r = 0.78$ — which indicates an almost *moderate* reliability according to norms for standard test construction.† The scatter plot of Figure 5.5 shows percent hit deviations of one half (X) against the other half of the data (Y). It can be seen that the scatter is stretched out to the right, which indicates that the reliability of hit scores improves with increasing hit score levels.

Split-half correlations were also obtained separately for low-hitters

*This total is smaller than the grand total because samples 1998 and 1999 completed four ball test runs only.
†By using eight instead of six runs, the reliability of the ball test would rise to $r = .83$, 16 runs would yield $r = .91$. Eight runs require two hours of ball drawing work; 16 runs require four hours work, etc. Compare this to what is expected of testees subjected to ordinary intelligence test batteries.

among X-scorers and for high-hitters among X-scorers (the dividing point low-high, 12.6 hits per run on average, made two equal halves). Interestingly, the XY correlation for low-hitters is near zero (amounts to $r = -0.11$), while the correlation for high-hitters is $r = 0.89$ (again Spearman-Brown corrected). The difference is large and apparently due to the fact that psi is not normally distributed. On the one hand, many participants do not deploy psi ability at all — for them inter- and intraindividual ball test variance is random. On the other hand, variance for participants with actual psi-dispositions is not random, but is due rather to varying degrees of psi power whose stability turns out to be quite consistent.*

Why Are Hit Rates So Large?

"One truth about psi phenomena which every parapsychologist learns the hard way is that they are not just elusive, in the sense of being difficult to pin down, they are, or at any rate they seem to be, actively evasive," says John Beloff in an Epilogue to his *Concise history of parapsychology* (Beloff 1993, p. 230), and his view finds support from others. One well-known contemporary experimentalist (William Braud) has spoken of the "self-obscuring" aspect of psi. In view of many *non*elusive, *non*evasive, and *self-revealing* psi effects observed during five years of ball drawing experiments, an explanation of these observations is warranted. Six possible questions might be asked:

1. *Did the experimenter falsify his data?* A tremendous amount of work would be required for producing "good misses" (see Appendix 5-A) and other earmarks of psi contained in this database, aside from producing excessive main effects and their differential variations. Such artfulness would require unusual talents of a genius that I could not compare with on resourcefulness or craft.

2. *Was the experimenter unconsciously biased?* Perhaps yes. "Lingering doubts of possible error somewhere have haunted some of the most enthusiastic supporters of psi research" (Rao 1993, p. 4). But the question is not whether the experimenter was biased, but whether his bias could affect his results. Most subjects completed this test at home at self-selected times, so the experimenter's desires or fears could hardly have much impact on their records. Moreover, unexpected findings (psi-missing by an interacting mate, good misses, strange patterns among misses, etc.) can hardly be due to biased expectations.

Seventeen hits per run (41.7 percent surplus), averaged for one series of six runs, might be taken, with considerable confidence, as an indicator of psi ability. An average of 16 hits (33.3 percent surplus) is still reasonable for selected participants.

3. Did experimenter effects produce or enhance results? "There is much reason to consider the experimenter the psi source as any of the designated subjects. I am certainly not the first person to point that out" (Palmer 1993, p. 50). Indeed, the research literature indicates that certain psi experimenters report predominantly psi-positive results while others never take off from *MCE*. Are ball drawing results Ertel-dependent? This is conceivable, but I doubt that this effect, if present, would be large. The experimenter's suggestive "personal field," capable perhaps of eliciting or inhibiting psi phenomena of his subjects in his presence, can hardly affect them equally much in their home settings. Moreover, several participants were successful in the lab when under the control of helpers. This question needs further attention. If experimenter effects are larger than is suggested here, test-taking conditions would lack constancy so that additional problems for test development and application would have to be solved.*

4. Did the participants juggle the data? Participants are generally eager to know whether they have psi abilities or not, so they would thwart their curiosity if they fudged the records. In addition, fraud would probably be detected by subsequent lab tests (as already stated) and this might appear somewhat dangerous to the students who want to succeed in a science discipline. What motives could student beginners have that might lead them to spend more time than necessary with no apparent benefit (i.e., fudging records is more time-consuming than filling out records properly)? Above all, the majority of results obtained subsequently under lab control were actually positive, thus rendering proof that deviations from chance, attributable to psi, did occur, irrespective of whether individual frauds might have remained undiscovered

This is not to say that each recorded number of the present database is free of error. Some participants might occasionally misread the numbers on the balls, possibly more often numbers that they missed. Critics might dramatize this possibility. But even if this effect were large, say, if one wishful misreading occurred in every run (1.6 percent), this could not give rise to 40 percent to 130 percent hits above *MCE*. After all, I would certainly have noticed here a leak for artifacts, if it existed, across 19,320 ball test trials (322 runs) that I made myself. Finally, misreading numbers

---

A sample of 30 students at Professor M. Stadler's Institute of Psychology, Bremen University, performed the ball test under home conditions. Deviations from chance were less conspicuous compared with Göttingen results, even though significant. They also differed from Göttingen results in that they included two very extreme psi-missing cases, both of whom exceeded by far psi-missing cases among 238 Göttingen participants.

can hardly occur for "good misses" and other quirky observations, nor does it apply to ball tests under controlled conditions.

5. *Is the participant's home atmosphere indispensable for hit scores above MCE?* Home atmospheres are not indispensable, as has been demonstrated, but they seem to be particularly psi-conducive. "Subjects score best … [when] they are more comfortable in the test situation, thereby better able to exercise the relaxed spontaneity thought to be necessary for high scoring" (Palmer 1977, p. 197).* But doesn't the ball test lack precautionary control, a condition that most researchers in this field are trained to set up in any circumstance? Yes, it lacks it, but control need not be precautionary — "post-cautionary" control (letting "relaxed spontaneity" freely develop first) can be equally effective. Researchers must watch out for signs of artifacts when the data are delivered, and high-hitters at home sessions may be tested later under controlled conditions to make sure that their home records were genuine. Bierman and Gerding (1992) seem to have been the first to escape the obsession of precautionary control, with insight into its psi-lowering effects — at least for individual cases.

However, critics may remain unconvinced of the results of psi research. They should be reminded here of their own common practice of handing out questionnaires, inventories and such material to their students in class to be filled out at home, often under the protection of anonymity. They seem unaware of their double standard, since they demand excessive control over research in fields they distrust, while they leave the doors open to fraud in fields they endorse. They will regard, with tolerance, noise in their data, caused by possibly dishonest participants. This is, no doubt, a legitimate and common practice because participants who "fake out" researchers are certainly rare exceptions anyway. It is the one-sidedness of critics of psi research that deserves severe criticism.

6. *Is the ball drawing activity psi-conducive?* Yes — in fact, the design itself seems to be the prime reason for its success. The fact that hit scores from ball drawing tests, obtained even under controlled conditions, exceed traditional card guessing results, seems to be due to favorable test attributes. The participant's activity combines motor activity (shaking the bag, moving, picking and drawing balls) and sensory perception (auditory sensations as balls are being bounced, tactile sensations as balls are being touched, visual sensations as when drawn balls, held between thumb and forefinger, are being looked at). The participant's action is akin to every-

*Pratt (1962) found that "the psychological factor of familiarity with the surroundings appeared … important, although not absolutely essential" (p. 128). His conclusion was based on a survey of the first 22 volumes of the Journal of Parapsychology. It had "disclosed 43 instances in which subjects met the pertinent criteria of 'high scorers.'"

day actions like searching for something that cannot be seen (e.g., a lost key at night or a coin in one's trouser pocket). By contrast, the psi-test participant of traditional research does not move, touch, hear, or search for anything. His or her task is not embedded in any naturalistic context. His or her mind only is challenged and activated, but such activity is restricted to call out simple words ("cross," "square," "circle," etc.), pressing keys in silence like an automaton, or "sending out" mental images, with closed eyes, or waiting for some imagery to intrude into his or her thoughts. The atmosphere is stern and formal, not game-like as in the ball test. Russel and Rhine (1942) already noted that a participant's psi performance declines due to a "change from a free, game-like test situation in the informal tests to one of work and strain in the formal" (p. 284). More insight into optimal psi-eliciting conditions requires further methodological research.

How Innovative Is the Ball Drawing Test?

With hindsight, I realized that Ramakrishna Rao's (1992) "new look at our research strategies" almost predicted the ball drawing test. He traced his ideas back to Gardner Murphy (1961/1970). Murphy claimed that the normal may call upon the paranormal for aid and the two kinds of functions may be blended: "The normal may be the fuse that ignites the paranormal or simply the base on which the paranormal is mounted" (Rao 1992, p.7). Rao then stated that traditional psi research was entirely inadequate: "[O]ur testing procedures themselves may be psi-inhibitory. ... [T]hey may mask or filter out psi to the point of effectively reducing it to a trickle that we can afford to ignore" (p. 4).

Rao's way out of this dilemma is one that I fully endorse. He refers to Kreitler and Kreitler (1974) whose plea for fusing normal and paranormal phenomena is quoted. The Kreitlers demanded "a new strategy for studying normal-paranormal interaction which, if successful, would yield results that could not be ignored, because they would be too striking and significant in their import" (p. 7).

Rex Stanford's model of Psi-Mediated Instrumental Response (PMIR) is appropriate here. Stanford attempts to place psi processes in contexts of everyday need-propelled actions: "The organism uses psi (ESP), as well as sensory means, to scan its environment for objects or events relevant to that need and for information crucially related to such objects or events" (Stanford 1977, p. 841). PMIR thus links psi intimately with ordinary sensory processes. Both are needed instrumentally to obtain meaningful information for evolving ordinary behavior. Psi might therefore be elicited to its full potential with experimental opportunities to assist sensory perception instead of cutting psi off from the senses, which unfortunately has become common practice. It might be Rhine's introducing the term "extra"-sensory that misled researchers into conceiving of psi as functionally unrelated to visual, auditory, olfactory, and tactual processes. The term "co"-sensory (*co-sensory psi information* or similar) might have better indicated what psi actually is.

Rao seems to have almost foreseen the present endeavor: "[A] tangible and consistent effect, even when obtained under conditions that may not have the best of controls, could be very valuable in understanding the phenomenon" (p.7). Rao envisions a radical fusion:

> What if psi functions ... in juxtaposition or in coalescence with other modalities including the sensory? ... What if the sensory and other processes are needed to sustain, guide, channel, trigger, and focus on the paranormal? And what if psi merely supplements rather than supplants the sensory and motor functions? If we would give credence to these possibilities, we would be in a totally new ball park, playing a different game with a completely new set of rules [Rao 1993, p. 6].

With the help of sufficient pioneers in our community, a new "ball park" (let us take it literally) with a "completely new set of rules" might eventually take shape.

Conclusion

Parapsychological experiments are encumbered with problems: (1) Psi phenomena (ESP and PK) may not come to the fore without huge experimental effort; (2) Participants are demotivated by monotonous tasks; (3) Psi effects are tiny in spite of the great effort getting them; (4) Psi effects tend to decline, or are elusive, or are often not replicable; (5) Large effects raise suspicions about methodological error or fraud; (6) Proof-oriented research inhibits process-oriented research (i.e., experimenters, who have a hard time showing that psi is there at all, barely get to discover the factors that are key in the underlying paranormal process).

Do parapsychologists have to put up with these quandaries forever? The novel approach described above is based on a new naturalistic procedure that is deemed less problematic. The advantages of the ball drawing test are as follows: (1) The test requires a minimum of an experimenter's time; (2) most participants enjoy shaking the bag and drawing balls using their arms and hands; (3) the average hit surplus above mean chance expectancy for unselected student participants is considerable (roughly 23% of 238 students came up with $p = .05$ or less, 11 percent with $p = .001$ or less, and 6% with $p = .0001$ or less); (4) hit surpluses of psi-gifted participants (showing surpluses of 40 percent or more), even though fluctuating to some extent, are rather stable; (5) an experimenter's fear of being suspected of bias or fraud is greatly diminished with additional results obtained under controlled conditions and by unfakable secondary psi indicators; (6) insight into factors determining psi-processes is gained by design variation.

In view of the results presented in this chapter, the ball drawing procedure may serve as a standardized psi test with ordinary psychometric properties (reliability, validity) as demanded by mainstream science. The test may even be used for recruiting psi-gifted people serving as participants for subsequent studies in parapsychological laboratories.

REFERENCES

Beloff, J. (1993). *Parapsychology: A concise history.* New York: St. Martin's.

Bem, D. J., and C. Honorton (1994). Does psi exist? Replicable evidence for an anomalous process of information transfer. *Psychological Bulletin* 115, 4–18 [data from p. 11].

Bierman, D. J., and J. L. E. Gerding (1992). Towards a reduction of experimenter control in the study of special subjects. In E.W. Cook, ed., *Proceedings of the PA-conference* (pp. 302–316). Las Vegas.

Blackmore, S. J., D. J. Bierman, and M. Johnson (1981). Reliability and other ignored issues in parapsychology. In W. G. Roll and J. Beloff, eds., *Research in parapsychology, 1980* (pp. 14–15). Metuchen, N.J.: Scarecrow.

Boller, E., and H. Bösch (2000). Reliability and correlations of PK performance in a multivariate experiment. Proceedings of Presented Papers: *The Parapsychological Association's 43rd Annual Convention*, 380–382.

Braud, W. G., and M. J. Schlitz (1991). Consciousness interactions with remote biological systems: Anomalous intentionality effects. *Subtle Energies* 2, 1–46.

Broughton, R. S. (1991). *Parapsychology: The controversial science.* New York: Ballantine.

Carpenter, J. C. (1977). Intrasubject and subject-agent effects in ESP experiments. In B. B. Wolman, ed., *Handbook of parapsychology.* (pp. 202–272). New York: Van Nostrand.

Coly, L., and D.S. McMahon, eds., (1993). Psi research methodology: A re-examination. *Proceedings of an International Conference held in Chapel Hill, North Carolina, October 29–30, 1988.* New York: Parapsychological Foundation

Dunne, B. J., and R. G. Jahn (1992). Experiments in remote human/machine interaction. *Journal of Scientific Exploration* 6, 311–332 [data from p. 315].

Haraldsson, E., J. M. Houtkooper, R. Schneider, and M. Bäckström (2002). Perceptual defensiveness and ESP performance: Reconstructed DMT ratings and psychological correlates in the first German DMT-ESP experiment. *Journal of Parapsychology* **66**(3), 249–270.

Honorton, C., and D. C. Ferrari (1989). Future telling: A meta-analysis of forced-choice precognition experiments, 1935–1987. *Journal of Parapsychology* **53**, 281–307.

Jahn, R. G., B. J. Dunne, G. J. Bradish, Y. H. Dobyns, A. Lettieri, R. D. Nelson, J. Mischo, E. Boller, H. Bösch, D. Vaitl, J. M. Houtkooperm, and B. Walter (2000). Mind/Machine Interaction Consortium: PortREG Replication Experiments. *Journal of Scientific Exploration* **14**, 499–556.

Kreitler, H., and S. Kreitler (1974). Optimization of experimental ESP results. *Journal of Parapsychology* **38**, 383–392.

Milton, J. (1998). A meta-analysis of waking state of consciousness, free-response ESP studies. In N. L. Zingrone and M. J. Schlitz, eds., *Research in parapsychology 1993* (pp. 31–34). Lanham, MD: Scarecrow Press.

Murphy, G. (1970). *Challenge of psychical research: A primer of parapsychology.* New York: Harper & Row (original work published in 1961).

Nabours, R. K. (1943). The masquerade of ESP. *Philosophy of Science* **10**, 191–200.

Newcombe, R. G. (1998). Two-sided confidence intervals for the single proportion: Comparison of seven methods. *Statistics in Medicine* **17**, 857–872.

Nelson, R. D. (1994). Effect size per hour: A natural unit for interpreting anomalies in experiments. Technical Note PEAR 94003. School of Engineering and Applied Science. Princeton University, Princeton, NJ, 08544.

Palmer, J. (1977). Attitudes and personality traits in experimental ESP research. In B. B. Wolman, ed., *Handbook of parapsychology* (pp. 175–201). New York: Van Nostrand.

Palmer, J. (1993). Confronting the experimenter effect. In L. Coly and D. S. McMahon, eds., *Psi and clinical practice* (pp. 44–97). New York: Parapsychology Foundation.

Pratt, J. G. (1961). On the question of control over ESP: The effect of the environment on psi performance. *Journal of the American Society for Psychical Research* **55**, 128–134.

Radin, D. (1997). *The conscious universe: The scientific truth of psychic phenomena.* San Francisco: Harper.

Radin, D., and D. C. Ferrari (1991). Effects of consciousness on the fall of dice: A meta-analysis. *Journal of Scientific Exploration* **5**, 61–83.

Radin, D. I., and R. D. Nelson (1989). Evidence for consciousness-related anomalies in random physical systems. *Foundations of Physics* **19**, 1499–1514.

Rao, K. R. (1993). Are we throwing the baby out with the bath water? A plea for a new look at our research strategies. In L. Coly and D. S. McMahon, eds., *Psi and clinical practice* (pp. 1–20). New York: Parapsychology Foundation.

Rosenthal, R., and D. B. Rubin (1989). Effect size estimation for one-sample multiple-choice-type data: Design, analysis, and meta-analysis. *Psychological Bulletin* **106**(2), 332–337.

Russell, W., and J. B. Rhine (1942). A single subject in a variety of ESP conditions. *Journal of Parapsychology* **6**, 284–311.

Schmeidler, G. R. (1964). An experiment on precognitive clairvoyance: II. The reliability of the scores. *Journal of Parapsychology* **28**, 15–27.

Stanford, R. G. (1967). Response bias and the correctness of ESP test responses. *Journal of Parapsychology* **31**, 280–289.

_____. (1977). Conceptual frameworks of contemporary psi research. In B. B. Wolman, ed., *Handbook of parapsychology* (pp. 823–858). New York: Van Nostrand.

Steinkamp, F., J. Milton, and R. L. Morris (1998). A meta-analysis of forced-choice experiments comparing clairvoyance and precognition. *Journal of Parapsychology* **62**, 193–218.

Storm, L., and S. Ertel (2001). Does psi exist? Comments on Milton and Wiseman's (1999) meta-analysis of Ganzfeld research. *Psychological Bulletin* **127**, 424–433.

Storm, L., and M. A. Thalbourne (2000). A paradigm shift away from the ESP-PK dichotomy: The theory of psychopraxia. *Journal of Parapsychology* **64** (3), 279–300.

Timm, U. (1982). Methodologische Probleme bei der Planung und Auswertung differentieller Psi-Experimente [Methodological problems at designing and analyzing differential psi-experiments]. *Zeitschrift für Parapsychologie und Grenzgebiete der Psychologie* [*Journal of Parapsychology and Related Areas of Psychology*], 23 (3), 140–160.

Ullman, M., and S. Krippner (1970). *Dream studies and telepathy*. Parapsychological Monographs No. 12. New York: Parapsychological Foundation.

Wilson, S. (2002). Psi, perception without awareness, and false recognition. *Journal of Parapsychology* **66** (3), 271–289.

Wolman, B. B. (1977). *Handbook of parapsychology*. New York: Van Nostrand.

Appendix: Methodological Issues

Memory Leakage

One might object that drawing guessed numbers correctly is possibly facilitated by implicit memory processes. Participants, when putting a ball back into the bag, might roughly keep in mind in which corner of the bag the ball fell or was placed. Perhaps they do not turn and shake the bag as the instruction demands it so that a just-drawn-number (JDN) is likely to become a hit at their next trial after calling that number. If this occurs often enough, significant hit surpluses might arise through "memory leakage," even without conscious intention and awareness.

Of course, such a suspicion should give rise to a testable hypothesis, not outright rejection. The hypothesis of memory leakage was tested as follows. First, if guessing JDNs facilitates hit occurrence due to memory leakage, then guessing JDNs would be continuously reinforced by successes. Consequently, guessing JDNs should gradually be preferred by participants, through operant conditioning, perhaps subconsciously. But it turns out that participants do not guess JDNs very often. Figure 5.A1(a) shows that guessing JDNs is even largely avoided (apparently participants are biased towards making sequential variations).

What does the box chart of Figure 5.A1(a) show?: Without bias, JDNs should be guessed, within one run of 60 trials, 12 times on average (see the dotted *MCE* line). But the majority of participants were biased in the negative direction — they guessed JDNs only 6.7 times per run (see the horizontal line in the middle of the box). The lower and upper sides of the box are determined by the 25th and 75th percentile of the sample, respectively, and the whiskers mark the distribution from the 5th to the 95th percentile. Results of two participants with the largest scores outside that range are shown individually. It can be seen that participants #122 and #120 lie far above the 95th percentile. Unlike the majority of the sample they guessed JDNs very often, for whatever reason. Now, if guessing JDNs is good for raising one's hit score, due to memory leakage, then participants #122 and #120 should have become high scorers. But their hit percentage deviations were low, numerically even below *MCE* (namely, -9.7 percent and -1.4 percent, respectively).

How about operant conditioning (learning effect) — do calls of JDNs increase across runs? No, they do not significantly increase. Apparently, participants have nothing to learn here, as is shown next.

Still, one might argue that subconscious information processing of #120 and #122 was possibly not sufficiently acute to turn off JDN calls to advantage. Even though students in general do not guess JDNs very often, they might generally gain some advantage from JDN storage whenever they make rare JDN guesses. In that case, a significant difference should be expected, regarding hits, between JDN guesses and other guesses.

Figure 5.A1(b) shows differences of percent hit deviations between JDN guesses and other guesses (Y-axis). Without memory leakage, the

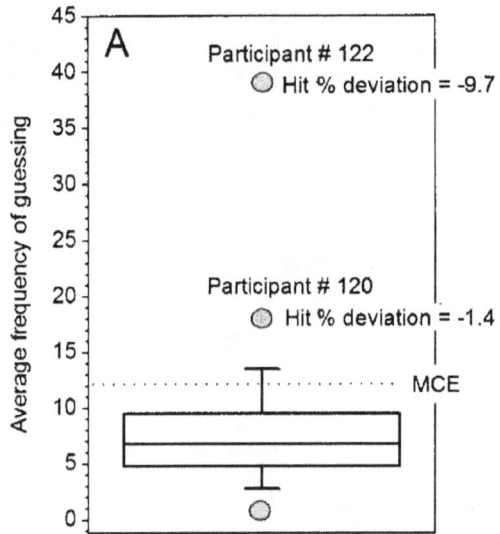

Figure 5.A1(a). Participants avoid guessing JDNs (just drawn numbers), thus foregoing possible advantages for raising hit rates.

average difference would be zero (see the dotted *MCE* line). If memory leakage was present, then the mean difference would be positive and significant (i.e., its level would exceed the line of expectancy). But as can be seen, the mean difference is close to the *MCE* level.

The two largest outliers are shown here again. Participant #26 obtained many more hits at guessing JDNs compared with guessing other numbers. Memory leakage, if it occurred, should have made #26 an excellent hitter. But the participant's overall hit score did not differ from *MCE*. The reason is that her count of hits for not-JDNs was unusually low. Her numerous JDN hits and rare not-JDN hits, when summed, evened out. The other outlier person (#49), however, might have gained a moderate advantage by guessing JDNs, because his overall hit excess was 27.5 percent. But if #49 took advantage from drawing JDNs, why did none of the best hitters gain an advantage from drawing JDNs (those with 100-percent hit excess and beyond)? C.G.— the highest-scoring participant (#1)— obtained almost equal hits from guessing JDNs as from guessing other numbers. One case with conceivable JDN influence, and 230 cases with actual lack of JDN influences, does not yet give vent for general suspicion.

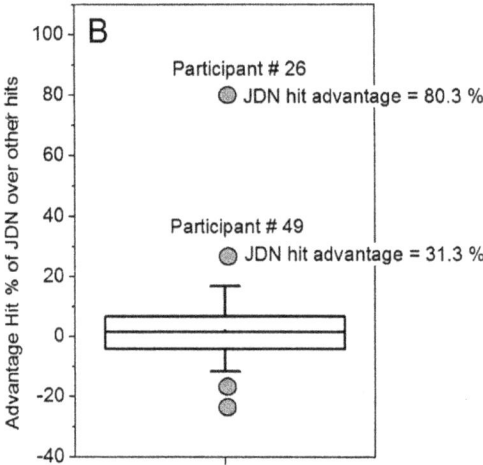

Figure 5.A1(b). Guesses influenced by JDNs were not more successful than other guesses.

More evidence against memory leakage might not be needed, but after having had continuous discussions with overly skeptical parapsychologists who insisted that some such artifact might be present, I provide another empirical argument. One particular ball test instruction demanded from participants to draw number 1 successively 12 times, then number 2 12 times, then number 3, etc., each number 12 times within one run. This condition (coded as "11111") should be *favorable* for memory leakage because for periods of 12 successive trials participants would need to store positions of balls for one number only, whenever that number is drawn. As a control, another condition was applied which was *unfavorable* regarding memory storage. Participants were told to draw the number series "1234512345," etc., (coded as "12345"). Here participants need to attend to all five numbers, and if they store them they have to place them separately in their working memory, which is difficult. In any event, if memory leakage exists, hit scores obtained under the "11111"-condition must be larger than hit scores obtained under the "12345"-condition.

Two participants, G.X. and T.X. — high-hitters under the standard condition — drew balls with the "11111" and "12345" instructions, 16 runs for each condition. G.X.'s hit surpluses were almost equal; she obtained 78.1 percent surplus under the "11111" condition, and 78.7 percent under the "12345"condition. T.X.'s hit surpluses were slightly different with predicted direction. She obtained 57.8 percent surplus under the "11111" condition, and 46.4 percent under the "12345" condition, but the difference was slight and not significant. I myself, without any psi-giftedness, but with no apparent deficit regarding storage by implicit memory, obtained 3.2-percent hit deviation above *MCE* under the "12345" condition and I did not improve, as I should with the help of memory leakage, under the "11111" condition (32 runs for each condition). Here, my hit deviation was even slightly worse: -0.26 percent below *MCE*. In other words, there is no indication whatsoever that memory leakage is effective. If such a factor exists at all, though, its effect would be undetectable and negligible. It could never explain hit surpluses as they are obtained under standard and other conditions.

Sensory Leakage

Another conceivable objection is that hit surplus might be due to *sensory* leakage. Participants touch the balls and might feel ink traces of written digits. Or they might sense varying temperatures of the balls (the temperature of their hand might be differentially transmitted). Finally, sensory stimulation of, as yet, unknown origin might help participants discriminate the balls and digits written on them, though conscious awareness is not needed (see Wilson 2002, on psi and "perception without awareness").

While still on this line of thought, a straightforward and testable hypothesis may be derived here: any information about numbers and balls leaking through sensory channels cannot be effective during *initial* test trials, as they would turn up gradually with sufficient practice, which is consistent with the usual laws of learning.

Figure 5.A2 shows percent deviations of hits from *MCE* across 60 trials, averaged over runs, separately for less successful runs (hit average per run 12.85 or less) and for successful runs (hit average 12.86 or more). This criterion divides the total into two equal halves. If hit surplus in this test was due to sensory leakage, the upper line (successful runs) should slope up, sooner or later, while the line below (less successful runs) should maintain its initial level. Figure 5.A2 shows, however, that the upper line does not slope up. The regression lines (dotted) of the two plots are equally flat (i.e., regarding hits across trials, no learning occurred). The sensory leakage hypothesis is not supported.

One's skepticism may still remain: participants, unable to learn and increase hit rates *within* runs, might nevertheless be able to learn and increase hit rates *across* runs. We took data from 136 students who completed six runs (those 95 who completed only four runs, and seven students who completed 32 runs were excluded). The percent deviations from *MCE* for runs #1 to #6 were obtained separately for 67 successful, and 69 unsuccessful students. The dividing point was an average of 12.7 hits per run (*MCE* = 12 hits). The upper curve of Figure

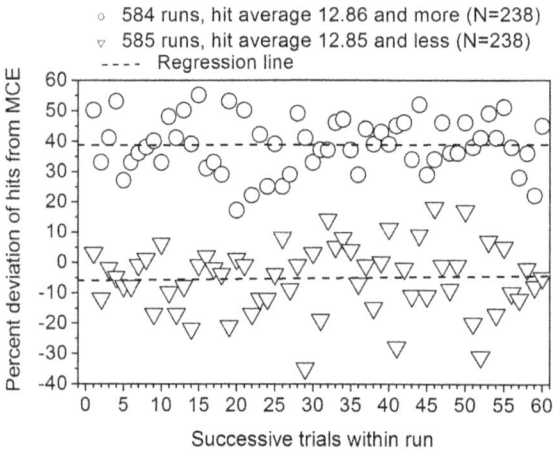

Figure 5.A2. Percent deviations from chance expectancy across 60 trials (one run). Averages for successful (above) and unsuccessful runs (below).

5.A3 shows that average hit rates of successful students did not increase across runs. Hit rates actually dropped slightly from runs #1 to #3, an increase from #3 to #4 was short-lived. The level of run #5 had the lowest average in this series. Most hits were obtained with run #6, but since this was not preceded by a gradual rise, the #6 peak cannot be interpreted in terms of a learning effect. A horizontal line, representing the hypothesis that learning did not occur, remains within error bars (95 percent confidence). Since no trend is present in this data set, the hypothesis that successes at drawing balls might be due to sensory leakage is not supported. It is not inconceivable that sensory cues might operate at rare individual trials, but conceivable exceptions need not be considered as long as the data total remains unaffected, as can be seen in Figure 5.A3.

The "Good Misses" Phenomenon

Excessive hit numbers in the ball test are *primary* psi effects. For good reasons, J. B. Rhine took pains at stressing the importance of what he called "earmarks of psi" (or "quirks"), which are *secondary* psi effects. Participants are unaware of such effects and therefore cannot produce them at will:

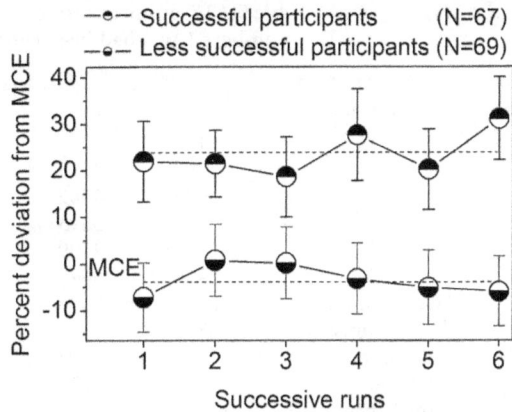

Figure 5.A3. Percent deviation from *MCE* of successful (upper curve) and unsuccessful students (lower curve). The dividing point is an average of 12.7 hits per run (expectancy = 12 hits). Confidence bars comprise 95 percent chance variation.

I can conceive of no stronger evidence of psi, even today after 30 years have passed. ... [It is] a kind of proof that allows no question of experimenter honesty to arise. ... Scores of times the more incontestable answers have come when I have discovered new hidden evidence which was unknown to the individual experimenter ... [Rhine 1977, p. 168].

In his chapter Rhine demonstrated position effects as "hidden evidence." He found that hits were unevenly distributed on his standard record page. More secondary psi effects were in store (i.e., displacement effects, lag effects, differential effects), and "new searches can be made for more new findings. No one knows how much more remains to be discovered" (Rhine 1977, p. 167).

By analyzing the ball test data, several such "quirks" have been discovered.* An account of only one finding is provided next — the "good misses" phenomenon. Suppose a participant misses number 1, which he called. Having missed number 1, number 2 or 3 or 4 or 5 may have been drawn, the probabilities being equal. How many times did 238 students draw numbers 2 to 5 instead of number 1, which was called? The counts

---

*Highly significant secondary effects found or confirmed are: (i) the "good misses" phenomenon; (ii) the preference paradox (higher hit proportions with less preferred calls), a "response bias effect" as already stated by Stanford (1967); (iii) Deviant succession of drawn numbers (repetition avoidance); (iv) Deviant sequences of hits and misses (runs of good luck or interrupted good luck); (v) Targeted number series displaced, across series of misses, using "11111," "12345," or "54321" targets; and so on.

Table 5.A1.Counts of numbers 1 to 5 drawn after
numbers 1 to 5 had been called (i.e., guessed)

Row #	Numbers drawn			Numbers called				
		1	2	3	4	5	Sum
1	1	**3489**	3793	3596	3210	2701	16789
2	2	3082	**4542**	3856	3261	2773	17514
3	3	2953	3893	**4343**	3289	2747	17225
4	4	2920	3709	3735	**3926**	2689	16979
5	5	2926	3676	3626	3322	**3143**	16693
6	"Good" misses	6035	7686	7591	6611	5436	33359
7	"Other" misses	5846	7385	7222	6471	5474	32398
8	Difference 6 -7	189	301	369	140	-38	961
9	Sum 6+7	11881	15071	14813	13082	10910	65757
10	Sum 1 through 5	15370	19613	19156	17008	14053	85200
11	"Good" misses	#2 #3	#1 #3	#2 #4	#3 #5	#4 #3	
12	"Other" misses	#4 #5	#4 #5	#1 #5	#1 #2	#1 #2	

N = 238 participants. The diagonal shows counts of hits, the rest counts of misses. Good misses (row #6) and other misses (row #7) are distinguished; Row #8 shows the difference, generally a preponderance of "good misses."

are 3,082 (2), 2,953 (3), 2,920 (4), 2,926 (5). That is, #2 was drawn more frequently than #3, and #3 more frequently than #4 *and* #5. This looks as if participants drew "call-near" numbers more frequently than "call-distant" numbers. Did they generally prefer "good" over "other" misses? Ball test participants do not make conscious distinctions among misses— drawing non-hit numbers is like drawing blanks in a lottery which all have equally low value. Table 5.A1 shows counts of draws of numbers 1 to 5, separately for called numbers.

Calls are distinguished by columns, draws by rows. Diagonal counts (bold) represent hits, all other counts are misses. Row 6 sums counts of two "good" misses, row 7 of two other misses, as defined in rows 11 and 12. Row 8 shows the main result (bold), all differences *good-minus-other* misses. Four of five differences are positive and considerable, thus indicating the suspected preponderance of good misses (number 5 is an exception, more on that below). The *good-minus-other* total, which is 961 (row 8 last column), deviates very significantly from what is expected by chance ($\chi^2 = 14,00, df = 1, p = .00001$). The deviation is not large, only 1.5 percent good misses occurred above *MCE*. Nevertheless, a highly significant occurrence of good misses, as observed here, confirms, beyond reasonable doubt, that psi effects are present in this database. In view of this feature, all skeptical insistence on memory or sensory leakage, or on the participants' fraud or an experimenter's bias, becomes irrelevant. The present result does not only show that psi is active when participants draw balls at home, but that psi is capable of making subtle algebraic distinctions among numbers without any intentional or other conscious support. Such observations might contribute to our understanding of how and why psi processes come into existence. The mere fact of their existence should long since have been taken for granted. Further proof than is already provided in the historical record of psi research (see Radin 1997) is actually not needed.

But why did a preponderance of the "good" sort of misses not show up for number 5? This may be due to the fact that for standard ball experiments number 5 is the last number in the series. Participants might have been attracted, subconsciously, not only by near-5 numbers, but also by numbers at and near the beginning of this series of five numbers.* Adjacent (4, 3) and opposite numbers (1, 2) might both have become attractors. A compromise between opposing tendencies might have occurred which hypothesis is testable by using (e.g., numbers from 1 through 6 for comparison).

The phenomenon of "good misses" warrants further scrutiny. Are good misses psi-power-dependent? Nine psi-power subsamples ranging from very bad hit rates to very good ones were formed, the worst runs were psi-missing runs (hit counts of 10 or less, see Figure 5.A4, on the left), the best runs showed 20 or more hits (see Figure 5.A4 on the right; *MCE* = 12). Next, the differences *good-minus-other misses*

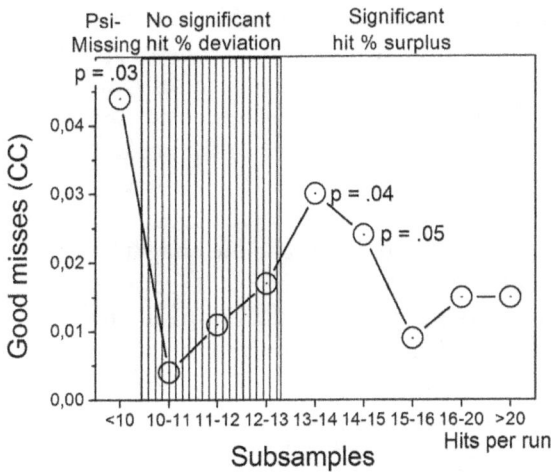

Figure 5.A4. The X axis represents psi-power, measured by hit rate, increasing from left to right. The Y axis shows good misses minus other misses. A preponderance of good misses is noted with psi missing (left) and moderate hit surplus (middle). The dashed area is the psi-free region.

A highly significant tendency of number 5 misses to be followed by number 1 misses, the beginning of the number series, has been found when participants had been instructed to draw numbers "1 2 3 4 5 1 2 3 4 5," etc., in that order, thus stressing the circular arrangement of the five numbers (N = 8, p =.001). An instruction to draw "5 4 3 2 1 5 4 3 2 1" led to a tendency of number 5 misses to be followed by number 4 misses (N = 5, p = .001).

were obtained, separately for the nine samples. It seemed reasonable to expect that the good-misses effect, a secondary psi-effect, would somehow correlate with hit levels, the primary psi-effect.

In Figure 5.A4, the middle part of the curve runs as expected: Good misses are not above chance, apparently because psi is missing — hit rates here are also not above chance. Good misses rise with increasing hit surpluses. But with still more increasing hit surpluses they drop and even disappear — this is the first problem, posed on the right end of this curve. The second problem is posed on its left end, in view of a surprising peak of good misses for runs with significant *psi-missing*. How does one explain all that?

The second problem seems easier to resolve. Psi-missing effects are psi-effects with intention-opposing direction. Apparently, hits are desired and avoided at the same time. This entails a strong kind of ambivalence comparable to unconscious conflict and "reaction formation." Reaction formation is a psychoanalytic defense mechanism by which impulses are not only repressed, but are also held in check by exaggerated opposite behavior. Psi-missing is in fact the result of an exaggerated resistance to ordinary psi-test intentions. Good misses, therefore, reflecting ambivalence straightforwardly, will tend to go along with psi-missing: plain hits are avoided, but choosing numbers close to hit numbers, even though still misses, is the best algebraic compromise one can think of.

If this explanation holds, the other problem mentioned might be settled in the same vein. Participants with slight hit surpluses of about 15 percent (13–14 hits) might possess stronger psi power than is manifested on that level. But a greater hit surplus than is actually manifested seems to be moderately suppressed (not to the point of reaction formation). Thus, an ambivalence of moderate surplus hitters comes to the fore by moderate counts of good misses. On the other hand, other psi-gifted participants had less inner restraint, less or no suppression occurred, so hit rates rose to more extreme levels, without ambivalence, and without the symptom of ambivalence, the good misses proportion level dropped to *MCE*.

An explanation of Figure 5.A4 results might eventually be simplified on that line by assuming that ambivalence regarding psi manifestation, whose symptom is good missing, is negatively correlated with actual psi manifestation, as measured by hit counts. The good misses curve should therefore peak on the left, as it does, and drop to *MCE* on the right, as it does, and a large dip in the good misses curve is expected and actually observed in between, in the psi-free region, where both, hit surplus and good misses, both psi-dependent, are absent.

This interpretation reminds one of the reported correlations between

ESP scores from the Defense Mechanism Test (DMT) which was designed to measure general inclination for defensive responses to submanifest anxiety (Haraldsson et al. 2002).* The present result seems also akin to one of Timm's observations. One of his participants mixed up significantly certain Zener card symbols. The participant's hit rate showed psi-missing, and his mixing up of symbols occurred with significant psi-missing runs only, not with runs on a chance level (Timm 1968). Timm asked: Did this participant evade plain ESP hits, or did his ESP merely make inadvertent misreadings? He probably evaded ESP hits — that is what the present finding suggests. Perceptual distances among Zener symbols (similarities, dissimilarities) are more difficult to define than are distances between numbers. Here, and on various other occasions of data analysis, the ball test's design of using numbers as targets, rather than Zener or other visual forms, did turn out to be a huge advantage.

Haraldsson et al. did not replicate earlier correlations between ESP and DMT — seven of 16 such correlations had been significant. The fact that they failed in their replication attempts might be due, aside from their own supposition (experimenter effect), to low psi abilities in their sample of only 50 subjects whose two indicators (clairvoyance and precognition) showed too small deviations from chance. They even contradicted in sign, and to a corresponding lack of reliability of these scores. Reliability coefficients, unfortunately, were not reported.

6

Forced-Choice ESP Experiments: Their Past and Their Future

*Fiona Steinkamp**

In this comprehensive review of the forced-choice ESP literature, Dr. Fiona Steinkamp comes to some profound conclusions about the future direction of an experimental domain
that has been consistently successful for over 120 years.
Specifically, she identifies "promising evidence" that low neuroticism, extraversion, and good social adjustment, among
other variables, are keys to success in forced-choice ESP
tests. On a more sobering note, however, Steinkamp argues
that parapsychology has to follow a clearer direction before it
can "walk among the sciences." (Editors)

There are at least two problems in trying to write about the future of
any discipline. The first one is that whatever one writes will, in retrospect,
probably appear misguided once that future has arrived. The second problem is that it seems rather presumptuous for any one person to prescribe
to others the directions in which that discipline should move. What one
can do is to take stock of the discipline's status at the time of writing and

*I would like to thank Bob Morris for his comments on this chapter, which was writ-
ten while the author was supported by grants from the Bial Foundation and the Perrott-
Warrick Fund.

to see if that itself is suggestive of where the field should go. This is the approach that I will take.

Parapsychology is the academic, primarily scientific, study of the so-called paranormal. It focuses predominantly on extrasensory perception (ESP) and psychokinesis (PK). ESP comprises three basic phenomena: telepathy (putative mind-to-mind communication without use of the known senses), clairvoyance (the ostensible ability to gain information about spatially distant events without using the known five senses), and precognition (the ostensible ability to gain information about future events without using the known senses). In all three, the percipient gains information that he or she could not have received normally. PK is the ostensible ability to exert a mental influence on a physical object. Here, the agent is exerting an influence on the physical world in a manner that cannot currently be explained by normal means. Psi is a neutral, umbrella term that can denote either ESP or PK (or both together). General ESP (GESP) is an umbrella term for clairvoyance and telepathy in cases where a distinction between the two cannot easily be made. For instance, in telepathy experiments in which a person is looking at a card and trying to communicate psychically to someone which card they are looking at, the receiver could theoretically gain that information either telepathically or by bypassing the sender altogether and just guessing the card clairvoyantly. Here, one would talk of GESP.

In this chapter I will focus on reviews of forced-choice ESP work in parapsychology. In a typical forced-choice experiment a participant is shown the back of a card and is asked to guess which of, say, five possible symbols is on the reverse of that card. This would be a test for clairvoyance, or possibly for telepathy if someone else is looking at the target card at the time of the participant's guess. Alternatively, the participant may be asked which of five cards he or she will later be shown. In this case the experiment is testing for precognition. In all cases the participant is forced to choose between several alternatives (hence "forced-choice"), each alternative usually having an equal probability of being revealed afterwards to be the target card. Thus, in the example here where the participant chooses between five cards, by chance the participant will guess the card correctly one in five times. Armed with the knowledge of how often a participant would get a correct guess by chance, statistical analyses can determine whether participants have guessed the correct card statistically more often than chance.

Forced-choice experiments are one of the simplest and oldest forms of formal ESP testing and they form a large body of research. Many researchers have tried to summarize the findings. This chapter will summarize major reviews of forced-choice work written in English that encompass more than one person's data unless one person is summarizing a body of research that comprises more than five studies from one person. The reviews were found by a manual search of volumes available in the Koestler Parapsychology Unit of: *Advances in Parapsychology*, the *Journal of the American Society for Psychical Research, European Journal of Parapsychology* (and *Research Letter*), *International Journal of Parapsychology, Journal of Parapsychology, Journal of the Society for Psychical Research* (and *Proceedings*), *Parapsychological Monographs*, the *Proceedings of the Parapsychological Association's Annual Conventions* and *Research in Parapsychology*. This chapter will omit reviews of psi-missing or psi-displacement data (e.g., Crandall 1991; Milton 1988); the issues here are complex and the conclusions are in any case generally obscure. It also omits reviews of physiological or physical variables that an experimenter cannot realistically manipulate with ease, for the aim of the review is to see how people can easily design their studies in the future for greater success. For an existing, if rather outdated, review of physiological research in conjunction with forced-choice tasks, see Beloff (1974); for a more general review see Alexander (2002). For the same reason, and to save space, reviews of multivariate findings have also been omitted. Additionally, this chapter focuses only on experiments with humans. Some reviews may be omitted if they have been superseded by more recent findings. Due to time constraints, I have not gone back to the original literature on which the reviews surveyed here were based; nor have I sought to update the reviews in the light of further findings, either.

My aims here are as follows:

1. To provide an overview of the findings from existing reviews of forced-choice research.
2. To determine the current state of parapsychology in this area.
3. To focus on what these findings suggest for the future of forced-choice research.

My approach will be broadly chronological. My hope is that even if the findings fail to predict the outcome of future studies, this chapter will nevertheless form a useful reference for researchers both now and in the future.

Review of Forced-Choice ESP Research 1880–1940

For many researchers Rhine, Stuart, Pratt, Smith and Greenwood's *Extra-Sensory Perception After Sixty Years* (*ESP60*), first published in 1940 and then reprinted in 1966, was the parapsychological bible. It contained a summary of the criticisms of parapsychological results, defenses against those critiques, and statistical summaries of the outcomes of research to that point.

ESP60 — Introduction

ESP60 covers the years 1880–1940. Before 1934, 203,775 trials had been conducted in experiments that were amenable to statistical analysis. These studies usually used ordinary playing cards. Participants had to guess either the *color* of the card (red or black) with a 1:2 probability of a hit, the *suit* (hearts, diamonds, clubs, spades) with a 1:4 chance of a correct guess, or the *exact card* (suit and number) with only a 1:52 chance. Between 1934 and 1939 most experiments were conducted with decks of 25 ESP cards, each deck comprising five cards of each symbol (square, wavy lines, cross, circle, star) and correspondingly offering participants a 1:5 probability of a hit. During this later period 3,026,936 ESP trials were conducted, of which 2,757,854 had a probability of a hit of 1:5. Thus, the majority of all trials conducted between 1880 and 1939 had a one in five chance of success and were conducted in the last five years of the survey. The results were highly significant, apparently indicating that ESP was possible.

For a relatively early summary statistical analysis, the methodology in *ESP60* is surprisingly sophisticated. All ESP trials from all experiments were summed, regardless of whether the experimental protocols had been for precognition, clairvoyance or telepathy. The trials were then systematically trimmed according to quality criteria (e.g., by excluding trials from studies in which participants may have obtained information from normal sources) and the remaining trials were reanalyzed to see if the effect still remained. Even early file-drawer analyses were conducted (see Appendix 6.A). That is, *ESP60* reported calculations to inform the reader how many unreported trials with chance results would be necessary to reduce the findings to being only just significant. If the number of trials required to reduce the findings is very large, one can assume that the results from the reported tests are unlikely to be due to experimenters reporting only their successful studies.

The results of trials in *ESP60* with a probability of a hit of 1:5 are presented in Table 6.1. They are presented in order of the increasing number of safeguards that the experiments employed. The safeguard criterion of excluding visual or auditory cues or both was particularly important. If participants could gain information about the target through normal means, no conclusions could be made about the possibility of ESP operating. For instance, early experiments used ESP cards that were not fully

Table 6.1. Summary of Results of Studies: 1880–1939
(probability of hit: 1:5) (SOURCE: *ESP60*)

Safeguards Employed	N Trials	Z-score	ES	Trial drawer	Number of reports
1. All studies, regardless of quality	2,758,354	79.37	.0478	6,380,767,413	45
2. As 1, excluding studies where sensory cueing possible	907,030	39.90	.0419	399,032,366	33 (8 by Rhine)
3. As 2, excluding studies without double-checking	468,630	34.40	.0503	203,285,366	21 (8 by Rhine)
4. As 3, excluding studies without independent recording	220,455	11.2	.0239	9,807,323	9 (6 by Rhine)
5. As 4, excluding studies with only one experimenter	72,750	7.82	.0290	1,566,426	6 (4 by Rhine)
6. As 5, but with additional safeguards	60,000	4.99	.0204	488,946	1 (Pratt & Woodruff 1939)

opaque when held up to the light; other experiments may have allowed a sender to provide the participant with a clue as to the target by, for example, tapping his foot according to an agreed code.

As the years went by, more safeguards were in place for other possible errors and Table 6.1 gradually trims the database according to how many safeguards were used. Hence the first row presents the results from all trials; the second row trims the database to those studies in which participants could not have gained sensory cues about the target; the third row presents only experiments which additionally employed some form of double-checking of the results; the fourth row offers reports in which the calls and the cards were also recorded independently of each other; the fifth row depicts studies with at least two experimenters; and the final row gives the results from a study that employed triple-checking, locked storage of the records and stamped record sheets. In Table 6.1, I have performed the effect sizes (*ES*) ($z/\sqrt{N}$) and "trial"-drawer calculations; all other information has been obtained from *ESP60*. Effect sizes are measures that show how strong the results of a study are. The effect size used here can range from 0–1; all effect sizes in this review are very small, which means that many trials have to be conducted before the effect can obtain statistical significance.

There are four points of interest in this table. First, there is a sharp decrease in the effect size at the point at which independent recording was introduced as a precautionary measure (see Table 6.1, row 4). Independent recording is necessary because if the experimenter is optimistically expecting the participant to give a correct response, the experimenter may accidentally record the guess as a hit even when it was not. Thus it is better if at least two people record the targets and the guesses independently. Remember, these studies were performed before computers were available to make automatic recording possible. Thus, although Murphy (anon 1938) downplayed the impact of recording errors on overall results, Kennedy (anon 1938) appeared to be justified in investigating them. However, as in any attempt to review data, it may also be that there was an uninvestigated factor that caused the drop in effect size between rows 3 and 4 in Table 6.1. Nevertheless, Murphy correctly claims that recording errors alone cannot explain the results, which are still highly significant even when there is independent recording. The findings do illustrate, though, that even just one systematic oversight in precautionary measures can make a relatively big difference to an estimation of the size of any putative effect.

Second, as the number of safeguards rises, it becomes clear that one experimenter (J. B. Rhine) predominates (see the final column of Table 6.1, which shows how many experimental reports included each row's safeguards). Although Rhine is not responsible for all the results, it is clear that the results come from only a handful of experimenters. This raises some problems about the generalizability of any effect found. If parapsychology is to provide convincing evidence for the existence of ESP, its results will have to be replicable by many experimenters and not just one or two.

Third, the sixth row, with the most safeguards, contains only one study. Moreover, this study is one of the most recent ones in this particular database, thus indicating that safeguards improved over time. Because there is only one study with the most safeguards, it is likely that parapsychology had not yet come to maturity at this point and that further errors were later to be corrected. Indeed, today there is more awareness of the problems of multiple analysis and, relatedly, of making post-hoc decisions about how to split the data. If experimenters conduct too many analyses on a body of data, by chance some of those analyses will give what appear to be significant results. Thus if experimenters have performed multiple analyses and report only those that are significant, this will offer the reader a misleading impression. Nevertheless, for the time, there was considerable experimental sophistication. *ESP60* lists 34 criticisms of ESP research and how the experimentation of the time dealt with them.

Fourth, the remaining study (Table 6.1, row 6) is also the row with the lowest effect size. If one thinks that the addition of safeguards will increase the credibility of the outcome, then if there is only one study with full safeguards, this not going to be sufficient to establish an effect.

Table 6.2. Moderator Variables for Forced-Choice ESP Experiments: 1880–1939 (SOURCE: *ESP60*)

Factors of no Impact	Rating	Psi-Conducive Factors	Rating	Psi-Inhibitory Factors	Rating	Factors about the Nature of ESP	Rating
Sex differences	**	1/5 chance of hit	*	Presence of visitor	*	Erratic	***
Age	**	Use of open matching	**	Long runs	**	Unconscious	***
Blind or Sighted	**	Adults best tested individually (not in group)	***	Delay in checking results	***	Pure telepathy	***
Psychopathic or Normal	**	Good experimenter-participant relationship	**	Formality (as opposed to fun)	**	Pure clairvoyance	***
Hypnotizability	**	Introduction of novelty	**	Frustration	**	GESP	***
Professional Psychics	**	Use of rewards	**	Externally fixed tempo	**	Unstable (e.g., it declines)	***
Intelligence	**	Children in competitive situation	**	Sodium amytal	**	Can't be learned/developed	***
Physical disorder (illness)	**	A little alcohol beforehand	**			Voluntary/dirigible	***
Self-induced trance	**					Temporal control is involuntary (e.g., can't say when will be successful)	***
GESP no better than pure telepathy or pure clairvoyance	**						
Size of target	***						
Distorted target	**						
Use of barriers	***						
Distance	***						
Location (e.g., in deck or as separate card)	***						
Matching vs. Calling	**						

* = suggested; ** = indicated; *** = established

Although Rhine et al. argue (1940/1966, pp. 236–237) that the decrease in effect is not systematic—for example, in Table 6.1 the effect size in row 3 is larger than that in row 2 with fewer safeguards and likewise the effect size in row 5 is larger than in row 4—the lower effect sizes in rows 4–6 compared to rows 1–3 are striking. Thus, although the result from that remaining study in row 6 is impressive, there appeared to be room for further research to replicate those findings.

Although there were not the statistical means in 1939 to analyze for moderator variables, *ESP60* also provides an informal summary of moderator variables in the experiments to that date. Moderator variables are variables that can be exploited to increase or decrease the probability of gaining good experimental results. For example, if women consistently outperformed men in ESP tests, the sex of participants would be a moderator variable because the different sexes perform differently in such tests. The potential moderator variables that had been examined in the first 60 years of ESP research and Rhine et al.'s (1940/1966) assessment of them are summarized in Table 6.2. Rhine et al. devised a rating scale of "established," "indicated" and "suggested." A finding was *established* if there were at least two experimental series yielding extra-chance results, with at least one conforming to all 34 safeguard criteria and the other excluding visual or auditory cues or both, or, if the finding was contentious, at least two independent studies should meet all 34 criteria. Interestingly, Rhine et al. note that on this criterion the Pratt and Woodruff study was the only one that established ESP. They also stress that "established" is not meant to imply "filed claims of accomplishment" (p. 252) but "an outline of partial and potential discovery" (pp. 252–253). A finding was *indicated* if an experimental series was significant and excluded visual or auditory cues or both or if there were three independent experiments that failed to meet the criteria and yet yielded the same results. There had to be at least twice as many series favorable to the hypothesis as opposed ones. A finding was *suggested* if the experimental conditions did not meet the safeguard criteria of excluding visual and auditory cues or if there were two experiments in favor of the hypothesis and one against.

By today's standards the number of studies available in *ESP60* to assess the moderator variables is rather small and thus the conclusions are based often on only a couple of studies. To this extent, the findings in Table 6.2 must not be taken too seriously.

From Table 6.2 it can be seen that variables that do not appear to matter (far left column) predominate and that many of the "established" characteristics (far right column) ultimately rest on the elusiveness of psi—i.e., that as soon as one tries to establish psi, it seems to disappear.

From a skeptical standpoint the predominance of factors that appear to be immaterial for the success of an ESP study would support the idea that the findings are ultimately due to chance, for if ESP results were all statistical artifacts one would expect none of the findings to replicate systematically. This, together with an established elusiveness of psi, will only support the view that the ESP results are ultimately illusory. If parapsychology is to progress, its aim should be to establish a number of conducive conditions. The aim of this review is to see which conditions these may be, based on reviews conducted to date.

In the light of post–1939 research it is interesting to see whether the conclusions from *ESP60* still appear to hold. I will discuss those aspects that have formed the basis of later reviews; after this I will turn to later reviews that have discussed additional variables.

Intelligence

In *ESP60*, intelligence was "indicated" not to be an important factor for ESP scoring. In 1958, Mangan published a monograph reviewing research conducted on personality variables in relation to ESP scoring level, including intelligence. In this review Mangan tentatively concluded that if the average score of the participants' best ESP sessions was used, this correlated positively with their score on an intelligence test. However, he also noted that most studies used few participants, different intelligence tests, and often the analyses on intelligence were performed only as a side-issue to the experiment. Thus, the results reported in the studies included in his review could be due to multiple analysis and, because studies use different tests to measure intelligence, there is no guarantee that the tests were always measuring the same thing. Similarly, Palmer (1978), too, found a tendency for a correlation between intelligence and good scoring in ESP tests, although, somewhat like Mangan, he argues that the relationship between intelligence and ESP may ultimately be due to those who have good personal adjustment scoring better on ESP tests. In sum, the findings that observe a link between intelligence and success in ESP tests are not well-established due to methodological problems and they could also be due to confounding variables rather than necessarily due to intelligence.

Spatial Distance

One of *ESP60*'s established findings was that distance did not play a role in ESP scoring. That is, at that point it appeared that participants could gain information by ESP regardless of how far away the target, or the agent looking at the target, was. Twenty-five years later, Osis (1965) took a closer look at forced-choice studies with at least 500 trials that examined whether ESP could operate over distance. He suspected that people may be assuming that spatial distance poses no barrier to ESP, when the experimental evidence did not support this claim. He provided a statistical summary of all forced-choice experiments with a 1:5 chance of success that were published in English and that were explicitly designed to address the issue of distance. All analyzed experiments were conducted over a distance of least 100 yards, which was the distance assumed to separate two buildings. Distance was measured around the globe's circumference and not via its diameter.

Osis omitted the "broadcast [Zenith radio] experiments" because they were too poorly conducted; these had originally been omitted from *ESP60*, too, for the same reason. He also excluded studies in which distance was examined alongside precognition or psychokinesis, because of the possible confounds. Otherwise, he did not select for the quality of the experiments and he notes that about half of the material involved multiple calling for the same set of targets, thus opening up the possibility of a stacking effect. That is, if many people are guessing at the same set of three target possibilities and, say, people tend always to pick the middle one of three, then all those people's guesses stack up for that choice. If that choice turns out to be the target, there will be a large number of apparent hits, but this will not necessarily be due to that many people psychically guessing the target, but due to the number of people naturally preferring that one target over the others. The number of hits is thus inflated. Osis was unable to correct for this artifact. Table 6.3 presents the results from his findings. I have calculated the z-scores (without continuity corrections) and effect sizes using the results from Osis's tabular summary (Osis, 1965, Table 6.1, p. 27). Osis's table includes only total runs and the run-score averages.

Osis's findings appear to indicate that ESP in forced-choice experiments declines over distance. Although the effect sizes are very likely to be inflated due to artifacts, the decline over distance does not appear to

Table 6.3. Osis's (1965) Summary of Forced-Choice Studies Examining ESP Over Distance

Distance in miles	Up to 1*	1.1–1,000	1,001–2,000	2,001–3,000	3,001–4,000	7,001–8,000
N trials	4,950	84,664	5,450	13,175	42,425	1,200
Z	43.21	7.57	1.55	1.84	2.27	0
ES	.614	.026	.021	.016	.011	0
N studies	4	9	2	1	4	2
N publications	3	6	2	1	3	1
N main authors	3	5	2	1	3	1

*There is one outlier study (Series A, Riess 1937) with an average run score of 18.24 ($MCE = 5$). No other run score average is above 8. If this study is removed, the data for this column become $N = 3100$, $z = 7.41$, $ES = .133$

be due solely to the stacking effect, for if this were the case one would expect there to be a relationship between the number of trials and the size of the effect. All studies were conducted with a distance of at least one building apart, so sensory cueing should have been less problematic. If one assumes that all studies were equally well (or badly) designed, the pattern is clear. However, the number of studies in each category is very small and it would need only a few of them to have a particularly serious flaw to give a false impression of the overall pattern. Moreover, as Palmer (1978) notes, the apparent decline over distance could be due to psychological effects, with participants perhaps feeling more daunted by studies where the target was placed a great distance away. Additionally, in his review, Palmer (1978) found that the decline over distance occurred only in studies in which uncontrolled variables (such as psychological effects) could account for the results. Other, better controlled studies appeared to show no such decline. However, Palmer also noted that no study showed an incline over distance. He argued that there may be a cut-off point at which psi can no longer operate. Additionally, in a personal communication, Robert Morris has noted that the final column in Table 6.3 with putatively null results is due to only one publication (Osis & Pienaar, 1956), which actually contained two significant results in opposite directions. It is only because these two findings cancel each other out that the overall outcome presented in the final column of Table 6.3 is at chance.

In sum, just as it was reckless for people to assume from the results given in *ESP60* that distance was of no relevance for success in ESP experiments, it would likewise be foolish to have too much confidence in the results offered by Osis. Nevertheless, these initial analyses do show that this might be a worthwhile area to investigate further. Indeed, given the central importance of this variable for model-building, it is surprising that more effort has not been invested in this direction.

Mental Illness

In *ESP60* it was further "indicated" that studies investigating whether "psychopathic" participants performed better than "normal" participants found no difference between the two. A survey by Rogo in 1975 supports this claim. His review included studies that examined psychosis, defining psychosis for the purpose of the review as schizophrenic reactions and affective states "without clearly defined physical cause or structural change within the brain" (American Psychiatric Association 1952) (Rogo 1975, p.120). Rogo was unable to draw any firm conclusions, mostly because the studies reviewed did not have an appropriate control group to which to compare to the patients. However, it appeared that some studies, at least, showed that psychotic patients could display positive ESP scoring; thus what was in question was whether they fared any better than the general public. Rogo noted that the forced-choice procedure may be not particularly good for this population, for it requires them to concentrate for long periods (participants are often required to do hundreds of trials at one sitting in a forced-choice experiment). Palmer's (1978) review also appeared to support Rogo's conclusions.

Sex, GESP, Experimenter Effects, Depressants and Monetary Rewards

In 1978, Palmer wrote an extensive review of ESP research findings, which will be discussed in more detail below. However, regarding the variables it considered that were also in *ESP60*, Palmer's (1978) findings agreed that (a) the participant's sex is not relevant to ESP scoring *per se*; (b) there is no evidence that GESP works any better than clairvoyance or precognition; (c) people outside the immediate experimental setting may have an influence on the study's outcome (for instance, the appearance of strangers may be psi inhibitory; people checking the statistical data may somehow psychically influence the outcome of these data); (d) participant-experimenter interactions appear to be important; (e) mental illness does not appear to affect results; whereas (f) central nervous system depressants reduce the ESP scoring level. Nevertheless, Palmer discusses also the studies that were in *ESP60* and so his findings are not entirely independent. The main conclusion in Palmer (1978) that runs counter to the findings from *ESP60* pertains to monetary (or tangible) rewards. Whereas *ESP60* indicated rewards to be psi-conducive, Palmer's review found that monetary rewards had little effect. However, Palmer notes that the concept of reward is itself ambiguous and if feedback is regarded as a type of reward, then studies that provided immediate feedback appear to do better. This will be seen more formally in the precognition database below.

Long Runs

The use of long runs was "indicated" in *ESP60* as psi-inhibitory. Analyses by Nash (1989) on the *ESP60* database seemed to confirm this finding. Nash found a negative correlation between the length of the experiment overall and the scoring rate, showing that people scored worse in larger experiments. Although Nash interpreted this finding as demonstrating a within-experiment decline (the idea that results systematically decline the longer an experiment goes on), an alternative explanation may be that, by testing over a greater number of trials, larger experiments provide more accurate estimates of the effect size, because results are not prone to normal fluctuations in data. Smaller studies may give an inflated effect size estimate, especially if there is a reporting bias with people tending to report only their more successful smaller studies. Nash also found a negative correlation between scoring rate and the average length of the subject's test. That is, the longer the individual was tested for, the worse that individual's performance in the test was. However, this last finding was one of many subsequent analyses and it may be an artifact of multiple analysis.

Hypnosis

ESP60 rated as "indicated" that neither hypnotizability nor self-induced trance had any impact on ESP scoring. However, Palmer's review in 1978 found that two out of the three forced-choice studies showed a relationship between hypnotic susceptibility and ESP scoring; this relationship did not hold for free-response studies. Since *ESP60* there have been, relatedly, several attempts to review the use of hypnosis in ESP research (e.g., Schechter 1984; Stanford 1992). In 1994, Stanford and Stein published a meta-analysis (a formal statistical summary) of 25 ESP studies that contrasted hypnosis and a comparison condition. Twenty-three used a forced-choice method for the ESP task and thus this meta-analysis can be understood as one applying primarily to the forced-choice database. Although the overall ESP scores obtained under the hypnosis condition were clearly significant ($z = 8.77$), whereas those obtained overall in the comparison condition were not ($z = 0.34$), the results differed greatly across investigators. When the analyses were performed using the effect size associated with a particular investigator, the contrast between the two conditions was not significant. That is, individual investigators did not tend to find a difference between the conditions and whereas some were good at obtaining positive ESP scores, others were less successful.

It is hard to draw conclusions from this body of literature. Moreover, Stanford and Stein report that the studies could have been better designed. None of the reports in the database had experimenters who were blind to whether the participant was in the hypnosis or comparison condition. Thus experimenter expectancy effects may have been possible. Nor was there sufficient information to assess the hypnotic susceptibility of the participants; thus the results may be due at least in part to hypnotic susceptibility rather than to hypnosis *per se*. None of the moderator variables in the meta-analysis produced significant results, although there was a relatively strong and surprising correlation indicating that suggestions for success during the hypnosis condition correlated with lower scoring. Stanford and Stein (1994) propose that if a participant already believes that hypnosis favors ESP, then suggestions of success during hypnosis may make the participant think that the experimenter is not confident that hypnosis alone will help. In sum, hypnosis research is fraught with difficulty and at this point in time, these difficulties have not yet been sufficiently well tackled by investigators. It may well be a fruitful avenue for research, but the research will be useful only if studies are better designed. Researchers are directed to the existing reviews mentioned above for information about pitfalls to avoid.

Post–ESP60 *Reviews*

Although *ESP60* analyzed around 40 variables, later reviews considered yet additional ones. These variables will be considered in the following sections, in chronological order of the relevant reviews.

Extraversion — (a) Mangan

As mentioned earlier, Mangan (1958) wrote a monograph summarizing psychological variables in ESP research. He found that in all the studies reviewed that used extraversion scales, extraversion was associated with higher forced-choice ESP scoring. Nevertheless it was unclear whether Bernreuter's Inventory (see Super 1942) and Factors T(hinking) and S(ocial) on Guildford's 1959 STDCR Inventory adequately measured extraversion or even whether the two scales measured the same personality trait. Twenty years later, Palmer's (1978) review also found that there was a likely relationship between extraversion and good forced-choice ESP scoring. This relationship will be discussed further in the context of Palmer's own review, later on in this chapter.

Mangan also reported that participants who scored high on the restricted Stuart (1946) Interest Inventory were often successful in ESP tests and he noted that the restricted form of Stuart's scale was weighted in favor of extraverted activities. Thus the findings from the studies examining extraversion and from those using Stuart's scale may both be due to the same trait. In similar vein, Palmer (1978) commented that it was hard to know exactly what the Stuart Interest Inventory was measuring. The scale is now no longer used. Further, Mangan's review revealed that participants categorized as expansive in a projective test for expansion-compression, using qualities of drawings, were better at forced-choice ESP tasks than their counterparts, although the "compressives" improved once they had warmed up. According to Mangan, Elkisch (1945; cited in Mangan 1958), who devised the scale, says that compression may be a symptom of a neurotically developed introversion. To conclude, it appears that extraversion could be a promising variable for forced-choice research.

Personal Adjustment

Mangan additionally found that most studies with participants scoring well on personal adjustment scales (e.g., Maslow, Hirsh, Stein and Honigmann 1945 Security-Insecurity Questionnaire), tended to show that well-adjusted participants performed better than those scoring low on the scale. Again, it is not always easy to know whether the different scales are measuring the same traits and Palmer (1978) has even surmised that the extraversion and personal adjustment scales may be assessing similar characteristics and that this is why both are relatively successful predictors of forced-choice ESP scoring. Thus, again, extraversion appears to be a promising trait, although it is unclear whether the relevant variable should be described as extraversion or as good personal adjustment.

Picture-Frustration Test

Mangan's review yielded only ambiguous results for Schmeidler's work with the Rosenzweig picture-frustration test. Here, participants view a series of cartoons of stressful events in which one person is blaming another. The participant has to respond on behalf of the frustrated person. Although this test may be useful, it seemed to interact with how participants perceived their ESP task and so it was not easy to assess. For instance, some participants may find the ESP test frustrating, whereas others may understand it to be fun and enjoyable, and these factors, together with the ratings from the picture-frustration test, may provide a fuller picture. Consequently, conclusions from this variable suggest that its relationship to ESP scoring may not be particularly easy to test.

Testing Real-Time ESP with Respect to Teacher-Pupil Relations

In 1959, Van de Castle reviewed ESP tests conducted between pupils and teachers in the classroom. These tests yielded significant results, perhaps supporting the claim in *ESP60* that group testing was inhibitory only for adults. However, any potential moderator variables in the classroom tests generally provided only conflicting evidence. For example, Van Busschbach's classroom work found consistently good results with pupils in sixth grade or lower (e.g., Van Busschbach 1953), whereas Anderson (e.g., 1957) and Anderson and White's set of studies (e.g., 1956, 1957) achieved better results with seventh-grade students or higher. Nevertheless, it may be that age is not a relevant factor, as was concluded in *ESP60*.

In his review, Van de Castle expressed frustration at the difficulty in comparing studies that do not directly replicate previous work. For instance, Anderson's work primarily used a clairvoyance procedure rather than GESP, making comparison between Anderson's and Busschbach's work difficult. Another example of this difficulty can be seen in Anderson and White's (1956, 1957) finding of a consistently better performance between pupils and teachers who mutually rated each other favorably (i.e., as more liked by them) than between those who independently rated each other less favorably. Hall (1958) attempted to replicate the Anderson-White findings but failed to find a significant difference between the two groups, although the scoring was in the right direction. Hall, however, used a different scale from the Anderson-White studies and thus, again, it is difficult to make a direct comparison. There was no clear evidence in these tests overall that any one sex performed better than the other, although Van de Castle suggested that it may depend on the relationship between the sex of the receiver and that of the sender (e.g., female participants may perform better with a male sender). However, it may simply be that sex is not a relevant factor, as was the conclusion in *ESP60*.

The most promising findings from the classroom studies appear to be the ones from Anderson-White's favorable-unfavorable distinction, which in turn may have a bearing on the issue of a psychologically mediated experimenter effect or on the "preferential effect" (discussed below).

Palmer's (1978) Review

Twenty years after Mangan's review, Palmer (1978) provided a comprehensive review of ESP research findings. The main findings from forced-choice studies in this review are summarized in Table 6.4; the categories heading the columns and the assignment of findings to them are my own, although I hope they are a fair representation of Palmer's conclusions.

Some of these findings may appear to be surprising, so I will discuss a selection of them.

Creative Participants

Readers may be puzzled to see that there is no evidence to indicate that creative people do particularly well. Although some free-response experiments have shown remarkable results using a creative population (e.g., Dalton 1997; Moss 1969; Schlitz & Honorton 1992), the variables in Table 6.4 relate only to forced-choice experiments. Thus, it is perhaps not

Table 6.4. Summary of Palmer's (1978) Paper Regarding Forced-Choice ESP (excludes variables covered by other, more formal meta-analyses)

No strong evidence	Weak evidence	Clear trend
Visualizing the target is better than intuitive guessing (+)	Immediate feedback is better than delayed feedback (+)	Participants with low neuroticism scores perform better (+)
Relationship between short-term memory and ESP scoring (+)	People outside immediate context can be influential (ESP60)	Extravert participants perform better (+)
Creativity is related to good ESP scoring (+)	Field dependence as measured on the Embedded Figures Test yields greater score deviations (+)	Participants taking central nervous system depressants perform worse (ESP60)
Good dream recall is related to good ESP scoring (+)	Spontaneity of participants yields greater variance (+)	
Twins are superior participants (+)	Experimenter-participant relations affect results (ESP60)	
Participants claiming psychic experiences are superior (ESP60)	Hyperthyroid psi-conducive (+)	
Participant's attitudes to psi (e.g., would like psychic abilities to be real) relate to ESP scoring (+)	Participants fare better on their preferred response mode (+)	
Monetary rewards help scoring (?)	Meditation before the psi task increases performance (+)	
Mental illness (ESP60)	Hypnotic susceptibility relates to good ESP scoring (?)	
GESP is superior (ESP60)	Expansiveness relates to positive ESP scoring and negative GESP scoring (+)	
Birth order (eldest children better) (+)		
Sex (ESP60)		
Simple mood questions relate to scoring (+)		
Confidence calls relate to success (+)		

Notes: (ESP60) = Consistent with *ESP60*; (?) = Finding differs from *ESP60*; (+) = Additional variable — not considered in *ESP60*

so surprising that creative people do not perform unambiguously well in a forced-choice setting in which participants' options are usually severely constrained to not more than five standard targets. Free-response experiments, in which participants can freely describe any impressions they have about what is usually a more artistic target (e.g., a video clip, a postcard-type picture, usually from a large target set), may well be more suitable for a creative population.

Psychic Experiences

It is perhaps surprising that Palmer's survey revealed that participants who claimed to have had a psychic experience were not necessarily better in ESP tests than other participants. This finding suggests that the sheep-goat effect found in Lawrence's (1993) meta-analysis (discussed below), which focuses on (a) the participants' belief that they would perform well in that specific experiment, and (b) participants beliefs in the paranormal, is distinct from participants' gaining belief in psi through their own spontaneous experiences. On the face of it, this is rather counterintuitive, although, clearly, having a spontaneous experience is quite different from thinking you could control it in an experimental setting overseen by an experimenter you do not even know. In sum, the message is that for forced-choice experiments there is no particular advantage in selecting participants who claim to have had psychic experiences.

Spontaneity

The tentative findings in the second column in Table 6.4 regarding (i) spontaneity and (ii) the Embedded Figures Test are probably not that useful for experimenters wishing to increase their study's hit rate, because both variables increased variance and thus neither predicted the actual direction of the scores. That is, they simply showed that scoring tended to diverge more from chance, but the scoring could either be in either a particularly positive or negative direction. In his update, Palmer (1982) found more evidence that spontaneity may enhance psi, so it might be a productive route to follow. However, no standard test for spontaneity has been used and sometimes it is a somewhat post-hoc categorization of the task at hand. It would be useful if future research could develop or use a standard measure.

Experimenter-Related Variables

The two experimenter-related variables (experimenter-participant interaction and the effect of other people on the experiment) can both be understood as supporting the findings from *ESP60*, yet the specification of what is necessary for experimenter-participant interaction to be psi-conducive is still vague. This is too complex a topic for this chapter, but those who want to learn more about the experimenter effect may wish to consult the existing reviews (e.g., Kennedy & Taddonio 1976; Thouless 1976; White 1976). Basically, the experimenter effect hypothesis holds that the experimenters' interactions with the participant may affect the outcome of the overall experiment, either by affecting the psychological setting for the participant or perhaps even by the experimenter implementing his own psi to obtain the results he wants. The bottom line in this literature is that there is still no clear understanding of what makes a psi-conducive experimenter, if there is such a thing. Similarly, there is no clear specification of the stage at which a person is regarded as no longer being able to have a psychic effect on the experiment. For example, do the people working in the same building as the experimenter but who have nothing to do with the experimenter's study also affect the outcome of the study?

Hyperthyroid

In the second column of Table 6.4, the potential for people with a hyperthyroid condition to be particularly good participants is an interesting one. Palmer notes that two of the highest-scoring card-guessing subjects in the history of parapsychology had hyperthyroid conditions. However, both studies were conducted in the 1930s and Palmer explains that at least one of them was not well-designed and permitted auditory cues to the participant. Thus, although these studies look promising, the findings may be artifactual. However, research in this area may be beneficial.

Meditation

Palmer found two studies in which participants meditated before taking part in a forced-choice psi task. Both studies found enhanced results after meditation. However, this putative effect could presumably be partly psychological in character, with participants having greater confidence after meditating, presumably with the belief that the experimenter thinks that meditation will help. Moreover, there are only two studies in Palmer's review. Thus, more studies in this area may be worthwhile, but the current findings must be taken with some caution.

Preferential Effect

Palmer also tentatively noted that participants in studies in which there were two modes of response tended to perform better in the response mode for which they expressed a preference. That is, if participants did two types of trial, for example, one in which they had to call out their guesses, and another in which they had to write them down, participants would usually perform better in, say, the calling mode if they stated beforehand that they preferred this mode. This "preferential" effect appeared to be more promising for studies alternating response type rather than for studies alternating target type. Thus, if, for example, participants sometimes guessed at a target in the form of a picture and sometimes at a target in the form of a word, the participants' previously expressed preference for, say, picture targets would not reliably result in more success on the picture targets. However, dividing the analysis into a preferential effect for response type versus a preferential effect for target type may mean that the tentative finding for response type is artifactual due to multiple analysis. Consequently, although the preferential effect may be a useful avenue of research, the evidence must currently be regarded as suggestive at most.

However, the preferential effect is reminiscent of the tentative evidence of success with the favorable-unfavorable distinction in the classroom studies, which were reviewed above. Nevertheless, Palmer offers a word of caution as to whether the preferential effect will promote the chances of psi-hitting in experiments in which there is no choice of response mode. That is, the preference may come about through participants having a choice rather than being due to anything intrinsic to that particular method.

Neuroticism

Perhaps the most promising variable arising from Palmer's (1978) review is that of neuroticism. He uses the term to refer broadly to "tendencies toward maladaptive behavior caused either by anxiety or by defense mechanisms against anxiety" (p. 178). The studies in this section of his review used at least 13 different objective scales and three projective ones (e.g., Rorschach TAT-like pictures). Thus the use of the term "neuroticism" here may be broader than normally understood. Palmer found that 20 forced-choice studies, testing participants individually, found that less-neurotic participants scored better in ESP tests, whereas only six studies, testing participants individually, found the reverse result. However, the studies used a variety of measures to test for neuroticism, again making comparison between studies difficult. Palmer notes that Cattell's (1965) scales have been the most successful (used four times).

In his later, updated review, Palmer (1982) noted that the relationship between low neuroticism and good ESP scoring still had some support, but was unclear due to a significant reversal of the effect in a forced-choice clairvoyance experiment by Haight, Kanthamani and Kennedy (1978). Schmeidler (1988) explains the somewhat conflicting evidence by arguing that more neurotic participants may do badly only when the experimental situation makes them nervous (e.g., in the laboratory, rather than at home) and they want to do well at the test.

In sum, neuroticism remains a promising variable, although the details may render the relationship more complex than it initially appeared.

Also, the trend is towards a deviation in scores rather than to less neurotic participants doing particularly well. A meta-analysis of this area may prove fruitful.

Extraversion — (b) Palmer

Like Mangan (1958), Palmer (1978) also found a relationship between extraversion and ESP, with extraverted participants scoring better, regardless of whether they were in a group setting or not. The neuroticism findings had held only for those tested individually. Schmeidler (1988) found an extra 38 studies (not specifying how many were forced-choice) between 1981 and 1986 examining extraversion, of which 29 showed this trend and 12 of those 29 were significant, thus further supporting Palmer's finding. She notes, however, that these findings may apply only to certain conditions. For example, if the psi task is particularly dull or repetitive, extraverts may perform worse.

Palmer notes that there is a strong correlation between the extraversion scales used in ESP research and neuroticism (p. 133) and because many of the experiments used both scales, it is difficult to separate out these two variables. Moreover, the relationship between ESP scoring and good social adjustment reported by Mangan (1958) is arguably also related to these findings. Additionally, Schmeidler (1988) thinks that openness may be a psi-conducive trait. This, too, may relate to low neuroticism, extraversion and social adjustment.

Unlike neuroticism, there has been a meta-analysis examining extraversion as a variable (Honorton, Ferrari & Bem 1998). Initially, the meta-analysis appeared to show that a significant correlation between extraversion and psi scoring in forced-choice ESP tests was artifactual. Honorton et al. (1998) found that the effect arose only for studies in which the extraversion scale was administered after the ESP test. They argued that scores on the ESP test may have affected the way in which participants answered the questions on the extraversion scale. However, Palmer and Carpenter (1998) showed that the alleged artifact was due to a confound between group testing and individual testing — that is, the difference between the ESP-extraversion relationship for pre- and post–ESP administration of the scale could be seen actually to be due to the difference in testing conditions. Participants tested individually showed a correlation with extraversion and ESP scoring and this was not due to participants being given the extraversion scale after the ESP task. That is, according to Palmer and Carpenter, the relationship between extraversion and ESP scoring was upheld when individuals were tested individually.

To conclude, extraversion is a highly promising variable, although some doubt remains as to whether it is confounded with neuroticism, low defensiveness, and personal adjustment.

Reviews after 1978

Vivid Imagery

George (1981) found that forced-choice studies using the Betts QMI (Quality of Mental Imagery) scale (see Richardson 1969) reported significant interactions with the measure, whereas free-response studies did not. However, the interactions were not always in the same direction and George notes that the scale's validity had been questioned by Honorton (1975). Consequently, George's finding is likely consistent with Palmer's (1978) finding that visual imagery fared no better than intuitive guessing.

Subliminal and Psi Perception

Roney-Dougal (1986) reviewed subliminal and psi perception. In the section on forced-choice studies she concludes, with Rao and Rao (1982), that both subliminal and psi perception are facilitated by altered states (e.g., dreaming, meditation) and that to this extent they may be similar. She notes, again along with Rao and Rao, that many of the studies did not use truly subliminal thresholds and that it may be that as soon as some sensory processing is activated, the similarity between psi and subliminal perception is lessened. She concludes that people who do better at a subliminal perception task after meditating will also do well at an ESP task. However, at the time of her review only two studies had directly investigated meditation, subliminal perception and psi perception simultaneously (Rao & Puri 1978; Rao & Rao 1982). Thus, again, there is much work to be done before any conclusions can be drawn.

Meta-analytic Review of Precognition

Introduction: The majority of the 45 studies analyzed in *ESP60* did not test for precognition (see Table 6.5, row 1), although after 1940, and especially from 1960 to 1980 (see Table 6.5, rows 4–5), forced-choice precognition studies became a major focus of interest. In the following, I will summarize the findings from the Honorton and Ferrari (1989) meta-analysis of forced-choice precognition studies from 1935 to 1987.

Database: Honorton and Ferrari (1989) located 309 studies by 62 senior authors in 113 publications. They found that these reports contained studies with "nearly two million individual trials and more than 50,000 subjects" (p. 283). This is substantially fewer trials than the 3 million trials

Table 6.5. Year of Publication of Forced-Choice Precognition
Reports Used in Honorton and Ferrari (1989)

Decade	Number of published reports
1935–39	3
1940–49	7
1950–59	12
1960–69	36
1970–79	41
1980–87	14

in *ESP60*'s forced-choice ESP database. Moreover, whereas *ESP60* reports over 2.75 million trials with a 1:5 probability of a hit performed in 45 reports over a five-year period, the precognition meta-analysis reports around a third fewer trials from two and half times more reports (113 reports) over a 10-times longer (50-year) period.

The difference is striking. There must either be significant differences in the ways in which ESP and precognition studies are conducted or for some reason there must have been a general decrease in the number of trials per published report over time. The former alternative appears unlikely to account for the difference, because one would actually expect precognition studies to have more trials. Precognition trials do not require a sender and they require fewer precautionary measures. Thus they are easier to conduct at length. Possibly, over time, shorter, nonsignificant studies may have had a better chance at being published and thus the mean number of trials per publication decreased.

There may also have been more social pressure to publish even small studies, again decreasing the mean number of trials per publication. Honorton and Ferrari included English-language published work that reported fixed-length studies in which direct hits could be calculated. They coded six safeguard criteria. This may seem small compared to the 34 criteria listed in *ESP60*, but precognition studies are less prone to sensory cueing than clairvoyance and telepathy studies. The criteria included the added safeguards of determining whether the analyses were preplanned and whether the sample sizes were prespecified.

There are many problems with assigning safeguard ratings to studies. For instance, authors of significant studies or, as Honorton and Ferrari argue (p.296), of studies using selected participants may feel more justified in including more details about the experimental procedure in their reports. Hence these reports may achieve better safeguard ratings than studies that are nonsignificant or that have used unselected participants.

Similarly, defining studies to be included as those in which the number of direct hits could be calculated will probably increase the number of studies in the analysis that have pre-planned the use of direct hits, thus perhaps artificially increasing the quality rating by increasing the likelihood of a positive rating for preplanned analyses. Consequently, a lack of correlation between study outcome and study safeguards should be treated with some caution. With this caveat, Honorton and Ferrari's analyses showed that none of their results could be explained through lack of appropriate safeguards. Interestingly, the mean effect size of all 309 studies (*ES* = .020) is the same as that discovered in the sixth, and most robust, experiment in *ESP60* (*ES* = .020). Honorton and Ferrari's major findings are summarized in Table 6.6.

Honorton and Ferrari performed a 10-percent trim on the database, eliminating the upper and lower 10 percent of the z-scores. This is referred to in Table 6.6 as the trimmed database; all moderator variable analyses in that table were performed on the trimmed database. The trimmed database showed no significant difference across the 57 remaining investigators, suggesting that the effect was a consistent one across many experimenters.

It is notable that the effect size of the trimmed database (*ES* = .012) is smaller than that for all studies (*ES* = .020). Presumably, one should choose the lower effect size for power calculations for future studies, assuming one does not regard oneself as a particularly psi-conducive or psi-inhibitory experimenter (if one thinks that experimenter issues are relevant) and one is conducting a study with the general population.

Honorton and Ferrari (1989) found that the mean number of trials was larger for significant studies than for nonsignificant studies (p. 284) and this is probably due to the larger studies having better power to detect an effect. Also, many wonder about how the older studies frequently gained

Table 6.6. Main Results from Honorton and Ferrari's (1989)
Forced-Choice Precognition Meta-Analysis

	Mean *ES*	Number of Studies	$t(df)$
All studies	.020	309	
Trimmed database	.012	248	
Selected participants vs.	**.051**	25	$t(246) = 3.16$
Nonselected participants	.008	223	$p = .001$
Individual testing vs.	**.021**	97	$t(200) = 1.89$
Group testing	.004	105	$p = .03$
Trial by trial feedback vs.	**.035**	47	Not available
Delayed feedback	.009	21	(post-hoc split)
Millisecond precognitive interval vs.	**.045**	31	Not available
1 month — 1 year precognitive interval	.001	7	(post-hoc split)

significant results, whereas today it seems less common. If experiments in *ESP60* had more trials, it may be that they had more significant results not just because they were more poorly designed, but also partly because they had better-powered studies. For an effect size of .01 the number of trials needed for a study with a power of 95 percent is 108,213.

I will now discuss the moderator variables.

Experimenter Interactions: Before trimming the database, Honorton and Ferrari (1989) found a significant difference ($p = .034$) in mean effect size across investigators, although they downplay this by calling it "surprisingly small" (p. 285), despite apparently according credence to the significant difference ($p = .03$) between individual and group testing (p. 296). The issue of experimenter-to-participant relations arose also in *ESP60* and this seems to be supported here obliquely by Honorton and Ferrari, if one thinks that different experimenters interact differently with their participants. The problem lies in the undefinability of the problem (e.g., is the so-called experimenter effect due to experimenter psi, experimenter-participant relations, systematic differences between the ways experimenters conduct studies etc.?) and if an experimenter effect of any kind exists, it no doubt adds to the problem of the so-called elusiveness of psi. Clearly, this is an area that needs to be understood better if parapsychology is to progress. However, if it can be established that other variables can produce a replicable effect regardless of experimenter, the issue of experimenter psi will be less important. The aim of this review is to see where and how we can best hope to establish a replicable effect.

Selected Participants: By "selected participants" Honorton and Ferrari (1989) meant those who had been selected on the basis of prior performance in other experiments. Thus the selected participants finding does not necessarily conflict with the indicated finding in *ESP60* that professional psychics do not perform any better than the normal population. The message from Honorton and Ferrari's finding is that it might be advantageous if investigators in forced-choice experiments first singled out those participants who have previously performed well in such tests.

Group Studies: The Honorton and Ferrari meta-analysis appears to replicate the indicated finding in *ESP60* that group studies are psi-inhibitory for adults. The difference between individual and group performance found by Honorton and Ferrari seems to come more from the poor performance of group studies than from any particularly impressive effect size from studies with individuals. Thus, whereas Honorton and Ferrari express their finding as favoring individual testing, the variable is probably better expressed instead as showing that group settings are psi-inhibitory. This could perhaps be regarded as weakly supported by a meta-analysis by Milton and Wiseman (1999), which showed that eight mass-media tests yielding over 1.5 million ESP trials provided non-significant results ($z = -1.60$; $ES = -0.005$). There is some ambiguity as to what constitutes a "group" experiment—for instance, does it include mass media studies where many participants may be taking the test alone at home, but in which they nevertheless understand themselves as being part of the nation? Are online tests over the Internet classified as group experiments, mass-media experiments, or as normal ESP tests on individuals but without the presence of an experimenter? The analyses in *ESP60* indicated that the group setting may be psi-inhibitory only for adults. Either there were not enough studies in the precognition database to examine this, or Honorton and Ferrari simply did not investigate whether the group findings differed for children.

Trial-by-Trial Feedback and Short Precognitive Interval: The variables of the apparent superiority of trial-by-trial feedback and that of a very short precognitive interval are confounded, as Honorton and Ferrari (1998) themselves remark (p. 298). That is, if the target is selected quickly after a participant's guess, the participant can gain feedback more quickly, too. Honorton and Ferrari additionally found that the short precognitive interval was advantageous only if one used unselected participants. They do not mention whether this difference between selected and unselected participants applied also to trial-by-trial feedback. If a short precognitive interval is advantageous only for unselected participants, psychological factors, such as feeling daunted by trying to guess a target that will not be selected until much later, may explain the apparent precognitive attrition over time. Consequently, these findings need to be treated with caution and it would be useful for theoretical work if studies could provide more information about (i) whether it is speed of feedback or the precognitive interval that is more important; (ii) whether moderator variables differ for naïve and experienced participants; and (iii) whether psychological factors can explain the decrease in effect size over length of precognitive interval. Palmer (1978) found that trial-by-trial feedback does not produce a consistent change in ESP scoring rate over time, although he did find that if there was a change, it was more likely to be an incline (i.e., enhanced ESP scoring). He suggests that trial-by-trial feedback may stabilize ESP scoring. In short, experimenters should use trial-by-trial feedback and work could be conducted to see if there are any confounding variables.

True Precognition: Initially, the findings suggest that the precognition database may have similar characteristics to that of the GESP database; both suggest that group testing of adults is psi-inhibitory, that immediate feedback is more favorable than delayed feedback, and evidence so far is that both databases have a similar effect size. These similarities may raise the question of whether precognitively gained information is actually gained in real-time. Honorton and Ferrari examined this possibility by seeing whether the apparent precognitive effect was confined to precognition studies that did not successfully rule out real-time explanations. For example, early precognition experiments required participants to guess the order in which a pack of cards would be after it had been shuffled. However, the successful results could be due either to the participant correctly guessing the future order of the cards (precognition) or to the shuffler psychically arranging the cards to match the participant's pre-existing guesses (clairvoyance or PK on the shuffler). Consequently, Honorton and Ferrari (1989) analyzed separately the studies that used a very complex method of determining the future target (Mangan, 1955). This complex method used a roll of dice followed by complex calculations (including the use of square roots and sines, etc.) to find an entry point into a random number table in order to determine the target. This methodology rendered it unlikely that any experimenter could work back through the calculations to determine which numbered dice he would need to throw in order to obtain a hit on the basis of psychic knowledge of the participants' guesses. Thus successful results from studies using the Mangan method or equivalent would be due to the participants' precognitive ability and not to real-time ESP. Honorton and Ferrari found that results from the studies using the Mangan method were not significantly different from those in the rest of the database, $t(45) = .38$, $p = .37$, two-tailed.

Nevertheless, Morris (1982) has noted that studies using stock market figures have tended to be nonsignificant. Moreover, Tart's (1983) meta-analysis of 85 forced-choice studies appeared to show that real-time ESP studies outperformed precognition ones. However, Tart used only those studies that reached significance for his analysis. But if precognition and clairvoyance studies have the same effect size, yet precognition studies have a larger number of trials, the better power in the precognition studies due to the larger number of trials would enable more precognition studies with a lower effect size to reach significance and hence to reach the criterion for inclusion in Tart's analysis (see Steinkamp, Milton, and Morris 1998). Thus Tart's (1983) analysis may artificially inflate the clairvoyance effect size.

Steinkamp, Milton, and Morris (1998) looked at the same issue from a different perspective. They analyzed 22 forced-choice experiments comparing clairvoyance and precognition from 1935 to 1997 to see whether clairvoyance experiments had a higher effect size. They argued that if precognition is due to using real-time psychic information to make a best guess, one would expect precognition to have a lower effect size because precognition would have more room for error or miscalculation. The results indicated that there was no difference in effect size between the results from the two experimental protocols. The effect size from the clairvoyance studies was .009 and the precognition effect size was .010. These effect sizes are fairly close to the final effect size in Honorton and Ferrari's (1989) trimmed sample (.012). This provides some confirmation of the prior findings, although there is considerable overlap between Honorton and Ferrari's database and that of Steinkamp et al., and so the similarity in findings should not be surprising.

Consequently, there is no clear-cut answer to the issue of whether true precognition is possible, but certainly precognition protocols not using stock market figures appear to be as successful as clairvoyance ones.

In sum, the precognition findings are very similar to the findings from forced-choice GESP experiments. Success in precognition experiments appears to decline as the precognitive interval increases and similarly GESP results appear to decline as the spatial distance increases. Yet both of these suggested findings have confounds and need to be examined with much more rigor before we can assert them with any confidence. Clearly, both issues are of extreme importance for any model-building and this is one area on which parapsychology could focus.

Sheep-goat effect: A variable that was not analyzed in either *ESP60* or Honorton and Ferrari (1989) is that of the sheep-goat effect. This is the hypothesis that believers in paranormal phenomena ("sheep") tend to score above chance in ESP tests, whereas those who are skeptical of the paranormal ("goats") tend to score below chance (see Schmeidler 1943). Lawrence (1993) conducted a meta-analysis of forced-choice ESP studies to look at this proposed effect. He included any forced-choice ESP study from 1947 to 1993 that "addressed the relation of [the] subject's attitude to the paranormal and its influence on ESP scoring" (p. 76). The results from the 73 studies were strongly in favor of a difference in performance between the two groups ($z = 8.17$, $p = 1.3 \times 10^{-16}$), demonstrating a mean trial-based effect size of the difference of .029. The sheep-goat effect did not appear to be related to study quality and the number of unpublished studies needed to bring the result down to just barely significant was 1,726. As in previous reviews, significant studies tended to have a larger sample size.

Lawrence investigated several sheep-goat measures (Bhadra 1966; Thalbourne and Haraldsson 1980; Schmeidler 1943 and Van de Castle and White 1955); these measures did not show any significant difference in predictive performance, although Schmeidler's (1943) question of: "Do you believe it is possible that ESP can be shown under the conditions of this experiment?" is the simplest and had the highest mean effect size of the difference (.032) jointly with Thalbourne and Haraldsson's (1980) scale. Nevertheless, Schmeidler's question has varied over time. Between 1948 and 1951, participants were classified as sheep if they answered Schmeidler's question with either "it is probable," "undecided," or "unlikely." Only those designating it as "impossible" were classified as goats. Thus even relatively skeptical participants were classified as sheep.

Although the mean effect size for the database overall includes studies in which the belief scale was administered after participants had taken part, and hence in these instances the participants may have responded to the scales according to how they had just performed, the 50 studies in which the scales were presented before the ESP test had a very similar mean effect size of the difference (.028) to the one overall (.029).

Nevertheless, the sheep-goat distinction is a relatively puzzling one, given that other reviews have consistently concluded that participants claiming to have had psychic experiences perform no better than those reporting no such experiences. One would expect those who report having had psychic experiences also to be more likely to be "sheep" regarding the paranormal than those reporting no such experiences. Moreover, the sheep-goat distinction appeared to hold even when the sheep-goat scales focused on paranormal belief rather than on the original issue of people believing that the experiment could elicit ESP. Consequently, any differences between those who believe ESP can be elicited in the experimental situation and those who believe that ESP is possible in ordinary life cannot supply the whole solution. Nevertheless, it may be that because the sheep-goat effect is relatively small, it can show up only when participants are separated in terms of their paranormal belief and not when participants who have had no personal experiences, some of whom may yet believe in the paranormal, are compared with those who have had personal experiences.* Additionally, if participants are not new to ESP testing and have been successful before in a previous experiment, they will be more likely to respond positively to Schmeidler's question. Thus the sheep-goat variable could be confounded with the finding that participants selected on the basis of prior testing perform better. The sheep-goat findings are not as clear as is perhaps generally believed.

Nevertheless, the results from the Lawrence (1993) meta-analysis suggest that the difference in performance between sheep and goats is a useful one to pursue; what it does not tell us is whether the difference is due, for example, to goats tending to perform significantly badly, with sheep

*I would like to thank Caroline Watt for this point.

scoring at chance or to sheep performing significantly well with goats scoring at chance (or something in between these two alternatives). Nor is it entirely clear whether this variable holds for both naïve and experienced experimental participants, and hence it is not entirely clear what the sheep-goat variable really measures. Further analyses or work in this area might help to specify more accurately what we need to focus on to achieve good results. For now, the meta-analysis does not necessarily suggest that selecting sheep for a test will in itself increase the overall results of any particular forced-choice study; the issue is rather to avoid testing goats. Lawrence correctly notes that the inclusion of goats may nevertheless provide us with more information on individual differences. Whether the sheep-goat effect holds also for free-response experiments or for PK studies remains an open question, too.

Super-sheep: In 1970, Beloff and Bate made a further distinction between sheep and super-sheep. The term super-sheep denoted sheep who expressed certainty that they could show ESP under the experimental conditions. Palmer (1978) found suggestive evidence that results from super-sheep showed greater variance. That is, they tended to perform both very well and very badly and thus overall tended to perform at chance. This may be related to the finding in *ESP60* that professional psychics did not provide better results. Nevertheless, at this stage the evidence regarding super-sheep is not strong, although it may be a useful avenue for further research.

Defense Mechanism Test: In 1995, Haraldsson and Houtkooper conducted a meta-analysis of studies examining the correlation between low defensiveness, as measured by a defense mechanism test (DMT) (Kragh 1969; Kragh & Neuman 1982), and good ESP scores in forced-choice experiments. They statistically combined 16 experiments to find an overall effect size for the correlation ($ES = 0.16$, $z = 3.87$, $p = .00006$, two-tailed), although the results declined over the years. The overall ESP score for the combined 10 Icelandic experiments was not significant ($z = -0.23$, $p = .407$). Nevertheless, a later paper (Haraldsson, Houtkooper, Schneider and Baeckstrom 2001) indicated that the DMT ratings, which had been performed by Martin Johnson (MJ), could not be replicated by another researcher and that the correlation between ESP scores and the DMT came solely from the nonobjective part of the DMT ratings. Haraldsson et al. (2001) concluded that perhaps the apparent correlation between DMT ratings and ESP scoring comes purely from a psi-mediated experimenter (or checker) effect. This raises serious doubts about the replicability of the supposed correlation, although even these doubts are themselves open to doubt. For instance, some of the scoring was also performed by Ulf Kragh

(UK). MJ and UK showed good interrater reliability (noted by Johnson and Haraldsson 1984; Watt 1990), thus indicating that MJs coding was not necessarily as subjective as one might initially believe. Also, Haraldsson et al (2001) note that MJ's coding strategy may have changed over time, and that this may be why it was hard for them to reconstruct and to replicate MJs coding.

In sum, this area of research has no clear answer and, to establish an effect, other criteria may be more immediately productive. Nevertheless, low defensiveness may be related to the extraversion, low neuroticism and good social adjustment scales that have already been seen in other reviews to be potentially psi-conducive. It does appear that a personality profile of potentially good participants is slowly emerging from the data.

Religiosity: Haraldsson (1993), and Haraldsson and Houtkooper (1995) also found a significant correlation between religiosity and forced-choice ESP scoring in their Icelandic experiments. Religiosity was measured by asking participants (i) how religious they considered themselves to be; (ii) how often they attended religious meetings; (iii) how often they read religious material; and (iv) how often they pray. Haraldsson (1993) notes, however, that religiosity may differ from culture to culture. For instance, he remarks that Icelanders often rate themselves as religious, which is similar to Americans. Icelanders, however, attend church less often. Thus different surveys may rate religiosity differently, according to culture. Haraldsson et al. (2001) did not replicate the relationship between religiosity and ESP scoring, although the results were in the right direction. Thus, this variable may be worth further investigation, although the evidence is not yet strong enough to warrant too much confidence and scales may need to be refined for cross-cultural use.

Replication

An important issue is that of replication. Hess (1982), though not interested in the replication issue specifically, asked five different questions of 45 replication studies. Namely (i) is there a difference in success rate of strict, close, and conceptual replications of successful original experiments?; (ii) is there a difference in success rate between strict, close, and conceptual replications of unsuccessful original experiments?; (iii) do more successful original experiments tend to be followed by stricter replications?; (iv) do replication experiments tend to be less successful than original experiments regardless of replication type?; and (v) do strict replications tend to be less successful than the original experiment?

Surprisingly, given the general confusion of findings in the literature reviews, only question (v) received an affirmative answer, although it may be that replication studies had equally disparate findings, regardless of replication type. Moreover, the number of studies was relatively small and there are no details as to how the experiments were coded for replication type and whether there could be a coding bias. A well-designed review along these lines could be of interest.

Conclusions

The challenge for parapsychology, if it wants to continue to follow the path of science, is to find the experiment that can be replicated by anyone, or, failing that, the experiment that can be replicated by experimenters of a clearly defined type. The effect obtained in parapsychology is small. Thus, forced-choice experiments are a good means by which to obtain a large number of trials with relatively little effort. The aim of this review has been to try to find which variables might stack the odds in favor of achieving this aim.

Unfortunately, there are few variables that have correlated clearly with success and even those which have are all to some extent ill-defined. Virtually all the reviews mention the difficulty of assessing the state of the field because of the sheer diversity and, underlying this claim, the lack of systematicity of the studies involved. Moreover, most of the variables examined have revealed conflicting evidence, with at least some of the evidence coming from poorly-designed studies that do not permit a strong conclusion. Indeed most variables tested provided little evidence either way as being ultimately psi-conducive (see especially, Table 6.7, far left column) and there were relatively few variables that appeared to be encouraging (see Table 6.7, far right column).

Additionally, although many variables have been tested, each variable often has only a few studies. Thus even potentially promising variables may later turn out to be false leads. Moreover, most studies are conducted with people who have never taken part in an ESP test before. Hence, the results really apply only to the general population of people taking an ESP test for the first time. Table 6.7 summarizes the simpler findings from all reviews summarized in this paper.

On a more positive note, meta-analytic methods should make it possible to gain a better idea of which methods really are the most promising. The second and third columns in Table 6.7 provide the most promising areas for future meta-analyses, although even variables in the first column may be worth further testing. Meta-analyses may also encourage more tightly designed studies by providing criteria by which studies

Table 6.7. Summary of Evidence for the Potential Relevance of Variables from the Reviews of Forced-Choice Experiments Surveyed in this Chapter

Little Evidence	Partial Evidence	Promising Evidence
Age (ESP60, VdC)	Open matching is best (ESP60)	Low neuroticism as psi-conducive (M, P, Sch)
Sex (ESP60, P)	A little alcohol beforehand is psi-conducive (ESP60)	Extraversion as psi-conducive (M, P, Sch)
Intelligence (ESP60*, M, P*)	Low defensiveness in DMT is psi-conducive (HH)	Good social adjustment as psi-conducive (M, P)
Sighted vs. blind (ESP60)	Spontaneity/novelty is psi-conducive (ESP60, P)	Selected participants on basis of prior testing perform better in precognition tests (HF)
Mental illness (ESP60, R, P)	Openness is psi-conducive (Sch)	Smallest possible precognitive time interval is better (HF)
Physical illness (ESP60)	Expansive is psi-conducive for clairvoyance (M)	Trial-by-trial feedback is better (ESP60, P, HF)
Birth order (e.g., eldest child best) (P)	Meditation before task is psi-conducive (P)	Adult group testing is psi inhibitory (ESP60, P, MW)
Twins (P)	Hyperthyroid condition is psi-conducive (P)	Goats score low (P, Sch, L)
Creativity (P)	Use of hypnosis is psi-conducive (P, StS)	Central nervous system depressants are psi inhibitory (ESP60, P)
Dream recall (P)	Hypnotic susceptibility is correlated with ESP scoring (ESP60, P*)	
Short-term memory and ESP scoring (P)	Religiosity correlates with ESP scoring (H)	
Confidence calls (P)	Long runs inhibitory (ESP60)	
Visualizing vs. Intuitive guessing (G, P*)	Visitors inhibitory (ESP60)	
Attitude to psi (e.g., like it to exist) (P)	Formality inhibitory (ESP60)	
Self-induced trance (ESP60)	People outside immediate experiment can influence results (P)	
Psychic claimant/experiences (ESP60, P)	Experimenter-participant relationship plays a role (ESP60, P)	
Monetary rewards (ESP60, P*)	Field-dependence in embedded figures test provokes greater deviation (P)	
Size of target (ESP60)	Preferential effect provokes difference in scoring (P)	
Distorted target (ESP60)	Super-sheep provide greater variance in scores (P)	
Barriers to target (ESP60)		
Matching vs. calling target (ESP60)		
Location of target (on own or in deck) (ESP60)		
Spatial distance of target (ESP60*, O, P*)		
GESP vs. pure ESP (ESP60, P)		

Notes: ESP60 = reported in ESP60; G = reported in George (1981); HF = reported in Honorton & Ferrari (1989); HH = reported in Haraldsson & Houtkooper (1995); L = reported in Lawrence (1993); M = reported in Mangan (1958); MW = reported in Milton & Wiseman (1999); P = reported in Palmer (1978); R = reported in Rogo (1975); Sch = reported in Schmeidler (1988); StS = reported in Stanford & Stein (1994); dC = reported in Van de Castle (1959); * = reviews provide contradictory conclusions; asterisked reviews support conclusion indicated here were quality rated and thus a clear set of criteria that future studies should ideally follow.

At this point in time, many parapsychological reviews and meta-analyses of forced-choice studies have to base themselves on a large proportion of historical findings with methodological flaws, which may or may not have been responsible for the results of some of the studies. Indeed, there are more trials in the last five years of the *ESP60* (1940/1966) database than there are in the 50 years of the Honorton and Ferrari (1989) one. Quality ratings may be a help, but they do not provide the whole picture and they may even furnish a rather misleading one. Moreover, even as recently as 1976, Rhine was still arguing that nonsignificant studies should not be published in full. Thus pre–1976 findings and beyond may to some extent be distorted by multiple analysis, if experimenters tried to find a significant result somewhere in their data so that they could publish it. Although it is probably fair to say that methodologically parapsychology has now come of age, until meta-analytic results are based on a longer history, their findings may be able to give us only a shadow of what the data really mean. Recent reviews of the hypnosis and the DMT literature are good examples of this; both sets of findings were in the end ambiguous due to methodological problems in the databases involved. Historical errors and improvements were a necessary part of parapsychology's maturation process. Hopefully, parapsychology can now look forward to an ever-increasing number of quality experiments in its history and an ever-increasing possibility of a realistic grip of its data.

On reading the reviews, it becomes clear how few studies there are for any one variable and how few direct replications there are. This lack of direction is doubtless in part due to the lack of funding for the field, and the lack of active researchers, both of which may foil any attempt to persist at any single research question. But it is all too easy to hide behind excuses; the fault lies with the researchers, too (I do not exclude myself from this). Generally, my impression from this review of reviews is that parapsychology has grown from a baby to a toddler. It has grasped the methodology of walking, but it has yet to learn how to walk in a specific direction. There is no view of a goal or of the quickest and easiest way to get to that goal. It is difficult to know whether it is psi that is elusive or whether it is the lack of direction that makes it appear elusive.

If one tries to construct the ideal, easily conducted forced-choice experiment from the research accrued in this review, it is immediately apparent how little we know even about the more promising variables. Should the ideal study select participants who have done well on previous testing or should it select extraverts, or should it select nonneurotic participants who are willing to think that the ESP experiment could be successful? Or do all these potential participants essentially belong to the same group or is there a particular variable which is more important? The ideal study should possibly use shorter runs, trial-by-trial feedback and include more spontaneity, but perhaps all of these variables are successful because there is an underlying factor common to them all? How do we define our terms?

From the reviews considered in this chapter, two of the most important factors that need to be understood for model-building purposes are the basic issues of whether psi declines over distance or over time or both. The former issue has been neglected in recent decades and a solid meta-analysis of this database might help us to understand this better. The meta-analysis should then be followed up by a large study to see whether or not the findings can be realized. The question of psi operating over time has received more attention, although, like the question of psi over distance, it is not clear how much psychological factors play a role, given that the finding that the later the target was selected, the less good the results were, applied only to nonselected participants.

Reviews consistently suggested that low neuroticism, extraversion, and good social adjustment may be positively related to forced-choice ESP scoring. Future studies need to build upon these findings, which are generally quite promising; a preliminary meta-analysis of neuroticism as a variable may be helpful. Additionally, a reexamination of the sheep-goat literature might reveal how often participants were experienced or new to parapsychological experimentation, whether experienced participants had previously gained positive results, and whether the overall scoring for sheep was positive or at chance. This is all important information.

Despite the apparent negativity expressed in this review, there is room for optimism. The effect sizes obtained have been remarkably consistent, which, if not due to experimental flaws from the older literature, might indicate that the effect size obtained is genuine. The very fact that reviewers have claimed that it is difficult to separate out low neuroticism, extraversion, low defensiveness, and good social adaptation and that all these traits seem to be associated with good forced-choice ESP scoring suggests that the relationship between these traits and ESP scoring may indeed be a real one. Similarly, the similarity between the need for spontaneity or novelty, the worse performance on longer runs and with extremely formal proceedings may also indicate that a real finding may be underlying their association with psi-hitting. Unfortunately, their similarity means that overall there is a paucity of variables associated with enhancing psi-scoring in forced-choice experiments. The more easily implementable findings are to use trial-by-trial feedback, to test people individually, to avoid using goats or super-sheep, and possibly to use shorter runs. There is a need for research to interact with mainstream findings and to link up with them. If parapsychology is to walk among the sciences, it has to learn to walk with a direction and to follow what evidence there is. I hope this review will serve to help parapsychology fulfill this aim.

REFERENCES

Alexander, C.H. (2002). Psychic phenomena and the brain: An evolution of research, technology, and understanding. *The Parapsychological Association 45th Annual Convention. Proceedings of Presented Papers* (pp. 9–24).

American Psychiatric Association, Mental Hospital Service (1952). *Diagnostic and statistical manual of mental disorders.* Washington, D.C.: American Psychological Association.

Anderson, M. (1957). Clairvoyance and teacher-pupil attitudes in fifth and sixth grades. *Journal of Parapsychology* 21, 1–12.

Anderson, M., and R.A. White (1956). Teacher-pupil attitudes and clairvoyance test results. *Journal of Parapsychology* 20, 141–157.

_____, _____. (1957). A further investigation of teacher-pupil attitudes and clairvoyance test results. *Journal of Parapsychology* 21, 81–97.

Anon (1938). The ESP symposium at the APA. *Journal of Parapsychology* 2, 247–272.

Beloff, J. (1974). ESP: The search for a physiological index. *Journal of the Society for Psychical Research* 47, 403–420.

Beloff, J., and D. Bate (1970). Research report for the year 1968-1969. *Journal of the Society for Psychical Research* 47, 403–420.

Bhadra, B.H. (1966). The relation of test scores to belief in ESP. *Journal of Parapsychology* 30, 1–17.

Blackmore, S.J. (1980). The extent of selective reporting in ESP ganzfeld studies. *European Journal of Parapsychology* 3, 213–219.

Cattell, R.B. (1965). *The scientific analysis of personality.* Baltimore: Penguin.

Crandall, J.E. (1991). The psi-missing displacement effect: Meta-analyses of favorable and less favorable conditions. *Journal of the American Society for Psychical Research* 85, 237–250.

Dalton, K. (1997). Exploring the links: Creativity and psi in the ganzfeld. *The Parapsychological Association 40th Annual Convention: Proceedings of Presented Papers* (pp. 119–134).

George, L. (1981). A survey of research into the relationships between imagery and psi. *Journal of Parapsychology* 45, 121–146.

Guildford, J. P. (1959). *Personality.* New York: McGraw-Hill.

Haight, J.M., H. Kanthamani, and J.E. Kennedy (1978). Interaction of certain personality variables and feedback in a computerized ESP test. *Journal of Parapsychology* 42, 51–2 [abstract].

Haraldsson, E. (1993). Are religiosity and belief in an afterlife better predictors of

ESP performance than belief in psychic phenomena? *Journal of Parapsychology* 57, 259–273.

Haraldsson, E., J.M. Houtkooper, R. Schneider, and M. Baeckstrom (2001). Perceptual defensiveness and ESP performance: Reconstructed DMT-ratings and psychological correlates in the first German DMT-ESP experiment. *The Parapsychological Association 44th Annual Convention. Proceedings of Presented Papers* (pp. 118–134).

Hess, D. (1982). Resistance, belief and replication. In W.G. Roll, J. Beloff, and R.A. White, eds. *Research in parapsychology 1982* (pp. XX–XX). Metuchen, NJ: Scarecrow Press.

Honorton, C. (1975). Psi and mental imagery: Keeping score on the Betts scale. *Journal of the American Society for Psychical Research* 69, 327–331.

Honorton, C., and D.C. Ferrari (1989). Meta-analysis of forced-choice precognition experiments. *Journal of Parapsychology* 53, 281–308.

Johnson, M., and E. Haraldsson (1984). The Defense Mechanism Test as a predictor of ESP scores: Icelandic Studies IV & V. *Journal of Parapsychology* 48, 185–200.

Kennedy, J.E., and J.L. Taddonio (1976). Experimenter effects in parapsychology. *Journal of Parapsychology* 40, 1–33.

Lawrence, T. (1993). Gathering in the sheep and goats. A meta-analysis of forced-choice sheep-goat ESP studies. *The Parapsychological Association 36th Annual Convention. Proceedings of Presented Papers* (pp. 75–86).

Mangan, G.L. (1955). Evidence of displacement in a precognition test. *Journal of Parapsychology* 19, 35–44.

Mangan, G.L. (1958). *A review of published research on the relationship of some personality variables to ESP scoring level.* New York: Parapsychology Foundation.

Maslow, A. H., E. Hirsh, M. Stein, and I. A. Honigmann (1945). A clinically derived test for measuring psychological security-insecurity. *Journal of General Psychology* 33, 21–41.

Milton, J. (1988). Critical review of the displacement effect (part 1). *Journal of Parapsychology* 52, 29–56.

Milton, J., and R. Wiseman (1999). A meta-analysis of mass-media tests of extrasensory perception. *British Journal of Psychology* 90, 235–240.

Morris, R.L. (1982). Assessing experimental support for true precognition. *Journal of Parapsychology* 46, 321–336.

Osis, K. (1965). ESP over distance: A survey of experiments published in English. *Journal of the American Society for Psychical Research* 59, 22–42.

Osis, K., and D.C. Pienaar (1956). ESP over a distance of seventy-five hundred miles. *Journal of Parapsychology* 20, 229–232.

Palmer, J. (1978). Extrasensory perception: Research findings. In S. Krippner, ed. *Advances in parapsychological research. 2: Extrasensory perception* (pp. XX–XX). Plenum Press: New York.

_____. (1982). ESP research findings: 1976–1978. In S. Krippner, ed. *Advances in parapsychological research 3* (pp. XX–XX). Plenum Press: New York.

Rao, K.R., and I. Puri (1978). Subsensory perception (SSP), extrasensory perception (ESP) and transcendental meditation (TM). *Journal of Indian Psychology* 1, 69–78.

Rao, P. V. K., and K. R. Rao (1982). Two studies of ESP and subliminal perception. *Journal of Parapsychology* 46, 185–208.

Rhine, J. B., J. G. Pratt, C. E. Stuart, B. M. Smith, and J. A. Greenwood (1940/1966). *Extra-sensory perception after sixty years*. Boston: Bruce Humphries.

Richardson, A. (1969). *Mental imagery*. New York: Springer.

Rogo, D.S. (1975). Psi and psychosis: A review of the experimental evidence. *Journal of Parapsychology* 39, 120–128.

Roney-Dougal, S.M. (1986). Subliminal and PSI perception: A review of the literature. *Journal of the Society for Psychical Research* 53, 405–434.

Scargle, J.D. (2000). Publication bias: The "file drawer" problem in scientific inference. *Journal of Scientific Exploration* 14, 91–106.

Schechter, E.I. (1984). Hypnotic induction vs control conditions: Illustrating an approach to the evaluation of replicability in parapsychological data. *Journal of the American Society for Psychical Research* 78, 1–27.

Schlitz, M., and C. Honorton (1992). Ganzfeld psi performance within an artistically gifted population. *Journal of the American Society for Psychical Research* 86, 93–98.

Schmeidler, G.R. (1943). Predicting good and bad scores in a clairvoyance experiment: A preliminary report. *Journal of the American Society for Psychical Research* 37, 103–110.

Schmeidler, G.R. (1945). Separating the sheep from the goats. *Journal of the American Society for Psychical Research* 39, 47–49.

Schmeidler, G.R. (1988). *Parapsychology and psychology. Matches and mismatches*. Jefferson, NC: McFarland.

Stanford, R.G. (1992). The experimental hypnosis–ESP literature: A review from the hypothesis-testing perspective. *Journal of Parapsychology* 56, 39–56.

Stanford, R.G., and A.G. Stein (1994). A meta-analysis of ESP studies contrasting hypnosis and a comparison condition. *Journal of Parapsychology* 58, 235–270.

Steinkamp, F., J. Milton, and R.L. Morris (1988). A meta-analysis of forced-choice experiments comparing clairvoyance and precognition. *Journal of Parapsychology* 62, 193–218.

Stuart, C. E. (1946). An interest inventory relation to ESP scores. *Journal of Parapsychology* 10, 154–161.

Super, D. E. (1942). The Bernreuter Personality Inventory: a review of research. *Psychological Bulletin* 39, 94–125.

Tart, C.T. (1983). Information acquisition rates in forced-choice ESP experiments: Precognition does not work as well as present-time ESP. *Journal of the American Society for Psychical Research* 77, 293–311.

Thalbourne, M.A., and E. Haraldsson (1980). Personality characteristics of sheep and goats. *Personality and Individual Differences* 1, 180–185.

Van Busschbach, J.G. (1953). An investigation of extrasensory perception in school children. *Journal of Parapsychology* 17, 210–214.

Van de Castle, R.L. (1959). A review of ESP tests carried out in the classroom. *International Journal of Parapsychology* 1, 84–102.

Van de Castle, R.L., and R.R. White (1955). A report on a sentence completion form of sheep-goat attitude scale. *Journal of Parapsychology* **19**, 171–179.

Watt, C.A. (1990). Defensiveness and psi: Problems and prospects. *The Parapsychological Association 33rd Annual Convention. Proceedings of Presented Papers* (pp. 361–377).

White, R.A. (1976). The limits of experimenter influence on psi test results. Can any be set? *Journal of the American Society for Psychical Research* **70**, 333–369.

Appendix

Rhine at al.'s (1940/1966) own formula for a file drawer calculation is presented in the footnote on pp.136–137 in *ESP60*. However, my own calculations did not appear to confirm their formula in a robust way. Also, they based their calculations on a model of reducing the *z*-score to $p = .01$ (one-tailed), whereas today $p = .05$ (one-tailed) is more common. Consequently, I have used the following "trial drawer" formula to determine how many additional, unreported chance trials would be necessary to bring an existing extra-chance deviation down to just $p = .05$:

$$\text{Total } N = ((\text{dev}/\sqrt{pq})/1.65)^2$$

$$\text{Trial drawer} = \text{Total } N - N$$

where Total N = the total number of trials necessary for the observed deviation to produce a *z*-score of 1.65 ($p = .05$, one-tailed); Trial drawer = the number of unreported, chance trials that one must add to the observed number of trials to reduce the z-score of the observed deviation to 1.65; dev = observed deviation; N = total number of trials actually conducted; p = probability of a hit; q = probability of a miss.

The term "trial drawer" should be credited to Emil Boller. There is some argument about whether the supposed unpublished trials should be assumed to be at chance — as the calculation above assumes— or whether they should be assumed to have a slightly negative deviation because the studies with positive results have been published and thus the average of the remaining, unpublished reports will tend to have a more negative deviation. Rhine et al argue in *ESP60* that in parapsychology there is equal pressure to hide significant results and that the unpublished reports tend to be more favorable to the ESP hypothesis (see the discussion in *ESP60* pp.74–76). Blackmore (1980) has also found that there is no evidence that the file or trial drawer consists predominantly of unsuccessful studies, at least for the ganzfeld database. Statistically, though, arguments favor the conclusion that the file drawer should be assumed to comprise studies that deviate somewhat negatively from chance (Scargle 2000). Rhine et al themselves concede that they are more likely to know about the unpublished, significant results, although they observe that investigators with non-confirmatory studies tended to hasten more to the press. Readers need to bear this controversy in mind when drawing conclusions from the results presented here.

Section III

THEORETICAL ISSUES

The Future of Psi Research: Recommendations in Retrospect

Stanley Krippner and
*Gerd H. Hövelmann**

In 1986, Drs. Hövelmann and Krippner published 11 recommendations for the future of psi research. These recommendations attracted quite a bit of attention from various quarters. Another team (Millar, Jacobs, and Michels 1988) provided a critique of each of these "11 Commandments," whose critical response is reproduced below the positive content of the recommendations, and followed by a response from Hövelmann and Krippner. The present authors thus weigh their recommendations in the light of the 17 years that have elapsed since their original publication. In the interim they have come up with six more recommendations. The fact that the original recommendations are still germane, and that their additional recommendations follow close behind, indicate their utility and their significance. (Editors)

The Chair for Consciousness Studies of Saybrook Graduate School supported the preparation of this chapter, and the authors respectfully dedicate it to the memory of Professor Marcello Truzzi, whose brilliant reflections on the status of parapsychology are echoed in many of our recommendations.

For as long as human beings have kept records of their experiences, they have described reveries that appeared to transmit thoughts of another person, dreams in which they seemed to become aware of faraway events, rituals in which future happenings supposedly were predicted, and mental procedures that were said to have produced direct action on distant physical objects. These purported occurrences may have been instances of phenomena that psi researchers (or parapsychologists) now call telepathy, clairvoyance, precognition, and psychokinesis. Collectively, they are referred to as "psi"—reported interactions between organisms and their environment (including other organisms) in which information or influence has occurred that appears to violate mainstream science's understanding of time, space, force, and their constraints.

"Psi research" attempts to study these interactions, using the tools and technologies of disciplined inquiry associated with other scientific enterprises. Nevertheless, mainstream science tends to write off psi research as "pseudoscience" because it allegedly masks actual scientific enterprises, but is loaded with untestable assumptions, unfalsifiable concepts, and unrepeatable experiments (e.g., Leahy & Leahy 1983).

Parapsychologists, in fact, constantly carry what most women carry in large purses: much that is useless, a few absolutely essential items, and then, for good measure, a great number of items that fall in between. Parapsychologists' greatest difficulty lies in establishing which is which. Parapsychologists, of course, do not transport those items physically because their trove of possessions is essentially mental. Now and then they add a few items: a new body of data, a new experimental idea, a new theory; now and then they reluctantly clean out the trash; and now and then they pause to sort out all their belongings and reconsider their value, their mutual relations, and their possible future relevance.*

In the 1980s, we presented 11 recommendations for the future of psi research (Hövelmann & Krippner 1986a). The suggestions we made received quite a bit of attention from colleagues in parapsychology and elsewhere, and we got the impression that, in practical parapsychological work and presentation over the ensuing 17 years, they have exerted at least some subterranean influence.

---

*In the 1980s, one of us was asked to predict the future of psi research; as a result, he and a colleague provided three scenarios (Krippner & Hastings 1981). In one of these scenarios, psi had been employed by third-world nations as a cost-effective defense against the manipulations of the superpowers. In another scenario, psi had been employed for benevolent purposes by the superpowers themselves. The editors deleted a third scenario, one in which minimal progress in understanding and utilizing psi had been made by the year 2001; in retrospect, this scenario was by far the most prescient.

Our paper was reprinted in its original English version (Hövelmann & Krippner 1987a) and translated into German (Hövelmann & Krippner 1986b) and Japanese (Hövelmann & Krippner 1993). It was favorably received and commented upon both on the popular fringes of parapsychology (see the long, sympathetic commentary by Fuller 1987, and our reply in Hövelmann & Krippner 1987b) and in more conservative parapsychological circles (Eeman 1986, pp. 202–204, who has a reputation as an inside critic of parapsychology, published a lengthy summary and supportive commentary in Flemish), as well as by card-carrying skeptics such as Kendrick Frazier (1987), the editor of CSICOP's *Skeptical Inquirer.* Dutch skeptic Rob Nanninga (1988, pp. 281–282) also included a complete listing of our recommendations in a book and endorsed them. In addition, summaries were published, for instance, by Irvin Child (1987, p. 204) and included in the second edition of Patrick Grim's *Philosophy of Science and the Occult* (Grim 1990, p. 77).

Our canon of recommendations even seemed to be considered a model for discussions in a different area when Geoffrey Dean used an extensive summary of them as a hand-out (Dean 1987b) "to stimulate discussion" in a "debate on the best directions for future research in astrology" (Dean 1987a) that he was leading during the 1987 annual London Conference on Research in Astrology.

On the other hand, suggestions for future scientific practice, talk and behavior are not likely to remain unchallenged. Thus, McConnell (1987) took issue, in particular, with the first of the 11 suggestions we made (see below; for our rejoinder, see Hövelmann & Krippner 1987c).

Little Sympathy for the Devil

Another team of authors, all of them from the Netherlands, referred to our suggestions as the "11 Commandments," and provided a critique of each from the devil's advocate point of view (Millar, Jacobs, & Michels 1988).

1. **Thou shalt not represent parapsychology as a revolutionary science:** According to Hövelmann and Krippner (1986a, p. 2), the claim is often made that parapsychology is a revolutionary science, that its findings have revolutionary implications for humankind, and that parapsychologists are in the vanguard of a revolution. They discussed more than half a dozen conceivable meanings of the term "revolutionary," and rejected them all as either misleading, inadequate, self-contradictory

or intrinsically meaningless. The term "revolutionary" may imply, for instance, that psi researchers have dismissed scientific methodology; if this implication is incorrect, psi research cannot portend a "revolution" no matter how dramatic its findings may appear to be.

Critique: If a medical researcher were to find a new anticancer drug, this would be considered a part of mainstream science. However, if on injecting that substance, the patient were to become invisible, the term "revolutionary" would not be inappropriate. Psi researchers of the "revolutionary" school hold that there is the possibility that parapsychological data may produce results of this magnitude, and that such data would initiate drastic changes in many of the other sciences (Millar, Jacobs, & Michels 1988, p. 6).

Response: As far as solid, repeatable empirical evidence for psi and its eventual utilization is concerned, most parapsychologists would probably agree that the situation has not dramatically improved during the 17-year period since our paper was published. The basis for revolutionary claims therefore does not seem to have become much firmer than it was back then. So as long as we do not have very much in our hands that is suited to shake the foundations of the mainstream sciences' worldviews, we are well advised to stay back from any revolutionary pretensions. Also, as long as there are no convincing, viable alternatives, we continue to be reasonably comfortable with the prevailing worldview.

That parapsychology produces evidence that compels change of a magnitude deserving to be termed "revolutionary" (in a sense that, in the event, would have to be specified explicitly) still remains to be shown. And, in all frankness, we parapsychologists are the ones who will have to make that case. In addition, parapsychologists will have to demonstrate yet another matter that often goes unrecognized: that the "conventional" sciences in their current shape are not up to the task of dealing with whatever we might be able to confront them. We are not convinced that we are yet in a position to do anything that comes even close to fulfilling one or both of those obligations. Given those circumstances, to merely insist, as Millar, Jacobs, and Michels do, that we envision ourselves as revolutionaries is not by itself revolution. It is rebellion.

As for the medical researcher evoked by our critics, the one who turned his patient into an invisible person instead of curing his potentially fatal disease, a case could be made for calling that a tragic accident (if not something worse)— not a revolution, but an instance of apparent maltreatment.

2. **Thou shalt not put much emphasis on survival research:** Hövelmann and Krippner (1986a, p. 2) suggested that it seems very unlikely that survival-related research can produce empirical knowledge about survival or otherwise contribute to a solution to the survival problem. The results of life-after-death research, on the other hand, can tell us much about the dying process specifically and the human condition in general (also see Hövelmann 1988a), but there are so many alternative explanations of near-death experiences (Hövelmann 1985b), "past-life" reports, mediumship, and related data that survival claims may be unverifiable (also see Cardeña, Lynn, & Krippner 2000).

Critique: Mediumship studies, conducted in the heyday of survival research, yielded information about deceased persons that were many orders of magnitude better than the best of contemporary psi data produced in the laboratory. Survival research is more understandable, and probably more amenable to funding, than other aspects of psi research, hence the current unfashionable status of these investigations makes little sense (Millar, Jacobs, & Michels 1988, p. 6).

Response: Millar, Jacobs, and Michels who, from their other writings, are known to basically agree with our second recommendation are careful not to pretend that the old mediumship studies they refer to have evidential value of a strength that would contribute significantly to a solution to the survival question. They are, of course, well aware of the problems that exist with the evaluation of historical evidence, the documentation of which did not always attain, to say the least, the minimum standards that today would be required.

However, the authors seem to suggest that survival research (as opposed to *survival-related research* in the sense specified above) be continued for mainly opportunistic reasons, that is, because of its arguably greater marketability. We question both the wisdom and the ethics of this policy. "Selling" research on a given question (e.g., the survival hypothesis) while one is convinced that, for the various methodological and conceptual reasons we outlined in our 1986 paper and elsewhere, even moderately promising results that might suggest empirical confirmation or rejection of that hypothesis will not be forthcoming, is very unlikely to serve the field in the long run.

While we believe that *survival-related research* (i.e., the investigation of human experiences and beliefs which appear to be related to the concept of survival) can be well worth our time and efforts and may be of great potential importance to our knowledge about death and dying (Hövelmann 1988a), the centrality of the survival hypothesis to parapsychology has always been a major impediment to the acceptance of the field by our scientific peers. Therefore, Harvey Irwin (2002) advocated a "redefinition of parapsychology and the relegation of the survival hypothesis to minor status." (p. 19). Mostly for the same reasons that we put forward in 1986, Irwin concluded that "it is foolhardy to persevere with this intractable and severe compromise to the standing of parapsychological research as a legitimate scientific endeavor. The survival hypothesis needs to be substantially set aside as a provocative but ultimately unproductive facet of the history of parapsychology" (p. 25). We agree.

3. **Thou shalt not attribute much weight to non-experimental material:**
   According to Hövelmann and Krippner (1986a, pp. 2-3), parapsychologists should not rely too heavily on so-called evidence from spontaneous cases or from data obtained in quasi-experimental settings. The flaws that often accompany these types of investigations tend to be untraceable after the fact, as well as open to overinterpretation and projection. Nevertheless, these reports often stimulate more rigorous types of investigation, and can be used to derive testable predictions.

   Critique: Psi experiments are still only sporadically successful, and cannot be produced on anything like a production-line basis. As a result, spontaneous cases and informal observations should not be ignored; computer analyses of existing collections of spontaneous cases (e.g., Schouten 1979; Persinger 1988) have yielded data arguably as vital as anything emerging from the laboratory (Millar, Jacobs, & Michels 1988, p. 6).
   Response: There is, as far as we can ascertain, no substantial difference between what we suggested in our recommendation and the comments advanced in the critique. As a matter of fact, we fundamentally agree that the areas and types of study highlighted by Millar, Jacobs, and Michels "should not be ignored," and we said as much in our paper. These areas form, and have always formed, important parts of parapsychological practice and they have contributed considerably to the overall case for psi that the field is able to make today.
   Rather, what we tried to point out is the difference in evidential value that exists between insights gained from spontaneous case reports, field studies and case collections on the one hand and data obtained from more rigorously controlled studies and experiments in laboratory settings on the other. There are two long-established factions in parapsychology, the "experientialists" and the "experimentalists." While the latter principally acknowledge the necessity and desirability of less formal studies of presumably spontaneous psi events as a source of stimulation for more strictly

controlled experimental research, the former sometimes appear far less generous. They seem to be content with the spontaneous events of at least uncertain evidential power and prefer, as they might say, experiencing psi in the real-life setting to exorcising it in the lab.

In response, we can hardly do better than to quote an entirely unsuspicious source. Carlos Alvarado (2002), one of the foremost spokespersons of sophisticated spontaneous case studies, reminded his colleagues: "We should be aware that research is done from one's interest and training and that we cannot expect those who conduct other types of research to do research we want to see done. They simply have other priorities and views" (p. 116).

And then he went on to describe our concern, which he apparently shares, in no uncertain terms:

> My impression over the years is that a segment of those concerned with the study of spontaneous phenomena are not interested in explaining or understanding the phenomena. They seem to be happy to maintain the mystery for its own sake. In their view, the phenomena is [sic] something sacred that should not be probed too much [p. 117].

Alvarado added:

> My impression is that some of those interested in survival of death or in conceptualizing psychic phenomena as manifestations that point toward non-physical or spiritual aspects of human beings are generally not interested in showing how cases relate to aspects of the natural world. ... [They] feel it is more important to establish survival, spirituality, or the like because of the implications of these concepts for the nature of human beings. Perhaps those who see the study of spontaneous phenomena in this way do not want the topic associated with mundane physical, biological, and psychological correlates because such correlates undermine the more spiritual views they prefer [p. 119].

4. **Thou shalt not take the name of psi in vain:** Hövelmann and Krippner (1986a, p. 3) argue for a terminological reform in psi research, emphasizing that the current terms (especially "extrasensory perception" or ESP) are negative in form, stating what ESP is not, not what it is. At the very least, parapsychology should discriminate between explanatory and descriptive terms; instead, it appears as if psi researchers are explaining an anomaly when they are merely identifying one. The proposition, "The bend in that spoon must have been caused by a psychokinetic force" is grammatically correct but is actually a nonexplanation.

Critique: Any attempt to impose a neutral, atheoretical terminology is doomed to failure before there are more substantial results based on sound theoretical concepts. In the meantime, an atheoretical terminology is as useful as an alcohol-free Scotch (Millar, Jacobs, & Michels 1988, p. 7).

Response: At least part of the purpose we had in mind when we conceived this particular recommendation has been fulfilled in the meantime: the awareness among parapsychologists of their terminological problems has increased remarkably over the past two decades, and the necessity of a terminological reform has been widely acknowledged by our colleagues. Some even ventured to present their own more or less far-reaching terminological suggestions (e.g., Mabbett 1982; May, Spottiswoode, Utts, & James 1995; May, Utts, & Spottiswoode 1995; Palmer 1986, 1988). Even so, some of these valiant efforts often were marred by the same old problems or new, formerly unrecognized ones (e.g., see Braude 1998; Hövelmann 1988c). So the diagnoses seem clear-cut and generally accepted, but as yet there admittedly are no proper remedies on the horizon.

5. **Thou shalt not doubt the ultimate serviceability of psi:** Some parapsychologists claim that they are dealing with unreplicable, elusive phenomena (Hövelmann & Krippner 1986a, p. 3). However, this claim may be premature (see Bem & Honorton 1994). Further, psi research methodologies may not yet be fully adequate for the task. Psi is a complex event; even so, its underlying processes may eventually be understood, allowing robust, stable, and replicable results to be forthcoming.

Critique: After over one century of unrepeatable experiments, the possibility that unrepeatability is inherent in parapsychology should at least be considered (see Friedman 1984; Hansen 2001).

Response: Richard Broughton (1988), in his 1987 presidential address to the Parapsychological Association, reminded us, "If you want to know how it works, first find out what it's for" (p. 187). Both parts of this prescription--the notions that something is expected to "work" and that it is instrumental in accomplishing certain goals or in fulfilling certain needs that an organism may have — logically presuppose a minimum of systematic functional reliability, robustness and repeatability of the supposed underlying psi ability or process.

As long as there is no positive proof whatsoever that unrepeatability is inherent in parapsychology and that reliable "serviceability" and need-serving characteristics of psi are chimeras, the search for a functional significance of psi remains the best way to go.

6. **Thou shalt listen to and respond to outside criticism:** Parapsychology has nothing to lose and potentially much to gain by listening to and collaborating with its critics (Hövelmann & Krippner 1986a, p. 3). Outside criticism has varied in terms of its scope, subtlety, relevance, fairness, and objectivity. Nevertheless, an active exchange and even a collaboration with the most astute of these critics would eliminate the dichotomy of "proponents" and "critics" that currently exists, permitting an active collaboration of all those who sincerely desire a solution to the problems posed by the anomalies emerging from reported psi occurrences.

Critique: Time is money, and there is only so much of it. Given the choice between carrying out a new experiment and debating some criticism of previous work, it would be more cost-effective to favor the former alternative. Many of the criticisms repeated most often come from writers whose respective knowledge of the relevant literature is sparse, and their education should not be a priority of the field (Millar, Jacobs, & Michels 1988, p. 7).

Response: No doubt, the characterization that Millar, Jacobs, and Michels provide of the majority of self-declared scoffers is correct (see Hansen 1992; Hövelmann 1985a). "Educating" those persons cannot reasonably be considered one of our priorities. Nevertheless, our commentators' critique dissimulates the fact that in the protracted disputes around parapsychology we encounter many more shades of gray than is usually recognized. The reality of the psi debate thus is far more complex than is portrayed in the critique. In fact, as one of us has demonstrated elsewhere (Hövelmann 1988b), sufficiently identifying a parapsychologist or a skeptic, or reliably telling the one from the other, can be much more difficult than propagandists on both sides of the controversies around the legitimacy of parapsychology would have us believe. Hence, the need for active exchange and, ideally, cooperation between all camps continues to exist.

However, practical collaboration appears to have become increasingly difficult in recent years. And there is a specific reason for that. As Honorton once observed, opposition to early parapsychological laboratory research had been virtually silenced by 1940 (Honorton 1975). We may be in a comparable situation today. As can be clearly inferred from, for instance, the pages of the *Skeptical Inquirer*, organized skepticism has largely shifted away its attention from mainstream parapsychology to concentrate on easier (and sometimes virtually nonexisting) targets. And the few controversies around parapsychological research proper that still flare up from time to time tend to be much less unfair and acrimonious than the ones we experienced during the early 1980s.

Any feeling of relative security may be treacherous, though. As Honorton has also shown, new generations of self-styled skeptics (perhaps more properly termed "scoffers") are likely to turn up once in a while, and past experience provides little hope that the majority of them will have learned the lessons from their and our joint past. We therefore continue to believe that it will be in our own best interest to keep in close touch with the few knowledgeable and relatively moderate skeptics who are currently active.

7. **Thou shalt not associate with "true believers":** Psi researchers need to commit themselves to critical judgment and intellectual self-discipline; therefore, they should separate themselves from claimants who put forward untestable, unfalsifiable notions permeated with supernaturalism (Hövelmann & Krippner 1986a, p. 3).

Critique: Why should one associate with stated or potential "enemies" while differentiating oneself from stated "friends"? One never knows when a metaphysical group will provide financial assistance or other forms of aid.

Response: We do not see the necessity, nor do we feel any inclination, to discuss scientific or rather, in this particular case, science-political matters in terms of alleged "enemies" (presumably, the skeptical organizations) and "friends" (the "metaphysical groups"). The vague hope that the latter might provide us with the financial assistance that is urgently needed also does not impress us as a proper reason for compromising our scientific integrity and credibility. Being in touch with the "true believers" or the naïve metaphysical groups may be quite useful at times as far as obtaining new research ideas from their theoretical or practical orientations. But associating with their organizations or even adopting their ideologies would be courting disaster, always a price too high to pay.

8. **Thou shalt provide complete data:** When publishing an experiment, complete data will not only make replications easier but will prevent critics from making unjustified accusations (Hövelmann & Krippner 1986a, p. 3). If nothing else, a footnote could be added to the article stating where the complete experimental protocol is available. In addition, a consortium of journals and researchers could set up a canon of guidelines about how the data that cannot be published in full can be treated and made accessible.

Critique: When publishing an experiment, a rather detailed description should be given of the procedure, analyses, results, etc. In particular, data should not be withheld about portions of the research that did not produce the expected results. But how complete do the published data need to be? A complete listing of hundreds of trials is out of the question. No matter how extensive the write-up, psi researchers inevitably know more about an experiment than what appears in print (Millar, Jacobs, & Michels 1988, p. 7).

Response: Millar, Jacobs, and Michels' comments essentially are a paraphrase rather than a critique of most of what we said in the respective section of our paper. There does not seem to be a real disagreement about the desirability, or even the necessity, of providing experimental documentation that is as detailed and complete as possible. Given the current prevalence and prestige enjoyed by meta-analytical procedures, this need is even more urgent today than it was 17 years ago. Hence, the question is not so much whether complete data should be provided, but how this could be done. This is essentially a matter of reaching agreements on the best ways to preserve and, if necessary, to provide to justifiably interested parties all information about an experiment that is conceivably relevant for the subsequent new evaluation and analysis of that experiment. Here leaders of scientific organizations and journal editors probably are in the proper position to join forces for the development of suggestions for practicable solutions.

9. **Go forth and replicate:** Parapsychologists should spend more time replicating their own and each other's research (Hövelmann & Krippner 1996a, p. 3). It is true that funds for psi research are extremely limited, thus it comes as no surprise that parapsychologists are eager to break new ground with the little money that they have. However, this does not excuse psi researchers from attempting to repeat important studies or from examining the data for trends, patterns, and promising leads.

Critique: There are more attempted replications in parapsychology than there are in mainstream psychology. Given the limited resources available, it is quite possible that other activities will often have a higher priority (Millar, Jacobs, & Michels 1988, p. 7).

Response: Again, this critique largely repeats in an affirmative way what it pretends to be criticizing, and so we will basically make a nonresponse to a noncritique. Breaking new ground no doubt is important. However, this can only be undertaken with a realistic hope for and expectation of success if our feet rest firmly on past achievements. Actual or conceptual replication of important past and current experiments will broaden the basis (and, as a matter of fact, provide a secure place for retreat) from which groundbreaking endeavors can be launched.

10. **Thou shalt devote thyself to planning and cooperation:** Parapsychologists should devote themselves to more long-range planning and interlaboratory collaboration (Hövelmann & Krippner 1986a, p. 3). The latter would promote more long-range planning rather than the "fits and starts" that has characterized psi research over the decades. Interlaboratory cooperation would be an appropriate response to the limited funds available as well as to the importance of international communication.

Critique: Interlaboratory cooperation may not be as cost-effective as one might suspect, given the differing agendas that may exist at each laboratory. Again, there are probably more important ways to utilize the available funds for psi research (Millar, Jacobs, & Michels 1988, p. 7).

Response: This, of course, is a non sequitur, and Millar, Jacobs, and Michels know that quite well. There cannot possibly be meaningful *general* (as opposed to *concrete*) objections to the friendly recommendation that researchers at different laboratories, or even entire institutions, join forces and constructively work together. And, in fact, our critics do not put forward any substantial objection. Experiences over the past one-and-a-half decades have confirmed our position and shown that interlaboratory collaboration indeed is increasing. This apparently has been due, at least in part, to the (at least temporary) availability of new funding sources, mainly originating in Germany and Portugal.

11. **Thou shalt study psi-like effects that are not psi:** Parapsychologists should devote themselves to the whole range of allegedly paranormal phenomena, regardless of which type of explanation turns out to be most useful (Hövelmann & Krippner 1986a, pp. 3–4). When the early societies for psychical research were first activated, hypnosis, multiple personalities, and near-death experiences formed proper parts of the research agenda. This legacy has been nearly forgotten, even though it contributed to the understanding of human consciousness and was coopted by mainstream psychology, which proposed plausible explanations for them. If this trend continues, psi researchers will become "yet more isolated rather than sharing their expertise and experience with others" (Blackmore 1982, p. 142). It would be in psi research's best interests to attempt an understanding of the entire

range of anomalies in consciousness regardless of what type of explanation turns out to be most useful. If parapsychology adopts this approach, it will be more than likely to make a genuine contribution to scientific knowledge, even if this approach eventually leads parapsychology back into mainstream science.

Critique: Most parapsychologists have focused their efforts on what they suspect to be "real psi" rather than anything else. Why should they be encouraged to investigate phenomena that are likely to be understood in a way that precludes psi? In addition, psi researchers have backgrounds in diverse disciplines and may not be qualified to investigate the psychological phenomena that constitute quasi-psi effects (Millar, Jacobs, & Michels 1988, p. 7).

Response: This indeed continues to be a very serious question that still seems to be divisive within the parapsychological community. Should we follow our phenomena and experimental results and study the entire range of anomalies in consciousness wherever that may lead us? Even if that may force us to adopt an increasing range of nonpsi approaches and eventually bring us back into mainstream science? Or should we rather insist on being the ones who investigate "real psi" and nothing else — at the risk of eventually finding ourselves left with no subject matter at all?

The position we take on this issue has been quite clear from our 1986 paper and from the above summary, and has not changed in the interim. Investigating mysteries for the sake of mysteries is not basically a scientific attitude. If we really are interested in scientific answers to the questions that have plagued most of us most of the time we will have to follow wherever our well-considered scientific methods will lead us.

The alternative is quite obvious: parapsychology might turn into an ever-shrinking field with ever-shrinking competence and relevance, and it eventually might lose its subject matter altogether once the other scientific disciplines have taken over and provided the nonpsi (or maybe even the sort-of-psi) explanations we have been searching for all along. The field, then, would be likely to disintegrate and disappear like the grin on the Cheshire Cat and to end up as a meager footnote in the future sourcebooks on the history of science — or, even worse, as one of the curious exhibits in a future Museum of Modern Oddities, in one of those intellectually disturbing collections of marvels and monstrosities, of the bizarre and the uncanny, that have been so impressively described by historians of science and culture such as Badou (2000), Bondeson (1999a, 1999b), Daston and Park (1998), Jay (1999), Michell and Rickard (2000), Purcell (1997), and Weschler (1998). We still have the freedom to decide.

Frankly, the arguments that Millar, Jacobs, and Michels volunteer in defense of the psi-and-nothing-but-psi approach rather remind us of what the late writer Philip K. Dick (of *UBIK* and *Blade Runner* fame) once remarked about science fiction authors:

> Science fiction writers, I am sorry to say, really do not know anything. We can't talk about science, because our knowledge of it is limited and unofficial, and usually our fiction is dreadful. A few years ago, no college or university would have considered inviting one of us to speak. We were mercifully confined to lurid pulp magazines, impressing no one. ... We longed to be accepted. We yearned to be noticed. Then, suddenly, the academic world noticed us, we were invited to give speeches and appear on panels—and immediately we made idiots of ourselves. The problem is simply this: What does a science fiction writer know about? On what topic is he an authority? [Dick 1995, pp. 259–260].

Surely, much of this will have a familiar ring to parapsychologists.

The "Tame Psi Lab" and the "9 to 5 Parapsychologist"

The extensive critique by Millar, Jacobs, and Michels (1988) seems to require a few additional, more general remarks that put their comments into proper perspective. Why this is relevant to the present discussion will become apparent as we proceed.

The critical authors have decided to read our recommendations, which we admit were not always modest ones, as "11 Commandments" and, consequently, they have couched their comments, sometimes with a self-confessed parodistic undertone, in quasi-Biblical language. This cannot dissimulate, however, that they really are in basic agreement with the gist of at least some of our suggestions. Thus, the comments they make, for instance, on our recommendations #3, #5, and #6 as well as #8 through #10 hardly contain much that comes close to being a critical commentary. They even state that "in our heart of hearts we are already establishment scientists. This is surely the underlying reason that we can so unreservedly embrace Hövelmann and Krippner's recommendations" (Millar, Jacobs, & Michels 1988, p. 8).

Yet, even though they actually agreed with much of what we wrote, they did not wish to say so in so many words. And there is a reason for that. There was a hidden (but still easily recognizable and transparent, for those who know the background) agenda to their commentary. In fact, their paper basically forms Brian Millar's final reckoning with establishment parapsychology in general and with his former employer, the Parapsychology Laboratory at the University of Utrecht in the Netherlands, in particular. While Sjef Jacobs and Hans Michels undoubtedly had their input and eventually agreed to the final version of the article, the essence of the detailed comments and of the general discussion was recognizably written by Brian Millar.

And he did so with a clear intent that becomes apparent in section 3.3, which forms the final third of the article. There, under the heading "Warning—'The Tame Psi Lab' and the '9 to 5 Parapsychologist,'" Millar reveals his disenchantment with parapsychology and particularly with the Utrecht Laboratory and its personnel by using a mix of irony, caricature, sarcasm, and roughly disguised slander to describe a supposedly fictive scenario that is meant to both illustrate the dreadful consequences of following the Hövelmann and Krippner recommendations for progress in parapsychology and, especially, to portray the experiences he claims to have made during the four years he spent at the Utrecht lab.

For those who would like to go back to the original article to (re)read Millar's description, the following explanation of names (a mixture of mostly Dutch words with real names) of the "9 to 5 parapsychologists in the Tame Psi Lab" may be useful: We there encounter *Imnix Proph* (read: "I am not a professor"—that is, Sybo Schouten), *Bink Boemelkop* (read: "Genius gone to seed"—that is, Henk Boerenkamp), and *Stom Jones* (read: "Speechless Jones"—that is, Professor Martin Johnson). The *Boring Journal of Parapsychology*, of course, is supposed to be the *European Journal of Parapsychology*, and *Krall Zipper*, *Stom Jones*'s favorite philosopher, is easily identified as Karl Popper.

Even though we know many of the historical, internal details and personal circumstances, we have no intention here to comment on the contents of these fairy tales from Utrecht (as far as it seemed necessary, *Imnix Proph* himself has done that already with a masterful counterparody to Millar's caricature, see Schouten 1988). What we would like to point out, however, is that Millar's tale, whatever one may think of it in terms of fairness and professional ethics, does illustrate the kind of disenchanting consequences the lack of funds and permanent employment opportunities may have for an aspiring young researcher who is trying to devote himself permanently and full-time to the science of parapsychology.

By hindsight, this also makes more easily understandable both the many references to the lack of funding that we find in the critical commentaries as well as in several other places in the paper by Millar, Jacobs,

and Michels (1988) and their apparent and repeatedly stated willingness
to put up with intellectual compromise in favor of being funded for doing
parapsychological research. The situation for young (or even older)
researchers, we are sorry to say, has not significantly improved in early
twenty-first-century parapsychology.

Some More Suggestions for Parapsychology's Future

As we stated in the introduction to our 1986 paper, "our canon of recommendations makes no pretension to completeness" (Hövelmann &
Krippner 1986a, p. 2). Therefore, we may be permitted, after nearly two
decades, to add a few more recommendations for the consideration of psi
researchers. We will start with one that we have borrowed from our colleague Robert Morris, who suggested it in a recent attempt to present a
conceptual basis for experimental strategies in the investigation of mind-
matter interaction (MMI) effects. Therefore, it will be quoted in Morris'
own words:

12. **We Need Demonstration Plus Understanding:** "The creative energy
    of researchers has largely gone into identifying the basic research
    strategies needed to rule out various alternative interpretations that
    have been offered by critics for the MMI evidence; or, for many,
    attempting to demonstrate the reality of MMI by statistical analyses
    which can be seriously questioned when used in that context. Statis-
    tical evidence in itself is never sufficient as a contribution to the cor-
    pus of scientific knowledge; it must be linked to a testable model or
    even theory of some sort. Most research to date has involved relatively
    gross or *ad hoc* measurement and unsystematic analysis techniques,
    not designed to extract the maximum information available to char-
    acterize degree of absolute or differential resemblance. This situation
    is starting to change, but only to the extent that we move on to the
    stage of understanding and not just demonstrating. Then we will be
    clearly beyond the stage of appearing to be studying a set of effects hav-
    ing only negative definitions" (Morris 1999, p. 575).

One of us (Krippner 2001) has recently made four additional recommendations for the future of psi research, embedded in a discussion of the
prospects for psi in the postmodern age.

13. **We Need Friends and Allies:** "Parapsychology could more rapidly
    attain salience if it attempted to forge alliances with some of the move-

ments that share its skepticism regarding the reigning meta-narrative of Western science as it is currently constructed. For example, many physicists do not see psi phenomena as inconsistent with quantum theory (e.g., Bohm 1980). Holonomic theory suggests that psi phenomena simply reflect the presence (to some extent) of all information at all levels of reality (e.g., Pribram 1986). General systems theory and chaos theory could easily subsume psi at one or more levels of a living system (e.g., Hardy 1998; Krippner, Ruttenber, Engelman, and Granger 1985). In biological synergy (e.g., Bleibtreu 1969) and human ecology (e.g., Bateson 1979), psi may play an important role in mediating mind-body and organism-environment interactions. Moving into closer collaboration with these potential friends and allies would increase the power base necessary for psi research to be more influential and to become a formidable contender in the scientific scene" (Krippner 2001, p. 15).

14. **Utilize Parapsychology's Uniqueness:** "The role available to psi research is unique (Darby 1999). Parapsychology has developed methods and techniques of investigating anomalous events that, by and large, are more sophisticated than those to be found in any comparable field. These approaches were derived from modern science, but if combined with the contributions of postmodern critiques, they could yield disciplined, rigorous means of research eminently suitable for the tasks ahead. Purported psi phenomena are not the only anomaly that needs to be taken seriously by scientific investigators in the twenty-first century. Even so, parapsychologists could lend their expertise to researchers of near-death experiences, out-of-body experiences, alien-abduction experiences, and a host of other reports that have been too long ignored" (Krippner 2001, pp. 15–16).

15. **Be Open to New Models:** "From a postmodern perspective, the conceptions and possible applications of psi might take on forms radically different from those that characterize it at the present time. This is not surprising because the models of psi are the results of the modern worldview. Psi in the postmodern age might be simpler, more elegant, and more parsimonious than can be imagined today. The current dichotomies between 'brain' and 'mind,' between 'body' and 'psyche,' and between 'matter' and 'spirit' may be resolved in favor of a systems-oriented interactionist model of consciousness. What today is considered 'extrasensory' may tomorrow be conceptualized as 'supersensory'; current conceptions of 'psychokinesis' may be subsumed by

discoveries of an organism's 'biological fields' and their distant influences (e.g., Laszlo 1996)" (Krippner 2001, p. 16).

16. **Take a Multiple Approach:** "Postmodern psi research can present a multiple approach. On the one hand, laboratory work and controlled observations should continue, but with the recognition that this task reflects a complex interlocking of research participant, researcher, time, and place — any one of which can skew the results in a way that may accentuate 'local truths' rather than 'universal truths.' At the same time, the investigation of 'texts' of people's exceptional experiences can adhere to William James's (1902/1985) call for 'methodological pluralism,' using heuristic, hermeneutic, and phenomenological methods that may yield insights into psi phenomena that are more profound than anything captured in the laboratory" (Krippner 2001, p. 16).

17. **Don't Be Afraid:** Parapsychology as a scientific endeavor still has not had the success and has not achieved the scientific recognition that it has been hoping for. On the other hand, we can claim with some self-confidence that our findings are stronger, our methodologies are better (sometimes even exemplary) and our intellectual rigor is greater than even moderate pessimists would have predicted. While we cannot claim to have established "psi" (in the original meaning of the word) as a scientific fact, we have sufficiently demonstrated that we are dealing with genuine anomalies of communication and interaction that deserve wider scientific attention. The scientific community, perhaps understandably, is still taking its time to realize that we are on the track of something that may be of importance to various disciplines. This growing awareness of the role we might potentially play in the long run is something to build on. There is no reason for being unduly enthusiastic about the future of our field. But there likewise is no reason for being afraid so that we do not miss the opportunities that may come from our slowly but visibly growing recognition.

Conclusion

Earlier, we metaphorically suggested that parapsychologists carry both essential and nonessential items in large purses, noting that parapsychologists' greatest difficulty lies in establishing which is which. We then made several recommendations to help psi researchers clean out the useless debris and prioritize what remains.

Parapsychologists continue to lead a precarious existence. Funding is unpredictable, and the reception of mainstream science to even the most robust results of psi research is mixed, ranging from dismissal to debunking to genuine curiosity. The facts that our original recommendations are still germane, and that our additional recommendations follow close behind, indicate their utility and their significance. We have not proposed new models, new paradigms, or new qualitative nor quantitative projects. We simply have called for a streamlining of our field that may utilize the available funds and personnel to the maximum advantage. We hope that these recommendations will be seen as cost-effective and, more important, valuable in obtaining a more complete picture of humanity and the world it inhabits.

REFERENCES

Alvarado, C.S. (2002): Guest editorial: Thoughts on the study of spontaneous cases. *Journal of Parapsychology* 66, 115–125.

Badou, G. (2000). *L'énigma de la vénus hottentote*. Paris: Jean-Claude Lattès.

Bateson, G. (1979). *Mind and nature: A necessary unity*. New York: Dutton.

Bem, D.J., and C. Honorton (1994). Does psi exist? Replicable evidence for an anomalous process of information transfer. *Psychological Bulletin* 115, 4–18.

Blackmore, S.J. (1982). Parapsychology — with or without the OBE? *Parapsychology Review* 13, 1–7.

Bleibtreu, J.N. (1969). *The parable of the beast*. New York: Collier.

Bohm, D. (1980). *Wholeness and the implicate order*. London: Routledge and Kegan Paul.

Bondeson, J. (1999a). *A cabinet of medical curiosities: A compendium of the odd, the bizarre, and the unexpected*. New York: W.W. Norton.

_____. (1999b). *The Feejee Mermaid and other essays in natural and unnatural history*. Ithaca, NY: Cornell University Press.

Braude, S.E. (1998). Guest column. Terminological reform in parapsychology: A giant step backwards. *Journal of Scientific Exploration* 12, 141–150.

Broughton, R.S. (1988). If you want to know how it works, first find out what it's for. In D.H. Weiner and R.L. Morris, eds., *Research in parapsychology 1987* (pp. 187–202). Metuchen, NJ: Scarecrow Press.

Cardeña, E., S.J. Lynn, and S. Krippner, eds. (2000). *Varieties of anomalous experience*. Washington, DC: American Psychological Association Press.

Child, I.L. (1987). Criticism in experimental parapsychology, 1975–1985. In S. Krippner, ed., *Advances in parapsychological research, Vol. 5* (pp. 190–224). Jefferson, NC: McFarland.

Darby, R. (1999, October). Bringing psychical research into the mainstream. *Paranormal Review*, 3–7.

Daston, L., and K. Park (1998). *Wonders and the order of nature, 1150–1750*. New York: Zone Books/MIT Press.

Dean, G. (1987a). Personal communication to S. Krippner, 7 September 1987.

_____. (1987b, November). *Suggestions for improving psi research*. Unpublished manuscript.

Dick, P.K. (1995). How to build a universe that doesn't fall apart two days later. In L. Sutin, ed., *The shifting realities of Philip K. Dick: Selected literary and philosophical writings* (pp. 259–280). New York: Vintage Books.

Eeman, W. (1986). Abstracts. *Psi-Forum: Orgaan van de Werkgroep Parapsychologie* 3, 195–205.

Frazier, K. (1987). Articles of note. *Skeptical Inquirer* 11, 299–302.

Friedman, J. (1984). Love and parapsychology. *Journal of the Society for Psychical Research* 52, 253–260.

Fuller, C. (1987): I see by the papers. *Fate* 40, 7–8, 10, 12, 14, 16.

Grim, P., ed. (1990). *Philosophy of science and the occult* (2nd, revised). Albany, NY: State University of New York Press.

Hansen, G.P. (1992). CSICOP and the skeptics—An overview. *Journal of the American Society for Psychical Research* 86, 19–63.

_____. (2001). *The trickster and the paranormal*. New York: Xlibris.

Hardy, C. (1998). *Networks of meaning: A bridge between mind and matter*. Westport, CT: Praeger.

Hövelmann, G.H. [with M. Truzzi and P.H. Hoebens] (1985a). Skeptical literature on parapsychology: An annotated bibliography. In P. Kurtz, ed., *A skeptic's handbook of parapsychology* (pp. 449–490). Buffalo, NY: Prometheus.

Hövelmann, G.H. (1985b). Evidence for survival from near-death experiences? A critical appraisal. In P. Kurtz, ed., *A skeptic's handbook of parapsychology* (pp. 645–684). Buffalo, NY: Prometheus.

_____. (1988a). On the survival question: A clarification. *Journal of the American Society for Psychical Research* 82, 186–188.

_____. (1988b). Parapsychologists and skeptics—problems of identification. *SRU Bulletin* 13, 125–132.

_____. (1988c, October). "Psi-conducive states": Problems of definition. Paper presented at the 1st Euro–PA Conference, Vught, The Netherlands.

Hövelmann, G.H., and S. Krippner (1986a). Charting the future of parapsychology. *Parapsychology Review* 17, 1–5.

_____, _____. (1986b). Thesen zur Zukunft der Parapsychologie. *Zeitschrift für Parapsychologie und Grenzgebiete der Psychologie* 28, 207–218.

_____, _____. (1987a). Charting the future of parapsychology. *SRU Bulletin* 12, 5–13.

_____, _____. (1987b). Position statement. *Fate* 40, 111–112.

_____, _____. (1987c). Correspondence: Gerd Hövelmann and Dr. Krippner reply [to R.A. McConnell]. *Parapsychology Review* 18, 12–13.

_____, _____. (1993). Charting the future of parapsychology [in Japanese]. In T. Kasahara, ed., *Chojougenshou no toraenikusa [The elusiveness problem of psi]* (pp. 59–69). Tokyo: Shunju-Sha Publishing.

Honorton, C. (1975). Error Some Place! *Journal of Communication* 25, 103–116.

Irwin, H. (2002). Is scientific investigation of postmortem survival an anachronism? The demise of the survival hypothesis. *Australian Journal of Parapsychology* 2, 19–27.

James, W. (1985). *The varieties of religious experience: A study in human nature.* New York, NY: Penguin Books. (Original published in 1902.)

Jay, R. (1999). *Learned pigs and fireproof women* (2nd ed). New York: Farrar, Straus and Giroux.

Krippner, S. (2001). Psi and postmodernity in the twenty-first century. *International Journal of Parapsychology* 12, 1–28.

Krippner, S., and A. Hastings (1981). Parapsychology. In A. Villoldo & K. Dychtwald, eds., *Millennium: Glimpses into the 21st century* (pp. 105–119). Los Angeles: J.P. Tarcher.

Krippner, S., A.J. Ruttenber, S.R. Engelman, and D. Granger (1985): Toward the application of general systems theory in humanistic psychology. *Systems Research* 2, 105–115.

Laszlo, E. (1996). *The whispering pond.* London: Element Books.

Leahy, T.H., and G.E. Leahy (1983). *Psychology's occult doubles: Psychology and the problem of pseudoscience.* Chicago: Nelson-Hall.

Mabbett, I.W. (1982). Defining the paranormal. *Journal of Parapsychology* 46, 337–354.

May, E.C., S.J.P. Spottiswoode, J.M. Utts, and C.L. James (1995). Applications of decision augmentation theory. *Journal of Parapsychology* 59, 221–250.

May, E.C., J.M. Utts, and S.J.P. Spottiswoode (1995). Decision augmentation theory: Toward a model of anomalous mental phenomena. *Journal of Parapsychology* 59, 195–220.

McConnell, R.A. (1987). Correspondence: Dr. McConnell objects. *Parapsychology Review* 18, 12.

Michell, J., and R. Rickard (2000): *Unexplained phenomena: Mysteries and curiosities of science, folklore and superstition.* London: Rough Guides.

Millar, B., J.C. Jacobs, and J.A.M. Michels (1988). Hövelmann and Krippner's eleven commandments: The devil's advocate speaks out. *Parapsychology Review* 19, 6–9.

Morris, R.L. (1999): Experimental systems in mind-matter research. *Journal of Scientific Exploration* 13, 561–577.

Nanninga, R. (1988): *Parariteiten. Een kritische blik op het paranormale [Pararities: A skeptical look at the paranormal].* Utrecht: Uitgeverij Het Spectrum B.V.

Palmer, J. (1986). Terminological poverty in parapsychology: Two examples. In D.H. Weiner and D. Radin, eds., *Research in parapsychology 1985* (pp. 138–141). Metuchen, NJ and London: Scarecrow Press.

Palmer, J. (1988). Conceptualizing the psi controversy. *Parapsychology Review* 19, 1–5.

Persinger, M.A.(1988). Increased geomagnetic activity and the occurrence of bereavement hallucinations: Evidence for melatonin-mediated microseizuring in the temporal lobe? *Neuroscience Letters* 88, 271–274.

Pribram, K.H. (1986). Behaviorism, phenomenology and holism in psychology: A scientific analysis. *Journal of Social and Biological Structure* 2, 65–72.

Purcell, R.W. (1997). *Special cases: Natural anomalies and historical monsters.* San Francisco: Chronicle Books.

Schouten, S.A. (1979). Analysis of spontaneous cases as reported in "Phantasms of the Living." *European Journal of Parapsychology* 2, 408–433.

_____. (1988). *From Imnix Proph.* Unpublished manuscript, privately distributed under the name of "Imnix Proph."

Weschler, L. (1998). *Mr. Wilson's cabinet of wonder.* New York: Pantheon.

8

The Theory of Psychopraxia: A Paradigm for the Future?

Michael A. Thalbourne

The theory of psychopraxia has been most fully expounded in Thalbourne (2004). Nevertheless there remain various issues arising from that discussion. It is the purpose of this chapter to address some of these issues and in so doing clarify the theory of psychopraxia. These issues include the nature of the self, the so-called pro attitude, and the necessary conditions that must be present to allow a psi effect to occur. (Editors)

> *It is doubtful, of course, whether this god [Apollo] merely predicts the future or whether he directs it by his oracular declarations.*
> Lucan, *Pharsalia*, v. 91–93, c. A.D. 65

When Adrian Parker was confronted by the word "psychopraxia" before he had even read about the theory he commented that the vocabulary of parapsychology was already "overburdened" (personal communication, October 10, 2000). I must disagree. Parapsychologists have never shrunk from adopting new terms to describe new techniques and new phenomena. Thus we have "autoganzfeld" and "intuitive data sorting," or Parker's (1977) own neologisms, "psi-conducive" and "psi-inhibitory."

But, certainly, the onus is on the neologist to justify the introduction of a new term. I believe that sufficient justification has been given for "psychopraxia," at length (Thalbourne, 2004, which I shall refer to simply as "the monograph"), more briefly (Storm and Thalbourne 2000; Thalbourne 2000; Thalbourne 2001), and more concisely again (Thalbourne 1982). Nevertheless, in what follows I shall give a few introductory remarks. The main purpose of this chapter is to discuss some relevant issues that were not addressed in depth in the monograph — discussion which is desirable for elucidating ramifications of the theory of psychopraxia. Reference will also be given towards the end to some empirical attempts to test the theory.

The term "psychopraxia" is derived from two Greek words* which together mean something like "the self achieving goals." According to Storm and Thalbourne (2000, p. 280) there are four components which are central to the theory of psychopraxia: (1) the self; (2) the so-called pro attitude, or preference for a particular outcome; (3) the set of necessary conditions which, together with the pro attitude, are sufficient for the outcome; and (4) the outcome, or goal-state itself. Psychopraxia may operate endosomatically (i.e., within the mind-body complex) or exosomatically as "psi," to use the traditional term. In a very real sense this theory can be said to be the spirit of Thouless and Wiesner's (1947) Shin theory, with the self replacing their concept of Shin and psychopraxia replacing the dualistic pair of processes which they named psi-gamma (i.e., ESP) and psi-kappa (i.e., PK). The theory of psychopraxia postulates that there is not a dichotomy but only one, unitary paranormal process by which goals of a variety of sorts — mental or physical — are achieved. More recently, Heath (2000) has come to the same conclusion: She used the phenomenological method to analyse features of both spontaneous and intentional "PK" experiences. One of these features was the experience of overlap between ESP and PK, which is highly consistent with the view espoused by psychopraxia: five of her eight experients described simultaneous ESP and PK; two participants stated that ESP and PK are both active, energetic processes; five participants said that the same altered state of consciousness facilitated both ESP and PK; two participants said that the physical sensations for ESP and PK are the same or similar; and one participant stated that overuse of one (PK or ESP) may prevent success with the other (p. 64). Of course the samples are very small here, but despite that Heath concludes with the following timely remarks:

*The word "psyche" actually means "life-force" or "soul." "Praxia" comes from "prattein," "to accomplish," "be successful."

While this study cannot determine for certain if PK and ESP are the same process, their overlap in ASC and energetic qualities raised the question that ESP and PK may, in fact, be the same experience, with the apparent differences being more superficial than real. It is possible that their outward differences have blinded us to their similar core essence, and that PK and ESP may be the same process ... [Heath 2000, p. 70].

The Nature of the Self

Few theories in parapsychology refer to the self, preferring to talk of "the individual" or "the organism" (e.g., Stanford 1990, p. 62). However, though the concept of the self is essential to the theory of psychopraxia, the monograph presented relatively scant description of that notion: "the 'I' of personal identity, the witness of mental and physical events, not to be identified with mind but present as a common denominator of all experience" (p. 102). Storm and Thalbourne (2000) gave a similar definition: "the self, which is not defined further than that it is inclusive of the 'I' — the common denominator of all experience and the agent of all action (this description allows for additional agency of the 'unconscious' component of the self)"* (p. 280). The task of definition is not an easy one, as anyone who tries will almost certainly discover for themselves.

Part of the definitional problem seems to arise from the fact that the word "self" is used differently in different circumstances. I refer the reader to Figure 8.1.

Starting at the bottom of the diagram we find personal space, the invasion of which can seem to be an intrusion upon the self. The self thus considered surrounds and protrudes somewhat from the physical body. Speaking of the physical body, we often refer to those bodies as being the self, as when we say "I cut myself this morning while shaving," or when we look at "ourselves" in the bathroom mirror. On the other hand, we seem to be referring to the mind or its aspects as the self when we say "I'm angry at myself," or even "Know thyself!" And we seem to refer to both mind and body when we threaten to "kill ourselves" in suicide ("-cide" = "the slaying" + "sui" = "of the self"). These are common usages of the word "self," but the suspicion may remain that there is a more fundamental sense of selfhood. What is the self in this case?

---

*Cf. Stanford (1990, p. 104): "contemporary cognitive theory is moving strongly toward views of cognitive function that would support meaningful, nonconscious processing of information and the related production of behavioral tendencies."

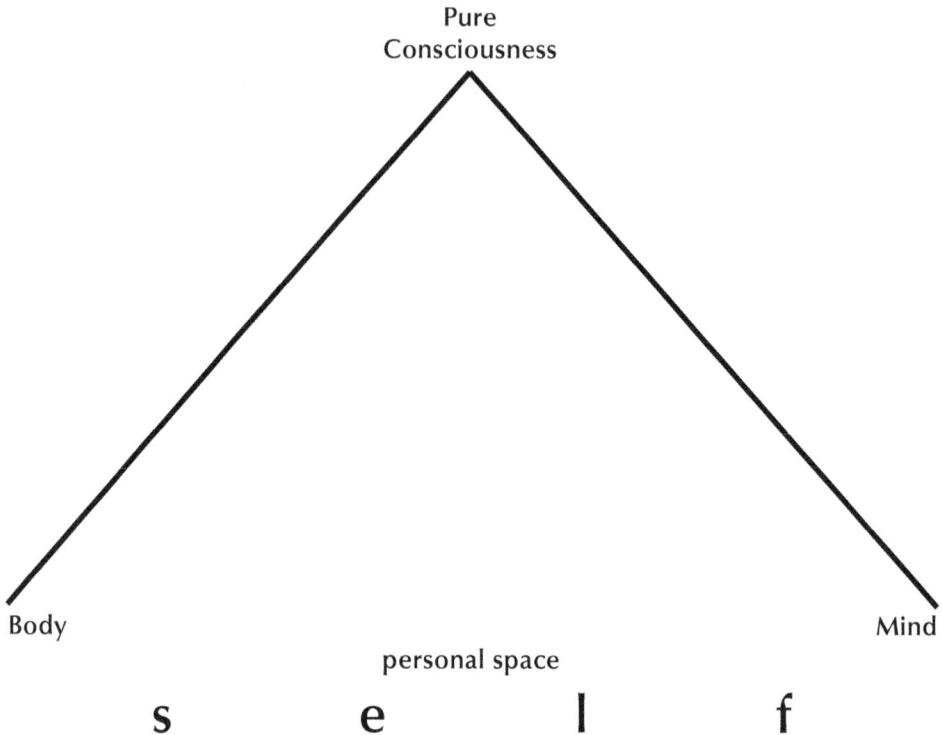

Figure 8.1. The various concepts of self.

The answer — *an* answer — to this question may involve the top part of the diagram — pure consciousness or pure awareness. In order to argue that such a state exists, let me quote four passages where such a state of consciousness is held to occur:

> One of Bjerre's patients, for instance, told of a "... most wonderful sensation, a feeling of concentration of one's self with one's body as if one were isolated within one's self. Everything disappears, only the I-consciousness is left. This concentration is like the most absolute rest one can imagine" [Ellenberger 1970, p. 150].

> A systematic method [= transcendental meditation] has been developed that enables an individual to experience directly the pure state of Being [= pure consciousness]. It is done by consciously entering into the experience of the subtle strata of a thought, eventually arriving at the direct experience of the subtlest state of the thought and then arriving at the very source of thought. Then the conscious mind attains the pure state of Being [Maharishi Mahesh Yogi 1963/1966, p.

21]. ... Experience shows that Being is bliss-consciousness, the source of all thinking. ... It lies beyond relative existence, where the experiencer ... is left awake in full awareness of itself without the experience of any object [p. 28].

In a survey I [Adrian Parker] recently carried out on 63 students, about 22% of them answered *yes* to the question: "Have you ever experienced a state of consciousness in which your consciousness became intense and focused, so much so that it could be described as a state of being conscious of being?" [Parker 2001, p. 237].*

Finally, even these [signals and inputs] are transcended as the meditator disentangles himself [sic] from the world of form altogether. At this point he starts to experience moments of "no-thought" as he regards the pristine consciousness of the Ground itself, devoid of content, uncolored by ego, unmixed with particular thoughts, feelings, or instinct: being as being. This pure consciousness ceaselessly flows from a center of measureless energy that dwells at the core of the self. These moments are rare and fleeting, but are shot through with unparalleled bliss [Nelson 1994, p. 354].

If we may take these quotations at face value, they all seem to be pointing to a self which is pure consciousness. Yet we rarely experience this state, and therefore do not act from it. Most of the time, the I to be found in pure awareness is commingled with the psychophysical organism, and we identify with other aspects of the self lower down in the pyramid shown in Figure 8.1. I hazard a hypothesis that action — normal and paranormal — is more effective the closer the person's self is to pure consciousness. This may be why certain altered states of consciousness, such as those induced by meditation or the ganzfeld, seem to be more productive of exosomatic psychopraxia — paranormal goal-achievement (Honorton 1977).

In a critique, Storm (2001, p. 254) points out that it is unclear how the self should be able to witness itself without this being a mental process, when the self is not the mind. A reply to this is to concede that the self is indeed mental (perhaps the acme of mentality), or a physical state whose physiological correlates can be revealed by EEG techniques. Alternatively, it could be argued that self-witnessing is transmental and transphysical, and that the self is therefore transcendent, but this conclusion would remove the self from the domain of empirical science.

---

*Parker (2001) in fact has a number of useful contributions to the debate about the nature of self.

The Pro Attitude

It would be good to define again the concept of the pro attitude. A person may be said to have a pro attitude towards state S when they would prefer S rather than not-S *if* those two alternatives were to be brought to their attention. Under this heading fall goals, intentions, needs, wishes, and dispositions, be they conscious or unconscious. Thus, even "non-intentional psi" has at base a pro attitude of some sort, albeit non-conscious. It is conjectured in the theory of psychopraxia that psi-missing is the result of some pro attitude towards low results. (If a pro attitude is *not* at the basis of a paranormal action then the theory can be said to be falsified: in that case, *some* paranormal actions may be psychopractic, but others would not be. Research will eventually disclose which of the two situations pertains.)

As an example of a pro attitude, let me consider the following. I once lived in Missouri, the slogan on whose automobile license plates was "The Show-Me State." It is in honor of that slogan that I name the following causal relations—"show me relations."

The evidence that I proffer for these relations is introspective. I claim that anybody can be aware of the same relations if they introspect sufficiently carefully.

In a "show me" relation, I adopt the pro attitude "I wish to see, spread out in front of me, the events in sequence of situation X." That situation X could be a fantasy, or an anxiety (which is a kind of fantasy) or even a memory. The pro attitude is the seed from which the other states of consciousness develop. These other states are usually visual, but can occur in other modes of consciousness. The self adopts the pro attitude, and immediately creative resources are accessed which draw on information from the subliminal consciousness to produce a movie-like sequence in supraliminal consciousness. "Show me" relations can be consciously brought to a halt in many cases by a pro attitude towards stopping, but not necessarily in all cases, such as chronic anxiety. "Show me" relations could also be named "What if...? sequences." In either case, they are usually an example of psychopraxia operating on the endosomatic level.

I wish to consider now the likely scenario where *two* or more pro attitudes may compete for ascendancy. It seems logical to propose that the stronger pro attitude wins out, strength of pro attitude being determined by some appropriate empirical technique. I want to consider the situation of the classic approach-avoidance conflict (see also Stanford 1990, p. 150).

In an approach-avoidance conflict as traditionally conceived there exists on the one hand an impulse *towards* a desired object, and an impulse *away* from that object. If one impulse is strong and the other weak, the stronger wins out: if the approach motive is stronger, then there is movement towards the object; if the avoidance motive is stronger, then there is movement *away* from the object; if the motives are equally strong, action is suspended and frustration ensues.

We can look at the approach-avoidance conflict from the psychopractic point of view. On the one hand we have a pro attitude to *achieve* the goal-state; on the other hand there is a pro attitude towards the *absence* of that achievement. (Classical fear of psi situations may be an example of this circumstance.) Bearing in mind the assumption that the stronger pro attitude results in achievement, if one pro attitude is stronger than the other then its goal will be achieved; if the pro attitudes are about equal in strength, then conflict arises, no achievement is attained, and frustration arises. There can be an up-down oscillation in strengths of the pro attitude, as, for example, by switching attention from one to the other, leading to a to-ing and fro-ing. Perhaps, when the goal to be achieved is exosomatic psychopraxia, and there exists at least one strong pro attitude towards its absence, the existence of this particular pro attitude tends to nullify other psychopractic action, if it is strong as, for example, in the case where it is paid utmost attention. The theory of psychopraxia may also entail the interaction of a number of different pro attitudes, other than those of the participants, such as those of the experimenter, and perhaps even those of colleagues and persons aware of the research (or with unconscious attitudes towards it). Isolation of the efficacious pro attitude is a top priority, but liable to be difficult in practice. Sometimes it may even be necessary simply to state that exosomatic psychopraxia occurred, but that we do not have a clear picture as to the locus of its causation. Further research on the conditions necessary for the paranormal effect should help clarify this impasse.

The Necessary Conditions

The monograph (pp. 94–96) makes clear my point of view, like that of Stanford (1990, pp. 102–104, 113, 157), that paranormal causation is not magic. In magic we have just the wish, and somehow the effect occurs. The origins of the notion of magic may have been in the self's interaction with its own mind-body complex, where a wish or volition is frequently, and often almost instantaneously, fulfilled in reality. So, if in the mind-body complex, why not also in the external world? But this magical view is prohibited by the theory of psychopraxia: it is postulated that even when the self adopts a particular pro attitude, there are additional conditions that must be met in order for the goal-state to be achieved. (A little thought and some introspection will reveal that the same is in fact the case for endosomatic psychopraxia.) The process may *look* like magic, but it is not; the question of whether real magic occurs is a moot one.

I speak of necessary conditions because I am following the theory of cause put forward by John Stuart Mill (see Hospers 1967, ch. 15), to the effect that cause equals sufficient condition, this being the summation of the conditions that are necessary. Hospers, in referring to J. S. Mill, points out that:

> In our daily causal talk, ..., we talk as if one event by itself caused another event, but this is in fact not so: for various practical reasons we isolate one condition and talk as if this were the cause, though in fact there may be many causal conditions all of which would be required before we had a condition that was sufficient. When the causal factors are extremely numerous, as they are in the realm of human behavior, we are more than ever inclined to speak in this way....
>
> Often we call that one factor the "cause" and all the others the "conditions." But Mill concluded that there is no basis for such a distinction: all of the factors are causally relevant to the occurrence of the effect [Hospers 1967, p. 294].

It follows from this discussion that in order to produce exosomatic psychopraxia — psi — we need to assemble so far as possible the conditions necessary to provide the (or *a*) sufficient condition. Perhaps psi is produced to such a paltry degree in most experiments because the necessary conditions are not assembled very often or in many participants, and when they are, like the raising of my arm, we do not know all the relevant necessary conditions. Even in the most successful ganzfeld experiment the majority of participants do not score a direct hit. It perhaps then follows that a greater attempt should be made to assemble putative necessary conditions in our experiments. But what *are* some of these necessary conditions?

Stanford (1990, pp.138–139) may be relevant to our discussion inasmuch as he writes of factors which *limit* the opportunity for so-called psi-mediated instrumental response (PMIR). For example, he mentions behavioral *rigidity* ("the inclination to follow undeviatingly preset plans and to allow little or no deviation"). He next discusses inhibition, which "includes a disinclination to act on impulse and the tendency to seek clear justification for one's actions." After that is mentioned *stereotypy*, which "means the tendency to repeat a particular action or action sequence just as it has been done before." *Response chaining* "involves one act tending automatically to follow another, as in the case of habits that are regularly strung together in time." And finally we have *strong preoccupations*, which "implies a situation that tends to preempt one's attention and effort because of its outstanding interest or its intrinsic quality." (As Stanford remarks, "Each of the above factors puts constraints on behavior and can diminish the spontaneity that is necessary for the occurrence of PMIR" [p. 139]) In the wake of Stanford's comments, I suggest that the *absence* of these limiting factors may be necessary conditions for exosomatic psychopraxia. These are, we can say, *negative* necessary conditions.

Let us turn to some positive conditions, which contribute to the effect by their *presence*. I have chosen as illustration the previously mentioned work by Heath (2000). Fourteen "necessary conditions" were found for all "PK" experiences, with two more that appear in intentional "PK." They are, slightly adapted from Heath: (1) the presence of an altered state of consciousness; (2) a sense of connection to the target or other people that involves a transcendent level of interconnectedness; (3) a feeling of dissociation or detachment from the individual ego identity; (4) suspension of the intellect; (5) the presence of playfulness or peak levels of emotion; (6) a sense of energy, that may have a transcendent quality; (7) the physical state may contribute to, or reflect, PK energy; (8) awareness is focused; (9) a frequent release of effort or attention; (10) an altered sense of time; (11) investment in the outcome; (12) a sense of openness to the experience; (13) positive impact on feelings or worldview from the experience; and 14) a sense of "knowing." With intentional PK there are also: (16) the feeling that the process is guided in an interactive (or reactive) manner; and (17) there is trust in the process.

It is perhaps too much to expect that *all* these constituents be present in a paranormal attempt, but with some ingenuity a number of them could be assembled, perhaps making it more likely that a sufficient condition is set up and exosomatic psychopraxia occurs.

Like Stanford, Heath also mentions conditions whose *absence* appears to be necessary for paranormal performance: (1) bystander hostility; (2) self-frustration; (3) effort (lack of trust in the process); (4) analytical thinking (inability to suspend the intellect); (5) ego (lack of dissociation); (6) inability to focus awareness; (7) investment (cf. above #11); and (8) overuse of ESP.

I insert here a caveat that I may have inadvertently left ambiguous in previous writing on psychopraxia, and that is that there is not necessarily just *one* set of necessary conditions to bring about a paranormal effect. Take as an example endosomatic psychopraxia. Suppose I wish to press the letter P on my keyboard. The self adopts the appropriate pro attitude (e.g., I want to press the letter P), this is translated into efferent neural impulses, and this results, if all goes well, in my pressing the P key. But suppose I want to press the Q key. The pro attitude for Q-pressing is similar to, but at the same time different from, that for P-pressing, and slightly different neural conditions are innervated to get the hoped for response. In both cases there is a pro attitude, but slightly different in each case. In both cases there are other necessary (physiological) conditions, but again slightly different in each case. Also, the conditions for pressing P with my right index finger could be altered so that I use my left finger, so the conditions that are sufficient in one case may be different from those in another. That is, there may be multiple sufficient conditions to achieve the same goal. It is not the case that one and the same set of conditions is necessary for all goals: the ensemble is task-dependent. But still the general psychopractic process is the same. This should also be the situation with exosomatic psychopraxia — conditions necessary in one experiment may be to a greater or lesser extent necessary in another.

As an example of this way of thinking, let us take the ganzfeld procedure and enumerate its components and steps. I refer the reader to Figure 8.2.

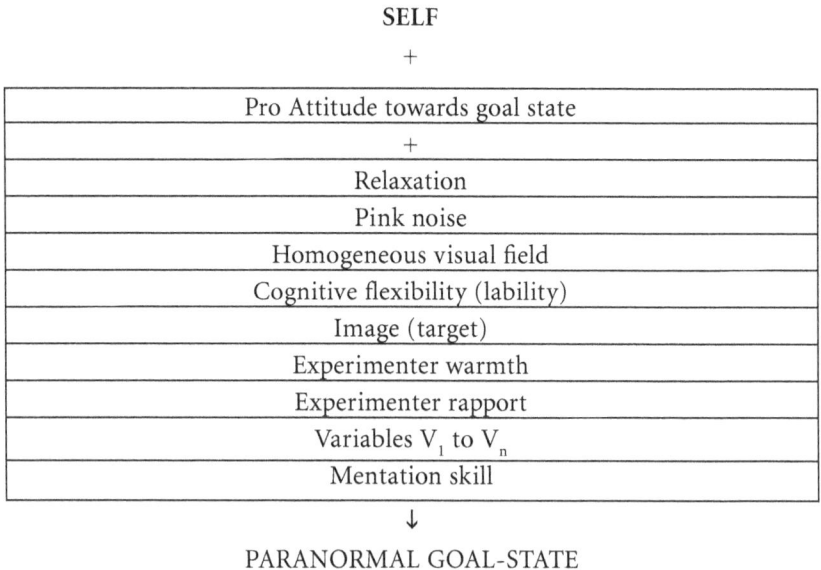

SELF

+

Pro Attitude towards goal state
+
Relaxation
Pink noise
Homogeneous visual field
Cognitive flexibility (lability)
Image (target)
Experimenter warmth
Experimenter rapport
Variables V_1 to V_n
Mentation skill

↓

PARANORMAL GOAL-STATE

Figure 8.2. The necessary conditions involved in producing a paranormal goal-state from the ganzfeld procedure. Note that while some conditions are sequential, others are simultaneous.

These conditions seem by consensus to be necessary for the production of a hit in the ganzfeld. However, notice the box labelled V_1 to V_n, which contains all the necessary conditions that are not yet specified. A major task for ganzfeld experimenters is to verify the necessity of the specified conditions and to seek out *additional* conditions which are necessary.

The final issue with which we shall briefly deal in this section has to do with the question of how to determine that a condition is necessary. A factor which appears to be causal in one study may just as easily fail to replicate in the following study. Why the failure? Surely the condition is "necessary" in an absolute sense, or it is not. I believe that the failure may lie in the fact that not all the necessary conditions were assembled in the failed replication, so that even if a psi-conducive factor was present (like relaxation: see Storm 2001) other factors may not be, and so the ensemble is unsuccessful. Only further research with multiple psi-conducive factors will succeed in getting around this problem. In the meantime, any putative necessary condition should be regarded as tentative until replicated on sufficient occasions. Meta-analysis may prove useful here. Moreover, experiments which entail examination of *multiple* necessary conditions are, with appropriate caveats (such as wariness about the effect of multiple analyses), to be encouraged over those which look merely at one. In fine, it should be emphasized that, as in endosomatic psychopraxia, different ensembles of necessary conditions may lead to different goal-states.

Nomenclature

No matter how appealing a new theory may be, the fact of the matter is that parapsychologists must have appropriate linguistic tools at their disposal in order to talk about their science. If we are persuaded not to talk of "ESP" or "PK," how are we to describe our experiments? Storm and Thalbourne (2000, p. 286) have compared nine of the common paranormal domains: DMILS (direct mental influence on living systems), ganzfeld and autoganzfeld, RNG, dice-throwing, forced-choice, free-response, clairvoyance and future-telling (for ostensible precognition, which may alternatively turn out to be clairvoyant extrapolation). In all these domains we find effects which may be better termed exosomatic psychopraxia.

Instead of "endosomatic psychopraxia," Stokes (1987, p. 170) speaks of "internal psi." But according to Beloff (1985):

Unfortunately, the term *psi* has become so firmly connected with the exosomatic manifestations of Shin that to use it in connection with normal psychology, for the endosomatic manifestations of Shin, now appears as a contradiction in terms. In these circumstances a new term is clearly needed that would encompass both the exosomatic and endosomatic manifestations of Shin [p. 226].

The same objection would apply to the otherwise creative shorthand $\psi\pi$ (psi-pi) suggested by my colleague Lance Storm (personal communication, August 30, 2001).

Thus, if the worst comes to the worst, and the term "psychopraxia" is not widely adopted, then it may survive in the hypothesis that psi operates in a psychopractic manner.

Empirical Studies

The first experiment to be carried out with the theory of psychopraxia in mind was probably by Storm and Thalbourne (1998-1999). They deliberately elicited a paranormal phenomenon that was ambiguous as to whether it was ESP or PK. Storm and Thalbourne made unconventional use of the ancient Chinese art of divination the *I Ching*, which is a book that contains 64 readings accessed in modern times by the throw of three coins six times. This process produces a "hexagram" and its associated unique reading. They created a Hexagram Descriptor Form, containing 64 pairs of adjectives succinctly describing the respective hexagrams. The primary task of the participants (mainly university students) was to select 16 (i.e., 25 percent) of the descriptor-pairs, one of which they thought would turn up as a result of the throw of the coins, this result being called a "hit." Storm [and Thalbourne] (2001c) found that the obtained effect size significantly exceeded chance. They proceeded to carry out a replication study, which yielded an even greater proportion of hits (Storm & Thalbourne 2001a, b). The question arises, as in so many other studies (see Storm & Thalbourne 2000, p. 283, for a representative list): "Is the paranormal effect to be called ESP (in this case precognition of the outcome of the hexagram-decoding procedure) or PK (physical influence on the coins to make the hexagram come up appropriately)?" (This is the import of the quotation at the beginning of this chapter.) It was concluded that a more parsimonious explanation was psychopraxia, where there was a pro attitude toward the preselected hexagrams coming up and this goal being achieved to a greater-than-chance extent. These two experiments were thus aimed at undermining the ESP-PK dichotomy and producing evidence better explained by the concept of exosomatic psychopraxia. Storm and Thalbourne plan a future experiment consisting of participants from the general rather than the university population.

According to Robert Morris (2000):

> A colleague once noted how boring it was to read original research reports that simply looked for evidence of psychic ability but that made no attempt to test any hypothesis derived from theoretical considerations. This observation is important, because far too much research has been done in a theoretical vacuum, aimed solely at obtaining evidence of psychic functioning, to persuade oneself and others that it actually exists [p. 131].

Research by Storm and Thalbourne —carried out as tests of aspects of the theory of psychopraxia —cannot be said to have been conducted in such a vacuum. Their third experiment (Storm & Thalbourne 2001d) was predicated on the hypothesis that when *normal* perception fails, *paranormal* perception might take over as a substitute: a free-response experiment with drawings as targets was administered to 42 vision-impaired participants and a matched group of sighted controls. In this particular instance, though the overall group scored significantly above chance, the sighted participants did *better* than the vision-impaired participants, and thus the psychopraxia-derived hypothesis was not supported. Totally blind participants, however, obtained a larger effect size than the rest of the sample. Storm and Thalbourne noted informally that there seemed to be personality differences between the two experimental groups, and future studies of the vision-impaired should take this observation into account.

In a fourth study (Storm 2001, Chapter 8)—carried out by computer — participants were first administered the 18-item forced-choice Australian Sheep-Goat Scale (Thalbourne 1995). Participants scoring above the median on this scale were classified as believers, and were given 50 trials of a computer-run Zener card test. Participants scoring *below* the median were classified as skeptics: one randomly chosen subgroup of skeptics was told that scores considerably below chance were nothing more than chance, while the other subgroup were ostensibly educated into believing that scores exceedingly below chance were a result of negative ESP (psi-missing). Thus, there were two groups of skeptics: naïve and sophisticated. Some sophisticated skeptics believed in the possibility of psi-missing (these were called converts), while others did not (these were called entrenched). All skeptics were given a further run of 50 trials, and it was predicted that naïve participants would persist in their scoring while "converted" sophisticated skeptics (but not the entrenched) would score significantly close to chance in an attempt to falsify the psi-missing hypothesis. The results were that there was (a) a moderately high sheep-goat effect among the converted skeptics; (b) converted skeptics' scoring did improve, but not significantly, in accordance with their new pro attitude, and (c) entrenched skeptics showed no changes in scoring, which was expected since their pro attitude did not change.

This experiment, novel though it was, was conducted under less-than-optimal conditions: the experimenter usually was not present and therefore could not foster psi-conducive conditions; due to a computer error there were extremely small sample-sizes for the skeptic groups, and a call to the local skeptics association produced no volunteers; moreover, ethical considerations prevented deception from being used with the skeptic subgroups (i.e., telling them after the first 50 trials that they had scored *significantly* below chance regardless of what score they had actually achieved). Future studies should try to rectify these shortcomings.

Storm's (2001, Chapter 7) last Ph.D. experiment was modelled on a gambling scenario. The participant's aim was to locate, paranormally, in five trials, each of five aces of spades, and simultaneously to avoid five aces of clubs. In this way it was hoped to confirm the specificity of the pro attitude. Participants started with five chances to win a prize (on an "instant scratchies" ticket), one of which was removed for every ace of spades not identified. Before taking part in this experiment participants were administered questionnaire scales on belief in good luck, on attitude to gambling, and on a Jungian personality test. Few significant results were found, but moderate scorers on the Gambling Attitude Scale were more likely to produce significant correlations between hitting on spades (and on clubs) and extraverted intuition and introverted intuition.

One criticism of the experiments thus far is that there is no direct measure of the pro attitude — only indirect ones such as sheep-goat measures and the Transliminality Scale. Whether or not it is true to say that psi-hitting results from compliant pro attitudes is an *empirical* question. The best way to test it is to have a direct measure of a compliant pro attitude in the experiment, and see whether scores on this measure correlate positively with the psi scores. Admittedly, there is a serious potential problem of demand characteristics in trying to assess the pro attitude directly (participants may dissemble and thereby invalidate their measurement on the scale) but that is a challenge that must be faced if a good test of the hypothesis is to be forthcoming. It is not a good idea to infer the pro attitude directly from the psi scores. In a practical demonstration of the *I Ching*, Storm (2002) asked his participants "On a scale of 1 to 7, how much do you want to score a hit as a result of your coin-throws? Rating 1 was juxtaposed to "I'm not interested at all," while rating 7 was juxtaposed to "It's very important to me."

It must be said that psychopraxia experiments have produced mixed results. However, it is very early days yet, and it is imperative that other researchers undertake replication of these experiments (such as the one with sophisticated and naïve goats) to begin to build up a database for meta-analysis.

Conclusion

It might be objected that the theory of psychopraxia is merely a statement of the fact that a paranormal effect has a cause, among whose many necessary conditions are just two— the self and its pro attitude — and that most all of the intervening necessary conditions remain to be assembled. There may be some truth in this view. But experiments thus far have been fairly successful — tentative necessary conditions have been found, the concept of the pro attitude is highly useful, and there are some experimental results in the theory's favor. The theory of psychopraxia leaves behind many of the problems faced by investigators in the past century, and is therefore a theory very much oriented towards research in the twenty-first century. I wish parapsychology every success in the process of assembling the sufficient condition(s) for psychopractic effects.

REFERENCES

Beloff, J. (1985). Robert Henry Thouless 1894-1984: An appreciation. *Journal of Parapsychology* **49**, 221–227.
Ellenberger, H. F. (1970), *The discovery of the unconscious. The history and evolution of dynamic psychiatry*. London: Allen Lane, Penguin Press.
Heath, P. R. (2000). The PK zone: A phenomenological study. *Journal of Parapsychology* **64**, 53–71.
Honorton, C. (1977). Psi and internal attention states. In B. B. Wolman, ed., *Handbook of parapsychology* (pp. 435–472). New York: Van Nostrand Reinhold.
Hospers, J. (1967). *An introduction to philosophical analysis*. Englewood Cliffs, NJ: Prentice-Hall.
Maharishi Mahesh Yogi (1963/1966). *The science of being and art of living*. London: International SRM Publications.
Morris, R. L. (2000). Parapsychology in the 21st Century. *Journal of Parapsychology* **64**, 123–137.
Nelson, J. E. (1994). *Healing the split. Integrating spirit into our understanding of the mentally ill*. (Rev. ed.) Albany, NY: State University of New York.
Parker, A. (1977). Parapsychologists' personality and psi in relation to the exper-

imenter effect. In J. D. Morris, W. G. Roll, and R. L. Morris, eds., *Research in parapsychology 1976* (pp. 107–109). Metuchen, NJ & London: Scarecrow Press.

＿＿＿. (2001). What can cognitive psychology and parapsychology tell us about near-death experiences? *Journal of the Society for Psychical Research* 65, 225–240.

Stanford, R. G. (1990). In S. Krippner, ed., An experimentally testable model for spontaneous psi events: A review of related evidence and concepts from parapsychology and other sciences. *Advances in parapsychological research 6* (pp. 54–167). Jefferson, NC: McFarland.

Stokes, D. M. (1987). Theoretical parapsychology. In S. Krippner, ed., *Advances in parapsychological research 5* (pp. 77–189). Jefferson, NC: McFarland.

Storm, L. (2001). *A parapsychological investigation of the theory of psychopraxia: Experimental and theoretical researches into an alternative theory explaining normal and paranormal phenomena.* Partly published Ph.D. thesis, Department of Psychology, Adelaide University, South Australia.

Storm, L., and M. A. Thalbourne (1998-1999). The transliminal connection between paranormal effects and personality in an experiment with the *I Ching*. *European Journal of Parapsychology* 14, 100–124.

＿＿＿. (2000). A paradigm shift away from the ESP/PK dichotomy: The theory of psychopraxia. *Journal of Parapsychology* 64, 181–194.

＿＿＿. (2001a). Studies of the *I Ching*: I. A replication. *Journal of Parapsychology* 65, 105–124.

＿＿＿. (2001b). Studies of the *I Ching*: II. Additional analyses. *Journal of Parapsychology* 65, 291–309.

＿＿＿. (2001c). Research note: Effect size in "The transliminal connection between personality and paranormal effects in an experiment with the *I Ching*" by Storm and Thalbourne (1998-1999). *European Journal of Parapsychology* 16, 107–108.

＿＿＿. (2001d). Paranormal effects using sighted and vision-impaired participants in a quasi-ganzfeld task. *Australian Journal of Parapsychology* 1, 133–170.

Thalbourne, M. A. (1982). *A glossary of terms used in parapsychology.* London: William Heinemann.

＿＿＿. (1995). Further studies of the measurement and correlates of belief in the paranormal. *Journal of the American Society for Psychical Research* 89, 233–247.

＿＿＿. (2000). The theory of psychopraxia. Paper distributed at the Third Bial Foundation Symposium, Porto, Portugal, 6–8th April.

＿＿＿. (2001). A layperson's guide to the theory of psychopraxia. *Australian Journal of Parapsychology* 1, 127–132.

＿＿＿. (2004). *The common thread between ESP and PK.* New York: Parapsychology Foundation.

Thouless, R. H., and B. P. Wiesner (1947). The psi processes in normal and "paranormal" psychology. *Proceedings of the Society for Psychical Research* 48, 177–196.

9

A Critique of the
Theory of Psychopraxia

*Lance Storm**

> Dr. Lance Storm undertakes a two-stage assessment of the
> theory of psychopraxia as discussed by Dr. Michael
> Thalbourne in the previous chapter (see Chapter 8). The
> psychological and philosophical issues related to the theory
> involve a consideration of the definitions of self, pro attitude,
> and necessary conditions. This chapter concludes with a
> consideration of future paths for research and experimental
> investigation that may prove fruitful for the theory of
> psychopraxia, and more generally, for the field of para-
> psychology. (Editors)

*Psychological and Philosophical Considerations
of the Theory of Psychopraxia*

In Chapter 8, Thalbourne described three major components underlying the psi process in his theory of psychopraxia — the self, the pro attitude, and necessary conditions. Readers should refer back to that chapter
for a basic outline of the theory. In the first section of the present chapter, each of the three major components will be put under the spotlight.

*The author wishes to thank the Bial Foundation, Portugal, for its support during the
writing of this chapter.

The second section, will consider psychopraxia's future, but first, the terminology used in the theory of psychopraxia, beginning with the self.

The Self

In the previous chapter, Thalbourne (Chapter 8, pp. 191–193) described the nature of the self. Before dealing with the psychopractic aspects of the self, a distinction must be made between two types of self commonly referred to in the literature, often under very different guises. These distinctions follow Western empirically based models, rather than those drawn from (say) Eastern introspectively derived models that have not been experimentally tested. First, there is the empirical self, also referred to as the ego, or the "I," by the psychoanalytic schools (cf. Freud 1949; Jung 1987). The empirical self is mental (i.e., of the psyche) rather than corporeal. It is characterized by its central relationship with consciousness—that is, it has a pivotal role as sole arbiter of experience. This self, also referred to as ego, has acknowledged links with the body and body consciousness, as indicated in the early stages of psychoanalytic history, by Adler (1928) and Freud (1949), and later by the learning theorists Miller and Dollard (1941).

Experimentally, this self is empirical because it is verifiable, having been tested using all manner of measures, such as attitude scales, IQ tests, personality tests and the like (cf. Reber 1985). The empirical self, therefore, has reached general acceptance, whether taken as a construct or entity, simply because it is empirically verifiable as the sole agent of thought and deed. More recently, the empirical self has encouraged much speculation as to its constructed nature and purpose (cf. Markus & Kitayama 1991; Neisser 1988; Spinelli 1989).

Second is the broader concept of self that is hypothesized to extend beyond the limits of the ego, and is therefore not entirely empirical because it is claimed to have an unconscious component. Like the concept of the ego, this self too originates in the psychoanalytic schools (again, see Freud 1949; Jung 1987). For Freud (1949), the self is a composite of the ego, superego, and the id, therefore coming close to Jung's (1987) self, which is a concept that "designates the whole range of psychic phenomena in man [sic]" and "expresses the unity of the personality as a whole" (para. 789). This self is "potentially empirical" because of the unconscious component, also referred to as the Cognitive Unconscious (cf. Parker 2001, p. 233). As a concept, no direct equivalence can be made with the psychoanalytic self and the corporeal body, and Jung, for example, makes reference only to the relationship of self with body when he refers to the influence of the self at the "organic level" (i.e., on the organs of the body). Note that the concept of, and evidence for, psychosomatic illness extends from this hypothesized relationship.

Conventional psychology (for recent examples of its representatives, see again Markus & Kitayama 1991; Neisser 1988; Spinelli 1989) has always been criticized by "depth" psychologists (cf. Edinger 1996; von Franz 1980) for failing to venture beyond the realms of consciousness into the domain of this other aspect of the self, by assuming that there is only the individual and his choices made in consciousness. This attitude appears to eliminate the need for any further debate about other possible determinants of action and thought. In fact, it is possible that these determinants have sources within the same mental or brain structure as consciousness, but nevertheless remain unconscious to the individual. The outcomes of unconscious processes suggest this other, hidden component of the self (for examples, see Edinger 1996).

As far as the theory of psychopraxia is concerned, Thalbourne (Chapter 8, p. 191) regards the self as the causal agent of psychopractic action, but his statements about the self sometimes appear ambiguous, so that it is not always clear where this action supposedly originates. Thalbourne refers to:

(i)   the self as "I": "the 'I' of personal identity" (Thalbourne, Chapter 8, p. 191). Tentatively, this self could also be the ego, given that "I" in Latin is ego, which might refer to the empirical self, or it may refer to the total personality, or perhaps it may be the less conceptual "person-as-physical-being."

(ii) the self as other than "mind": "the witness of mental and physical events, not to be identified with mind" (Thalbourne, Chapter 8, p. 191). This self appears to be conceptual like the mind, but is not the mind. It is not clear how this self should be able to "witness" itself, that is, *apperceive* (which is a mental event and therefore of the mind), but apparently the distinction derives from introspective experience.

The ambiguity in points (i) and (ii) is not resolved when Thalbourne says that "the self is indeed mental (perhaps the acme of mentality), or a physical state" (Chapter 8, p. 193). He also identifies the self with a heightened state of consciousness distinct from the mind, but infused with it (see Chapter 8, p. 193).

Thus, there is a degree of ambiguity in Thalbourne's definitions of the self. It seems, at one time or another, that all "selves" may be the cause of psychopractic action. However, from the perspective of locating the source of action, the "psychopractic subject" could be either (a) the empirical self as ego, or "I," (b) or the body of the individual (i.e., the biological organism along with its inherent needs, desires, and drives), or even (c) the "potentially empirical" self that is inclusive of the unconscious. Of course, the self may be all three, (a), (b), and (c), and in some sense, they can be seen as collapsing together as an integrated whole for the most part, with the differences existing only in discourse. However, the ambiguity is still there when the experimenter is asked to consider who or what Thalbourne's (2002) preferred term "agent" (p. 70) actually refers to, even though Thalbourne is certain that the agent is the "I" who, in his example, "set[s] off the process" of information acquisition (2004).

Further consideration reveals that it is not adequate to dispense with all the above terms and speak only of "agents," "experimental participants," "individuals," or even "human beings" (we must also recognize the poverty of such nebulous terms as "individual" and "organism"). This ambiguity is not unlike the problem that arises when we ponder whether a test of a person's sporting ability tells the same thing about the processes of the "self" as does a test of that person's intelligence. Clearly, one and the same participant (or agent, if preferred) is being tested in both cases, but the causal factors underlying both organic processes are not the same, thus indicating that intelligence is not causally located in the musculature, just as physical strength is not causally located in the brain. In selecting a student for higher education by his intelligence alone, or selecting a player for a football team by his strength alone, these issues do not matter, but experimentally, when limits to agency must be set, self does not denote a subject or an object of critical investigation. In such cases, the agent of the self as causal factor of both physical and mental processes, no matter how well Thalbourne defines it (Chapter 8, p. 191), does not inform our knowledge of process.

To clarify this point, if psychopractic action has an agent, if a pro attitude can be held, if some entity or other can hold a goal, the experimenter needs to know what he or she is testing from one moment to the next in a given experiment (e.g., mind, or autonomic systems, or semiautonomic systems, or executive functions of the brain, which may or may not equate with ego functioning, and so on). If the specific causal components that underlie agency cannot be identified during an experiment, the experimenter can never claim knowledge or understanding of (say) paranormal process. Thus, the problem is not merely philosophical or discursive, but the self as a concept, as useful as it has been in establishing a dimension to personality heretofore undiscovered and now unbounded, has created a dilemma in experimental research. This is not to criticize the theory of psychopraxia because the problem is broader than that. In parapsychology, knowing that the potential of the participant may be unbounded does not help isolate the cause of paranormal processes, but merely increases our uncertainty about the process. Self as causal factor underlying psychopractic action can only be a working hypothesis until the experimenter can really point to a more sharply defined center of the cause of action.

The Pro Attitude

To restate the definition of the pro attitude: "a person may be said to have a pro attitude towards state S when they would prefer S rather than -S [not S] if those two alternatives were to be brought to their attention" (Chapter 8, p. 194). Thalbourne recognizes the fact that an unconscious pro attitude may exist, which may remain forever unconscious (supposedly -S as far as the person is concerned, were it conscious, but actually S as far as the unconscious self is concerned). This unusual state of affairs may be more common that might at first be assumed. For example, a consciously preferred pro attitude to win at a gambling task may be usurped by an unconscious pro attitude to lose. This situation may be typical of the compulsive gambler who simply cannot prevent himself or herself from indulging in games of chance in which he or she is fated to fail due to an unconscious pro attitude towards making unwise decisions in situations where wiser decisions are possible (e.g., safe betting, knowing when to stop. Cf. Ibanez et al. 2001, who found that "gamblers with comorbid psychiatric disorders had gambling scores and psychological scale scores indicating greater severity of gambling and psychopathology," p. 1,733).

Since some individuals are defined by their failures, it may be more important for them to fail and preserve what little identity they have, than succeed and risk an identity crisis (cf. Ingram 1985, who claims that the "losing behavior of pathological gamblers serves to fulfill a life script as a loser. ... [The] script is a decision ... made early in life to accommodate to parents perceived as threatening and omnipotent. The decision, once made, is carried unwittingly into later life and is reenacted repeatedly," p. 89). Given psi, such failure may be more often than chance would explain (i.e., what is traditionally called psi-missing). Thus, a pro attitude towards failure may be explained by the possibility that reinforcement can take forms other than cash prizes. It must, therefore, be acknowledged that pro attitudes may be intimately enmeshed with concepts involving issues of self-image and self-esteem (or lack thereof), and the maintenance of these concepts.

The pro attitude may be adjusted to meet the criteria of *a priori* prerequisites that are unconscious. An unconscious pro attitude for failure may be stronger than a conscious pro attitude for success. Thus, the "person" may consciously prefer success, but the self may not. Of course, as long as the pro attitude can be unconscious, the issue of measurement with (say) questionnaires poses a problem. While John Palmer (personal communication, January 31, 2002) recognized the problem of demand characteristics that can result from *explicit* measures, he did not comment on the *implicit* nature of the pro attitude. The same problem exists in achievement motivation research in which it has been found through meta-analysis (see Spangler 1992), that the correlation between *explicit* (i.e., self-attributed) need for achievement and *implicit* need for achievement is extremely weak.

To continue this train of thought, Thalbourne (Chapter 8, p. 194) locates the cause of action in the agency of a self-system where conscious and unconscious or "non-intentional" processes can be applied. Thus, he considers the approach-avoidance conflict, where "there exists ... an impulse *towards* a desired object, and an impulse *away* from that object" (Chapter 8, p. 194), as driven by (say) fear of psi. (Note that Kennedy 2001, has listed fear of psi as a prime possible cause of the elusiveness of psi.) This conflict is key in determining the final psychopractic outcome. In addition, there is the possibility that pro attitudes may come from sources other than the participant (e.g., the experimenter, or group of researchers involved in the experiment, or persons aware of the research). Relevant to this claim is Kennedy's (2001) hypothesis that the elusiveness of psi is caused by the "net result" of "all the people who eventually learn about or would have an interest in a psi result" (p. 234). These people could have positive or negative effects on psi.

Since, Thalbourne (2004) makes it clear that conscious and unconscious processes underscore the pro attitude, the self he refers to must be the "potentially empirical" self, defined as "the whole range of psychic phenomena" in the individual, which is taken to be the unified or whole personality (Jung 1987, para. 789). Therefore, as comprehensive as the above definition of the pro attitude is in its current form, it is only accurate insofar as the "person," which incorporates the potentially empirical self, is the causal agent. In fact, the unconscious aspect of the self may be the actual agent, while the person (unconscious of any hidden agenda) may be a mere proxy to the self. This specification of actual agency is only tacit in the current definition of the pro attitude.

From another perspective, there is a commonsense aspect to the term pro attitude that defies criticism. On the basis that the pro attitude is itself the primary necessary condition that defines the causal chain that ends in goal achievement, it is hard to imagine how an organism could act of its own volition in the paradoxical situation of it not being the agent of its own goal achievements (notwithstanding the possibility of experimenter effect!). If it does not decide, devise, implement, or design, its own actions and goals, who or what does?* Given the implication of the concept of the pro attitude in terms of its relevance to causal factors, it is not surprising that the idea of the "pro attitude" has its origins in philosophy. Thalbourne admits borrowing the term "pro attitude" from Davidson (1966), who applies it in a common sense way, as does Thalbourne. Apart from that, Thalbourne (personal communication, November 16, 2001) borrows very little from the arguments put forward by Davidson.

Davidson (1966) coined the term "pro attitude" to describe "some-one [doing] something for a reason" (p. 221). The person thus has a "pro attitude towards actions of a certain kind" (p. 221). Davidson regarded the reason (i.e., he regarded rationalization) as an "ordinary causal explanation" in the sense that "reason rationalizes the action" (p. 221). Thalbourne (2004) states that he uses the term in a different sense to describe "a positive preference for a particular end state of affairs" (p. 65, n4), rather than just an action. Thus, Thalbourne (personal communication, November 16, 2001) sees the person as having some sort of pro attitude towards a goal rather than towards an action that leads to a goal.

Davidson (1966) claims that: "Giving the reason why an agent did something is often a matter of naming the pro attitude" (p. 222). Naming the pro attitude, however, may be harder than Davidson thinks. He goes to great efforts to show how constructions in language can represent pro attitudes, and he points out the ambiguity that may arise, and the absence of rationalization that may be implied, if syntactical representations are poorly expressed. While such efforts are essential in philosophy, since philosophers depend on the precision of words (there not being other instruments and measures), the empirical psychologist may find great redundancy in this effort. For example, child psychologists will be well aware of the ongoing stream of nonsyntactical desires, "wantings," and needs entertained by the "polymorphous perverse" prelinguistic infant. Suffice it to say, the infant holds pro attitudes regardless of its inability to express them.

The only way the psychologist (or indeed, parapsychologist) can proceed in the enterprise of understanding more fully the pro attitude as a first condition is to adopt the idea that "mental representations" (e.g., images, scenarios, etc.) can be pro attitudes too. In fact, it may be better

*Note that Thalbourne explains cases of poltergeists and RSPK (recurrent spontaneous PK), which appear to be acausal, as being due to unconscious pro attitudes (for examples, see Roll 1977).

to dispense altogether with philosophical "syntax criteria" and describe a pro attitude, not by its representation in language, but by the implied form it may, or must, take in the experimental situation. In speaking of preferences, which take the forms of targets or goals, rather than word statements, Thalbourne has probably circumvented the verbal problems towards which Davidson's theory necessarily inclines.

The Necessary Conditions

Following on from the pro attitude in the normal chain of psychopractic events are the so-called "necessary conditions" needed to bring about the paranormal effect (Chapter 8, pp. 195–199). Thalbourne's (2004) definition of psychopraxia stipulates that "certain conditions" must be in place before a pro attitude can be fulfilled in reality. This component of the theory delivers the theory from out of the domains of "magical causation" and "teleological causation" into the realm of testable science. As long as it is possible to explain a paranormal result in terms of the conditions that brought it about, there is a demonstrable causal chain of conditions that allow for the establishment of predictable models of the psi process. Thalbourne emphasizes this aspect of the necessary condition by pointing out that "we need to assemble so far as possible the conditions necessary to provide the (or a) sufficient condition" for exosomatic psychopraxia (Chapter 8, p. 196). Each of these conditions is seen as causally relevant in bringing about an effect. Figure 8.2 (see Chapter 8, p. 198) is an example of an ensemble of such necessary conditions that constitutes a sufficient condition. Thus, for Thalbourne, various combinations of psychopraxia-conducive conditions work like dominoes lined up in a series (see Figure 9.1)—take one condition out of the "line-up" and a psychopractic effect may fail to eventuate.

Note that the mechanical analogies shown in Figures 8.2 and 9.1 introduce chronological and mediational dimensions to the psychopractic process that may not exist. In fact, psychopractic causation may also depend on a "concomitancy" of conditions that must be effected simultaneously in "real" time, and not necessarily contiguously as in the ganzfeld or domino analogies. Furthermore, a necessary condition in one situation may not be necessary in another.

Thalbourne notes too that these necessary conditions are not fully specified as yet, but he lists a number of them, many of which have been found to be psi-conducive through experimentation (Chapter 8, p. 197). The list is not comprehensive, and is not meant to be, which still leaves the investigator of psychopraxia the job of hypothesizing or discovering which (of possibly many) other conditions must be sought out and tested

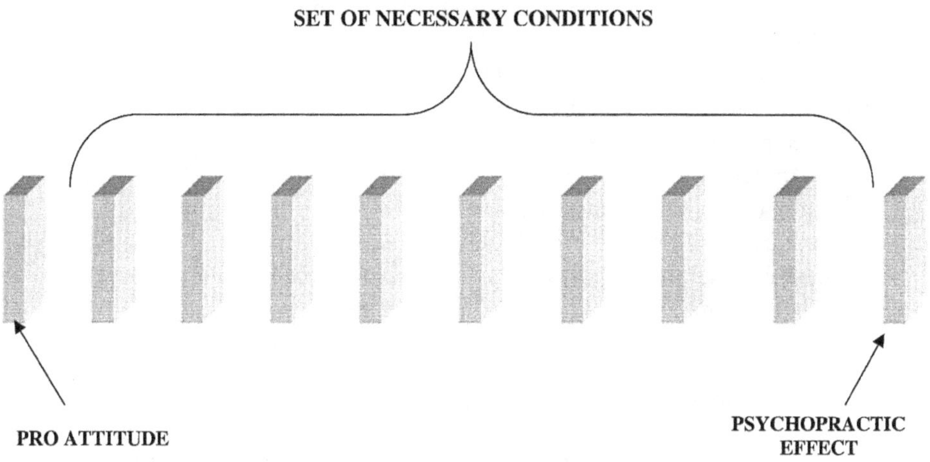

SET OF NECESSARY CONDITIONS

PRO ATTITUDE

PSYCHOPRACTIC
EFFECT

Figure 9.1. The domino analogy of psychopraxia.

as being necessary for a psychopractic effect. These conditions may be pre-dictors, or moderating or modifying variables, or psi-conducive condi-tions, or they may even take the form of the negation of, or reduction in, the effects of certain psi-inhibitive factors (Thalbourne lists some of these factors, Chapter 8, pp. 196–197). Unfortunately, the human subject, together with all its typical and not-so-typical behaviors, is still too broad-based a domain for the search to be all that easily and fully accomplished. Usually a theory imposes certain restraints or parameters that restrict the investigator to specific lines of inquiry. Thus, a theory may have only a short "shelf life" if a point is reached where there is absolutely no ques-tion that all of its formal expressions and terms have been tested and found wanting. The theory of psychopraxia may never meet this fate, not because it will ultimately be shown to be valid, but because it can never be wrong.

It might not be such a problem if a list of proposed necessary condi-tions were exhaustible, even though that might still keep testing of these conditions going almost indefinitely, since this circumstance is true of many theories. For example, Einstein's theory of relativity was proposed near the turn of the twentieth century, but some of its basic tenets were not proved until decades later. Delays in validation of a theory do not reflect badly on a theory. The shortcoming of the theory of psychopraxia is in the demands it places on the investigator, who is required by the usual methods of scientific endeavor (such as intuition, deduction and induc-tion, and even trial and error), to not only test hypothesized necessary conditions, but to find them as well. However, deficits like these might simply be *de rigueur* for parapsychology given the exceptional and elusive nature of psi.

One final issue related to necessary conditions concerns the degree to which it can be stated that a condition is *always* necessary or *always* sufficient, for where there is doubt, we can only say that the condition is psi-conducive. Thalbourne (borrowing from John Stuart Mill) believes "that cause equals sufficient condition, this being the summation of the conditions that are necessary" (Chapter 8, p. 196). This sentence means that a specific ensemble of necessary conditions *must* be in place before we can have the sufficient condition for a cause. But is this always true? Peter Delin (personal communication, November 30, 2001) points out that:

> a "necessary" condition is one without which an outcome cannot occur. Its presence by no means guarantees the outcome. A "sufficient" condition is one which, even if it is not necessary, does guarantee the outcome. Of course, some conditions can be both. A condition may be "conducive to" an outcome without being either necessary or sufficient.

But, of course, Thalbourne is talking about an ensemble of conditions, not any given condition on its own. He also admits that the necessity or sufficiency of a condition may only be circumstantial — "any putative necessary condition should be regarded as tentative until replicated on sufficient occasions" (Chapter 8, p. 199). Here, the so-called necessary condition is like the null hypothesis: we can never say it is true — we can only fail to reject it.

Where does the logic of these statements take us? If we consider relaxation — a psi-conducive condition — we might be able to answer that question. The general finding for relaxation is that, while it has been shown to be psi-conducive, it has never been shown to be *always* necessary. However, if the psi effect, *on a given occasion*, cannot be made *stronger* without the relaxation treatment, it then becomes a necessary *and* sufficient condition. This kind of conditional nomenclature is not entirely in keeping with the rigorous demands of science where terminology is expected to be precise. It is perhaps not surprising that John Palmer (personal communication, January 31, 2002) sought to avoid the issue by preferring the all-embracive term "conducive" over the terms "necessary" and "sufficient." Of course, avoiding the issue only leaves the researcher forever guessing about causes, which is ultimately undesirable for an allegedly progressive science like parapsychology. After all, we need to do more than optimistically set up psi experiments where there is a good *a priori* probability that an effect will be elicited because we have a handful of psi-conducive conditions. To do more than that, we need to find the indisputable and indispensable links in the chain that give us that effect — and induction tells us that there must be such links. For example, to take an example from the everyday world, who would dispute the fact that concentration while driving on the road is *always* a necessary condition, without which *excellent* driving performance could not be guaranteed, and in fact would be dangerous? This is the general impression that Thalbourne is trying to convey.

The Future of the Theory of Psychopraxia in Parapsychology

The future of the theory of psychopraxia will be determined by a number of factors. While it is true that consistently nonsignificant results may, after some initial curiosity about a given theory, result in certain dismissal (or at least marginalization) of that theory by a broad range of investigators inside and outside the discipline of parapsychology, it is naïve to assume that significant and consistent results will ultimately lead to an immediate and general acceptance of the theory. If the latter scenario were the case for the theory of psychopraxia, there is still no guarantee that it will not meet the same reception as, for example, the ganzfeld paradigm where there was much opposition to results, which led to accusations of selective reporting, methodological flaws, etc. (e.g., see Hyman & Honorton 1986).

The theory of psychopraxia has been psychologically, philosophically and theoretically examined in this chapter. Experimentally, however, only some effort has been made to test the theory (see the Chapter 8, pp. 200-203; see also Storm 2001, 2002, 2003). From these studies, only partial support for the theory's two basic propositions (pro attitude and necessary conditions) has been achieved. These propositions need to be considered in turn.

The Pro Attitude

The work in achievement motivation research (see Spangler's 1992 meta-analysis) has pinpointed an important difference between implicit (nonconscious) and self-attributed (conscious) motivations. Like research into the sources of motivation, pro attitude research cannot be regarded as complete or even valid unless it includes recognition of unconscious states of mind. Work needs to be done using projective measures of pro attitude that draw out implicit responses as possible indicators of unconscious pro attitudes as opposed to those that are only explicit (i.e., indicators of conscious pro attitudes).

Neurobiofeedback studies may also give some insight into the brain processes that take place when pro attitudes, (a) are held in consciousness, (b) slip into and out of consciousness, (c) are unconscious, and (d) conflict with alternative pro attitudes. In fact, an answer to the question of what can and cannot be achieved by the pro attitude is crucial in understanding the limits of the human psyche in its day-to-day functioning.

On a related note, not only the presence and strength of the pro attitude needs to be understood, but also its duration. When should psi be expected to take effect, and how long might a psi effect be expected to last after the pro attitude ceases? Evidence already exists to suggest that psi does not eventuate immediately, or stop once it has started. Matthew Manning's attempts to bend a key were not successful until later in the experiment, while he was still "hooked up" to an EEG amplifier. Manning claims this delayed effect occurs on occasion when he psychically bends metal objects. Peter Delin (personal communication, 2002) gives a similar account of having one of his keys still paranormally bending the day after Uri Geller held it in his hand. These delayed and enduring effects recall the effects of inertia and momentum dealt with by physicists. Understanding these effects as they pertain to psi will tell us more about the nature of the pro attitude.

Necessary Conditions

Here there is a problem a little more complex than the concept of the pro attitude. Investigations into the *causal* aspects of necessity are needed, but while it is relatively easy to show that some conditions can be psi-conducive (and some may be necessary or sufficient), the real challenge, in keeping with the expectations of science, lies in finding evidence that there are conditions that are *always* necessary or *always* sufficient. Certainly such categories of conditions must exist. To be better able to confirm that claim, more work needs to be done with dichotomous conditions, rather than conditions with variability. Future investigations, therefore, will require more than just looking for significant performance differentials between treatment and control groups (or "high"- and "low"-scoring groups) because that only provides evidence of the effect of a psi-conducive condition, the necessity or sufficiency of which may only be tentatively inferred. That is, we need to circumvent the moot point that *some* participants in the control group, or (say) the low-scoring group, may have exhibited psi *without* the condition. The conservative response to that claim would be to attribute all seemingly anomalous outcomes (few as they may be) to chance if they are in the control or low-scoring group, but we need to be more responsible than that. What we can say is that we are probably dealing with an alternative necessary and sufficient condition that sets up a completely different formula for those few who did use psi in the control or low-scoring group.

But to really settle the debate over the said necessary and sufficient condition, evidence of psi-hitting would need to be found for *all* participants in the treatment group, whereas psi-missing would need to be found for *all* participants in the control group.* Interestingly, we could then say that the cause of the psi-missing was not exclusively due to the *absence* of the given condition, but may have been due to either (a) another condition, or (b) the *presence* of the polar opposite of the given condition, as in (say) paranormal disbelief, which is the polar opposite of paranormal belief.

A perennial problem in parapsychology, however, is that for both types of hitting, we cannot discern the chance cases from the cases where psi was really effected. But in the above extreme case, this is actually a pseudoproblem because we are interested in *general* causes. That is, it would still be true that a necessary and sufficient condition was involved, and may *always* be involved *as a cause* (assuming sufficient replication) because the cause, assumed to be the condition, must account for at least a sufficient number of hits, if not all of them.

Conclusion

The theory of psychopraxia proposes some interesting and challenging concepts, which may be met with criticism, both good and bad. This is not unusual for any theory, and it will not necessarily stand as a lasting indictment for or against Thalbourne's theory that it is right or wrong always, simply because it is right or wrong today. The most valid criticisms will be those that are founded on the results of future research. On that basis, this chapter may come to represent the first step only in the direction of continued investigation and inquiry into the theory of psychopraxia.

*Such outcomes are not impossible, but are rare. One way to avoid this problem is to test individuals, not groups (John Palmer, personal communication, January 31, 2002).

References

Adler, A. (1928). *Understanding human nature.* (W. B. Wolfe, trans.). London: Allen and Unwin.

Davidson, D. (1966). Actions, reasons, and causes. In B. Berofsky, ed., *Free will and determinism* (pp. 221–240). New York and London: Harper & Row. [First published in *Journal of Philosophy* 1963, LX, 685–700.]

Edinger, E. F. (1996). *The Aion lectures: Exploring the self in C. G. Jung's Aion.* Toronto: Inner City.

Freud, S. (1949). *An outline of psychoanalysis.* New York: Norton.

Ibanez, A., C. Blanco, E. Donahue, H. R. Lesieur, I. Perez de Castro, J. Fernandez Piqueras, and J. Saiz Ruiz (2001). Psychiatric comorbidity in pathological gamblers seeking treatment. *American Journal of Psychiatry* **158**, 1733–1735.

Hyman, R., and C. Honorton (1986). Joint communiqué: The psi ganzfeld controversy. *Journal of Parapsychology* **50**, 351–364.

Ingram, R. (1985). Transactional script theory applied to the pathological gambler. *Journal of Gambling Behavior* **1**, 89–96.

Jung, C. G. (1987). *Psychological Types.* (H. G. Baynes, trans., revised by R. F. C. Hull.) Princeton, NJ: Princeton University Press. (Original works published in 1921.)

Kennedy, J. E. (2001). Why is psi so elusive? A review and proposed model. *Journal of Parapsychology* **65**, 219–246.

Markus, H. R., and S. Kitayama (1991). Culture and the self: Implications for cognition, emotion, and motivation. *Psychological Review* **98**, 224–253.

Miller, N., and J. Dollard (1941). *Social Learning and Imitation.* New Haven, NJ: Yale University Press.

Neisser, U. (1988). Five kinds of self-knowledge. *Philosophical Psychology* **1**, 35–59.

Parker, A. (2001). What can cognitive psychology and parapsychology tell us about near-death experiences? *Journal of the Society for Psychical Research* **65**, 225–240.

Reber, A. S. (1985). *The Penguin dictionary of psychology* (2nd ed.). London: Penguin.

Spangler, W. D. (1992). Validity of questionnaire and TAT measures of need for achievement: Two meta-analyses. *Psychological Bulletin* **112**, 140–154.

Spinelli, E. (1989). The Perception of Self. In E. Spinelli, *The interpreted world: An introduction to phenomenological psychology* (pp. 77–104). London: Sage.

Storm, L. (2001). *A parapsychological investigation of the theory of psychopraxia: Experimental and theoretical researches into an alternative theory explaining normal and paranormal phenomena.* Partly published Ph.D. thesis, Department of Psychology, University of Adelaide, South Australia.

_____. (2002). A parapsychological investigation of the *I Ching*: Seeking psi in an ancient Chinese system of divination. *Australian Journal of Parapsychology* **2**, 44–62.

_____. (2003). "RV" by committee: Remote viewing using a "multiple agent–multiple percipient" design. Submitted for publication.

Thalbourne, M. A. (2000). The theory of psychopraxia. Unpublished manuscript.

Paper distributed at the Third Bial Foundation Symposium, Porto, Portugal, April 6–8, 2000.

_____. (2004). *The common thread between ESP and PK.* New York: Parapsychology Foundation.

Von Franz, M.-L. (1980). *On divination and synchronicity: The psychology of meaningful chance.* Toronto: Inner City.

10

Tackling the Mind-Matter
Problem from a
Consciousness Perspective

Christine Hardy

> Dr. Christine Hardy's semantic fields theory attempts a
> merging of the concepts of matter and mind (which includes
> the psi function) by stressing the importance of conscious-
> ness in the universe. Dr. Hardy's "law of connective-dynamic
> emergence" (a major component of semantic fields theory)
> provides the means by which the worlds of matter and mind
> can be envisioned as an intricately linked, interactional sys-
> tem. Dr. Hardy believes that mind and the psi function are
> evolving in us, and as human beings, we have the potential to
> solve our greatest problems by the "co-creation" and applica-
> tion of "complex intelligent and task-oriented cognitive sys-
> tems." (Editors)

The creation of meaning is a major self-organizational force at work
within the mind. However, it is also working as a (low-level, mostly unconscious) two-way informational exchange and interinfluence between
minds and natural, cultural, or individual, semantic systems or "fields."
Both these dynamics— of which psi is like the tip of the iceberg — exhibit
self-organization, nonlocality, and goal-directedness. Consciousness is
thus viewed as an organizing and negentropic force in the universe. Devel-

oping the above premises, semantic fields theory shows a very deep inter-mingling of mind with matter, to the point of diffusing the mind-brain or mind-matter "gap" into numerous "micro-gaps." I then propose that through a *law of connective-dynamic emergence*, totally distinct types of sys-tems (whatever their type of processes) interact dynamically, adjust, and coevolve, and thus create an emergent system with emergent properties. Tackling and hopefully shedding light on the mind-matter problem could, in my view, amount to a substantial achievement for parapsychology.

Then I address the issue of the evolution of mental and psi human capacities. Basically, the strong intention of developing a mental or psi capacity may act as a force potent enough to reorganize the individual mind toward favoring the emergence of the said capacity. Finally, what about the possibility of psi abilities becoming widespread worldwide? Could enhanced psi sensitivity be a deeply buried solution to our endan-gered species and Earth? Could it just be the right trigger for us to develop empathy with others, which, in its turn, would lead us to a greater per-sonal integrity and caring for humanity and the planet?

Psi in the Crack Between Paradigms

Let us take the famous metaphor of the flatlanders and twist it a bit. This metaphor was used to show that imaginary beings living in a flat world of two-spatial dimensions (length, width) — the said flatlanders — would be unable to grasp the existence of a third dimension: height, that is, a world in volume. The metaphor, then, was used to make us conceive of a third spatial dimension.

My point, in this revisited metaphor, is to imagine how flatlanders could guess or infer the existence of a third spatial dimension if the only indirect proof of something belonging to the third dimension was anom-alous shadows cast by light sources outside their two-dimensional world.

Suppose our flatlanders are tiny water spiders, but endowed with intelligence, living on the surface of a pool which has a few "round walls" impossible to trespass, in the middle of the water (they are canes sticking out of the water). They have no depth vision and are unable to see the sun with their tiny eyes, only a cycling of "obscure" and "light" periods; how-ever they have remarked that an elongated "black spot" (shadow) turns around each cane, without impeding their sliding on the surface for reach-ing the "hot clear surface." And thus, the only signs of a third dimension are oddities on their "hot clear surface" world. (We take for granted that they are not aware of their bodies having volume). Now, let us imagine our smart spiders have developed a rigorous science: all their methods to accrue their knowledge will be adapted to a two-dimensional world. Suppose now they are so sophisticated as to have extracted a general law of shadow-motion that describes perfectly all the movements of the black spots. Since all subsequent observations meet the law's predictions, they feel they have accounted for all observable phenomena. They have a vague presupposition that the dark spots are due to the "round walls" since the shadows always turn around them. One day, they do stumble on a set of shadows in an unexplored corner of their world that are anomalous: not only do they appear during the obscure period (instead of the light-period), but they do not move at all (they are created by branches in front of a street lamp overlooking the pool). The anomaly reveals their presupposition was false, because there exist some shadows that originate far from the "round walls."

The conclusion is that the existence of a new dimension can only be indirectly revealed through what appear in a lower-dimensional world as unexplained phenomena or anomalies. It did not dawn on our flatlanders that they had not really explained why canes had shadows in the first place. Neither have we explained why the galaxies are elliptical; or why half of the universe's matter is untraceable.

While physicists pose new dimensions in novel theories (e.g., six dimensions in quantum mechanics, 10 dimensions in string theory), only matter dimensions are being conceived of. Basically, we are still dealing with good old matter, even if this matter is becoming more and more strange—for example, mass has disappeared altogether in the new zero-gravity field. Lengthy debates have been going on for decades in physics about whether quantum mechanics (QM) is complete or not (i.e., whether QM is a complete description of reality). However, how can we assume a description of reality is complete when a substantial part of that reality is excluded altogether from the description—namely mind and consciousness?

In this paper I propose to formalize psi as a range of processes included in cognitive dynamics and belonging to a *semantic dimension* which can only be adequately described by specific semantic parameters. In this semantic dimension, mind and matter are deeply intermingled—what Carl Jung called a *psychoid reality*. All cognitive processes, including psi, present anomalies to classical physics and quantum mechanics because they reveal a more complex semantic dimension that instantiates nonlocal properties escaping space-time constraints. To keep up with our revisited flatlander story, let us start by these anomalies.

Psi, Physics, and Fields Theories

Psi points to a whole new dimension of reality that definitely does not abide by the laws of Newtonian physics, stating that objects have a causal effect on other separated objects, and move in a past → future time arrow. This is the reason why a number of theorists in parapsychology have relied on QM to explain some of the weird features of psi — such as, in precognition, information seemingly moving in the future → present time arrow, that is, apparent retrocausality, and the influence of an observer on matter.

In QM (the Copenhagen school), Schrödinger's equation poses that the wave-function describing a quantum system is the superposition of all possible states of that system. When a measurement is made, the superposed possibilities "collapse" and the system settles into one of its possible states — a particle described by space-time coordinates and endowed with specific properties. Prior to measurement and the collapse of the wave-function, the quantum system exhibits a fundamental indeterminacy. However, after the measurement, it becomes a system described by coordinates (of either waves or particle). Therefore, it is assumed that the result of measurement (the quantum system once measured and described by coordinates) is already the product of an interaction between the wave-function and the observer who did the measurement.

QM thus poses that the influence of the observer on the observed reality (an idea introduced by Heisenberg) occurs at the moment of measurement. However, this influence has been understood in several ways.* For some physicists, it is produced by the measuring device itself, something difficult to admit since the device has been conceived by minds and expresses a set of scientific laws. Others have proposed that the observer, or the act of perception, is crucial. The mathematician von Neumann and the physicist Eugene Wigner explicitly implicated consciousness in the collapse of the wave function, without implying that consciousness would *determine* the observed state of the system.

Observational theories (OT) move a step further in proposing that observation introduces a "biasing" of measurement outcomes. Physicist Evan Harris Walker (1975, 1984) argues that the act of observation creates an interaction (a nonlocal coupling) between internal brain processes and the external quantum system. Consequently, consciousness would be able to influence external microevents, in the same way it can direct its own internal brain

*About the diverse interpretations in quantum mechanics, see: Casti (1989); Bohm (1980); Costa de Beauregard (1989); and Herbert (1985). The physicists who imply consciousness in the collapse are Heisenberg, Von Neumann, and Wigner.

processes (e.g., willing a certain gesture). Extending the OT approach, physicist Walter Von Lucadou (Von Lucadou, 1983; Von Lucadou and Kornwaf, 1987) postulates an influence of mind on macro systems: under certain circumstances, individuals and physical systems would form a metasystem, a more inclusive whole having its own individuality or "organizational closure." Then, nonlocal correlations would link the person's mental state with the external system and produce temporary "mind-over-matter" effects.

Investigations of micropsychokinesis (micro–PK) in parapsychology are highly pertinent to this issue: several decades of experiments involving random number generators (RNGs, also referred to as random event generators or REGs)* provide evidence that individuals can intentionally bias microphysical events supposed to be probabilistic, in the sense that the normally random output of RNGs is slightly, but consistently, skewed in accordance with the intentions and mental state of subject-observers.† However, there exist some fundamental divergences between QM framework and some facts well supported by experimental research.

Psychological Factors

Parapsychological experiments suggest that several psychological, relational and sociocultural factors have a clear-cut, statistically significant influence on the results. These include the sheep-goat effect (influence of beliefs), openness to others, correlations with Jungian categories (MBTI test), etc.§ In the experiments on micro–PK, subjects' task is to influence the behavior of a purely random system (i.e., a random number generator), toward an aim selected randomly prior to the testing (e.g., moving a data feedback curve upward or downward). These tests also suggest that psychological

---

*Random number generators (RNG), or random event generators, are based on microphysical processes such as electronic noise or radioactive decay.

†Dean Radin and Roger Nelson (1989) conducted a meta-analysis of 597 experiments, employing RNGs and involving 68 investigators, conducted over the past 25 years. The combined result of all experimental studies on micro–PK ($z = 15.58$, $p = 1.8 \times 10{-35}$) shows that the RNG results deviate significantly from pure randomness in accordance with subjects' intentions. However, there are two main theories to explain these results. Proponents of the "psychokinesis" model hold that RNG functioning is itself perturbed by subjects' psi, that is, the random distribution becomes skewed. However, in the DAT model (developed by Edwin May and his collaborators in 1995 and known as "decision augmentation theory") the effects are explained by precognitive information enabling the subjects to trigger the RNG sampling at the very moments it would be biased in the sense of expectations. See Radin and Nelson (1989); and May, Utts, and Spottiswoode (1995).

§On psychological factors in parapsychology experiments, see: Braude (1986); Broughton (1991); Jahn and Dunne (1987); Mishlove (1993); Radin (1997); Rogo (1975); and Varvoglis (1992).

and relational factors may have an influence on results. If indeed psychological factors influence experimental results, then psi research could bring a different perspective to some obscure facets of QM, albeit in a very paradoxical way. Let me explain.

QM proposes that an observer has an effect on the quantum system *at the moment of observation*. Yet psychological factors shown to be influential through laboratory experiments are long-term personality traits— such as beliefs, interrelation style, openness, intuition, etc. Obviously, these psychological factors start to have an influence on the quantum system way upstream from the moment of observation and not only at that precise moment. In Schmeidler's (1973) experiment on the sheep-goat effect, the questionnaire on beliefs was filled out by the subjects just prior to taking the psi test. However, subjects held these beliefs a long time before coming to take the test, and they did build up expectations about the future test from the moment they knew they were going to participate in it (e.g., in Psychophysical Research Laboratories telepathy experiments in Princeton, announcements were made in the local press, asking interested individuals to contact the lab.)

That is, to go back to our revisited flatlanders metaphor, the anomalies appearing through parapsychological experiments are 1) that *psychological factors* are able to influence a purely random electronic or physical system (in micro–PK experiments); and 2), that the time-frame of the influence of psychological factors may imply the whole period of preparation prior to a test, and even long-term beliefs and personality traits. At the minimum, the influence of psychological factors suggests that parameters beyond the sole physical substrate have to be considered, and not only as a general principle, but as specific parameters to be taken into account in a complete theory of mind-matter.

Experimenter Effect

Another extremely interesting finding of parapsychology has been the experimenter effect, that underlines the influence an experimenter may have on his results. This goes beyond the simple psychological effects explained by Rosenthal (1984) (and thus called the Rosenthal effect), which showed how, given a certain hypothesis and a set of beliefs, the many choices of experimenters would be slightly biased toward proving their hypothesis. In parapsychology, we are talking about an experimenter having a psi effect on the results: indeed, if psi exists and is able to have an influence on outside systems, then all minds connected to an experiment will have a psi influence on it — and not only subjects' minds— something Murphy (1945) had already proposed.

To account for such facts, von Lucadou (1987), taking a QM and systems' framework, holds that the whole experiment and all the participants have to be viewed as a system. In his model of pragmatic information (MPI), psi is distributed among all the minds connected within an "organizational closure"—a view I share. Von Lucadou then goes on deducing that experimental psi results not only are nonrepeatable, but also bound to show decline effects in their results—a prediction I do not make. But let me give a quick review of the main theories of psi that implicate psi fields (i.e., *fields theories*).

Carington (1945), in his association theory, viewed the "field of consciousness" as consisting of "associative groupings of psychons," that is, sensory inputs and images. He spoke of a "common subconscious" that would favour associations in the minds of subjects, thus leading to psi information being activated. Murphy (1945, 1949) proposed the concept of "interpersonal field" and believed psi was fundamentally "transpersonal," grounded in the relationships between individuals. Psi, he thought, would be enhanced if people were to become more attuned to each other. Price (1939) proposed a "psychic ether" in which images-fields would dwell, thus enabling sensitive people to decode the information they were carrying. Roll (1965, 1983) introduced "psi fields" to explain some macro-PK phenomena such as poltergeists.

A series of experiments was conducted by Roger Nelson and colleagues (Nelson et al. 1996) of the PEAR laboratories at Princeton University in order to test what he called "fieldREG anomalies." His assumption was that a strong mental cohesiveness achieved in a group situation would affect an REG set up in the gathering room, whether people knew about it or not. He obtained quite positive results while testing different settings, such as professional, scientific, or religious gatherings. The REG would show peaks of deviation from the baseline during particularly intense and interesting moments of the gathering. For example, at a 1993 meeting of a research group on healing, the REG showed a highly significant deviation from chance during a specific presentation highly appreciated by the audience. Nelson et al. (1996) proposed that "the emotional/intellectual dynamics of the interacting participants somehow generate a coherent 'consciousness field,' to which the REG responds" (p. 137).

Nelson then went on to conceive of, and set up, the Global Consciousness Project (GCP)* which is a network of fieldREGs called "eggs" and distributed all over the planet. Nelson works with Dick Bierman of

*See Roger Nelson Web site: www.global-mind.org/ *and more precisely the World Trade Center attacks at* www.noosphere.princeton.edu/terror.htm.

the University of Amsterdam and Dean Radin of the Institute of Noetic Sciences. They analyze the distribution of randomness to find possible shifts at the very moment great world events or catastrophes occur at the planetary level. Indeed, they found peaks of exceptional strength were synchronous with most worldwide events. Of particular significance was the fact that on September 11, 2001, a peak of major proportions started at 5 A.M., whereas the first tower of the World Trade Center was hit only around 8 A.M.— an unexplained phenomenon that, in my own view, may suggest a form of precognition in the collective unconscious.

Nelson's experiments on fields/REGs and the Global Consciousness Project have shown results that, in my view, give credence to a theoretical stand based on fields. However, there are also some shortcomings to such a position, namely that:

(i)   psi does not show a uniform spreading as in a EM field;
(ii) psi does not show a decrease of the psi effect in function of distance; and
(iii) psi is not blocked by shields known to block EM energies.

On this basis, most psi researchers hold that we know at least for sure that psi *is not* EM energy. Thus, if psi involves energy, it would have to be anything but EM (i.e., the energy would have to be of a form that has not yet been discovered, and thus not bound by the three principles listed above). Furthermore, experiments suggest that psi may be directed and focused on an objective (the aim or target of the test), and this is yet another argument against psi involving known forms of energy. In my opinion, this signifies that mind is able to control such semantic energy — a basic tenet of this theory.

Several theorists have considered that psi escapes the normal dimensions of space and time: in short, psi is "transpatial and transtemporal," as Murphy (1949) puts it. Price (1939) introduced a parameter of "proximity" between "image fields" that cancels spatial distance. Roll (1983) proposed "psi contiguity" between people and their past and present homes, their psi-field leaving a persistent trace in the place. Similarly, Nelson et al. (1996) proposed "subjective parameters" such as "attentional proximity" and "intensity of subjective investment" (p. 137).

The semantic fields theory (SFT) posits that minds are semantic fields— that is, dynamical networks of processes, constantly interacting with other semantic fields and evolving (Hardy 1998). The theory aims at addressing the specific properties of mind and consciousness dynamics, as being independent of space-time. I (Hardy 2000) therefore postulated certain parameters, which are nonlocal in nature and relevant to mental levels in particular. I have currently identified four parameters specific to the *semantic dimension* that may describe mental and psi dynamics, such as semantic proximity, recurrence, intensity, and linkage types. *Semantic proximity* is a nonlocal parameter that bridges spatial distance between individuals who have a very strong bond, and who therefore tend to feel they are always connected, even when they happen to be far away from each other. All these semantic parameters instantiate nonlocal connections between distant semantic fields and create a complex web of mutual influences. I propose that communication at a distance between individuals (e.g., telepathy) is a dynamical interaction implying these nonlocal parameters. While interacting regularly with people, we develop nonlocal connections with them that, given sufficient recurrence and intensity, may become quasipermanent "semantic bridges." Thus, when one person undergoes a strong experience, his or her friend may get the information through the spontaneous activation of these semantic bridges between them, whatever the distance separating them. The only difficulty would then be that this information could remain unconscious, deeply buried in the semantic field.

The Mind-Matter Gap

A theoretical postulate that gathers the unanimity of psi researchers is that psi phenomena are first and foremost mind (or consciousness) phenomena. Whether some of them may show an added "something else" is an open debate. (For example, when shamans say that they "talk to nature spirits" the only thing we are absolutely sure of is that they experience a mental phenomenon, a state of consciousness—and this *fact of consciousness* will be fundamental and certain, *whether or not* such spirits exist.)

Thus, since psi is a mind phenomenon, a theory of psi must be tied to a theory of mind: It is my deep conviction that a theory of psi must be logically derived from, and grounded on, a cognitive theory. This is due to the fact that psi, as a mental fact, shows properties and dynamics that are radically at odds with "normal" properties of mind as viewed by classical cognitive theories (of course, as we mentioned, it is even more at odds with Newtonian physics). These theories belong to two paradigms: the first one, materialism (monism), denies that mind is anything beyond brain processes, and has been discarded by most researchers. The second one, the Cartesian dualism, proposes that mind and brain are two radically different "stuffs." It was revisited as the "computational paradigm" that poses mind as software running on the brain as hardware. And it gave rise to interactionism (Sperry 1976), which underlines the interaction between them.

These theories and their presuppositions are still widely held by scientists — whether explicitly or implicitly in the way research is conducted. However, they are unable to explain such a normal, self-evident fact as the interaction between mind and brain. The point is, no cognitive theory has adequately accounted for the "gap" existing between the mental level (experiences as being meaningful to *us*, to a subjective "I," that is, a "first-person perspective"), and the neurological level — brain and neurochemical processes, that is, a "third-person perspective."

As it is, in my view, *the Cartesian dualism (mind and brain as radically different) is the very type of framework that creates the "gap" in the first place.* And in interactionism, while mind and brain are viewed as interacting, the way they are supposed to do so is less than satisfying. The best case has been made by the "one-to-one correspondence" — one mental event linked causally to one neural event. However, this is bound to fail right from the start as an explanation since there is no adequate definition of either *one* mental event or *one* neural event (there are so many layers of organization, that each "event" is included with, and includes, all kinds of other events.) Furthermore, the correspondence has been generally viewed as causal and deterministic (whether in the top-down perspective of Eccles (1989) or the bottom-up one) — something hardly able to explain the exquisite flexibility and evolutionary dynamics of the mind.

The case has been made by Chalmers (1996) and has met general agreement among cognitive scientists who agree that the subjective "I" perspective is "the hard problem" in theory, and not something to be swept under the carpet. Consequently, there has been in the mid-'90s a general understanding that specific properties of the subjective experience of consciousness have to be addressed and accounted for if a cognitive theory wants to be deemed "complete" (thus giving the final blow to reductionism and materialism).

To resume, for a cognitive theory to be deemed adequate, it should account for:

(i)   At the minimum: different sets of qualities, dynamics, and properties, shown on the one hand by the mental and subjective levels, and on the other hand those shown by the brain and neuronal levels.
(ii) A two-way mind-brain interaction (both top-down and bottom-up) of extreme flexibility, that is, nondeterministic and evolving.

(iii)   An adequate explanation of such mind capacities as innovation, creation, learning, the ability to adjust, choose, will, imagine, etc.

As it is, all theories that have equated thinking to pure reason (starting with Descartes and then the whole computational paradigm that viewed mind as software running on the hardware of the brain) have been unable to explain learning (and generally, they have skipped the subject altogether), and even less so the subject of innovation. Why is this so? Because logic is a set of fixed rules, and the result of applying a rule is always logically contained within the rule-system. The only possible evolution of the rule-system is a combination of rules: However, combining rules can only lead to a combined result — a far cry from Shakespeare's plays or Einstein's theory!

As has often been the case in science, it is the very way a theory is structured that creates an insoluble problem — that is, insoluble by this specific theory! Any dualistic framework brings with it the gap problem. And the gap problem cannot be resolved unless we shift to another theoretical framework.

Connective-Dynamic Emergence

Tackling the issues I have just mentioned, I was led to build a theory grounded on largely different premises that shifts the perspective away from categories of substances (mental vs. neural) to focus instead on the connective dynamics between a vast array of processes and their self-organizing properties. The basic principle of the theory, or *law of connective-dynamic emergence*, is as follows:

> *Totally distinct types of systems of processes (whatever their type), through internal self-organization and a connective dynamic, are able to adjust between them, to interact dynamically and coevolve, and henceforth to create an emergent system with emergent properties.*

The principle of dynamical self-organization I am proposing is a complex mix of both network properties and complex-dynamical systems properties.

Self-Organization in Neural Nets

In a multilayered net, an ensemble of hidden units to which an output (or goal) is given, will learn to code for this output. The goal can be a shape, a letter, a word, a logical function or proposition, a pattern of activation, a molecular structure, a sound, etc. The learning capacity of neural nets is accrued in multilayered networks that use back-propagation and allow for the spontaneous self-organization of hidden units. At each step, the actual state of the network is compared to the expected output or goal, and the error-signal is back-propagated. Rumelhart and McClelland (1986) present a three-layered network that contains two hidden units (intermediary layer). While the stimulus patterns are presented repeatedly, the two hidden units learn to specialize spontaneously and after 210 sweeps, the first unit becomes a detector of the OR logical function, while the second one is able to detect the AND (see also, Bechtel & Abrahamsen 1990). The learning process ends when the network is able to recognize perfectly all the goal forms. A neural net may learn to recognize a great number of such forms (e.g. all the letters in the alphabet). Each internal configuration, coding for a form, has been equated by Jordan (1986) to an *attractor* of the system, thus making the link between neural nets and chaos theory.

Self-Organization in Complex Dynamical Systems (or Chaos Theory)

The principle is that of *dynamical emergence*, that is, creation of novel global orders through bifurcations and modifications of the attractors. In short, chaos theory poses that a global pattern (the attractor) governs the behavior of the system, while there is randomness at the micro level.

Note that in the self-organization of neural nets, the object the net is going to code for could be anything (as we mentioned, it could be a shape or a sound). In other words, the network consists of a group of units, in a multilayered system of such units, that are set in motion by the reiteration of a simple rule (or algorithm). The rule itself has nothing to do with the configuration the net will find (the attractor coding for the object), other than being a dynamical trigger.

In a similar way, the goal shape (or image, etc.) does not have anything in common with the net itself. What is important in the *law of connective-dynamic emergence*, is that two systems may interact and influence each other, whether or not they are of a similar structural or organizational type. Thus the law grounds the possible interaction and interinfluence between totally different systems such as: a pattern of neuronal activation in the brain AND a feeling AND a creative state AND decoding abstract signs AND painting skill (procedure, gestures) AND recognition of global patterns (e.g. a face) AND iconic, sensory memory, AND declarative, conceptual memory, etc.

To conclude, the *law of connective-dynamic emergence*— in posing the possibility of interconnectedness between systems whose internal structure (type of elements and processes) are not similar — solves the gap problem between mind and matter. What we have now is that the large variety of systems of processes existing in a living organism (chemical, neural, electric, magnetic, physiological, motor control, complex actions, procedures, concepts, images, subjective sensations, etc.) can exchange dynamical information between themselves without having a similar structural communication unit. In other words, it uses *"dynamical barter"* — that is, dynamical adaptability and coevolution between systems— and not a common substrate such as bits of information (as in the computational paradigm). Thus there is an infinite number of interconnections and exchanges between multiple mind-brain-psyche-body systems, thus allowing numerous microgaps to be bridged dynamically.

In this cognitive architecture made of dynamical multilayered networks, self-organized through connective dynamics, the mind-body problem does not exist anymore and instead, all complex dynamical systems participate in the cocreation of complex intelligent and task-oriented cognitive systems.

Coevolution and Emergence

Imagine we have two systems that start to interact between themselves and learn how to adapt to each other. For example, let us imagine two people who have just met and start developing a friendship or a love relationship. If we look at what is happening in terms of networks, each person is the "input" of the other one. Each good psychological connection (e.g., supportive, stimulating, response; shared values; harmonious state of consciousness, etc.) is an attractor in a shared semantic field.

In SFT, each person is a very complex semantic field, comprising many systems of coevolved processes— which I call semantic constellations or SeCos. Each SeCo has many attractors. For example, the "Painting-SeCo" contains several attractors (or organizational states) corresponding to the artist's creative states, such as artistic contemplation, listening, enjoying a landscape, actively painting, painting while listening to music, etc.

Let us say that both friends (M, N) are painters and thus share the same passion. M, in his Painting-SeCo, has an array of artistic states or attractors (a), thus the array may be represented by M $\{a_1, \ldots, a_n\}$ and similarly N $\{a_1, \ldots, a_n\}$.

Each time M is in a given state, then N develops a complementary, synchronized, or antagonistic state N(M); and so does M vis-à-vis N, building up some M(N) state. So basically the two friends develop a common semantic space that I call interface–SeCo. This interface–SeCo has an ideal number of states that corresponds to all possible states of M plus all possible states of N (and that includes all their complementary states). And the attractors of this common semantic space — which correspond to their shared past — are common attractors (i.e., all N[M] states plus all M[N] states).

However, let us remember that each person is having new experiences in the outer world all the time and is setting up new relationships, and that is sufficient for him or her to keep building new states and new attractors. And consequently the interface–SeCo is in a constant flux, not only from state to state, but also from creating new emergent states; and that of course will constantly modify its set of common attractors.

Emergent Self-Organization

The question now is: "Given that systems may be interconnected, what triggers the connective dynamic, and thus the self-organization of these systems?"

As the SeCos are the product of the organizational dynamic built by individuals to deal with specific tasks, knowledge, or aspects of their life (e.g., artistic know-how, professional knowledge, travel procedures, specific cultural and scientific constellations, social interactions and networks, love life, etc.), each person has, in any period in his or her life, a specific set of SeCos being activated in order to manage ongoing social and intellectual activities. This being said, let us pose that whenever two individuals interact in a deep and meaningful way, only a small number of SeCos are conjointly activated in both interlocutors. Let us build further on our previous example: the friends M and N are presently discussing sci-fi films and futuristic science while N is driving through town. Of course the SeCo of their friendship is activated, together with "sci-fi films," "futuristic science," "driving," and "town-roadmap." Given that driving is semi-automatic, and they have been friends for quite a while, the creation of meaning — the semantic dynamic — is mostly happening through the discussion they have.

We saw this in detail earlier, if M is in a given state, then N will react and adapt to that state — whether positively, negatively, or neutrally (i.e., N does not care). In his turn, M, will respond to N's state by entering a new feeling state, while N adjusts to the new state of M. The attractors then keep shifting slightly or drastically, as the process is going on. However, this is a crude description — just intended to illuminate the dynamics— because in reality the two persons keep interacting and interinfluencing each other simultaneously and in a continuous process (thus, it is not a cybernetic loop system, but what I have described elsewhere [Hardy 2001] as a multilevel web system.)

Thus, emergent self-organization is what is happening between subsystems interacting and coevolving within a greater whole — for example, two friends, individuals within a group, groups of cells within an organism, or else, systems coupled with their environment (such as fishes and the sea water they live in). The best example of emergent self-organization, in terms of MBP dynamics, is the skill developed by surfers, and in which they are constantly adapting their body (posture, muscular tension, equilibrium, weight, etc.) to the constantly changing state of the waves.

Intended Evolution

Whatever the complexity of a living system (such as a plant or a mind), such a system has needs that prod it into intentional actions in order to fulfil these needs. Endowed with self-reference, human minds are able to choose voluntarily their own objectives and actions in order to fulfil their many desires and needs. They experience a great number of needs beyond mere survival needs. For example, love and attraction are great forces that bridge the gap with others in a harmonious and open fashion. Furthermore, the psychiatrist Carl Jung added to the Freudian basic drives a "religious drive" that expressed the universal implication that human cultures are driven to develop forms of religious ritual and spirituality. It instantiates a basic need for understanding and knowing, a very deep urge to make sense of the world, to nurture and expand our consciousness. In his PMIR model, Stanford (1974) had proposed that needs were the force driving the emergence of psi abilities. I agree with him, but I would rather expand the dynamical trigger to all intentional processes; that implies the generation of meaning (desiring, hoping, praying), as well as conative processes (will, choice, etc.).

I thus view "intention" as the broader semantic force inciting us to evolve psychologically and mentally (and also evolve in terms of psi abilities). Intention includes desiring, anticipating, and acting voluntarily for the fulfilment of not only survival needs, but also affective, intellectual, and spiritual trends and needs. Survival needs are mostly automatic and redundant (such as the drive to sleep), whereas the more refined needs (e.g., relational or spiritual) are extremely changing and evolving in their content. In that sense, we can define *intention* as the setting of an aim and a proactive behavior in order to fulfil this aim.

But let us look at what our mind is doing at a lower level when we build a complex new intention. According to SFT, thought is a connective dynamic that creates constellations of linked processes. I have shown (Hardy 2003a) that intention and anticipations are creating a very complex system — *a sigma web* — that puts in interaction our aim (or project), how we envision it (its future form, key concepts, beliefs, values, etc.) and possible actions and steps to fulfil it. This sigma web exhibits weird properties: for example, the web is stretched in time from the present to the future time of realization; our objective creates an *attractor* in the future that sends its influence backward toward the present. As a result, there is a constant forward and backward flow of influence, which creates grounds for synchronicity (Hardy 1998). Synchronicity, as Carl Jung (1960) has shown, is not just positive coincidence, it often offers a solution to problems in life (see also, Jung & Pauli 1955). For example, synchronicity may provide the right information or contacts we need for realizing our project, or at the very least, it may help us stay focused in our aims (see also, Combs and Holland 1995; Peat 1987). This is how people sometimes get the impression that a true "serendipity" (i.e., a series of synchronicities) has happened to them. Thus, intention sets both a proactive and a retroactive flow that creates a dynamical attraction toward the intended future, triggering synchronicities in its wake. However, when we ponder the *meaning* of conscious life, we realize intention is much more than a two-way dynamical flow: intention is also a fundamental energy of meaning, a *semantic energy*. When what is intended is the attainment of a spiritual state of consciousness or knowledge, then it has the power to trigger an internal reorganization of our mind-psyche, that favors the growth of our Self (the spiritual self or soul). Jung called this process of spiritual growth the "individuation process" and he underlined the fact it was present and known in all traditional cultures as a path of initiation, as in shamanism's knowledge paths, or Eastern yoga (Tibetan and Zen Buddhism, Taoism, Hinduism, etc.).

I do believe that setting up for ourself the profound intention to open a path of spiritual growth and awakening is sufficient to trigger a reorganization of our mind-brain that will render it possible. This may be a somewhat far-fetched idea, one reminiscent of Lamarck's theory of evolution which preceded that of Darwin, and was later viewed as concurrent and antinomic to it, notwithstanding the fact that Darwin himself had not sought to discard it. Since random mutations have lately been shown to be much more rare than predicted by Darwin, and thus an unlikely candidate to explain evolution all by itself, some of Lamarck's ideas are being reconsidered, not any more *opposed to* random mutations, but as another evolutionary dynamics. Lamarck held that specific biological traits could be acquired during the life of one individual and, from there on, could be transmitted as hereditary traits to the descendants. As Arthur Koestler (1972) has shown in his biography of biologist Kammerer, the latter had successfully performed some experiments on toads that suggested this was possible in terms of biological traits (he was unfortunately drawn to suicide by the violent rebuttal he suffered at the time).

My point is that it could also be true in terms of psychological or mental abilities such as psi. So let me develop my point, somewhat derivative, but slightly divergent from Lamarck's theory: the strong intention of developing a skill, a gift, or a mental capacity, is in itself a very potent semantic energy, acting as an organizing force in the mind-brain-psyche. Intention, as a force, has the power to reorganize the individual mind and links within neuronal networks, toward favoring the emergence of the said mental or psi capacity. In my view, we are witnessing at the present time such an emergence of psi abilities in the general population across the planet. As several scientists have shown through analyzing surveys, there seems to be a progressive rise in the percentages of spontaneous psi experiences. A pragmatic personal way to assess this trend (if you are not a psi researcher or involved in the domain) is to count the number of people you know directly who have had such psi experiences in their life and to compare it with a decade or two ago.

If we are indeed witnessing such an emergence involving psi and spiritual self-development in humanity, then many disastrous predictions concerning both the planet and humanity could be reviewed. Such an evolutionary possibility would make sense in terms of the survival of our species and Earth. The dangers facing the human species, the quick extinction of thousands of human cultures, as well as animal and flora species, the ecological disaster looming over our planet — all of them mostly due to crass ignorance of ecological interconnected dynamics, and to a lack of a planetary consciousness— all this could trigger the frantic search for a solution by the collective unconscious, or Gaia consciousness.

Indeed, according to James Lovelock (Lovelock & Thomas 1990), the Earth is alive and endowed with consciousness, a concept that has some similarities with Jung's concept of collective unconscious. On these premises, I propose that "*a human being, when confronted with a situation of high risk or lethal danger, will draw from his unconscious all the possible knowledge and latent mental and psi capacities that could help him solve the crisis.*" Among these latent capacities are specific psi abilities, such as telepathy and clairvoyance — a sensitivity to fellow beings and to the state of the environment that is not bound by distance.

In my anthropologist's perspective, this is a form of communication at a distance that is instinctive in human beings (see Hardy 1991), dolphins (Lilly 1981), pets (Sheldrake 1981), and many living species, and that is rooted in a social instinct and a coupling between animals and their environment. Furthermore, according to Varela et al. (1991), the cognitive system itself is the product of a constant coupling between perception, action, and the environment.

However, all traditional lores as well as sacred books in the East state that practicing a form of yoga or of self-development technique will trigger the emergence of mental and psi capacities. Since the 1970s, many people have felt the urge to turn to some self-development technique, and we are, more and more, setting our intention on becoming spiritually conscious, and many are taking the shaman's path of knowledge (Feinstein & Krippner 1997). Then it is no wonder that we would experience the emergence of latent psi abilities, especially at the moment our collective unconscious would sense that the dangers facing our species and the planet are soon reaching an unprecedented level of lethality and irreversibility.

I will move a step further and propose a hypothesis to ponder on: *the massive emergence of latent psi abilities in the human population, especially since it is coupled with a scientifically oriented civilization going global, will, at a certain threshold, give rise to an abrupt emergence process of a totally novel type of consciousness endowed with new forms of psi.*

My hunch is that this abrupt emergence will be distributed throughout the whole planet (all cultures and walks of life). It will evolve in a quantum leap fashion — that is, through sudden shifts in states of consciousness for all sensitive minds, and their accessing heightened awareness and potentials, whatever the ground from which one is leaping (Hardy 2003b).

The whole collective process of emergence is bound to head toward a higher spiritual conscience, respect for life, social ethics, and sense of global responsibility — or else Armageddon is facing both humanity and life on Earth. The awareness of such a dire alternative, without so much as any sensical escape route, is what is, sadly so, raising our chances and making the taking of the first road all the more probable. Another line of reasoning that assists in the computation of our chances of survival is to weigh up how the process is set in motion and how it evolves: what is happening is that emergence leaps are triggered by the harm done to the planet and its life forms, including human societies and individuals. The result would be a sharp rise in awareness, a new ecological, ethical, spiritual and collective conscience. Due to the fact that it reflects a new sensitivity to divergent cultures and other intelligent life-forms (such as dolphins and elephants), to the probability of intelligent life in the cosmos, and the woe of our planet, even in a world shaken by terror and counterterror shockwaves, we have a reasonable hope that the emergence will follow the healing-the-planet path.

See, for example, how the data of the Global Consciousness Project (or GCP) started by Nelson, suggest that the normal distribution of randomness may be modified by the collective unconscious, or, as Radin (1997) puts it, by negentropic "ripples" moving around the planet (see also, Varvoglis, 1997). Let us proactively and positively hope that we are heading toward the *noosphere* envisioned by Pierre Teilhard de Chardin, that is, the progressive construction of a spiritual collective consciousness that at the end, at its *omega* point as he called it, will instantiate a harmonious whole in a tightly woven network of heightened Selfs!

Conclusion

A last point I would like to address as a conclusion is: what kind of social interactions could be envisioned in the prospect of psi becoming more widespread? Say some psi abilities become normal human capacities worldwide, what is going to be our subjective experience in terms of relationships and social interactions? My deep conviction, rooted in my own experience, is that the spreading of telepathic sensitivity would lead people to develop a greater personal integrity as they feel that their recourse to lying may have a greater chance of exposing them and putting them in a compromising position. By a mirroring effect, we would pay more attention to our own behaviors and discourses, and develop the courage to face our own shortcomings, to acknowledge them and put off the compulsion to hide them.

As a result of individuals taking their own, and others', qualities and faults at face value, and by confronting the serious problems, we would be less inclined to lie or manipulate others, but would rather resort to constructive dialog in order to solve these problems. It seems evident that deep divergences in worldviews, cultures and personal beliefs, would be made much more understandable if we were to be more "empathic," that is, more sensitive to the other's mind state. A good telepathic or empathic grasp could endow us with an "inside view" of others, and give us the ability "to put ourselves in the others' shoes." The global benefit would be to diminish tensions and to reduce the instinctive refusal of whatever appears different. We would understand and welcome the richness of a world of divergent outlooks and perspectives, whose diversity is the true warrant, not only of global democracy, but also of boundless creativity, innovation, and evolution.

REFERENCES

Bechtel, W., and A. Abrahamsen (1990). *Connectionism and the mind: An introduction to parallel processing in networks.* New York: Blackwell.

Bohm, D. (1980). *Wholeness and the implicate order.* London: Routledge & Kegan Paul.

Braude, S. E. (1986). *The limits of influence: Psychokinesis and the philosophy of science.* New York: Routledge & Kegan Paul.

Broughton, R. (1991). *The controversial science.* New York: Ballantine.

Carington, W. (1945). *Telepathy.* London: Methuen.

Casti, J. (1989). *Lost paradigms.* New York: William Morrow.

Chalmers, D. (1996). Facing up to the problem of consciousness. In S.R. Hameroff, A.W. Kaszniak, and A.C. Scott, eds., *Toward a science of consciousness.* Cambridge, MA: MIT Press/Bradford.

Combs, A., and M. Holland (1995). *Synchronicity: Science, myth, and the trickster.* New York: Marlowe.

Costa de Beauregard, O. (1989). Relativity and probability, classical or quantal. In M. Kafatos, ed., *Bells theorem, quantum theory and conceptions of the universe* (pp. 117–125). Kluwer Academic Publishers.

Eccles, J.C. (1989). *Evolution of the brain: Creation of the self.* New York: Routledge.

Feinstein, D. and S. Krippner (1997). *The mythic path.* New York: Tarcher/Putnam.

Hameroff, S. R. (1994), Quantum coherence in microtubules: A neural basis for emergent consciousness? *Journal of Consciousness Studies* 1, 91–118.

Hardy, C. (1991). *Le vécu de la transe.* Paris: Le Dauphin.

_____. (1998). *Networks of meaning: A bridge between mind and matter.* Westport, CT: Praeger.

_____. (2000). Psi as a multilevel process: Semantic Fields Theory. *Journal of Parapsychology* 64, 73–94.

_____. (2001). Self-organization, self-reference and inter-influences in Multilevel Webs: Beyond causality and determinism. *Journal of Cybernetics and Human Knowing* 8, (3), 35–39.

_____. (2003a). Multilevel webs stretched across time: Retroactive and proactive inter-influences. *Systems Research and Behavioral Science* 20, 201–215.

_____. (2003b). *Complex intuitive dynamics in a systemic cognitive framework.* CD-ROM of the Proceedings of the 47th annual meeting of the International Society for the Systems Sciences (ISSS), Crete.

Herbert, N. (1985). *Quantum reality: Beyond the new physics.* New York: Doubleday.

Jahn, R. and B. Dunne (1987). *Margins of reality: The role of consciousness in the physical world.* New York: Harcourt, Brace, Jovanovich.

Jordan, M.J. (1986). An introduction to linear algebra in parallel distributed processing. In D. E. Rumelhart and J. L. McClelland, eds., *Explorations in the microstructure of cognition; Vol. 1: Foundations* (Chapter 9). Cambridge, MA: MIT Press/Bradford.

Jung, C.G. (1960). Synchronicity: An acausal connecting principle. Princeton, NJ: Princeton University Press.

Jung, C.G., and W. Pauli (1955). *The interpretation of nature and the psyche.* New York: Pantheon.

Koestler, A. (1972). *L'étreinte du crapaud.* Paris: Calmann-Lévy.

Lilly, J. (1981). *The deep self.* New York: Warner Books.

Lovelock, J., and L. Thomas (1990). *The Ages of Gaia.* New York: Bantam-Doubleday-Dell.

May, E. C., J. M. Utts, and S. J. P. Spottiswoode (1995). Decision augmentation theory: Toward a model of anomalous mental phenomena. *Journal of Parapsychology* **59**, 195–220.

Mishlove, J. (1993). *The roots of consciousness.* Oklahoma: Council Oak.

Murphy, G. (1945). Field theory and survival. *Journal of the American Society for Psychical Research* **67**, 117–129.

Murphy, M. (1949). Psychical research and personality. *Proceedings of the Society for Psychical Research* **49**, 1–15.

Nelson, R. D., G. J. Bradish, Y. H. Dobyns, B. J. Dunne, and R. G. Jahn (1996). FieldREG anomalies in group situations. *Journal of Scientific Exploration* **10**, 111–141.

Peat, F.D. (1987). *Synchronicity: The bridge between matter and mind.* New York: Bantam.

Price, H. (1939). Hauntings and the "psychic ether" hypothesis. *Proceedings of the Society for Psychical Research* **45**, 307–343.

Puthoff, H., R. Targ, and E. May (1981). Experimental psi research: Implications for physics. In R.G. Jahn, ed., *The role of consciousness in the physical world* (pp. 37–86). Boulder, CO: Westview.

Radin, D. (1997). *The conscious universe.* San Francisco: Harper-Edge.

Radin, D., and R. Nelson (1989). Evidence for consciousness-related anomalies in random physical systems, *Foundations of Physics* **19**, 1499–1514.

Radin, D., J. Rebman, and M. Cross (1996). Anomalous organization of random events by group consciousness. Two exploratory experiments. *Journal of Scientific Exploration* **10**, 143–168.

Rogo, S. (1975). *Parapsychology: A century of inquiry.* New York: Dell Publishing.

Roll, W. (1965). The psi field. *Proceedings of the Parapsychological Association* **1**, 32–65.

_____. (1983). The psi structure theory of survival. *Research In Parapsychology 1982.* Metuchen, NJ: Scarecrow Press.

Rosenthal, R. (1984). *Meta-analytic procedures for social research.* Newbury Park, CA: Sage.

Rumelhart, D., J. McClelland, and the PDP Research Group (1986). *Explorations in the microstructure of cognition: Vol. 1. Foundations* (Chapter 8). Cambridge, MA: MIT Press/Bradford.

Schmeidler, G. R., and R. A. McConnell (1973). *ESP and personality patterns.* 2nd edition. West-Connecticut: Greenwood Press.

Sheldrake, R. (1981). *A new science of life: The hypothesis of causative formation.* London: Blond and Briggs.

Stanford, R. G. (1974). An experimentally testable model for spontaneous psi events. I. Extrasensory events. *Journal of the American Society for Psychical Research* **68**, 321–356.

Sperry, W. (1976). Mental phenomena as causal determinants in brain functions, in G. Globus, G. Maxwell, and I. Savodnic, eds., *Consciousness and the brain.* New York: Plenum.

Teilhard de Chardin, P. (1965). *Phenomenom of man.* New York: Harper Torch Book.

Varela, F., E. Thompson, and E. Rosch (1991). *The embodied mind.* Cambridge, MA: The MIT Press.

Varvoglis, M.P. (1992). *La Rationalité de l'Irrationnel.* InterEditions: Paris.

_____. (1997). Conceptual frameworks for the study of transpersonal consciousness *World Futures* **48**, 105–113.

Vasiliev, L.L. (1976). *Experiments in distant influence.* New York: Dutton.

Von Lucadou, W., and K. Kornwaf (1983). On the limitations of psi: A system-theoretic approach. In W. Roll, J. Beloff, and R. White, eds., *Research in parapsychology 1982* (pp. 85–89). Metuchen, NJ: Scarecrow Press.

Von Lucadou, W. (1987). The model of pragmatic information (MPI), *Proceedings of the 30th Annual Convention of the Parapsychological Association.* Edinburgh, Scotland: Edinburgh University.

Walker, E. H. (1975). Foundations of paraphysical and parapsychological phenomena. In L. Oteri, ed., *Quantum physics and parapsychology* (pp. 1–53). New York: Parapsychology Foundation.

Walker, E. H. (1984). A review of criticisms of the quantum mechanical theory of psi phenomena, *Journal of Parapsychology* **48**, 277–332.

Zohar, D. (1990). *The Quantum self.* New York: Quill/William Morrow.

11

Subjective Anomalous Events: Perspectives for the Future, Voices from the Past

Vernon M. Neppe and John Palmer

This chapter is about the concept of Subjective Paranormal Experience (SPE), a term which was coined by the first author, Dr. Vernon M. Neppe. He and co-author Dr. John Palmer argue that the study of such experiences— subjective though they may be — is important for integrating parapsychology into the rest of science, particularly psychiatry. To illustrate their points, they analyze in detail the psychological and physiological theories proposed to explain the out-of-the-body experience (OBE) and the near-death experience (NDE). The authors predict some possible correlates of the OBE and NDE on the assumption that the various theories are true. (Editors)

> *"Those who forget the past are condemned to repeat it."*
> *Santayana 1905*

George Santayana's words are well remembered in any article dealing with the future of a discipline. The future for most scientific disciplines may be predictable: more research, data accumulation, theoretical models and practical applications. But we must learn from the past.

Parapsychology should be like this, too, but is different. This is so as the basic tenets under which it functions are disputed by the scientific community. Questions remain as to its basic legitimacy. We could continue trying to prove the same phenomena over and over again to satisfy the critics that ESP and PK exist or to argue the evidence on controversial areas such as survival. Parapsychology might not have advanced as rapidly as it could have over the past century, and yet has made great strides in rigidity of methodology and statistical analysis and awareness of confounding variables. In the future, we may see entirely different approaches from experts in physics and magic to study such areas. We recognize the importance of continuing this approach within our disciplines.

But also our approach emphasizes understanding how other disciplines may in the future integrate parapsychology and particularly subjective paranormal experiences. This involves detailed phenomenological analyses and classification of events so that we may compare and analyze similar experiences as well as achieve knowledge by perceiving the differences. It is clear to us that the future of parapsychology requires a classification system for anomalous events and that the human sciences must also be involved.

Subjective Paranormal Experiences

To the authors, one of the major theoretical changes which has occurred is the awareness that one cannot scientifically "prove" most spontaneous psi experiences. This means the rise of subjective analyses and this allows for a whole new perspective on "anomalistic psychology."

This theoretical shift from objectification to the subjective approach effectively impinges on two related disciplines, namely anomalistic psychology and what Neppe (1982) calls parapsichiatry — the discipline impinging on questions of psychopathology and anomalous brain function. Neppe (1980a) developed the term "subjective paranormal (Psi) experience" (SPE) to analyze reported paranormal events through their "subjective" experiences. This allows a more nonprejudicial interpretation of this phenomenon, or, for that matter, research on subjective phenomena of a possibly anomalous kind — ESP and PK. But effectively it allows such SPEs to be analyzed in the same context as anomalous cognitive brain phenomena such as "hallucinations," "flashbacks" and "déjà vu" or curious other-body distortions. In all these experiences, the distinguishing characteristic is their external nonvalidation and their subjective nature. For this reason, using quality and quantity of SPEs as a measure, criteria can be used to separate out a group of "subjective paranormal (SP) experients" from "nonexperients." These groups are usually derived from an "ostensibly normal" population (Neppe 1979). Experients have a large number of SPEs of predefined different qualities (e.g. waking ESP, OBEs, mediumship phenomena, PK); nonexperients have never acknowledged any SPEs (Neppe 1980b). This approach can allow analyses of specific aspects of brain physiology, anatomy or symptoms, or analyze some psychological function such as personality or attitudes. Patients with normal or abnormal brain functioning can be analyzed for such SPEs, just as they are for hallucinations or delusions, which are other kinds of subjective experiences (Neppe 1982). This subjective approach can diminish the threatening elements of parapsychology substantially. An objectively researched psi event necessarily constitutes a threat to the universality of currently accepted scientific theories, introducing entirely different philosophical frameworks. *These frameworks allow broader research approaches for parapsychology in the future.*

What common themes exist relating to the future of such research? Phenomena are generally perceived from within the framework of one's training. Persons who describe finding themselves outside their body such that they "could see their physical body from the outside, and could not move it," would be described by the parapsychologist as having had an "out-of-body experience." The psychiatrist may record the experience as pathological and "ego-splitting with sleep paralysis" (Neppe & Ewart Smith 1982). Both these specialists have described a single experience within the perspective of their discipline. From the parapsychological standpoint, frequent "out-of-body experiences" would be described as normal; the psychiatrist may delve deeper into such frequent episodes. He/she will generally regard this as a "symptom" of underlying abnormality and may explain ego-boundary disturbance possibly as due to a defense against anxiety. Thus basic terminology in psychiatry often labels SPEs psychopathologically using an all-encompassing medical model.

There is a need to reconcile these poles. *The first future requirement may be to educate psychiatrists and psychologists about basic approaches to parapsychology, and to reestablish diagnostic nomenclature and narrow what is regarded as abnormal.* Once parapsychology becomes part of a routine teaching curriculum in other scientific endeavors such as psychiatry and undergraduate psychology, the potential for others to research the area will increase by an order of magnitude.

The Subjective Approach to Anomalous Experience in the Psychopathological Context

This chapter is concerned with the future of phenomena generally classified as "psychic" ("psi," "paranormal"). It is not concerned with whether such experiences are objectively paranormal or not. It analyses only the phenomenological facets of such experience. These are essentially subjective. Whereas the most fundamental way to a nonprejudicial approach may be the SPE, the mention of terms like paranormality to the psychiatrist appears to prejudice the issue, encouraging the labeling of such phenomena along a psychopathological continuum (Neppe 1988a, 1988b).

Psychiatric understanding of SPEs is based on the medical model, which perceives subjective experience as "symptoms," and phenomena which one elicits via examination of the patient or subject as "signs." Because the majority of SPEs are perceptual in nature, these would be symptoms. Those SPEs which involve an objective change in objects or events (i.e. psychokinetic experiences) may theoretically allow the eliciting of positive physical signs because environmental change would have occurred. In practice, the information obtained is almost always retrospective, and even ostensible psychokinetic phenomena would be elicited via talking, and thus could technically be regarded as a symptom (Neppe 1993). *Again, extension of what is normal behavior to include SPEs is necessary.*

Normality and Psychopathology

It is necessary to distinguish the apparent normality of the paragnost — so-called psychic or diviner or mystic —from the perceived abnormality of the psychiatrically ill. Normality can be conceived, inter alia, within statistical, sociological and psychological frameworks. A practical conceptualization involves a functional definition with a sociocultural base: the normal person is able to cope adequately at intrapsychic, interpersonal, familial, occupational and leisure levels. Conversely, the psychiatrically ill person does not cope on at least one of these levels, often resulting in behavior perceived as abnormal within their culture.

Moreover, such behavior is ethical — appropriate within the fabric of their religious background and belief systems, including those pertaining to anomalous phenomena, and does not cause trauma to others. The normal person does not manifest biological symptoms in their coping (Neppe 1999).

Normality implies coping at the ethicobiopsychofamiliosociocultural level (Neppe 1999).

Paragnosts generally functions well within their community: they have no major problems with coping and are therefore perceived as "normal" (Greyson 1977). On the other hand, mentally ill persons may or may not perceive themselves as ill — if they do not (as occurs frequently in the psychotic, who by definition is out of touch with reality), their culture generally does (Neppe 1983c, 1984, 1988a, b). However, the paragnost may live in a culture which does not accept any purported paranormal experiences. The authors believe this rejection may cause the person to react in one of at least five fundamental ways. First, they may deny such experiences and consciously or unconsciously suppress them; this may express itself in a variety of compensatory behaviors. Second, they may become distressed because of their social rejection: this may interfere with their functioning and manifest as anxiety or other neurotic features. Third, they may find their idiosyncratic experiences difficult to handle. They may be uncertain as to whether their experiences are real or just a figment of their imagination: this may disturb their reality testing, as they have no baseline against which to compare their idiosyncratic experiences (Neppe 1987a). Consequently, psi experiences could potentially precipitate psychosis— subjective paranormal experience psychosis (Neppe 1984). Alternatively, paragnosts may reject the rejection by their culture and accept their experiences, thereby producing feelings of alienation. Finally, they may join a subculture which accepts them, although to the broader culture this shift in group identity may be interpreted as not coping (Dudley 2002; Lange and Houran 1997; Neppe and Ewart Smith 1982). There is a need to understand these different contexts of SP experients. *Future research may focus on the differences in SPEs in these different subgroups. Ultimately, pooled analyses across cultures may clarify the existence of such nosological groups, and the awareness of them may change the attitudes of the macroculture.*

Such knowledge is necessary anthropologically, as well. Certain non-Western cultures may accept as "psychic" people who exhibit the biochemical and clinical abnormalities of the psychotic or of the epileptic. This is so because their aberrant pattern of behavior may be perceived as part of the magical ritual of inducing psi, and their delusional thinking and hallucinatory perceptions may be interpreted as paranormal knowledge (Neppe & Ewart Smith 1982). *This awareness of the psychopathology spectrum in the future should include a carefully theorized set of criteria describing each kind of SPE.* This is analogous to the origins of the various editions of the psychiatric Diagnostic and Statistical Manual, for which the criteria for psychiatric conditions are initially theorized and then are empirically tested (Committee 2000). How the experiences are defined has a lot to do with how they have been studied, and thus what we know about them. Investigators should agree on what the definitions should be.

Much of the remainder of this chapter describes a way of developing criteria for future research as to the properties of an anomalous experience and therefore allow for analyses of common SPE epiphenomena, differentiating them from psychopathology.

Specific Psychiatric Examples: Hallucinations, Delusions and SPEs?

There is some literature —for example, Ehrenwald (1973, 1975), Ullman (1973, 1977), Eisenbud (1982a) and Neppe (1993)—dealing with the psychopathology of psi and SPEs. But there is very little literature discussing specifically the psychiatric interpretation of subjective paranormal experience. One useful perspective, however, is Reed's (1972) excellent treatise on "anomalous experience." This book outlines the cognitive psychological explanations of several kinds of claimed "psychic" experiences. Although there are certain psychiatric guiding principles to this problem, psychiatry itself is not a discipline which allows unanimous consensus in either eliciting or interpreting such "symptoms." Indeed, the major psychiatric concepts of "hallucinations," "delusions," and "disturbed ego-boundaries" all parallel the framework of the SPE.

A hallucination is a false sensory perception occurring in the absence of any relevant stimulation of the sensory modality involved. Hallucinations may involve any perceptual type — auditory, visual, olfactory, gustatory, kinesthetic, somatic, vestibular or tactile; occasionally they may even be synesthetic — where one modality is perceived as another (e.g. hearing a color). Hallucinations are generally regarded as "abnormal" by psychiatrists except when they occur during certain physiological altered states of consciousness, e.g. just prior to sleep (i.e. hypnagogic) and while waking from sleep, i.e. hypnopompic (Neppe & Ewart Smith 1982). We will analyze these briefly.

Hallucinations are, generally, regarded as indicative of a psychotic condition when they occur spontaneously, are frequent, or are of long duration. They often have complex content, intrude on the whole personality and refer to the percipient himself. They have cognitive or emotional significance, with their content frequently interpreted by psychiatrists as part of the experient's needs or fears. They may occur suddenly, fully formed and clear; they involve a conviction as to their being outside the person's own space (i.e. they are external and objective), and they are regarded as concrete reality. Usually they are not under voluntary control. Thus, hallucinations in the psychotic have a special form (Neppe & Ewart Smith 1982).

However, hallucinations have also been described in a significant proportion of ostensibly normal people, far higher than the one in 30 or so that we would expect to exhibit psychotic thought in the absence of recreational drugs. Three British surveys, each 50 years apart—the first very large (Sidgwick & committee 1894) involving 17,000 not quite randomly chosen subjects, the second smaller but still substantial (West 1943) involving 1519 subjects—found life-time incidences of 9.9 percent and 14.3 percent respectively (West 1948a, 1948b). Sidgwick's study, although limited methodologically by today's standards, found that the number of unexpected death coincidences involving hallucinations exceeded chance probability by a factor of 440 (Sidgwick & committee 1894). Finally, Ohayon's (2000) study in Britain, Germany and Italy used representative samples of the noninstitutionalized general population, aged 15 years or over (N=13,057). Overall, two-fifths of the sample reported hallucinatory experiences, and about a fifth reported having these experiences less than once a month. Daytime hallucinations were reported by a quarter of the sample, many fold the incidence of psychotic disorders in this sample (Ohayon 2000). Because of this, parapsychological hypotheses have been suggested (Neppe & Ewart Smith 1982).

SPEs commonly involve hallucinations. They may particularly involve extrasensory perception (ESP) occurring while awake, and most commonly the perception of "presences," particularly "apparitional experiences," which are well-developed presences, usually visual, with or without other sensory modalities. Hallucinations occur as detailed waking ESP when a paragnost sees, hears, or otherwise experiences impressions seeming to come from outside themselves, relating to events in the past, present or future. They may interpret such a spontaneous phenomenon as "paranormal" if it were unusual and of a noninferential character, and if it had a close temporal and meaningful relationship to an actual event, which they may or usually may not be able to confirm. Thus, a dichotomy exists pertaining to hallucinations in the parapsychological-psychiatric context. The two poles of criteria listed may, theoretically, easily differentiate such subjective experiences, but at times the differentiation is muddier. These SPEs are hallucinatory in that there is no relevant external stimulus to induce such a perception. They appear to occur commonly in "normal" people. Thus, Neppe (1981) found that 59.6 percent of his 57 elderly subjects had perceived "presences," 14 percent frequently and Haraldsson et al.'s (1977)

Icelandic survey showed that 31 percent of his population ($N=902$) had experiences of apparitions of the dead and the living.

The psychiatric interpretation of *presences* usually relates to an increased level of suggestibility that fulfills a need within the generally depressed, elderly, widowed percipient. The sense of "presence" is culturally perpetuated by the legend of such occurrences, and is predisposed to by fatigue and loneliness. It pertains to an apparent cognitive set of impressions resulting from the patient's pathology (Reed 1972). The experience is not necessarily hallucinatory; instead, it may be illusory—in this instance, a special perceptual stimulus (such as a curtain moving in the dark) which is misinterpreted. It is highly probable that the hallucination-illusion explanation of the "sense of presence" is the most suitable one for the majority of such experiences. However, it is more difficult to explain cases of collective apparitions (40 percent according to Tyrrell)—and some of the detailed cases described by Tyrrell (1953), and later by Green and MacCreery (1975).

In contrast to the hallucination is the *pseudo-hallucination*: this is an unprovoked perception experienced *within* the percipient's inner space (i.e., in his head); it is subjective, does not appear to be part of external reality, and is nonsubstantial. The "pseudo-hallucination" is probably the most common kind of psychiatric equivalent to the ESP "feeling" or "impression," or the paragnost suddenly and often spontaneously obtaining an impression inside their head of an event which turns out to be contemporaneous, (i.e., in the present), precognitive (i.e., in the future) or—rarely—retrocognitive (i.e., in the past) (Neppe 1983c). It is usually auditory or visual, but it is sometimes just described as "meaningful," not involving specific modalities. Frequently, such an "impression" has a great deal of conviction. It is usually fragmentary and often colored by the conscious or unconscious images, memories or emotions of the percipient (Reed 1972). As with the hallucination proper, the interpretation of such a pseudo-hallucination should be in the full context of who is experiencing it, and whether it is compromising the subject's normal function.

A third ambiguous symptom is the *impression or feeling*. These again become strongly fixed in the experient's belief system. They may rise to the level of a belief, the truth of which is firmly held despite others regarding such a belief as patently untrue or extremely unlikely. The experient may, further, not regard such an impression as illogical. In this instance, the "impression" may fulfill qualities of a delusion. To other members of his culture it would be regarded as a "false," fixed belief that is held against objective and obvious contradictory proof to the contrary. The paragnost and the parapsychologist may regard these impressions as SPEs, but the psychiatrist would see them as delusional (Neppe 1983c; Reed 1972).

Delusional thinking is a hallmark of psychosis, as its content indicates that the experient is out of touch with reality. In the context of the paragnost, his hallucinatory or pseudo-hallucinatory perception may lead to interpretations in which he firmly believes; alternatively, he may develop a vague knowledge (a "feeling") of some kind of impending event, about a particular object or person. This appears irrational and may therefore be a *delusional idea*; the SP-experient may describe first "a sinister, awry sense of something being different," and this *delusional atmosphere* may lead them to be "aware" of certain specific or vague information. Thus, such awareness, interpreted as psychic, may alert the experient to certain information on which they may act. The situation may be further complicated by the "psychic" believing that outside agencies such as dead spirits or a higher power are guiding them. But to the psychiatrist, these fixed ideas are either delusional or perceived as not deviant within the spiritualistic or other validating microculture to which the "psychic" may belong. The situation is even more complicated, however: Rogo (1981) stresses how psychotics may be drawn into the psychic community and have their delusions reinforced. On the other hand, given that many normal functioning "psychics" may have belief systems which contradict their wider culture, would this imply they are psychotic? Unfortunately, the post-hoc validation of events cannot be interpreted as necessarily helpful. Thus, if the psychic's "delusion" comes true, doctors cannot use this fact to relabel it as "nondelusional": psychiatrists must base their interpretations on the here-and-now, realizing that future objective validation of the ostensibly strange ideas may never occur. *Clearly, these are important areas to research in the future. The very fabric of SPEs must be properly defined.*

Neppe (1984) argues that a prime differentiator of psychotic and psychic delusions must relate to the degree to which the experience interferes with the experient's functioning. The degree of self-reference and influence these ideas have most probably will parallel the actual degree of psychopathology. For example, a patient was presented for the first time with the awareness that she will die that year in December and was able to elaborate numerous previous subjective paranormal experiences. She became extremely anxious, because of, or concomitant with, her awareness. Such awareness is, in our opinion, delusional, irrespective of whether the self-fulfilling prophecy of "dying in December" occurs, and irrespective of whether she has influenced her microculture to accept her awareness. It requires management because it constitutes a danger to the patient.

Another guiding principle in analyzing SPEs psychiatrically is the concept of "ego-boundary disturbance." The "ego" is that part of one's psychological functioning that mediates between the person — their instincts, needs and moral behavior — and the reality of the outside world. Intactness of the ego-boundary relates to the ability of the ego to differentiate the real from the unreal and to discriminate between self and not-self (Neppe & Ewart Smith 1982).

Ego-boundaries are characteristically greatly disturbed in schizophrenia, as the patient has a disorder in which his thoughts, emotions, drives and instincts may be perceived by him as controlled or influenced by external agencies. Alternatively, patients may believe that their thoughts are not private, that they are being extracted from them, broadcast, or interfered with or blocked. Greyson (1977) points out how such ego-boundary disturbances could be regarded as disturbances of extra-sensory communication and, in fact, how commonly schizophrenics believe they have telepathic abilities (40 percent; $N = 20$). Such impressions could be falsely based. Studying the incidence of SPEs and psi abilities in psychotics by developing measuring instruments and procedures better adapted to the psychotic is important for future research. However, patients may be too paranoid to report such SPEs. Ullman, in fact, stresses his clinical impression that the prepsychotic is more sensitive to ESP than the normal. Such a finding led Greyson (1977) to question whether telepathy in mental illness was the deluge causing illness or the delusion — a result of illness.

Another condition in which ego-boundaries are grossly disturbed is hysterical dissociation. In dissociative states there is a sudden, temporary alteration in consciousness, identity, or motor behavior. Subjects may not remember what they have done during this period, and one extreme example of dissociation (either hysterical or schizophrenic) is multiple personality, now called dissociative identity disorder (Committee 2000). The relevance of such phenomena to the trance state in mediumship is obvious. Trance mediumship can be explained as an altered state of consciousness in which dissociation occurs such that a group of unconscious mental processes in the medium may be verbalized or otherwise expounded, and yet is denied by the medium as having its source in their unconscious. It is easy to see how such phenomena can be attributed to outside agencies such as discarnate spirits.

Such studies as the famous "Philip experiments" in Canada (Owen with Sparrow 1976) and similar replications elsewhere of material deriving from the unconscious in trance mediumship, received from a specially developed fictitious "discarnate" personality, suggest that the sitters' unconscious may play major roles (Owen 1978). *The replication and further development of such experiments is certainly important for the future of para-psychology.*

In the future, there is a need to study the impressions of the psychotic and nonpsychotic psychiatric patient in a nonprejudicial form. Neppe has revised one of his instruments—the INSET (Inventory of Neppe of Symptoms of Epilepsy and the Temporal Lobe)—to include more items pertaining to possible SPEs. It is relatively rare in his outpatient population for patients to deny all events on the INSET, despite information to the contrary. Because other validity scales such as those in the MMPI-2 are routinely used, as well as numerous other related tests, Neppe has found he is likely to uncover those who are denying such events despite their occurrence. This is a ripe area for future research. As an aside, so is studying patients with possible temporal lobe disorders or seizures in the same way (Palmer & Neppe 2003).

Neppe has suggested a resolution to the diagnostic nomenclature dilemma at two levels—firstly, the functional, and secondly, the psychopharmacologic. Using the functional framework of the ethicobiopsychofamiliosociocultural system (Neppe 1999), defects at any of these levels producing noncoping, or nonoptimal coping, can be perceived as psychopathologic. No matter how strange the patient's experiences are, they are not perceived as abnormal unless they distinctly interfere with the patient's functional and coping skills (Neppe 1984, 1988b). This is a good, basic, empirically derived definition that allows paragnosts to experience realities which others may not be able to conceive of, but which do not produce labels of psychopathology.

The second, related approach, actually fits within this first, and involves emphasizing the biological components of psychiatric disorder (Neppe & Wessels 1979) by analyzing psychopharmacologic responsiveness and toleration of psychotropic medication to psychiatric diagnoses. This is a very conventional, useful, underused and underemphasized diagnostic test. The normal person could not handle such crazy medications. Whereas labels such as schizophrenia, schizoaffective illness, organic delusional syndrome, or mood disorder may have descriptive meaning, the proper diagnostic classification of patients may be far more homogeneously represented by this responsiveness to specific combinations of psychotropic medication, irrespective of diagnosis. *Future research may allow differentiation of the biochemical tolerance and responsiveness indicators of psychopathology from the chemically different paragnosts. It may also allow a fertile source for studying SPEs in the context of seizure disorders,* a method that has been used by the authors in a population in the United States (Palmer & Neppe 2003).

An Example of a Legitimate Approach: The OBE and NDE

Let us look at specific content details of SPEs that require phenomenological analysis. We briefly take the *out-of-body experience* (OBE) and the *near-death experience* (NDE) as examples. The NDE is somewhat more complex than the OBE, and the OBE is often a component of the NDE. NDEs vary widely in content, and frequently occurring components of NDEs have been noted (Moody 1975, Ring 1980). At the cognitive level, they include, in addition to the experience of being outside the body, passing through a dark tunnel, being bathed in a bright white or yellow light, meeting with deceased relatives or religious personages, and a rapid, panoramic recall of one's past life experiences. At the emotional level, the tone is usually positive, involving a sense of calmness, peace, and joy. However, in a minority of cases, often associated with attempted suicide, the mood is decidedly negative (Ring 1980).

The future must contain definitions of precise SPEs. We believe these definitions should reflect what has motivated investigators to study the phenomenon, as represented by the label they chose for them. In the case of OBEs (at least for parapsychologists), this is the possibility that the experience might be literally true, in the sense that a mind or soul leaves the body during an OBE. From a phenomenological viewpoint, this possibility is best represented by the conviction that the experience gives to the person that they were really "out." (We are not suggesting that this conviction is valid as scientific evidence of externalization, only that it captures what investigators have found of most interest about the phenomenon — subjective not objective paranormal experiences.)

This principle led Palmer (1978a) to define the OBE as any experience that leads the person to conclude, at the time of the experience, that their consciousness is localized in space outside the body. He stresses "at the time of the experience" and also "localized" to distinguish the OBE from the mystical experience, in which the person experiences their consciousness as being universal, or "everywhere."

This definition is generally very broad. But Michael Whiteman (1980) conceived the OBE even more broadly. He described different stages of separation of the out-of-body experience, including the sense of being out of the body but, nevertheless, unable to subjectively "see" the physical body. Whiteman also described how in some OBEs, the consciousness is not necessarily detached but is both in and out of the body. Whiteman's conceptualization, therefore, includes states of subjective nonseparation of consciousness from the body and separation and nonseparation. Conversely, an example of a limiting criterion would be Tart (1975). He, for example, has argued that the experience must be real in the sense that "consciousness seems completely clear and normal" (p. 149). We think such limitations are premature. The broader definitions prime investigators to ask a crucial question, namely, what kinds of experiential content and quality generally lead people to conclude that they are out of their body? *Future research may want to debate exactly what these lists would contain.* No experiences that have met the conviction test in a nontrivial number of cases should be *excluded* from the OBE category.

The above rationale can also be applied to NDEs. The interest in NDEs arose from dying people having mental imagery of a quality that did not appear possible given their compromised brain function (Morse & Neppe 1991). Just as with OBEs, NDEs were seen as providing at least suggestive evidence of the mind acting independently of the brain. This led to a definition of NDEs based, once again, not on the phenomenology of the experiences, but on the external circumstances under which they occur, i.e., impending death. This rationale is clearly represented by Moody's (1975) original definition of the NDE: "any conscious perceptual experience which takes place during ... an event in which a person could very easily die or be killed ... but nonetheless survives, and continues physical life" (p. 124).

Once the list of experiences that meet the criteria for OBEs and NDEs have been established, *these experiences not only can but should be studied in other contexts as well.* For example, the realistic imagery of passing through a dark tunnel is not only appropriate but desirable to study in any other contexts where it might occur. Indeed, the range of circumstances under which it occurs could provide valuable clues toward its explanation.

The Multiplicity Problem

The primary purpose of defining OBEs and NDEs is to demarcate the subject matter. Both the OBE and (especially) the NDE include under their umbrella a large number of specific experiences or types of experience. In fact, it is a huge mistake to talk about *the* out-of-body experience and *the* near-death experience. Rather, we should be talking about out-of-the body experience*s* and near-death experience*s* (plural). Nowhere is the problem more acute than in the physiology of NDEs. Several theories have been proposed to explain the physiology of *the* NDE (Greyson 2000), and all of them have been attacked, justifiably, for applying to some aspects of *the* experience and not others. In the future, there may never be a single physiological explanation for *the* NDE because there is no such thing as *the* NDE, a point recognized early on by Blackmore (1992).

One reason why a single physiological explanation for all the NDE components is so unlikely is that even within the ND context the experiences arise from a variety of different neurological circumstances (Blackmore 1992). Recall that NDEs struck the interest of investigators primarily because people with compromised brain function due to events like anoxia were having experiences not to be expected under those circumstances. This is fine for people who are close to death as a result of a debilitating illness, but what about those perfectly healthy folks who have a brush with death because of a deliberate choice (i.e., suicide) or a fall from a cliff? Do their brains have the same capacity at the time of the experience as a person undergoing a cardiac arrest? We assume not. This implies we should develop subcategories of NDEs based on the neurological circumstances at the time of their occurrence. For example, Twemlow, Gabbard, and Coyne (1982) were able through the use of cluster analysis to classify NDE components in terms of five preexisting conditions: low stress, emotional stress, intoxication, cardiac arrest, and anesthesia. Although this is not exactly what we proposed above, it does show that certain groups of NDE components tend to cluster together and these clusters arise from different preexisting circumstances. We might ask, for example, if there are any specific neurological consequences of a cardiac arrest that would likely result in the particular phenomena found in Twemlow et al.'s (1982) cardiac arrest cluster, as opposed to or more so than those found in other clusters? Such statistical techniques should be used to study other SPEs as well.

The multiplicity problem is somewhat less acute for psychological explanations of NDEs, at least insofar as motivation is concerned, because crucial antecedent circumstances are likely to be more uniform. Regardless of whether a person is close to death as a result of a cardiac arrest, a fall, or a pending suicide, we can safely assume that death is on their mind and, at least subconsciously, evokes some fear. This is not to say that finding a uniform psychological explanation of NDEs will be easy and it may prove impossible, but at least it is a goal worthy of effort.

Theories of the OBE and NDE: Current Status and Future Prospects

In this section, we will first describe current theorizing on the OBE and NDE at both the psychological and physiological levels. Pointing toward the future, we will then list some ways in which these theories can be tested, a process that will lead to their further development or, on the contrary, their abolition.

Psychological Theories of the OBE

About 25 years ago, Palmer published a psychological theory of the OBE, which dealt primarily with the motivation behind the experience (Palmer 1978b). Although the theory employs some Freudian descriptors, it is not intended as an endorsement of Freud's theory. The Freudian terms in the theory are not the ones that are most controversial and the processes they refer to have been incorporated in dynamic psychology generally.

According to this theory, the OBE begins with a subtle change in the person's body concept, instigated by a change in the proprioceptive feedback the person receives from their body. The person should only be vaguely aware of the change, if aware of it at all. This alteration in the body concept threatens the person's self-concept, or sense of individual identity, again at an unconscious level. The mind then struggles to reinstate some concept of the self, but because the threat is unconscious, the resolution is governed by what Freud called the primary process, which creates fantasies or hallucinations that are guided by the same "irrational" principles that govern the content of our dreams. On some occasions, this unconscious process results in an OBE, which redefines the self as an entity localized in space outside the body. The experience must be realistic in order to convince the ego that the new self-identity is genuine. However, the OBE is only one of several options the person may employ to reestablish self identity. Another option is the lucid dream, through which the person establishes their identity as a dreamer having a dream. The OBE ends when the establishment of the identity is complete or when some external stimulus rouses the ego and a secondary process solution, which is always preferable to a primary process solution (except perhaps in a baby). In either case, the beginning of the secondary process solution is heralded by the person returning to the body and "waking up."

The theory addresses voluntarily induced OBEs by making reference to Freud's concept of "regression in the service of the ego": the ego consciously accesses the primary process material that led to the OBE and uses it to reproduce the experience or something like it, much as an abstract painter like Van Gogh would access unconscious material for his art. The theory predicts that only people who have had spontaneous OBEs can induce them voluntarily, because the memory of the spontaneous experience is needed as a template for the induced one.

The theory as such has never been tested, but there are data from the existing literature that support its premises, particularly the one about changes in the body concept preceding the OBE. The experience has been known to occur as the result of anesthetics, and in relaxed and hypnagogic states, all of which involve a reduction in proprioceptive stimulation. Additional evidence comes from a series of studies in which physiological recordings were taken while persons were experiencing voluntarily induced OBEs. These persons included Robert Monroe (Tart 1967), Keith Harary (Morris et al. 1978), Ingo Swann (Osis & Mitchell 1977), and a "Miss Z" (Tart 1968). The most consistent finding among all these studies was a reduction or lack of eye movements during the experience. Swann even reported that he intentionally blocked his eye movements during the experience. This finding is relevant to the theory because the proprioceptive feedback from eye movements can be conceived of as an important vehicle for establishing one's physical identity vis-à-vis the external environment. The high positive correlation between incidence of OBEs and lucid dreams is consistent with the notion from the theory that they have comparable functions (Palmer 1979).

Since the publication of the theory, two other major theories have been proposed. Irwin (1985, 2000) traces the origin of the OBE to extremely high or low cortical arousal creating a state of high absorption, accompanied by dissociation from proprioceptive stimuli. In support of this concept, Irwin (2000) found a measure of somatic dissociation to predict the occurrence and frequency of OBEs. The dissociation results in the impression that consciousness resides outside the body in a floating self. The proprioceptive image is transformed into a visual experience through synesthesia, or cross-modal processing. Supporting this latter notion is a report of an experimental subject describing a spontaneous, unsolicited OBE while engaged in producing synesthetic experiences (Holt-Hansen 1976). The realism of the OBE is attributed to the high absorption, and the content to the nature of the person's short-term needs.

The third major theory focuses on our cognitive models of reality (Blackmore 1992). In ordinary waking life, these models are guided by sensory input. In the absence of such input, the mind creates alternative models, one of which could be an OBE. Supporting this model are data indicating that OB experients who can induce the experience voluntarily are more adept than others at manipulating spatial imagery, such as being able to reproduce what a room with furniture would look like to a person hovering near the ceiling (Cook & Irwin 1983).

These three theories approach OBEs from different perspectives, and for this reason they are more complementary than competitive. We have no difficulty incorporating key components of the other two theories into Palmer's. Irwin's notion that absorption keeps the OB experient away from focusing on body sensations is very compatible with Palmer's notion that changes in the body concept must remain primarily unconscious if a primary process solution is to be provoked. Like Irwin, we also conceive of the changes in body concept as being primarily in the direction of a reduction of proprioceptive stimulation, although that was not explicitly stated (Palmer 1978b). Finally, this theory does not deal at all with the mechanism by which the proprioceptive experience becomes a visual experience, and we are delighted to incorporate synesthesia as the needed principle. Regarding Blackmore, although Palmer's theory states that the primary process is the main source for the OBE, there is room for stored memories of spatial configurations also to be drawn upon, as they satisfy the need for the experience to be realistic.

Palmer published his theory of OBEs shortly after Moody's (1975) seminal book on NDEs appeared, and at that time he was not sensitized to the close connection between OBEs and NDEs. As that is no longer the case, some discussion of how his theory might apply to NDEs is appropriate. Palmer's OBE theory is most compatible with those theories of the NDE that treat the latter as a psychological reaction to the threat of death (e.g., Ehrenwald 1974; Noyes & Kletti 1976; Pfister 1930). Fear of loss of self-identity and fear of death clearly bear some resemblance to each other from a psychodynamic perspective. Noyes and Kletti's (1976) theory has been criticized because of their embrace of depersonalization as a metaphor for how the fear of death is reacted to in NDEs. Critics have pointed out, for example, that OBEs are not characteristic of depersonalization, and that depersonalization is experienced as negative whereas most NDEs are positive (Gabbard & Twemlow 1984). But one can still adopt the overriding notion of the NDE as a psychodynamic response to the fear of death without embracing depersonalization.

Although ND experients do not score particularly high on measures of dissociation, it has been reliably found that they often were victims of abuse in childhood (Irwin 1993), a well-known precursor of dissociative tendencies later in life. Perhaps many learn how to dissociate as children to defend themselves against the psychological effects of the abuse. These "skills" remain dormant but could be evoked if the person is confronted with a comparable trauma, the fear of impending death, as adults. The capacity to dissociate could be seen as favoring NDEs, because dissociation can be conceptualized as a breakdown of the barrier between the conscious and unconscious mind. Expressions of dissociation are often unconscious, as evidenced by its starkest manifestation, dissociative identity disorder (Committee 2000).

Some theorists who think of the NDE as a response to the fear of death have invoked what Greyson (2000) calls the expectancy model to explain the content of NDEs. According to this view, "NDEs are products of imagination, constructed from one's personal and cultural expectations, to protect oneself from facing the threat of death" (Greyson 2000, p. 332). This model has been criticized on the grounds that NDEs often contradict people's expectations (Abramovitch 1988; Ring 1984). Palmer's OBE theory simply states that the content is influenced by the person's "psychological set." For the NDE, this psychological set would be awareness of impending death, and the theory would simply say that this awareness would lead to death-related imagery in the NDE, which may or may not be concordant with what the person expects death or the afterlife to be like. In terms of Palmer's theory, we would want to reject the word "expectation" and replace it with "hope," which could be unconscious. For instance, atheists would presumably expect that there is no afterlife, but because of our basic survival instincts, at some level they likely would hope they are wrong, and their unconscious mind might draw upon this hope, plus their knowledge of how some religion depicts the afterlife (or even their fantasy of what an afterlife might be like *if* it existed) to script an NDE.

Critics of the explanatory model also have pointed out that sometimes children too young to internalize notions of the afterlife seem to experience NDEs strikingly similar to those of adults (Bush 1991; Serdahely 1991). But if they occurred before the child developed language skills, they must by definition be based on retrospective accounts that could be biased due to faulty recollection either of the content of the experience or when it occurred (Greyson 2000). If the NDE were reported by the child, then the child is old enough to have incorporated relevant information from the environment. Moreover, Serdahely's comparisons were based on structural aspects of the NDE, such as conformity to Ring's (1980) stages, rather than the content of the experience. It is the latter that is most relevant to cultural conditioning. Finally, if it could be established that the child reported material that he had never come into contact before (which is very difficult to prove), we would have to invoke a paranormal hypothesis, most likely ESP.

Physiological Theories of the NDE

The theories discussed in the preceding section are psychological and do not address the question of what the brain is doing during OBEs and NDEs. For that, we need physiological theories. Psychological and physiological theories should not be treated as competing with one another but as representing different levels of analysis. On the other hand, it is desirable that they intersect with one another such that, for example, the parts of the brain that are hypothesized to be involved in particular kinds of

OBE/NDE phenomenology are known to produce the corresponding types of cognition in other contexts.

There is virtually no discussion of physiology in the OBE literature, whereas there is quite a bit in the NDE literature. Not surprisingly, NDE theorists have focused on physiological processes that are characteristic of the dying brain. The most pervasive of such mechanisms in this literature is anoxia or hypoxia, the lack of oxygen to the brain. A challenge to these theories is that one would expect lack of oxygen to lead to deterioration of cognitive function, as with delirium. NDEs, on the other hand, are characterized by imagery, particularly visual imagery, that is often vivid and as realistic as sensory perception. The standard way around this problem is to postulate that inhibitory neurons are affected by the anoxia sooner than excitatory neurons, resulting thereby in disinhibition and cognitive arousal (Saavedra-Aguilar & Gómez-Jeria 1989). Such theories must assume that in NDEs the anoxia occurs very gradually, so that the time interval between the collapse of the inhibitory neurons and the collapse of the excitatory neurons is long enough to support a meaningful experience. Exactly what the anoxia causes to happen in the brain is not always specified. Morse and Neppe (1991) pointed out that in the OBE and NDE context memories are remembered in a coma despite ostensible inability to form memories during that time. Some theorists say that anoxia leads to microseizures in the temporal lobes, particularly the limbic system, that result in hallucinations (Carr 1974; Persinger 1999; Rodin 1984; Saavedra-Aguilar & Gómez-Jeria 1989). Another proposed explanation draws on the fact that some phenomenological aspects of NDEs, such as tunnels, bright lights, and encounters with mythical beings, are produced in response to the anesthetic ketamine (Jansen 1997; Jourdan 1994). Specifically, Jansen says that anoxia causes the release of glutamate, which if left unchecked would kill off neurons by overwhelming their NMDA receptors. This toxic reaction is blocked by ketamine, and Jansen postulates that so-called "endopsychosins," which have the same protective as well as psychoactive properties as ketamine, are produced endogenously. Morse, Venecia, and Milstein (1989) suggested that NDEs arising from psychological stress or certain drugs (LSD, ketamine) are caused by disinhibition of neurons in the temporal cortex and hippocampus, mediated by an increase in serotonin. Neppe (1989) focused on anomalous temporal lobe function, not as a limitation but as a possible state or trait that may allow subjects to experience endogenous or exogenous NDE realities that otherwise could not be experienced.

The euphoria that often accompanies NDEs is attributed to the release of various opiates or neuropeptides in the brain in response to stress

(Blackmore 1993; Carr 1984; Persinger 1999; Rodin 1984; Saavedra-Aguilar & Gómez-Jeria 1989). These include endorphins, enkephalins, and ACTH. Persinger once again specifies the mechanism as the production of microseizures in the limbic system, and he notes further that if the amplitude and coverage of these microseizures advances beyond a certain point the positive effect turns into negative effect, which could account for the modicum of unpleasant NDEs (Persinger 1999).

The more global theories are often adapted to account for specific NDE characteristics. Blackmore (1993) attributes the tunnel phenomenon to the progressive disinhibition of neurons in the occipital cortex, starting with those dedicated to the center of the visual field and gradually extending to the periphery (Blackmore 1993). Persinger (1999) suggests a very similar if not identical process. Siegel (1984) found reports of tunnel effects in the early stages of hallucinatory drug experiences, interpreting them as the action of phosphenes caused by the firing of neurons in the eye. Drab (1981) attributed the sense of movement through the tunnel to disturbances in the vestibular system of the cerebellum. The well-known astronomer Carl Sagan (1979) speculated that moving through the tunnel was a memory of passing through the birth canal, but this theory was discredited when Blackmore (1983) demonstrated that persons born by Caesarian section also experienced the tunnel phenomenon. Wettach (2000) picked up on the same general theme, speculating that the tunnel experience represents a memory of life inside the uterus.

Another distinctive NDE experience is the panoramic life review. Persinger (1999) attributes the flood of images to disinhibition of neurons in the hippocampus, while the simultaneous distortion of the sense of time is attributed to the disruption of the mesiodorsal thalamus or its input from the amygdala. Wettach (2000), on the other hand, attributes it to the reemergence of the memory fragments from the cerebral cortex as its function returns in the later stages of the NDE.

Finally, what do these theorists have to say about the OBE component of the NDE? The theorist who has devoted the most attention to the OBE is Persinger (1999), who thinks of the OBE as an alteration in the sense of self. He attributes it to what he calls "vectorial hemisphericity," which he defines as "a right-hemisphere homologue to the left hemisphere sense of self" (p. 91). Specifically, it occurs when left-hemisphere activation accompanies sudden right-hemisphere deactivation. Wettach (2000), who focuses more on the floating sensation, attributes the OBE to activity of the midbrain unaccompanied by the orienting information and spatial cues normally supplied by other parts of the nervous system.

It is important to note that all of these theories are speculative and based on little if any physiological data from actual NDEs. Rather, the speculations are grounded on knowledge of the functions that certain parts of the brain perform generally. There is, however, a modicum of data derived from circumstances in which epileptic patients underwent intracranial stimulation of specific parts of the brain in preparation for surgery. In a classic study, Penfield (1958) found that a patient reported sensations characteristic of OBEs when the temporal cortex was stimulated. More recently, Blanke, Ortigue, Landis and Seeck (2002) noted that a patient reported seeing part of her body from above, as well as a variety of other somatosensory and vestibular images, while stimulation was applied to the right angular gyrus. The fact that these two cases involved stimulation of different parts of the brain illustrates that it is unlikely we will be able to link OBEs and NDEs to particular brain loci (Neppe 2002). On the other hand, as noted above, OBEs and NDEs are really a range of experiences, and it is possible we might have more success localizing specific types of images, such as seeing the body from above. Looking at the matter a bit more broadly, most of the theorists consider the temporal lobes, especially the limbic system, to be the seat of most OBE/NDE phenomena.

Finally, it should be pointed out that these physiological theories have problems beyond their speculative nature. To establish a really satisfying link between a certain NDE component and a particular brain function, we would like two circumstances to be true: (1) that such experiences occur only when that brain function occurs, and (2) that no other types of experience occur when that brain function occurs. The physiological theories of NDEs meet neither of these conditions. OBEs, for example, frequently occur in various stages of sleep and relaxation when there is no threat of death whatsoever. Drug theories, such as those drawing analogies to ketamine, have been criticized on the grounds of marked differences between the typical drug experience and the typical OBE/NDE (e.g., Jansen 1997; Morse 1997). Point (1) has been countered by pointing out that experiences can have multiple causes (Blackmore 1993), but we don't know what those other physiological causes or correlates are. Point (2), that the same physiological processes can produce different experiences, tells us that our knowledge of the mechanisms causing particular experiences is incomplete. There must be unknown factors that determine why, say, anoxia sometimes produces experience X and at other times experience Y. The progressive inhibition hypothesis addresses this problem to some extent for anoxia, but more is needed.

Some Predictions

The various theories outlined above were formulated to be testable, in principle if not in practice. Although various kinds of data have already been cited in support of some of them, their credibility would be heightened if, in addition, they could generate hypotheses or predictions that are subsequently confirmed.

As a general rule, we think that, especially in the case of NDEs, predictions should be made for specific NDE characteristics such as the OBE, passing through the tunnel, and the past-life review. Where this is not allowed by our current knowledge, predictions must be made for OBEs/ NDEs generically, but the data should be analyzed for each characteristic, such that networks of correlates can be uncovered for them individually.

Space limitations generally prevent us from discussing the methodology for testing these hypotheses, but such methods can be developed by suitably trained professionals.

1) *Field-independent persons and persons with strong body images will be more likely to have OBEs than mystical experiences, and vice-versa*: Persons who conceive of their bodies as separate from the external environment will maintain this distinction in their hallucinatory experiences, whereas those for whom such boundaries are weak or nonexistent would be more likely to see themselves as merging with the environment or being "one" with it.

2) *People who are close to death will be more likely to have OBEs if they score high on measures of absorption and synesthesia than if they score low on such measures.* The idea here is simply that what has been found for OBEs in non-near-death contexts should also be found in near-death contexts. It is also noteworthy that the Tellegen Absorption Scale, or TAS (Tellegen 1982) contains several synesthesia questions. It would be interesting to score these two components of the scale separately to see if they both predict NDEs, as theory would suggest.

3) *Experimental inductions of OBEs will be most successful with persons who score high on measures of absorption and synesthesia.*

4) *Only persons who have had spontaneous OBEs will be able to induce them voluntarily.*

5) *Persons who can induce OBEs voluntarily will be better at manipulating spatial imagery than other persons, including persons who have had only spontaneous OBEs.*

6) *The induction of OBEs will be facilitated by the application of local anes-*

thetics to reduce or eliminate proprioceptive stimulation from eye (muscle) movements.

7) *People who are close to death will be more likely to have NDEs if they score high on measures of fear of death, or even loss of self-identity, than those who score low on such measures.* As these hopes could be unconscious, indirect or projective measures of the fear may be most suitable, but the operationalized predictions must be falsifiable.

8) *The content of NDEs will reflect people's hopes for the afterlife but not necessarily their expectations.*

9) *The more gradually anoxia takes place in a near-death context, the more likely is the person to have an NDE.*

10) *During an OBE, EEG measurements will show activation of the left cerebral hemisphere and deactivation of the right cerebral hemisphere, compared to the pre–OBE state.*

Finally, here are two suggestions for analyses to be conducted, but for which we would not wish to make predictions:

11) *The qualities and content of OBEs occurring in ND and non–ND contexts should be systematically compared.* This ideally should include a test in which the experiences are mixed together randomly without identification as to their origin and to see if a "blind" judge can successfully sort them into two categories.

12) *The content and quality of NDEs and ketamine experiences should be systematically compared, including the test described for #11 above.* These analyses also require collection of a sufficient number of ketamine experiences, which could be a challenging task.

Resolution of the Problem: Detailed Classification

We have stressed that even when findings on subjective paranormal experiences (SPEs), including OBEs, are referable to specific anomalous brain functioning, they neither confirm nor deny the veridicality of the SPEs (Neppe 1979, 1983d). Like pathological hallucinations, the SPEs may have endogenous origins within the brain; alternatively, a particular brain function pattern may allow experience of an outside, usually covert, reality.

Clearly, future research should work with educating others in the area and using a classification of SPE. Psychiatric explanations for SPEs implying their abnormality should be viewed very carefully because of the remarkably high incidence of all kinds of SPE in the general population demonstrated in at least six countries. Labeling all such SPEs "pathological" would result in most of the population being regarded as abnormal. *Thus surveys of incidence in samples knowledgeable on the subject should be performed.* The most fundamental dichotomy appears to be the emphasis of parapsychology on *content* of the experience, and phenomenological psychiatry on the *form* of the SPE. A shift of orientation would probably be worthwhile (Neppe 1993). So would the appreciation of the predominantly biopsychological model of the sick patient in medicine as contrasted with the more sociocultural model of the normal paragnost in parapsychology.

Leading from this, the subclassification analyses of SPEs and like events may allow greater evidence distinguishing why there are several different subtypes, one of which may be different enough that the likelihood of it being of paranormal origin may become more cogent. An example is déjà vu. For example, at least four distinct descriptive entities of déjà vu apparently exist and these occur in different diagnostic subtypes. Neppe (1981, 1983b) analyzed déjà vu in different subtypes using 55 different parameters and ultimately 22 different Euclidean dimensions. He demonstrated that there are at least four phenomenologically distinct subtypes of déjà vu. These four categories are also diagnostically distinct. Moreover, such phenomenological experiences may be used in subtyping of type, diagnosis and management — in itself, another descriptive criterion. These manifestations can explain the wide variety of déjà clinical manifestations. Temporal lobe epilepsy déjà vu occurs in some temporal lobe epileptics; associative déjà vu in so-called "normals"; déjà vu in schizophrenics; and, finally, subjective paranormal experience (SPE) déjà vu is characterized by specific anomalous time distortions in SP experients (Neppe 1983e, 1987b).

Thus, not only is déjà vu not easily localized, one can distinguish subtypes that likely have entirely different etiologies (Neppe 1983b). Conversely, these different etiologies can be used to predict these same consistent phenomenological subtypes (Neppe 1983e). Similar analyses have been done but rarely. Neppe (1983a) has also demonstrated that olfactory hallucinations of a specific kind occur in SP experients. Again, there is a phenomenological link with the temporal lobe (Neppe 1980b, 1983d). This has not been done yet in OBEs or NDEs, nor has it been demonstrated in almost all other SPE phenomena. Similar research on other psi phenomena needs to be performed to demonstrate that subtypes might exist.

There appears an urgent need to subdivide all apparently anomalous experiences with greater detail from the onset. This may allow analyses— creative human or mathematical, statistical or computerized or combinations—which ultimately will better allow the parapsychological researcher, the phenomenological psychiatrist or anomalistic psychologist greater insight into the presence of homogeneous entities.

Psychiatrists have for many years attempted to detail their diagnosis with other factors that may be relevant. Diagnosis is commonly linked for example with predisposing, precipitating and perpetuating factors in relation to the illness. The American Psychiatric Association has, in fact, formalized diagnosis into five axes, namely I psychopathology, II personality, III organicity, IV social precipitants and V recent functionality. Specific diagnostic or operational criteria have been adopted within each axis producing the internationally recognized Diagnostic and Statistical Manual—IV-TM (DSM 4 TM) (Committee 2000).

Future of SPE Research

What can we suggest for future research? First, SPE is a useful area. The broader edifice of science may be kept reasonably intact allowing greater intrusion into other scientific disciplines, but analyzing subjectivity can assist understanding.

Moreover, this area encourages the neglected framework of analyzing spontaneous psi events as opposed to the lab situation. It also allows for correlations with ostensible SPE phenomena: e.g., is the NDE part of the OBE spectrum? Or in fact, is it legitimately an SPE? What about déjà vu, or olfactory hallucinations? With SPE research we can study the multiple possible causes and presentations for what appear to be subjective descriptions of anomalous phenomena. For example, we can apply these lessons to analyzing links with the brain, particularly the temporal lobes of the brain, geomagnetic approaches, psychological test correlates and diagnostic patterning. Such work suggests new philosophical standpoints, but interpretations are necessarily dichotomous—we discussed how a correlation of the temporal lobe with SPE may imply that SPEs originate within the temporal lobe and are not veridical objectively, or it may imply that an outside pattern of experience is integrated or experienced in part by a particular part of the brain.

In the future, there is a potential marriage of such SPE analyses with the objective. This is particularly so with the availability of Internet research, such as testing ESP using random event mechanisms with dice or numbers or other shapes on the Internet. This marries the subjective with the accumulated data from the objective. We can screen SP experients and formally test them for psi skills. We can use control groups or large sample sizes or specific chosen subjects in this regard.

The past reinstates future research in these areas. Very little has been done. Pioneering initial contributions and provisional interpretations must be replicated, validated and expanded upon. This is the future of anomalistic psychology.

REFERENCES

Abramovitch, H. (1988). An Israeli account of a near-death experience: A case study of cultural dissonance. *Journal of Near Death Studies* 6, 175–184.

Blackmore, S. (1983). Birth and the OBE: An unhelpful analogy. *Journal of the American Society for Psychical Research* 77, 229–238.

Blackmore, S. J. (1992). *Beyond the body: An investigation of out-of-the-body experiences.* Chicago: Academy Chicago Publishers.

Blackmore, S. (J.) (1993). *Dying to live: Science and the near-death experience.* London: Grafton.

Blanke, O., S. Ortigue, T. Landis and M. Seeck (2002). Stimulating illusory own-body perceptions. *Nature* 419 (6904), 269–270.

Bush, N. E. (1991). Is ten yeas a life review? *Journal of Near Death Studies* 1, 5–9.

Carr, D. B. (1984). Pathophysiology of stress-induced limbic lobe dysfunction: A hypothesis relevant to near-death experiences. In B. Greyson and C. P. Flynn, eds., *The near-death experience: Problems, prospects, perspectives* (pp. 125–139). Springfield, IL: Charles Thomas.

Committee, A. P. A. (2000). *Diagnostic and Statistical Manual: DSM IV-TR* (4th ed.). Washington, D.C.: American Psychiatric Association.

Cook, A. M., and H. J. Irwin (1983). Visuospatial skills and the out-of-body experience. *Journal of Parapsychology* 47, 23–35.

Drab, K. J. (1981). The tunnel experience: Reality or hallucination? *Anabiosis* 1, 126–152.

Dudley, R. T. (2002). Order effects in research on paranormal belief. *Psychological Reports* 90, 665–666.

Ehrenwald, J. (1973). Psyching out psi. *American Journal of Psychiatry* 130, 328–329.

_____ (1974). Out-of-the-body experiences and the denial of death. *Journal of Nervous and Mental Disease* 159, 227–233.

_____ (1975). Cerebral localization and the psi syndrome. *Journal of Nervous and Mental Disease* 161, 393–398.

Eisenbud, J. (1982a). Differing adaptive roles of psi in primitive and nonprimitive societies. *Psychoanalytic Review* 69, 367–377.

_____ (1982b). *Paranormal foreknowledge.* New York: Human Sciences Press.

Gabbard, G. O., and S. W. Twemlow (1984). *With the eyes of the mind: An empirical analysis of out-of-the-body states.* New York: Praeger.

Green, C., and C. McCreery (1975). *Apparitions.* London: Hamish Hamilton.

Greyson, B. (1977). Telepathy in mental illness: deluge or delusion? *Journal of Nervous and Mental Disease* 165, 184–200.

_____ (2000). Near-death experiences. In E. Cardeña, S. J. Lynn and S. Krippner, eds., *Varieties of anomalous experience: Examining the scientific evidence* (pp. 315–352). Washington, DC: American Psychological Association.

Haraldsson, E., A. Gudmundsdottir, A. Ragnarsson, J. Loftsson, and S. Jonsson (1977). National survey of psychical experiences and attitudes toward the paranormal in Iceland [Abstract]. In J. D. Morris, W. G. Roll, and R. L. Morris, eds., *Research in Parapsychology 1976* (pp. 182–186). Metuchen, NJ: Scarecrow Press.

Holt-Hansen, K. (1976). Extraordinary experiences during cross-modal perception. *Perceptual & Motor Skills* 43, 1023–1027.

Irwin, H. J. (1985). *Flight of mind: A psychological study of the out-of-body experience*. Metuchen, NJ: Scarecrow Press.

_____ (1993). The near-death experience as a dissociative phenomenon: An empirical assessment. *Journal of Near Death Studies* 12, 95–103.

_____ (2000). The disembodied self: An empirical study of dissociation and the out-of-body experience. *Journal of Parapsychology* 64, 261–277.

Jansen, K. L. R. (1997). The ketamine model of near-death experience: A central role for N-methyl-D-aspartate receptor. *Journal of Near Death Studies* 16, 5–26.

Jourdan, J. P. (1994). Near-death and transcendental experiences: Neurophysiological correlates of mystical traditions. *Journal of Near Death Studies* 12, 177–200.

Lange, R., and J. Houran (1997). Death anxiety and the paranormal: the primacy of belief over experience. *Journal of Nervous and Mental Disease* 185, 584–586.

Moody, R. A. (1975). *Life after life*. Covington, GA: Mockingbird Books.

Morris, R. L., S. B. Harary, J. Janis, J. Hartwell, and W. G. Roll (1978). Studies of communication during out-of-body experiences. *Journal of the American Society for Psychical Research* 72, 1–21.

Morse, M. L. (1997). Commentary on Jansen's paper. *Journal of Near Death Studies* 16, 59–62.

_____, and V. Neppe (1991). Near-death experiences. *Lancet* 337 (8745), 858.

_____, D. Venecia, and J. Milstein (1989). Near-death experiences: A neurophysiological explanatory model. *Journal of Near Death Studies* 8, 45–53.

Neppe, V. M. (1979). *An investigation of the relationship betwen temporal lobe symptomatology and subjective paranormal experience — MMed Psych thesis*. Unpublished, University of the Witwatersrand, Johannesburg.

_____ (1980a). Subjective paranormal experience. *Psi* 2 (3), 2–3.

_____ (1980b). Subjective paranormal experience and temporal lobe symptomatology. *Parapsychological Journal of South Africa* 1 (2), 78–98.

_____ (1981). *A study of déjà vu experience: Thesis*. University of the Witwatersrand, Johannesburg.

_____ (1982). Psychiatric interpretations of subjective paranormal perception. *Parapsychological Journal of South Africa* 3 (1), 6–16.

_____ (1983a). Anomalies of smell in the subjective paranormal experient. *Psychoenergetics — Journal of Psychophysical Systems* 5, 11–27.

_____ (1983b). The different presentations of the *déjà vu* phenomenon: New research. *Parapsychological Journal of South Africa* 4 (2), 124–139.

_____ (1983c). The hallucination: A priority system for its evaluation. *Parapsychology Review* 14 (4), 14–15.

_____ (1983d). Temporal lobe symptomatology in subjective paranormal experiments. *Journal of the American Society for Psychical Research* 77, 1–29.

_____ (1983e). *The Psychology of déjà vu: Have I been here before?* Johannesburg: Witwatersrand University Press.

_____ (1984). Subjective paranormal experience psychosis. *Parapsychology Review* 15 (2), 7–9.

_____ (1987a). Anomalous experience and psychopathology. *Parapsychology Review* 18 (6), 2.

_____ (1987b). Déjà vu: 4. The differences. *ASPR Newsletter* 13 (4), 31–32.

_____ (1988a). Psychopathology of psi: II. A new classification system for psi experience. *Parapsychology Review* 19 (6), 8–11.

_____ (1988b). Psychopathology of psi: I. A perspective. *Parapsychology Review* 19 (5), 1–3.

_____ (1989). Near-death experiences: A new challenge in temporal lobe phenomenology? Comments on "A neurobiological model for near-death experiences." *Journal of Near Death Studies* 7, 243–248.

_____ (1993). Clinical psychiatry, psychopharmacology and anomalous experience. In L. Coly and J. D. S. McMahon, eds., *Psi and clinical practice* (pp. 145–162). New York: Parapsychology Foundation.

_____ (1999). *Cry the beloved mind: A voyage of hope.* Seattle: Brainquest Press (with Peanut Butter Publishing).

_____ (2002). "Out-of-body experiences" (OBEs) and brain localisation: A perspective. *Australian Journal of Parapsychology* 2, 85–96.

_____, and M. Ewart Smith (1982). Culture, psychopathology and psi: A clinical relationship. *Parapsychological Journal of South Africa* 3 (1), 1–5.

_____, and W. H. Wessels (1979). Psychotic toleration of neuroleptic medication. *South African Medical Journal* 56, 1147.

Noyes, R., and R. Kletti (1976). Depesonalization in the face of life-threatening danger: An interpretation. *Omega* 7, 103–114.

Ohayon, M. M. (2000). Prevalence of hallucinations and their pathological associations in the general population. *Psychiatry Research* 97, 153–164.

Osis, K., and J. L. Mitchell (1977). Physiological correlates of reported out-of-body experiences. *Journal of the American Society for Psychical Research* 49, 525–536.

Owen, I. M. (1978). ON the review of "Conjuring up Philip." *Journal of the American Society for Psychical Research* 72, 73–75.

_____, with M. N. Sparrow (1976). *Conjuring up Philip: An experiment in psychokinesis.* New York: Harper and Row.

Palmer, J. (1978a). ESP and out-of-body experiences: An experimental approach. In D. S. Rogo, ed., *Mind beyond the body: The mystery of ESP projection* (pp. 193–217). New York: Penguin Books.

_____ (1978b). The out-of-body experience: A psychological theory. *Parapsychology Review* 9 (5), 19–22.

_____, and V. M. Neppe (2003). A controlled analysis of subjective paranormal experiences in temporal lobe dysfunction in a neuropsychiatric population. *Journal of Parapsychology* 67, 75–98.

Penfield, W. (1958). Functional localization in temporal and deep Sylvian areas.

In *Research Publications Association for Research in Nervous and Mental Disease* (Vol. 36, Ch VI, pp. 210–226). Baltimore: Williams and Wilkins.

Persinger, M. A. (1999). Near-death experiences and ecstasy: A product of organization of the human brain. In S. D. Sala, ed., *Mind myths: Exploring popular assumptions about the mind and brain* (pp. 85–99). New York: Wiley.

Pfister, O. (1930). Shockenken und shockfantasien bei höchster todesgefahr [Shock thoughts and fantasies in extreme moral danger]. *Zeitschrift für Psychoanalyse* **16**, 430–455.

Reed, G. (1972). *The psychology of anomalous experiences*. London: Hutchinson University Library.

Ring, K. (1980). Commentary on "The reality of death experiences: a personal perspective" by Ernst A. Rodin. *Journal of Nervous and Mental Diseases* **168**, 273–274.

_____ (1980). *Life at death: A scientific investigation of the near-death experience.* New York: Cowar, McCann & Geoghegan.

_____ (1984). *Heading toward omega: In search of the meaning of the near-death experience*. New York: Morrow.

Rodin, E. A. (1984). The reality of death experiences: A personal perspective. In B. Greyson and C. P. Flynn, eds., *The near-death experience: Problems, prospects, perspectives* (pp. 63–72). Springfield, IL: Charles Thomas.

Rogo, D. S. (1981). Mental health needs and the psychic community. *Parapsychology Review* **12** (2), 19–24.

Saavedra-Aguilar, J. C., and J. S. Gómez-Jeria (1989). A neurobiological model for near-death experiences. *Journal of Near Death Studies* **7**, 205–222.

Sagan, C. (1979). *Broca's brain: Reflections on the romance of science*. New York: Random House.

Santayana, G. (1905). *Life of reason, Reason in common sense*. New York: Charles Scribner.

Serdahely, W. J. (1991). A comparison of retrospective accounts of childhood near-death experiences with contemporary pediatric near-death experience accounts. *Journal of Near Death Studies* **9**, 219–224.

Sidgwick, H., and committee (1894). Report on the census of hallucinations. *Proceedings of the Society for Psychical Research* **10**, 25–422.

Tart, C. T. (1967). A second psychophysiological study of out-of-the-body experiences in a gifted subject. *International Journal of Parapsychology* **9**, 251–258.

_____ (1968). A psychophysiological study of out-of-the-body experiences in a selected subject. *Journal of the American Society for Psychical Research* **62**, 3–27.

_____ (1975). The physical universe, the spiritual universe, and the paranormal. In C. T. Tart, ed., *Transpersonal psychologies* (pp. 115–151). New York: Harper and Row.

Tellegen, A. (1982). *Brief manual for the Differential Personality Questionnaire*. Minneapolis: University of Minnesota.

Twemlow, S. W., G. O. Gabbard, and L. A. Coyne (1982). Multivariate method for the classification of pre-existing near-death conditions. *Anabiosis* **2**, 132–139.

Tyrrell, G. N. M. (1953). *Apparitions*. London: Duckworth.

Ullman, M. (1973). Parapsychology—implications for medicine. *Journal of the Kentucky Medical Association* **71**, 237–240.

_____ (1977). Psychopathology and psi phenomena. In B. B. Wolman, ed., *Handbook of parapsychology* (pp. 557–573). New York: Van Nostrand Reinhold.

West, D. J. (1948a). A mass observation questionnaire on hallucinations. Part 1. *Journal of the Society for Psychical Research* **34**, 187–196.

_____ (1948b). A mass observation questionnaire on hallucinations. Part 2. *Journal of the Society for Psychical Research* **34**, 644–664.

Wettach, G. E. (2000). The near-death experience as a product of isolated subcortical brain function. *Journal of Near Death Studies* **19**, 71–90.

Whiteman, J. H. M. (1980). Separative experience. *Psi* **2** (1), 1–4.

Section IV

SOCIOLOGICAL AND PHENOMENOLOGICAL ISSUES

12

A Socioempirical Perspective
on Skepticism about Psi

*Lance Storm**

The future of parapsychology hangs in the balance between
pure scientific empiricism on the one hand, and sociological
forces on the other. Dr. Lance Storm uses a socioempirical†
approach to attempt a merging of these two opposing positions. He explores the current and possible future states of
parapsychology and its subject "psi." The main focus is on
skepticism from the point of view of polemicists who, in
regard to psi, have "already decided the issue" (Hansen 1991,
p. 202). He uses three forms of inquiry to ultimately challenge this extremely skeptical position. First, the singular yet
paradoxical nature of psi is scrutinized in terms of its specifiability as an "acceptable" scientific phenomenon in comparison with other allegedly specified scientific phenomena.
Second, the impact on parapsychology of the philosophical
and sociological factors of "paradigm incommensurability,"
"sociocognitive discontinuity," and "epistemological discontinuity" is examined. Third, the influences of belief, experience and the scientific method on attitudes towards the

*The author wishes to thank the Bial Foundation, Portugal, for its support during the
writing of this chapter.
†The term "socioempirical" is used here to describe a fusion of, or interrelatedness
between, sociological and scientific ideas and principles both of which underlie the so-
called "objective" findings and statements of scientists.

paranormal are considered. On the basis of these inquiries, Dr. Storm claims that those who deny the possibility of psi have not yet produced cogent arguments to justify that position. (Editors)

In any scientific field of research that involves experimental work and theoretical speculation there is a widely held assumption that such activities are conducted in a dispassionate way by investigators and theorists, as if the sociocultural and behavioral influences on that field had been isolated and removed as confounding variables. Far from being removed, they are actively present. But these influences are more than just variables since they not only underpin the whole enterprise of science, but also constitute its very core. A number of critics of science have already made these observations. For example, Latour and Woolgar (1979) state the case:

> Whereas we now have fairly detailed knowledge of the myths and circumcision rituals of exotic tribes, we remain relatively ignorant of the details of equivalent activity among tribes of scientists whose work is commonly heralded as having startling or at least extremely significant effects on our civilization [p. 11].

Collins and Pinch (1982) also recognize this state of affairs as problematic for science and society, and the following statement implies a solution:

> On the whole, science is done in "controlled conditions." It is done in laboratories, conferences, journals, books, universities, and, of course, it is done here and now. Thus while it is certainly not true that every influence upon scientific development is transparent, most of what happens in science today is associated with a visible and investigable "outcrop" [p. 3].

Collins and Pinch recommend an ongoing sociological investigation into the scientific enterprise. This approach may lead to an understanding of how science works, but without realization, or even a tacit acknowledgment from scientists that transparent influences (i.e., the social forces that act upon science) exist, they remain invisible and therefore uncontrollable. More to the point, even if these social forces are identified, scientists may still fail to see the relativity and the subjectivity of their claims and findings if they do not adopt a reflexive (i.e., introspective) attitude to those forces. Consequently, they will pursue the same time-honored course they have always followed. This state of affairs is analogous to a blinkered horse that can have no concept at all of the broader nature of its environment — not unless it bothers to turn its head and look.

Thus we may lack a keen insight into, or at least remain ignorant of, how these influences have had considerable effects on (a) the way experimental and theoretical problems are resolved, (b) the criteria for interpreting results, (c) the future path and attitude of the investigator, and (d) the direction of a discipline. Metaphorically speaking, these influences work in the same way as the invisible "forces" that shape an environment. To extend this environmental metaphor, if we want fully to comprehend and appreciate a new territory, then not only must we circumnavigate its borders and coastline, scale its peaks, and enter into its heartland, we must also consider the forces and actions that have shaped and are still shaping that territory.

In like manner, parapsychologists must not only seek to discover empirically verifiable phenomena through direct observation, whereupon they posit theories, but they must also consider the field's current status (specifically how it came to be that way) in terms of those crucial but sometimes invisible influences that help give shape and form to those theories. Thus, a careful consideration of the socioempirical forces that have shaped parapsychology as a discipline, and continue to shape that discipline, is a necessary undertaking in terms of the importance to the field of maintaining its consistent identity and purpose in a constantly changing social and intellectual environment.

The Problems of Specification and Replication in Parapsychology

The "landscape" metaphor used above is reasonably well applied in the case of parapsychology. Just as any territory is dominated and shaped by or held within the framework of specific environmental forces, the constantly changing "landscape" of parapsychology does find itself "conditioned" by a long-running sociocultural and historical process of paradigm construction and reconstruction. Often the process involves the so-called paradigm "shift" where new theories and ways of thinking are necessarily put forward that challenge the received view of psi (for examples, see Jung 1960; May, Utts, & Spottiswoode 1995; Rhine 1937/1950; Stanford 1977, 1978; and Thalbourne 2004. See also the reviews of theories compiled by Stokes 1987, and more recently, Irwin 1999).

Though manifold and disparate in principle, these constructions and reconstructions, sometimes incorporating philosophical ideas that may or may not be empirically testable, have nevertheless, helped "integrate" parapsychology into a unified field of inquiry, thus rendering it a "landscape" or unique *topos* in its own right. In fact, ironically, parapsychology has maintained its "integrity" strictly on account of the particular nature of its subject matter — alleged paranormal phenomena.

Skeptics have disputed the above claim (see Alcock 1985; Blackmore 1985a; Bunge 1991; Hansel 1966; Hyman 1989; Kurtz 1985), but parapsychology, having identified its subject matter more than 100 years ago—"all types of phenomena called parapsychological or paranormal"*— has achieved this unity by consistently refusing to be intimidated or impressed by the specious claim that its subject is unspecifiable (e.g., see Boring 1955, 1966).

To clarify this point about the specification of the "parapsychological or paranormal" from a socioempirical perspective, it is important to recognize that the related term "psi" is often used interchangeably as both a "construct" and a "paranormal phenomenon" (see Palmer 1988, pp. 155–156). Palmer warns that the "traditional" approach of positing paranormal theories to explain psi is sometimes confused with the goal of confirming the psi construct. For example, the oft-used existentialist question "Does psi exist?" suggests a need for "construct-validation" of psi in its descriptive capacity as an "anomaly" (Palmer 1987, p. 156), yet psi was validated in this way as early as 1886 — i.e., by the time of the founding of the American Society for Psychical Research. Palmer (1987) argues that the investigator might be more gainfully employed in seeking an "explanation of (ostensible) psi phenomena" as possibly being a paranormal process— clearly a different goal to that of the verification of the psi construct. Palmer's focus, then, is on reaching a greater clarity of understanding about psi than is currently circulating inside and outside the parapsychological community.

Before discussing paranormal phenomena any further, we must ask how it is that any phenomenon comes to be specified. Traditionally, specification has been regarded as a process of recognizing how different one phenomenon is from another phenomenon by means of a categorization procedure — that is, a phenomenon can be regarded as specified if it has a unique identity. But, here we fall victim to taken-for-granted discontinuities because some form of general agreement on what constitutes a system of difference must first be established (such systems are clearly vulnerable to arbitrary decision rules, exclusion criteria, and other "incommensurables"; Collins and Pinch 1982, pp. 9–10, introduce these ideas).

Specification has also been understood as a process that reveals the nature of a phenomenon by establishing a certain level of predictability

*From the frontispiece of the Journal of the American Society for Psychical Research.

of that phenomenon. Edge (1985) points out the flaw in this kind of thinking. It does not follow that a suitable theory set up to specify a phenomenon should emerge exclusively from the fact that the phenomenon is predictable. Prediction does not yield understanding, whereas a theory makes the phenomenon intelligible. (It will be seen shortly that even a good theory does not necessarily guarantee specification in any absolute way.)

Given these ambiguities, we need to see how a so-called normal phenomenon would bear up against the above criteria before we could accept that it is a valid means of specifying paranormal phenomena. We can show this by borrowing a construct from the field of physics (viz., "gravity") and by probing into the socioempirical derivation of that construct. The effect we know as gravity is a unique and well-accepted (because repeatable, and therefore predictable) phenomenon, so it came to be "talked about" as if it had been specified at some point in scientific history. This misappropriation (*pace* Newton) emerged, first, because gravity, whatever it is, was deemed a genuine phenomenon by *consensus omnium*,* and second, because Newton had the scientific insight to propose a good theory to explain the phenomenon. But only the effects, not the nature of gravity, were recognized and "explained" by Newton's theory.† Still, in the twentieth century, the search for gravity waves as opposed to the equally plausible hypothesized entity, the "graviton"—both given as possible "causes" of gravity—only proves that, by the very standards of empirical science, unspecifiable phenomena lurk in all corners, not just in parapsychology.

For gravity, repeatability of the phenomenon was a deciding factor in its acceptance as a real phenomenon (notwithstanding the relatively powerful predictive model proposed by Newton). Yet the community of scientists then, as now, failed to realize that there is no such animal as a "common criterion" or "preconceived notion" (to use Schlitz's 1985, p. 79,

---

*Radin (1997, p. 44) refers to this social phenomenon as the "herd effect," which describes the way scientists herd together and come to a mutual agreement about which ideas or techniques will or will not be taken up as acceptable. This ancient principle effectively describes the formative process of the Kuhnian paradigm (see below).

†Newton, in fact, had insight into the "problem" of gravity: "That Gravity should be innate, inherent and essential so that one body may act upon another at a distance through a vacuum without the mediation of anything else, by and through which their action and force may be conveyed, is to me so great an absurdity that I believe no Man [sic] who has in philosophical matters a competent a faculty of thinking can ever fall into it. Gravity must be caused by an agent acting constantly according to certain laws: but whether this agent be material or immaterial, I have left to the consideration of my readers" (Motte & Cajori 1962, p. 364).

words) in science that was not, or should not be construed as anything more than a construction in the sense that it was subjectively derived by way of consensus. On this basis, scientists accepted the "gravity" construct on the grounds of very real (i.e., repeatable and demonstrable), mathematically describable effects, and these "facts" were set up as the criteria underlying the general acceptance of gravity as an "entity" about which one could propose a theory. Only among a very limited circle of scientists in the twentieth century were these criteria and subsequent assumptions questioned.*

To specify the phenomenon of psi in a scientific way also requires a "common criterion" by which to assess that phenomenon — a "preconceived notion." And it seems that in most cases, the "common criterion" for assessing the existence of a phenomenon — the "preconceived notion" that assists in pronouncing with great certainty the overwhelming evidence of a phenomenon — is the prerequisite of repeatability, because predictability ensues, and as a consequence, theory can be gainfully tested.

But, how concrete is this repeatability construct? Schlitz (1985) protests that "there is no common criterion for assessing replication in science" (p. 79). In fact, to go further, it is not always possible to specify what the term "replication" itself is supposed to mean because, as implied above, replication would be dependent on acceptability and the "preconceived notions" that we use to interpret experimental results (Schlitz 1985, p. 79; see also Storm and Thalbourne 2000, who discuss the distinction between statistical and complete replication). Collins (1976) confirms the above point — when replication is claimed as occurring, it tends mostly to be the end product of negotiation among investigators and theorists, and has very little to do with objective facts. For example, Edge (1985a) noted that replication in science does not in fact take place as often as we are led to believe. A "replication" experiment is often the same experiment with improvements, or refinements, and these differences may be of such importance that they disqualify one experiment as being a replication of the other. To use Diaconis's (1991) words: "One cannot judge what 'really goes on' in most areas [of research], and it is impossible to demand wide replicability in others" (p. 386). For example, one "area," the discipline of physics (again!), delivers no more a consistency of results from experimentation

*Note how Newton's model is complemented by Einstein's theory that gravity should be perceived as geodesics in (possibly curved) spacetime. To complicate matters, masses do not "attract" each other, they simply follow a geodesic (a path of least resistance) in warped spacetime brought about by the effects of the masses on the spacetime continuum. Thus, the specification of gravity (and by induction, any scientific entity) can be seen as discourse dependent.

than do the social sciences. And Radin (1997) gives a specific example from that discipline by asking: "How many times does an effect need to be repeatedly shown before it is accepted as a 'real' phenomenon and not an artifact?" He was referring to the "omega-minus" particle, which has been found only twice in 200,000 observations. This particle is now considered "real" by a majority of physicists by dint of a "sufficient" albeit "poor replication rate" of production and observation of the said particle (Radin 1997, p. 49).

Clearly, specification and replication of a phenomenon are "social actions" undertaken in accordance with subjective decision rules and criteria, thus throwing into question the validity of any so-called "objective" investigation of a phenomenon intended to establish the express or definitive nature of that phenomenon. Outside the demands of conventional science and its often loosely defined criteria (like the expectation of replication), psi is no different from gravity, yet it is "acted upon" as if it were — a purely socioempirical response to an allegedly unspecifiable phenomenon claimed to be such by standards that are unspecifiable. Thus, the tacit assumption in science that repeatability (and its concomitants, unique identity and predictability) may lead to specifiability does not follow. In fact, the nature of any entity or construct is arguably unspecifiable.*

All the above statements may give rise to the assumption that the belief that specification has been achieved, because replication and its concomitants are somehow entity-confirming processes, is actually a defense mechanism of conventional science set up as a legitimate scientific principle for arriving at some kind of consensus (cf. McClenon 1984). In fact, if parapsychology can be criticized as having not demonstrated a repeatable phenomenon, then perhaps *all the disciplines* may often warrant the same criticism. As an aside, and as an *apparent* contradiction to the point made above, parapsychologists do not have to defend themselves so forcefully against the accusation that psi is not repeatable — in fact, new evidence suggests psi is repeatable. Admittedly, parapsychology has had to wait a long time for its day, but it did, in the closing decades of the twentieth century, yield statistical evidence of repeatable paranormal phenomena. The argument that parapsychology has failed to show replicability

*Laudan (1983, cited in Rockwell & Rockwell 1986) has demonstrated that the Aristotelean "know-why" of a phenomenon (the possibility of its being specifiable) was dropped by Galileo as a scientific criterion because he admitted no understanding of the "causes or essence of gravity" (Rockwell & Rockwell 1986, p. 107). However, he maintained the Aristotelean "know-how" because he could demonstrate how his results were "true." "Scientists no longer [claim] that science offer[s] apodictic [church-established] certainty" (p. 107).

can be countered by the cumulative evidence of the meta-analyses. Such findings and statements challenge, in quite compelling ways, the relevance and even the validity of the claim that unrepeatability is parapsychology's only finding (Blackmore 1985a).*

The earlier relativization of the demand for replication, in the sense that repeatability is not necessarily a *sine qua non* in science, does nothing to debase the validity of the repeatability principle as demonstrated in the meta-analyses. It is accepted that repeatability is a generally accepted hard-line principle for confirming the existence of phenomena. But the more important issue under consideration here is the way in which the demonstrated repeatability of a phenomenon has falsely led many researchers to hold the illusory twofold belief that (a) the said phenomenon is not likely to be an artifact of experimentation or demonstration because it is replicable, and (b) the unique and predictable nature of said phenomenon has been specified.

Realistically, one needs to recognize the implications for science of this dichotomy where replication is crucial while at the same time can be regarded as unnecessary, and one cannot make a sound judgment about these implications by the standards of the empirical scientist or the critical sociologist alone. On the one hand, repeatability is a means of identifying (i.e., confirming the *existence* of) a phenomenon by the frequency of its occurrence, but many, if not most, inferences about the *nature* (specification) of that phenomenon might best be classified as speculative, or even philosophical. On the other hand, repeatability is not always a possibility, but that circumstance should not give rise to any suspicion about the existence of the phenomenon. Most researchers would surely acknowledge these issues, but the literature does not always suggest it. Honorton (1993) puts forward a similar argument. He identifies the "speculative" nature of the terms ESP and PK, preferring the terms "anomalous communication" and "energetic processes," respectively. He even recommends that the "anachronistic" term "paranormal" be "abandoned" (pp. 210–211).

In summary, when parapsychologists are expected to specify and replicate psi, yet fail to satisfy the demands of skeptics, they are criticized on the basis of technicalities that just happen to lend themselves very well to an ideology of "skeptical scientism"† (to coin a term), which blazons

---

Other contributions to the repeatability issue have been made by Honorton (1985) and Rao (1985). See also Shapin and Coly (1985) and Murphy (1987) for further arguments which question the assumption that repeatability is even essential to the purposes of parapsychology.

†*I shall tentatively define "skeptical scientism" as an "anti-anomaly," pro-scientific position dependent upon doctrinaire scientific convention.*

itself as good science. Thus do the same skeptics (often the spokespersons of other disciplines) make unreasonable challenges against parapsychologists by issuing socioempirically derived demands they would not require themselves to fulfill. (See also Irwin's 1999 observation that the demand for repeatability is largely a rhetorical exercise underscored by ulterior motives.) To formulate a question based on the general statements posed in this section (viz., "Has the singular nature of psi been undermined by scientific criticism?"), it has been argued here that specification of a phenomenon is an idealistic notion falsely associated with repeatability and its concomitants. Some kind of scientific community must accept the phenomenon, identify it, name it, and make inferences about its nature. Like gravity, psi phenomena *have* been identified, and constructions and reconstructions have been formulated around them within the paradigmatic frameworks of scientific discourse. But psi phenomena, *like gravity*, maintain anomalous dimensions. To borrow from Rhine (1948/1954), it often seems more accurate to specify what we collectively *believe* about a phenomenon rather than what we *know* of it. In the past, researchers and theorists in parapsychology have held onto the belief that psi will one day be understood. This is also true in the present. However, the unblinkered reality of the situation is that in the future, parapsychology, as indeed all the sciences, may forever be in flux — the socioempirical view gives credence to the possibility that the world is unknowable.

The Nature of the Paradigm in Parapsychology

From the above arguments, it can be seen that certain criticisms leveled against the subject matter of parapsychology in terms of its existence cannot be founded on objective grounds so that the field gains "the benefit of the doubt," and therefore, psi may be taken as a workable phenomenon. However, the existence of possible disparities between various paranormal paradigms (or at least disparities that often exist between various theories*) is recognized. In fact, the Kuhnian (Kuhn 1962) concept of "incommensurability" between paradigms (and theories in many cases) could be seen as another threat to the integrity of the paranormal as a class of phenomena, and therefore the integrity of parapsychology. A split in the parapsychological community, however, has not yet surfaced, in spite of the very real opportunity for such an occurrence (cf. Honorton 1993, who considers the variety of hidden agendas held by parapsychologists).

See Stokes 1987, pp. 77–189.

Of course, other disciplines face these same difficulties, but they have the buffer of scientific hegemony supporting them when such threats arise (cf. Irwin 1999, p. 314.)

In terms of Kuhn's (1962) notion of "paradigm incommensurability," there may be no solution to the above-mentioned difficulties that might surface because there are supposedly no common measures by which ideas from one paradigm could be understood from within the context of another. Following Kuhn's way of thinking, a paradigm shift within para-psychology could imply a "revolution" in the way its subject matter is to be defined.

But there seems to be a flaw in Kuhn's thinking. Kuhn led us to under-stand that science is a progressive enterprise, the progress being gauged by the higher predictive power of the new, superior paradigm compared with the old, less-refined one. More broadly, he constructed science as a "collective" of disciplines that are supposedly forging ahead in some way, ultimately creating newer and better technologies and more advanced soci-eties in which to live. Paradoxically, the Kuhnian model seems to be an endorsement of the aesthetic of the objectively verifiable "trajectory" of modernism, yet it maintains the conflicting two-edged "postmodern" premise that (a) paradigm comparison is not a plausible undertaking, which leads to the inevitable conclusion that (b) progress cannot be deter-mined in ways other than subjective, and may not even take place at all by the standards of a relatively broader, more objective (i.e., less subjec-tive) criterion.

The argument seems clear: if paradigms are incommensurable with each other then there is no standard by which they can be compared. Thus, to state that progress (in a discipline, for example) can be objectively substantiated, undermines the relativist argument that Kuhn puts for-ward. However, this ostensibly logical conclusion can be given a radical twist. Collins and Pinch (1982) argue that whatever other arbitrary sys-tem of decision-making scientists might resort to in assessing new ideas, "scientists reserve their final commitment to [these] ideas until they are forced to accept them by logic, or experiment" (Collins and Pinch 1982, p. 16).

But to go further than Collins and Pinch, rather than being at a loss in deciding which knowledge to keep and which to reject when all avail-able "systems of decision-making" fail, the diverse contents of scientific epistemology are *always* evidently and productively a composite of the "old" and the "new." In the past, as in the present, these diverse contents have been drawn on like tools in a toolbox, with each tool designed for a specific job. Scientists *can* live with the dichotomous situations that are thrown up rather than necessarily being frozen in their tracks just because it seems they cannot make a "final commitment."*

For parapsychologists, then, it is almost business as usual. There seems to be no reasonable argument that would undermine the recommendation that business proceed as usual, providing that one major concession be made. Parapsychologists may accept or reject both old and new ideas according to their findings (as Collins and Pinch have noted), but allowances need to be made. It is now not just a matter of upholding the theory that does (or theories that do) the best job of explaining experimental outcomes. Inevitably, parapsychologists will commit unreservedly to multiple or plural paradigmatic viewpoints, since different paradigms speak to different phenomenologies according to the discursive constructs of those paradigms. In the past, this approach would have suggested a discipline that was fragmented (if not unscientific), but now it may be regarded as a major philosophical strength for parapsychology. In fact, in recent decades pluralist approaches have been attempted in parapsychology (see Irwin 1999).

Sociocognitive and Epistemological Discontinuity in Parapsychology

Apart from the term "incommensurability" (used above), Kuhn (1962) acquainted us with two more terms — "incompatibility" and "irreconcilability" — that also describe the schismatic relationships that can supposedly exist between paradigms. These three related terms effectively underpin the all-embracing concept: "sociocognitive discontinuity" (Collins and Pinch 1982, pp. 9–24, 47–65). Sociocognitive discontinuity describes the state of affairs that may exist between (say) two groups of scientists who use mutually exclusive epistemologies to inform their "social actions" (Collins and Pinch 1982, p. 9). Even when there is a consensus between groups on the facts about a phenomenon, they may differ about the ideas and conclusions that follow from those facts. Thus, in cases where groups (or, in fact, individuals) are opposed, argumentation may proceed with little chance of a resolution between the two (or more) factions.

---

*For example, in 1931 Kurt Gödel showed that by taking a few basic mathematical axioms, a proof of arithmetical law involving finite numbers could be established, but Gödel further established that an opposing "truth" was also possible using the same axioms. This dichotomous situation did not cause the mathematical community to "reserve their final commitment," even though logic and experimentation were to no avail. Today, mathematicians accept the axioms as if they were true and proceed accordingly.

Sociocognitive discontinuity can be demonstrated in the field of parapsychology. When, for example, Pratt (1960) regards psi phenomena as "precisely those psychological events which defy description in terms of any physical theory now available" (p. 25), we can see that he seems to "tell" what psi is by telling what it is not — that is, the fundamental concepts of parapsychology are "essentially negative" (to borrow from Flew 1987, p. 93). But, to argue tentatively in support of Pratt, his characterization of psi is in harmony with the psi hypothesis: psi may be incompatible with current scientific principles, but that should not preclude its existence when it may be the case that the problem lies with our scientific principles, not the psi hypothesis. After all, it is entirely consistent with our philosophical and scientific epistemologies to posit "x" and therefore "not-x," where "x" is normal (i.e., "regular") whereas "not-x" is psi (i.e., "irregular" or even "paranormal"). Psi phenomena would thus be anomalous only by dint of their being incompatible with current definitions of what characterizes nonanomalous ("normal" and even "abnormal") phenomena.

Of course, the philosopher can repudiate this kind of formulation. First, can there be a general agreement on what constitutes "x" so that we can posit "not-x"? Second, if "x" and "not-x" are in contradistinction to each other, can there be a mutually agreed-upon system for drawing out this distinction? The parapsychologist is usually oblivious to, or at least a little blasé about such questions, leaving these sorts of problems to the philosopher.* And justifiably so since, as science stands, the main point of the above argument is that Pratt's position is tenable and workable in practice.

The skeptic, who may also be oblivious to the above questions, may enter the debate at this point and start his argument, in agreement with Pratt, by also stating that psi phenomena are incompatible with scientific positivism. Recall Pratt's (1960) idea that the very real psi event "def[ies] description in terms of any physical theory now available" (p. 25). But the skeptic (assumed here to be one who avows a total allegiance to "scientism" alone) will be led to state that psi cannot exist because science cannot explain it. Collins and Pinch (1982) make reference to this paradox: "These two arguments have at their core the same claims regarding the incompatibility of psi phenomena and science though they are deployed respectively by skeptics and believers..." (p. 49).

---

*Thalbourne (2004) discusses what may essentially be called "the ontological question," where psi (as both ESP and PK) can be characterized from within three mutually exclusive philosophical systems: metaphysical dualism, metaphysical materialism, and metaphysical idealism. The distinction between "x" and "not-x" will depend on one's ontological perspective.

Believer and skeptic both agree on what psi is according to what science cannot explain. But for sociocognitive reasons they split at this point — the one convinced that science needs to be more flexible, the other certain that there is no room for psi according to the standards of scientific truth. These arguments create the sociocognitive discontinuity of which Collins and Pinch speak, but both arguments also result in *epistemological* discontinuity (i.e., a new state of dissonance in the epistemology caused by incomplete or inappropriate applications of preexisting knowledge claims). Both arguments are unsound because they are derived from situational presumptions. Thus, the believer introduces the condition that the scientific viewpoint must change (not necessarily true, but it does square with the evidence of science as an accumulative enterprise *qua* Kuhn, therefore fully endorsing the research ethic), whereas the skeptic introduces the condition that the scientific viewpoint need not change (not constructive for science because it undermines historical process, therefore implying that all breakthroughs are explainable, and even that proof can apply without experimentation!). These two conditions are, of course, irreconcilable. (Note that on the issue of belief, there are psychosociological reasons underlying the social category within which one chooses to be; viz., believer or skeptic. This issue is explored in the final section.)

However, in support of the believer's argument, the only truly responsible scientific action that would fairly represent the psi hypothesis (or any hypothesis) is that researchers proceed in their quest to accumulate an ever-increasing epistemology. In recognizing the implication of the skeptic's argument, though, researchers on both sides of the fence must not delude themselves into thinking that they have not undermined the fundamental Cartesian tenet of creating certainty out of doubt. This certainty may be based on knowledge claims already established and accepted when, on the one hand, the reality is that these claims may not have been fully applied, or on the other hand, they may have been carelessly applied to (say) the psi hypothesis (for examples of knowledge claims not fully applied, or carelessly applied to psi, see Collins and Pinch* 1982, pp. 47–65; Meehl and Scriven 1987). To do the latter responsibly, the practitioners of science (opposing groups of scientists) must be conscious of the perils that

---

It is taken, for example, that psi does not obey the inverse-square law, but "the inverse-square law does not necessarily apply, even to ordinary electro-magnetic radiations" (Margenau 1966, p. 222, cited in Collins and Pinch 1982, p. 58). And "the inverse-square propagation of energy is seldom realized in practice" (Rush 1943, p. 48, cited in Collins and Pinch 1982, p. 58). Thus the "radiation analogy" can be used to show that "psi radiation" need not conform to the inverse-square law (Collins and Pinch 1982, p. 58).

ensue when sociocognitive and epistemological discontinuities rear their ugly heads, as these can so often arise out of the presumptive thinking that attempts to eliminate doubt. These discontinuities ultimately propagate more doubt, not certainty. For the sake of a more solid future for parapsychology, researchers and theorists have to be more cautious about how they construct so-called "good" science, including "good" parapsychology.

Sociocognitive and epistemological discontinuity should but seldom do create cognitive dissonance amongst those prone to its effects. Antithetical statements can be drawn from a single observation, yet often neither the poverty of these statements, nor the ensuing irony of their contradictory natures are acknowledged, if they are ever noticed at all. The next section will focus on other ironies, with particular focus on the influences of experience, belief, and the scientific method as socioempirical forces that also give form to the field of parapsychology. These factors necessarily emerge from the issues just discussed. It will be seen how it is often very difficult to discuss experience, belief, and the scientific method independently of each other since there is so much conceptual overlap between them. But it will also be seen how all three factors have shaped the field of parapsychology, and how they continue to contribute to its evolution and our understanding of the anomaly called psi.

Experience, Belief, and the Scientific Method

Sociocognitive and epistemological discontinuity lead us back to the phenomenology of the paradigm. We may ask how paradigms are constructed, and what the key influences that maintain or disturb one's choice of social category might be (i.e., whether we choose to call ourselves believers or skeptics of psi). Kuhn (1962) proposed that new paradigms replace old paradigms because the old ones fail to answer new problems. These problems arise through observation and our capacity to reason. Scientific paradigms, therefore, are born of human reason, but reason cannot take place in a vacuum — it is influenced by the factors of experience* and the beliefs† we hold. These two factors are constantly changing — they

---

*John Locke advocated experience above all things — even rationalism — as the raw material of all knowledge and reason (Drever 1968).

†Quine and Ullian (1970, p. 92) hold that "in a person's web of beliefs there is no strand that does not help support some value judgment." Judgment is a subjective, nonintellectual process, like feeling-toned evaluation. The process, like thinking, can function in abstract mode, and is thus capable of arriving at sophisticated concepts and ideas about phenomena (Jung 1987, para. 724).

influence each other, and they in turn underscore the processes of paradigm construction.

Thus we conduct research in characteristically human ways, which yet involves thinking from within the perspectives of prior epistemologies—we need the old techniques (experimental design, statistical methods, etc.) to test new paradigms. The scientific method, then, as an "arsenal of research tools" and a "philosophical outlook" (Rosnow and Rosenthal 1993, p. 19), is a consistent and major force in its own right, thus constituting a third factor in the formation of scientific paradigms.

All the sciences must rely on these three major factors—experience, belief, and the scientific method—as the general means by which proof-oriented and process-oriented research may continue. There are undoubtedly other factors involved in scientific practice,* but for parapsychology, experience, belief, and the scientific method have a particularly unique and pivotal influence on the field, as will become clear. These three factors are formative elements of the socioempirical approach. For these reasons, they are discussed next.

Experience

Psi phenomena usually seem the most real when they are experienced first hand, and they have a numinous quality about them that "informs" and enhances that experience. Such an experience may derive from a spontaneous case. However, for the experimental parapsychologist, the "experience" (or better, "evidence") of psi is often represented only as a cumulative statistic, where individual trials in laboratory situations provide units of data that appear rather ordinary or chance-like on their own. Often, therefore, due to a failure to demonstrate psi directly (such as in the spontaneous case) or inferentially (through a statistic), many parapsychologists have probably entertained Beloff's (1990) doubt—the fleeting thought that "perhaps, the whole field had been misconceived from the start" (p. 11).

Beloff's Doubt (to coin a term) ultimately implies two possible assumptions. On the one hand, psi cannot be convincingly and consistently demonstrated (or better, induced at call) in the laboratory because it does not exist. Of necessity, therefore, the application of the parapsychological technique (including the parapsychologist's own influence, other-

---

*Rosnow and Rosenthal (1993, pp. 17–19) note that the orienting attitude of the scientist, which includes enthusiasm, open-mindedness, inventiveness, confidence, etc., has an influence on scientific practice. In fact, some of these "variables," known as "psi-conducive states" (Braud 1975) are claimed to have real psi influences on outcomes in parapsychological experiments.

wise referred to as the "experimenter effect") is really a redundant exercise.* On the other hand, if psi does exist, the way the parapsychologist goes about looking for it may be inappropriate given its phenomenology. There are many who agree with the former assumption (Hyman 1985; Hansel 1966, 1980), while others have expressed sympathy or agreement with the latter (Rhine† 1948/1954; von Franz 1980).

For most researchers the idea of questioning the techniques of laboratory investigations of psi, and the existence of the psi effect itself, would be considered unreasonable, whether or not these researchers have the "evidence" of first-hand experience. Such loyalty is praiseworthy, but a working lifetime devoted to a single ideal can create an insurmountable prejudice. Beloff (1990) has stated a profound truth in this regard: "By the laws of cognitive dissonance the longer you commit yourself to some cause and the more effort you devote to it the harder it becomes to renounce it" (p. 11).

True words, though not true for all. Many investigators in the past, armed with certain prejudices, have entered a field in order to disprove that field's major claims, only to be convinced otherwise by their own experience. For example, French psychologist Michel Gauquelin (1983) sought to prove a life-long belief that astrological relationships as proposed by astrologers did not exist between the inner planets of our solar system and the professional lives of certain eminent individuals. In correlational studies spanning more than 40 years of Gauquelin's working life, statistical analyses consistently gave significant results that challenged his prior beliefs (see also West 1992, who provides evidence of successful replications of Gauquelin's work).

Again, starting off with his own brand of skepticism, Walter Mischel (1968, 1973) was most emphatic in his criticism of the idea of a consistent personality (temporally and situationally) as proposed and explained by psychodynamic theories (Freudian, etc.). Not until he conducted his own longitudinal studies (showing that character traits, which developed in

---

*Akers (1984) has brought attention to "explanations" that skeptics have used to justify their doubt regarding the existence of psi, such as randomization failure, sensory leakage, cheating, and procedural errors. Added to the skeptic's list of "explanations" of the psi event are "delusion, ... coincidence, [and] unconscious inference" (Stokes 1987, p. 84). The notion that psi might be an artifact of the methodologies used in parapsychology is discussed below.

†Rhine acknowledged the general problem of the possible inappropriateness of testing in parapsychology. In speaking about the decline effect, for example, he said: "We destroy the phenomena in the very act of trying to demonstrate them. Evidently the tests themselves get in the way of the abilities they are designed to measure" (Rhine 1948/1954, p. 161).

childhood, could persist into adulthood) did he classify the findings of this work as being akin to that of the psychodynamic theorists (Mischel & Shoda 1995). Thus experience and the scientific method when taken together may temper our prejudices.

Experience, then, is an important component of scientific research, as it can determine the future path of an investigator. The history of parapsychology, too, has been dotted with examples of the effects that experience has had on its researchers. Susan Blackmore (1985b, 1986, 2001), for example, joined ranks with the skeptics when she repeatedly failed to demonstrate the presence of psi in her experimental studies (probably a case of Beloff's Doubt, perhaps indicating too that cognitive dissonance needs time to take effect). On the other hand, some researchers, like the late Charles Honorton, have run consistently successful experiments (see Beloff 1990), encouraging others to join or continue in the field.

The socioempirical value of experience should not be ignored or conceptualized out of existence on the grounds that its chance-like (i.e., coincidental) nature renders it unworthy as a contributing element towards scientific knowledge and the scientific enterprise. Utts (1991) has stated that "experience is a poor substitute for the scientific method" (p. 363), and she has also claimed that "there is little more [in the way of suggestive evidence of psi] to be offered to anyone who does not accept the current collection of data" (Utts 1995, p. 290). Perhaps she is correct for the most part, but as she herself has discovered, a large cross-section of the scientific community is not prepared to accept that which they would deem to be unexplained anomalies (Diaconis 1978; Hyman 1991).

Such denial, however, is typical of the outsider (specifically, the skeptic) bereft of a personal experience in the area of parapsychology (especially a direct experience of ostensible psi). So perhaps there is more to be offered to anyone who doubts the evidence. Of course, one cannot reject the fact that a novel encounter of the psi kind can wear off quickly — "every miracle, no matter how incontrovertible it may once have appeared, will lose its lustre" (Beloff 1990, p. 33) — especially if the "miracle" is not positively reinforced by replication. Beloff (1990) gives examples illustrating how difficult it is to quell doubt and "sustain," or even instill a belief in psi, even when the evidence seems beyond doubt (pp. 30–32). Little wonder that the lack of an experience gives good reason for some critics to follow their doubts and criticize mostly the methods used by parapsychologists (especially the statistics, but more on this shortly), there being little recourse to do otherwise.

While the efforts of many critics do help to fine-tune scientific methods in parapsychology, the psi experience still seems to count once again as a key influence towards believing in the paranormal (especially if recent techniques such as meta-analysis are questioned). In other words, skepticism may be instrumental in strengthening the methods of parapsychology, but nothing seems to inform an individual's belief about the paranormal quite like the direct psi experience, even though many may believe without it.

Belief

Quine and Ullian (1970) describe the complex processes of belief formation and modification that many of us employ: self-evidence, observation, testimony (i.e., vicarious observation), and hypothesis testing. Most researchers are familiar with these processes, since they may also be applied in the procedures of the scientific method. (In a formal scientific investigation, however, these processes may not necessarily result in any particular belief about the nature of the phenomenon under investigation.)

The discipline of philosophy has provided additional means of belief construction through deduction, induction, analogy, and intuition. Each of these approaches can be used independently or collectively as a means of arriving at a belief, and they may extend outside the formal disciplines to the layperson, even leading him or her to skepticism of, or belief in, paranormal phenomena.

As already noted, however, no amount of evidence may be enough to change the "closed-minded thought processes" or beliefs of the skeptic, to use Stokes's (1987, p. 84) words. To explain skepticism, Tyrrell (1945) argued decades ago that "the constitution of our minds, as a result of biological evolution, causes us to reject whatever is entirely foreign to the world of common experience." For many, such is the basis for the denial of psi phenomena too.

On the other hand, many millions the world over in modern (Westernized) and pre-industrial cultures do believe in anomalous acquisition of knowledge, communication with discarnate entities, and so on. One might almost surmise, therefore, that belief formation for all peoples cannot stem from the application of any one or more of the above-mentioned processes alone. For if the opposite were true, unanimity of belief about most phenomena, including psi, would have been reached by now in all populations. However, such is not the case. Thus, there appears to be more to belief formation than we might realize.

Having reviewed much of the literature on paranormal belief, Irwin (1993, 1999) discussed four hypotheses that may serve as more general explanations for belief in the paranormal — the *social marginality hypothesis*, the *worldview hypothesis*, the *cognitive deficits hypothesis*, and the *psychodynamic functions hypothesis*:

The social marginality hypothesis: Believers are seen as "isolated" in some way — by age, gender, socioeconomic status, ethnicity, or culture, etc., — so that belief acts as a buffer to the vicissitudes of a life so often associated with marginal status. (After an extensive literature review, Irwin 1999, p. 285, reports that this hypothesis has not been supported.)

The worldview hypothesis: Believers hold paranormal belief as only one subjective and esoteric aspect of a much broader picture of life, humanity, and the world in general, where mental and metaphysical religious beliefs and practices are incorporated into that worldview. (There is partial support for this hypothesis, according to Irwin 1999, pp. 285–287.)

The cognitive deficits hypothesis: Believers are said to have uncritical, naïve, and irrational thought processes based on deficits in education, lower average levels of intelligence and poor reasoning skills. (Evidence for this aspect of the hypothesis is inconclusive at this stage, according to Irwin 1999, pp. 287–289.) Believers may also have overly creative imaginations. (There is some support for this aspect of the hypothesis, according to Irwin 1999, p. 289.)

The psychodynamic functions hypothesis: Believers are seen as being in some way psychologically disadvantaged or maladapted, or socially deviant in respect of their personality characteristics so that paranormal belief is seen as fulfilling a psychodynamic need (see also Radin 1997, pp. 242–247). (There is "general support" for this hypothesis, but Irwin 1999, proposes that a "specific version of the hypothesis that posits more precisely the nature of the psychodynamics involved," p. 291, is required.)

Overall, there is some evidence supporting the last three hypotheses, with particularly strong support from the correlational studies for the *psychodynamic functions hypothesis*. In respect of this hypothesis, and as an extension to it, Irwin (1993, 1999) notes that paranormal belief may be the result of physical abuse and childhood trauma, a mechanism whereby a psychodynamic need is fulfilled by an "illusion of control" which the belief serves (1993, p. 28). There is no evidence, however, that such an etiology excludes paranormal ability. That is, while it might be found that some believers in the paranormal base their belief on illusory states of mind or fantasy proneness, it might also be based on genuine paranormal ability. (In fact, although controversial, it may not be all that unreasonable to propose that trauma may be a sufficient psi-conducive condition!)

In parapsychology, too, it must surely be more than a state of mind that motivates many or most investigators in their research. Irwin (1999) actually includes "anomalous experiences" (p. 291) as one of two possible threats to an individual's intellectual and emotional autonomy (the other, as mentioned, being "traumatic events"), so it is feasible that experiences of genuine paranormal phenomena may be among those anomalous experiences. Thus may any number of parapsychologists be of a type actively engaged in the scientific pursuit of an understanding of the paranormal based on personal experience of such anomalies. Their intellectual and emotional autonomy may not be "threatened" at all, but may be modified to include an openness to, and acceptance of, the reality of psi, based on an informed understanding or experience of the paranormal. In concurrence with this view, Irwin (1999) proposes that belief in psi might logically stem from "the data of parapsychological research" (p. 290), but he does not actually say that direct experiences of psi might be sufficient causes in themselves for belief in the very same phenomena.

To continue this argument, one "specific version" of the *psychodynamic functions hypothesis,* by which at least one underlying *psychodynamic* cause of belief in psi might be explained, lies in the mental and neuropsychological processes described in Thalbourne's (2000) theory of transliminality. Transliminality is defined as "a hypothesized tendency for psychological material to cross (*trans*) thresholds (*limines*) into or out of consciousness" (Thalbourne and Houran 2000, p. 853). Thalbourne (2000) has found significant relationships between transliminality and a number of factors, including belief in psi, but more to the point, transliminality has been shown to be a predictor of paranormal ability, as found and stated in Storm and Thalbourne (1998–1999):

> The highly transliminal individual was more likely [than the rest of the sample] to … believe in his or her own ability to achieve a successful outcome in a psi-task — a belief which was vindicated in part by the fact that 40 percent of the highly transliminal participants obtained a hit [where MCE = 25 percent], suggesting that they … might be "psi-able" [p. 115].

Storm (2002) has since replicated these findings using the pooled data of three separate *I Ching* studies, which suggest that belief in paranormal phenomena, and belief in one's ability to produce such phenomena, are involved in the *I Ching* process, thus leading to the generation of psi effects. In short, belief in psi need not necessarily be associated with pathology, but may follow from psi ability.

The argument does not end here: it may have been shown that paranormal belief can engender a feeling of control (Irwin 1999), but again, such control may not necessarily be an illusory one. Even if there is doubt about the results of the *I Ching* studies, there is still stronger evidence that belief in ESP is a psi-conducive factor, as has been borne out in the many "sheep-goat"* studies since 1947 (Lawrence 1993). Lawrence found that belief in ESP correlated positively with ESP scores. (See also Haraldsson 1993, where various forms of belief other than belief in ESP also correlated with ESP scores.) Certainly, the socioempirical effects of belief can determine the direction of scientific research, but belief also appears to have real motive force as well (psychologically and parapsychologically) so that it is indeed a variable of quite considerable impact worthy of continued investigation as a psi-conducive factor.

Belief, then, appears to have manifest potency, and this fact may give reason for the reverence in which we hold our beliefs. It is not surprising, therefore, that our beliefs are the very foundations of our truths. But however "true" our truths may seem, the often personal nature of such truths must not be overlooked. We run the risk of deceiving ourselves if the so-called truths, which arise from our beliefs, can be argued as misguided due simply to their being nothing more than something we firmly believe to be true (i.e., are found not to be substantiated). In such cases Irwin's (1993) *cognitive deficits hypothesis* holds certain validity.

A few years after Tyrrell wrote the words quoted above, Jung (1960, para. 821) drew a distinction between the unique, "just so" quality of the chance-like (coincidental) personal truth and the more scientifically acceptable "statistical truth." Jung claimed:

> Absolutely unique and ephemeral events whose existence we have absolutely no means of either denying or proving can never be the object of empirical science; rare events might very well be, provided that there was a sufficient number of reliable observations [cf. the omega-minus particle]. The so-called possibility of such events is of no importance whatever, for the criterion of what is possible in any age is derived from that age's rationalistic assumptions [1960, para. 821].

(These thoughts touch on an earlier discussion concerning scientific consensus.) One "rationalistic assumption" that can be made in order to verify empirically the possibility of a certain phenomenon is to show that its probability is not zero. One can go further and establish the actual probability of the phenomenon (achieved statistically), which in our "age" involves considering the frequency of the event in terms of its relation to chance. Thus enters the need for statistics, and more generally, the scientific method in parapsychology.

---

*Sheep are believers in ESP, and they tend to score significantly higher than goats, who are disbelievers in ESP.

The Scientific Method

In the nineteenth century, science became defined by its methodology — the scientific method — and in many disciplines, statistical analysis became one of the fundamental components of the scientific method. Having successfully made the transition to the behavioral sciences, the scientific method naturally became a crucial part of experimental parapsychological research, and has served the field remarkably well for over a century.* But in the process, the effects of which statistics is not designed to explain or give account (particularly psi effects) have been too easily labeled as artifacts, based on the assumption that statistical and methodological procedures may be fundamentally flawed.† For example, for some time there was the assumption that true randomness cannot be achieved in any finite system (Spencer-Brown 1957), but Scott (1958) refuted this claim (Spencer-Brown overestimated the importance of the argument of true randomness). Gilmore (1989) later warned that researchers in psi "should take account of the possible inappropriateness of classical inferential statistics" (p. 338).

Once again, the average parapsychologist would have no difficulty in rejecting as untenable the consequent idea that these effects, which they usually take as suggesting the presence of psi phenomena, are to be taken as the perennial artifact of fundamental flaws. Such a rejection seems warranted, given the vast improvements in methodologies over the last 150 years or so (see Pratt 1973; Braud 1991). Braud (1991), in particular, objected to the possibility that a "singularly powerful flaw" or "more subtle confounds" could be responsible for the "positive outcomes" in psi studies (p. 58). To argue the case, he cites a "vast number of successful experiments" by many different investigators, all of whom have used "very different methodologies" (e.g., ganzfeld, autoganzfeld, forced-choice, etc.).

To expand the range of techniques and statistical tools for assessing psi, and to help avoid hackneyed experimental and statistical approaches, Rosenthal (1986) and others (e.g., Schmeidler 1968; Morris 1991) have advised the use of additional methodologies, and even an alternative to significance testing of hypotheses. Rosenthal, for example, recommends "sub-division of studies as a function of different experimental procedures

---

*Richet (1884) and Edgeworth (1885, 1886) were the earliest to propose the use of statistical approaches to the analysis of data generated in psi experiments. Fisher (1924, 1929) followed with improved methods that credited "close" guesses in card-guessing experiments as evidence supporting the psi hypothesis.

†In defense of the statistical procedures used in parapsychology, see Mauskopf and McVaugh (1980).

or individual difference variables such as sex, age, degree of belief in psi effects, and the like" in order to arrive at "moderator variables" (p. 322). He also recommends the use of multiple dependent variables, and replicability considerations based on effect size (p. 322).

These advances would be (or have been) constructive for parapsychology, but a larger problem may lurk in the wings. If statistical procedures are flawed because classical statistics does not offer a valid model of reality, then *all* the claims of science, not just those of parapsychology, are in jeopardy in so far as they employ just such procedures. To use Mosteller's (1991) words: "if there is no ESP, then we want to be able to carry out null experiments and get no effect, otherwise we cannot put much belief in work on small effects in non-ESP situations" (p. 396).

Like researchers in other fields, the parapsychologist must continue as before in the belief that the "point null hypothesis makes some sense" (Utts 1991 p. 401). But, to be realistic, is such a criterion enough to satisfy even the most hardened skeptic? The likely answer is generally a resounding "No!" because often the skeptic believes only when everybody else believes. In order to justify this seemingly facetious remark, one has to consider the social ramifications of statistical findings. In some cases particular methodologies are not even given due recognition by reviewers of scientific journals, or the scientific community in general, regardless of the claimed validity of these methodologies (see Greenhouse 1991).

The issue of prejudice surfaces once again when "prevailing substantive beliefs and theories held by scientists at any given time" work against the parapsychologist (Greenhouse 1991, p. 387). When Jung (1960, para. 821) implied that "the possibility of [rare] events" was a "rationalistic assumption" decided by the *consensus omnium*, he failed to mention that the process could sometimes be a biased procedure. Our age's "rationalistic assumptions" are based on the epistemological foundations of our sciences, such as Newtonian physics, causality, etc. They form the commonsense basis by which we think and form our ideas, and we must remember, as Beloff (1990) claims, that a commonsense approach means doing "justice to the evidence while, at the same time, seeking to do the least violence to our reason and our general knowledge" (p. 13). (As it happens, relativity theory and discoveries in quantum physics are slowly modifying our commonsense approach, as well as our reason and general knowledge.)

Psi phenomena, therefore, are irrational according to generally held scientific precepts, and that adds to their anomalous nature. But it is to the highest degree ironic how the irrationality of emotions and other prejudices can lend support to arguments that criticize psi on the basis that psi is an irrational phenomenon (see Stokes 1987). Thus do some critics (perhaps many) try to have their cake and eat it too. It is even more ironic when we realize that the reasoned approach of statistical law can suggest the psi anomaly in the first place. Taking all the foregoing statements into consideration, we can see how experience, belief, and the scientific method may all intertwine and give us much food for thought.

Any responsible investigator who considers these issues and takes them seriously must be left with the resounding feeling that social factors form the undercurrent of a seemingly unimpeded flow of scientific progress. These factors combined with the business of science as usual, give a socioempirical structure to parapsychology as much as they do to science in general. The whole field of science is a human endeavor that requires of us that we give heed to that fact consistently and thoughtfully.

Conclusion

There are many problems that parapsychology has faced in the past, and will continue to face in the future. This chapter addressed some of those problems and tried to arrive at some solutions. Generally, a socioempirical approach to psi was proposed by which new viewpoints might yield new answers. First, it was shown that *specification* of psi phenomena — the scientific account of the nature of the subject matter of parapsychology — is no more or less a burden for parapsychologists than it is for investigators and theorists in any other discipline, when they honestly confront their own subject matter. The general feeling from skeptics, though, is that this is not the case. For them, invalidation of a phenomenon (e.g., psi) stems naturally and rightfully from the fact that preconceived notions must need serious scrutiny, but they rarely apply a reflexive criticism to the phenomena they hold as being manifestly self-evident and self-specifying — their own preconceived notions remain unscrutinized.

Second, the principles of replicability and repeatability were introduced as conventional means of arriving at agreement about the existence of a phenomenon — more correctly, its statistical reality only — but the principles themselves and allegiance to them were actually shown to create the false impression that less replicable phenomena were unspecifiable and probably even artifacts. Since that conclusion is not always true in science, it follows that a socially constructed "myopism" or prejudice exists against anomalous phenomena based on principles that are anything but scientific. For all that, the principle of replicability still holds a certain validity and workability so long as we can arrive at some kind of consensus as to what it is that has been replicated. It was concluded, therefore, that when a phenomenon is said to be specified in some way, that *way* of specification is inherently constructed, and is therefore a socioempirical process of definition making.

Third, thought must be given to the nature of any given paradigm. It is only an assumption that disparate systems of thought must necessarily be incommensurable, incompatible, or irreconcilable with each other. Scientific knowledge consists of ideas and theories that complement each other as much as contradict. Very often they are merely discursively different — they even speak from the same core ideas and values. Given these considerations, it was argued that scientists must put their concepts in the balance and identify the discontinuities for what they may be — the result of social actions based more on opinion and personal or in-group prejudice rather than fact.

Finally, this chapter discussed the ways in which three factors — experience, belief and the scientific method (statistics in particular) — have given shape and form to the field of parapsychology and its paradigms (including the psi construct). These three factors also influence the researcher's attitudes and prejudices and therefore, have a direct influence on the future of parapsychology. The social repercussions, then, of experience, belief, and the scientific method are of direct concern to the field of parapsychology because these factors ultimately influence the field's social status as a discipline.

The same three factors were also claimed to be persuasive mechanisms that can influence "closed-minded" skepticism (and indeed any belief system). Skepticism can thereby be somewhat ameliorated through the processes of a direct experience in the field (preferably of the paranormal type), a more centered consideration of belief formation (incorporating a critical or commonsense approach to the nature of belief), and improvements in scientific methodologies.

In closing, and to resurrect an earlier theme, it was noted how the elusive nature of psi gives cause for skeptics to undermine parapsychological research — they believe that the study of "unqualified anomalies" is a contradiction in terms, so that psi must therefore be unbelievable. While skepticism, wherever it exists, was argued above as being a somewhat myopic outlook on all kinds of anomalous phenomena, skepticism can indirectly be a productive force in its own right — even in parapsychology — because its critical approach to the procedures and methodologies used to investigate those phenomena serves to identify faults that may exist in parapsychological practice.

Thus, in giving fair representation to opposing viewpoints, parapsychology holds a promise that it will continue to flourish in the future because of its open-mindedness, though that may incompletely represent parapsychology. Thus are the arguments presented in this chapter meant to support that open-mindedness in order that parapsychology becomes an informed science, not just a socially acceptable, or politically correct science. Parapsychology must not resist the forces of social change, but must yield to them as part of an ongoing natural process that extends into the future.

REFERENCES

Akers, C. (1984). Methodological criticisms of parapsychology. In S. Krippner, ed., *Advances in parapsychological research 4* (pp. 112–164). Jefferson, NC: McFarland.

Alcock, J. E. (1985). Parapsychology as a "spiritual" science. In P. Kurtz, ed., *A skeptic's handbook of parapsychology* (pp. 537–565). Buffalo, NY: Prometheus.

Beloff, J. (1990). *The relentless question: Reflections on the paranormal.* London: McFarland.

Blackmore, S. J. (1985a). Unrepeatability: Parapsychology's only finding. In B. Shapin and L. Coly, eds., *The repeatability problem on parapsychology: Proceedings of an international conference* (pp. 183–206). New York, NY: Parapsychology Foundation.

_____. (1985b). The adventures of a psi-inhibitory experimenter. In B. B. Wolman, ed., *Handbook of parapsychology* (pp. 425–418). New York: Van Nostrand Reinhold.

_____. (1986). *Extrasensory perception as a cognitive process.* Unpublished Ph.D. thesis, University of Surrie, England.

_____. (2001). Giving up the ghosts: End of a personal quest. *Skeptical Inquirer* **25**, 25.

Boring, E. G. (1955). The present status of parapsychology. *American Scientist* **43**, 108–117.

_____. (1966). Introduction — Paranormal phenomena: Evidence, specification, and chance. In C. E. M. Hansel. *ESP: A scientific evaluation* (pp. *i–xxi*). London: MacGibbon & Kee.

Braud, W. G. (1975). Psi-conducive states. *Journal of Communication* **25**, 142–152.

_____. (1991). Implications and applications of laboratory psi findings. *European Journal of Parapsychology* **8**, 57–65.

Bunge, M. (1991). A skeptic's beliefs and disbeliefs. *New Ideas in Psychology* **9**, 131–149.

Collins, H. M. (1976). *Upon the replication of scientific findings: A discussion illuminated by the experience of researchers in parapsychology.* Paper presented at the First International Conference on Social Studies of Science. Cornell University, November, 1976.

Collins, H. M., and T. Pinch (1982). *Frames of meaning: The social construction of extraordinary science.* London: Routledge.

Diaconis, P. (1978). Statistical problems in ESP research. *Science* **201**, 131–136.

_____. (1991). Comment. *Statistical Science* **6**, 386.

Drever, J. (1968). Some early associationists. In B. B. Wolman, ed., *Historical roots of contemporary psychology* (pp. 11–28). New York: Harper and Row.

Edge, H. (1985). The problem is not replication. In B. Shapin and L. Coly, eds., *The repeatability problem on parapsychology: Proceedings of an international conference* (pp. 53–72). New York, NY: Parapsychology Foundation.

Edgeworth, F. Y. (1885). The calculus of probabilities applied to psychical research. In *Proceedings of the Society for Psychical Research* **3**, 190–199.

_____. (1886). The calculus of probabilities applied to psychical research. II. In *Proceedings of the Society for Psychical Research* **4**, 189–208.

Fisher, R. A. (1924). A method of scoring coincidences in tests with playing cards. In *Proceedings of the Society for Psychical Research* **34**, 181–185.

_____. (1929). The statistical method in psychical research. In *Proceedings of the Society for Psychical Research* **39**, 189–192.

Flew, A. (1987). Analyzing the concepts of parapsychology. In A. Flew, ed., *Readings in the philosophical problems of parapsychology* (pp. 87–106). Buffalo, NY: Prometheus.

Gauquelin, M. (1983). *The truth about astrology.* Oxford: Basil Blackwell.

Gilmore, J. B. (1989). Randomness and the search for psi. *Journal of Parapsychology* **53**, 309–340.

Greenhouse, J. B. (1991). Comment: Parapsychology — On the margins of science? *Statistical Science* **6** (4), 386–389.

Hansel, C. E. M. (1966). *ESP: A scientific evaluation.* London: McGibbon & Kee.

_____. (1980). *ESP and parapsychology: A scientific reevaluation.* Buffalo, NY: Prometheus.

Hansen, G. P. (1991). The elusive agenda: Dissuading as debunking in Ray Hyman's "The Elusive Quarry." *Journal of the American Society for Psychical Research* **85**, 193–203.

Haraldsson, E. (1993). Are religiosity and belief in an afterlife better predictors of ESP performance than belief in psychic phenomena? *Journal of Parapsychology* **57**, 259–273.

Honorton, C. (1985). How to evaluate and improve the replicability of parapsychological effects. In B. Shapin & L. Coly, eds., *The repeatability problem in parapsychology* (pp. 238–255). New York: Parapsychology Foundation.

_____. (1993). Rhetoric over substance: The impoverished state of skepticism. *Journal of Parapsychology* **57**, 191–214.

Hyman, R. (1985). A critical historical overview of parapsychology. In P. Kurtz, ed., *A skeptic's handbook of parapsychology* (pp. 3–96). Buffalo, NY: Prometheus.

_____. (1989). *The elusive quarry: A scientific appraisal of psychical research.* Buffalo, NY: Prometheus Books.

_____. (1991). Comment. *Statistical Science* **6**, 389–392.

Irwin, H. J. (1993). Belief in the paranormal: A review of the empirical literature. *Journal of the American Society for Psychical Research* **87**, 1–39.

_____. (1999). *An introduction to parapsychology* (3rd ed.). Jefferson, NC: McFarland.

Jung, C. G. (1960). *The structure and dynamics of the psyche.* London: Routledge and Keegan Paul.

_____. (1987). *Psychological types.* (H. G. Baynes, trans., revised by R. F. C. Hull.) Princeton, NJ: Princeton University Press. (Original works published in 1921.)

Kuhn, T. S. (1962). *The structure of scientific revolutions.* Chicago: University of Chicago Press.

Kurtz, P. (1985). Is parapsychology a science. In P. Kurtz, ed., *A skeptic's handbook of parapsychology* (pp. 503–518). Buffalo, NY: Prometheus.

Latour, B., and S. Woolgar (1979). *Laboratory life: The social construction of scientific facts.* Beverly Hills, CA: Sage.

Lawrence, T. R. (1993). Gathering in the sheep and goats: A meta-analysis of forced-choice studies, 1947–1993. *Proceedings of the 36th Annual Convention of the Parapsychological Association,* pp. 75–86.

Mauskopf, S. H., and M. R. McVaugh (1980). *The elusive science: Origins of experimental psychical research.* Baltimore: Johns Hopkins University Press.

May, E. C., J. M. Utts, and J. P. Spottiswoode (1995). Decision augmentation theory: Applications to the random number generator database. *Journal of Scientific Exploration* **9**, 453–488.

McClenon, J. (1984). *Deviant science: The case of parapsychology.* Philadelphia: University of Pennsylvania Press.

Meehl, P., and M. Scriven (1987). The compatibiltiy of science and ESP. In A. Flew, ed., *Readings in the philosophical problems of parapsychology* (pp. 230–233). Buffalo, NY: Prometheus.

Mischel, W. (1968). *Personality and assessment.* New York: Wiley.

_____. (1973). *Readings in personality.* New York: Holt, Rineholt and Winston.

Mischel, W., and Y. Shoda (1995). A cognitive-affective system theory of personality: Reconceptualizing situations, dispositions, dynamics, and invariance in personality structure. *Psychological Review* **102**, 246–268.

Morris, R. L. (1991). Comment. *Statistical Science* **6**, 393–395.

Mosteller, F. (1991). Comment. *Statistical Science* **6**, 395–396.

Motte, A., and F. Cajori (1962). *Sir Isaac Newton's mathematical principles of natural philosophy and his system of the world.* Berkeley, CA: University of California Press.

Murphy, G. (1987). The problem of repeatability in psychical research. In A. Flew, ed., *Readings in the philosophical problems of parapsychology* (pp. 254–267). Buffalo, NY: Prometheus.

Palmer, J. (1987). Have we established psi?" *Journal of the American Society for Psychical Research* **81**, 111–123.

_____. (1988). The psi controversy. In D. H. Weiner and R. L. Morris, eds., *Research in parapsychology 1987* (pp. 153–157). Metuchen, NJ: Scarecrow Press.

Pratt, J. G. (1960). Contribution to: Physicality of psi, a symposium and forum discussion. *Journal of Parapsychology* **24**, 23–27.

_____. (1973). *ESP research today: A study of developments in parapsychology since 1960.* Metuchen, NJ: Scarecrow.

Quine, W. V., and J. S. Ullian (1970). *The web of belief.* New York: Random House.

Radin, D. I. (1997). *The conscious universe: The scientific truth of psychic phenomena.* San Francisco: HarperCollins.

Rao, K. R. (1985). Replication in conventional and controversial sciences. In B. Shapin and L. Coly, ed., *The repeatability problem in parapsychology* (pp. 22–41). New York: Parapsychology Foundation.

Rhine, J. B. (1937/1950). *Frontiers of the mind.* Harmondsworth, Middlesex: Pelican/Penguin.

_____. (1948/1954). *The reach of the mind.* Harmondsworth, Middlesex: Pelican/Penguin.

Richet, C. (1884). La suggestion mentale et le calcul des probabilités (Mental suggestion and probability calculation). *Review Philosophique* 18, 608–674.

Rockwell, T., and W. T. Rockwell (1986). Review of "The demarcation between science and pseudoscience: Working papers in science and technology, vol. 2, No. 1." (Ed. by R. Laudan). *Journal of the American Society for Psychical Research* 80, 105–112.

Rosenthal, R. (1986). Meta-analytic procedures and the nature of replication: The ganzfeld debate. *Journal of Parapsychology* 50, 315–336.

Rosnow, R. L., and R. Rosenthal (1993). *Beginning behavioral research.* New York: Macmillan.

Schlitz, M. J. (1985). The phenomenology of replication. In B. Shapin and L. Coly, eds., *The repeatability problem on parapsychology: Proceedings of an international conference* (pp. 73–97). New York: Parapsychology Foundation.

Schmeidler, G. R. (1968). Parapsychology. In *International Encyclopedia of the Social Sciences* (pp. 386–399). New York: Macmillan and The Free Press.

Scott, C. (1958). G. Spencer Brown and probability: A critique. *Journal of the Society for Psychical Research* 39, 217–234.

Shapin, B., and L. Coly, eds., (1985). *The repeatability problem in parapsychology.* New York: Parapsychology Foundation.

Spencer-Brown, G. (1957). *Probability and Scientific Inference.* London: Longmans Green.

Stanford, R. G. (1977). Conceptual frameworks of contemporary psi research. In B. B. Wolman, ed., *Handbook of parapsychology* (pp. 823–858). New York: Van Nostrand Reinhold.

_____. (1978). Towards reinterpreting psi events. *Journal of the American Society for Psychical Research* 72, 197–214.

Stokes, D. M. (1987). Theoretical parapsychology. In S. Krippner, ed., *Advances in parapsychological research* 5 (pp. 77–189). Jefferson, NC: McFarland.

Storm, L. (2002). A parapsychological investigation of the *I Ching*: Seeking psi in an ancient Chinese system of divination. *Australian Journal of Parapsychology* 2, 44–62.

Storm, L., & Thalbourne, M. A. (1998-1999). The transliminal connection between personality and paranormal effects in an experiment with the *I Ching*. *European Journal of Parapsychology* 14, 100–124.

_____, _____. (2000). Correspondence. *Journal of Parapsychology,* 64, 347–350.

Thalbourne, M. A. (2000). Transliminality: A review. *International Journal of Parapsychology* 11, 1–34.

_____. (2004). *The common thread between ESP and PK.* New York: Parapsychology Foundation.

Thalbourne, M. A., and J. Houran (2000). Transliminality, the Mental Experience Inventory, and tolerance of ambiguity. *Personality and Individual Differences* 28, 853–863.

Tyrrell, G. N. M. (1945). Presidential address. *Proceedings of the Society for Psychical Research* 47, 301–319.

Utts, J. (1991). Replication and meta-analysis in parapsychology. *Statistical Science* 6, 363–378.

_____. (1995). An assessment of the evidence for psychic functioning. *Journal of Parapsychology* 59, 289–320.

Von Franz, M.-L. (1980). *On divination and synchronicity: The psychology of meaningful chance.* Toronto: Inner City.

West, J. A. (1992). *The case for astrology.* London: Arkana/Penguin.

13

Language and the Study of Parapsychological Phenomena

*Robin Wooffitt**

Dr. Robin Wooffitt demonstrates the advantages that might be gained for parapsychology if a sociological approach is taken to the conversations that take place during psi experiment-interlocutor, psychic-sitter, experimenter-subject interactions. Dr. Wooffitt argues that conversation analysis "allows us to explore the broader communicative practices through which information is depicted as having a paranormal origin and validated in subsequent exchange." Thus, showing how "cold reading" might work, although useful to researchers, is nonetheless peripheral to the broader applications of conversation analysis. Consider, for example, the "you said" preface, often used by the experimenter in (say) the ganzfeld setting, to elicit more information, or confirm or clarify information already recorded in the mentation report. Analysis of this device (among other devices) gives researchers useful knowledge about how experimenter and subject make sense of their interactions. Dr. Wooffitt's chapter offers a much-

*Part of the work reported here was undertaken while the author was a visiting researcher at the Koestler Parapsychology Unit at the University of Edinburgh. The work was supported by an award from the Perrott-Warwick Fund. The author thanks the Perrott-Warwick Committee for their generous assistance, and Professor Bob Morris and his colleagues at the KPU for facilitating this research and making him feel welcome.

needed consideration of what underpins "talk in interaction."
Readers may detect the tacit implications this kind of study
may have in regard to the experimenter effect. (Editors)

Many parapsychologists have argued that it would be to parapsychology's advantage to develop strong links with other research disciplines.
There would be intellectual rewards, such as a cross-fertilization of
research topics and methodologies; and there would be institutional
benefits, in that strong relationships with established disciplines would
strengthen parapsychology's academic standing (e.g., see Chapter 2). One
way for parapsychology to develop in the 21st century, then, is to develop
and nurture collaborative research programs with other disciplines.

Parapsychology has largely modeled itself on laboratory-based experimental psychology. It should be no surprise to find that parapsychologists might seek to develop links with other sciences. It is more surprising,
however, to observe the extent of the intellectual traffic between parapsychology and the social sciences, particularly sociology. So, parapsychologists have looked to methodological and theoretical developments largely
associated with sociology to suggest how existing research programs might
be refreshed (White 1993), or to offer more radical overviews (Hansen
2001). More recently, Zingrone has argued that it is useful for parapsychologists to be aware of sociological studies of scientific controversies, as
these illuminate the broader processes that underpin the discipline's continuing struggle to establish its scientific status. She also draws on these
studies to identify how parapsychologists may be more strategic in managing their relationships with other disciplines (Zingrone 2002; see also
McClenon 1991).

The paranormal, the occult and the supernatural are not traditionally taken to be central concerns of sociology. Yet there have been occasions when the sociological gaze has turned to anomalous events and their
relationship to wider social forces and cultural changes. Many sociologists
interested in scientific controversies have explicitly focused on the history
and practices of parapsychology to examine the social processes through
which the scientific community demarcates between true and false knowledge claims (Allison 1982; Collins and Pinch 1979; 1982). There have been
studies that seek to identify the social correlates of anomalous experiences
(Bourque 1969; Moody 1974; Wuthnow 1976; Warren 1970; Fox 1992; Hartman 1976; Hay and Morisy 1978; Zimmer 1984). There have been attempts
to identify the cultural or social preconditions that give rise to interest in
or experience of anomalous phenomena (Campbell and McIver 1987; Greeley 1991; Markovsky and Thye 2001; McClenon 1990; Nelson 1975; Truzzi

1974a; 1974b). And scholars of contemporary culture have examined how the narratives of belief in the paranormal reflect and embody broader ideological, political and religious contexts (eg, Hess 1994), and their implications for wider social institutions (Adorno 1994; McClenon 1994). Parapsychologists, then, have been keen to explore the methodological resources sociology (and social sciences more generally) have to offer; and sociologists have explored the social contexts of and influences on paranormal beliefs and experiences.

There is, then, a tradition of research that explores (and sometimes transcends) the boundaries between parapsychology and sociology. But is it possible to go further than this, and to find research projects that address core concerns of *both* disciplines? I think it is. In an early paper on the relationship between sociology and parapsychology, Lynch (1975) noted that, at that time, there was a growing recognition in sociology of the central role of language and communication in everyday social action. He went on to argue that:

> both parapsychologists and [some] sociologists are intensely concerned with the subtleties of human communication processes. This shared interest alone should provide a basis for future interdisciplinary studies [Lynch 1975, p. 304].

Since the publication of Lynch's paper, research on language and interaction has emerged as a core component in various social sciences. This "linguistic turn" in the social sciences— specifically, a method of analysis that has come to be known as conversation analysis— offers the possibility of a sustained and mutually beneficial interdisciplinary collaboration.

In this chapter, then, I want to develop Lynch's observations, first by showing how parapsychological research relies on ordinary human communicative practices. Then I will discuss conversation analysis (hereafter, CA). Finally, I will describe how CA can be used to explore a range of issues in parapsychological research.

Language and the Paranormal

Parapsychology relies on language, particularly talk-in-interaction: researchers, practitioners and respondents rely on everyday communicative skills in conducting experiments, demonstrating paranormal powers or making reports of spontaneous experiences.

To illustrate, firstly, the significance of talk in laboratory practice, we will examine the ganzfeld experimental procedure as exemplified by the experiments conducted at the Koestler Parapsychology Unit during the 1990s (Dalton et al. 1996).

A typical ganzfeld trial largely depends on the participants— subjects, experimenters, assistants— using everyday language to accomplish a variety of tasks. So, it is likely that the subject will be met by one of the experimenters, or a representative of the laboratory, when they present themselves at the laboratory at the arranged time. There will be greetings, and, in all likelihood, activities such as inquiries about health, discussion of travel problems (if any), comments on the weather, and so on. And unless the subject has previous experience of the ganzfeld procedure, there will be discussion of what is going to happen: there will be explanations and accounts, questions and answers, queries and clarifications and so on. The actual core of the experimental procedure also relies on discursive activities. In the mentation the subject has to rely on their everyday communicative skills to convey the sensations and images they are experiencing. And in the mentation review phase, both experimenter and subject will rely on their tacit knowledge of everyday communicative practices concerning, for example, the management of turn-taking, clarification and correction. The judging session will also be managed verbally. There might be a subsequent debriefing with the subject during which the experimenter and subject may discuss the experiments, or parapsychology in general. Finally, the subject may be escorted from the laboratory or the building, during which there will be another series of informal exchanges.

The importance of language in the laboratory has not gone unnoticed by parapsychologists. For example, Giesler (1986) has raised some interesting points about verbal communication and psi. He suggests that psi functioning may be linked to communication in laboratories, and wonders whether what he calls "the spirit" of a parapsychological laboratory might be described in terms of its overall communicative environment. And Stanford et al. used quantitative measures to study the relationship between linguistic features of mentation reports and psychological constructs (1989a; 1989b). These studies are clearly important. But they do not attend to the ways in which language is used to manage particular interactional activities associated with laboratory contexts, or which are integral parts of experimental procedures.

Contemporary parapsychology is a scientific, laboratory-based discipline. But initial interest in the scientific study of anomalous phenomena was stimulated by events in less formal settings. First, psychic practitioners seemed to be able to provide demonstrations of knowledge gained from various kinds of parapsychological cognition: communication from the dead, clairvoyance, and so on. And reports of spontaneous extraordinary experiences from ordinary members of the public offered suggestive evidence for the occurrence of a range of paranormal phenomena such as telepathy, precognition and apparitional appearances. Language is central to the claims of psychic practitioners and the production of accounts of spontaneous experiences.

It is well known that members of the public who consult mediums and psychics often believe they have been told information which the psychic could not have known by the use of the normal senses, and that the authenticity and accuracy of paranormal powers of cognition have been demonstrated.

During the late nineteenth and early twentieth centuries, the proof of paranormal abilities was often demonstrated through the appearance and manipulation of physical objects. But the manipulation of objects is uncommon in the demonstrations of contemporary psychic practitioners. With some notable exceptions (e.g., Keen et al. 1999), the proof of special cognitive powers is almost always demonstrated verbally. Any proof that is given, any evidence that is provided, is accomplished in the interaction itself; what is communicated between the psychic practitioner and the sitter is thus the primary basis from which judgments can be made about the authenticity of the psychic's claim to possess paranormal forms of cognition. Parapsychologists (Roe 1995) and sceptics (Hyman 1981; Randi 1981) have been aware of the importance of language in the production of information derived from ostensibly paranormal sources. But there has been little investigation of the interactional dynamics of exchanges between psychic practitioners and sitters; sceptical advocates of cold reading in particular have assumed a model of language in which communication is viewed as a passive medium for information transfer, rather than the vehicle through which complex and delicate interpersonal activities are managed (Wooffitt 2003a).

Finally: knowledge of spontaneous anomalous phenomena comes — at least in part — from verbal accounts provided by people who consider that they have had extraordinary experiences. Here again, tacit communicative skills come into play. For example, accounts of such experiences are multiunit stories: narratives built out of a variety of separate components. The production of these kinds of narratives requires careful coordination by producer and recipient: for example, normal turn-taking procedures have to be temporarily suspended to allow the speaker to deliver an extended report. Thus even these kinds of semiformal interviews have to be interactionally managed.

There is, then, an irony. Parapsychology is the study of *anomalous* communication: extraordinary interaction between mind and the environment; yet parapsychologists rely so much on *ordinary* communication: the way that talk is used in various interactional contexts. Yet we know so little about the ways in which it impacts on the practices of parapsychological research, and the activities which parapsychologists study. Conversation analysis offers a way to explore these issues.

Conversation Analysis and the Study of Talk-in-Interaction

Conversation analysis is a formal, qualitative method for the analysis of naturally occurring interaction. It developed out of the pioneering studies of Harvey Sacks and his colleagues Emmanual Schegloff and Gail Jefferson, and focuses on analysis of the socially organized, tacit communicative activities through which participants in all kinds of verbal interaction produce intelligible, meaningful conduct (Hutchby and Wooffitt 1998; Sacks 1992). CA seeks to show how turns in interaction collectively form highly regular patterns: sequences of interactions. These sequences are taken to be the site in which interpersonal activities are managed collaboratively by participants.

There are now several methodological approaches to the study of language use: ethnomethodological discourse analysis (Gilbert and Mulkay 1984; Potter and Wetherell 1987), critical discourse analysis (Fairclough 1995), narrative analysis (e.g., Plummer 1995), Foucauldian analyses of discourses (Burman and Parker 1993), and so on. All of these offer empirical claims about the way we use language to conduct interaction, and through which we give reports and accounts of our experiences. However, conversation analysis has emerged as perhaps the preeminent social science method for the analysis of how people use language. This is because it has some distinctive methodological features, many of which will be illustrated throughout this chapter. In this section, however, I want to provide a broad outline of the assumptions that inform empirical research.

Although known as *conversation* analysis, empirical research is not exclusively concerned with conversational activities. Researchers study many kinds of interaction which would not be considered conversational; indeed, one of the growing areas of research in CA is the study of institutional talk such as courtroom interaction, doctor-patient consultations, calls to radio talk shows and political interviews broadcast on television (Boden and Zimmerman 1991; Drew and Heritage 1992). CA is regarded as a method for studying all kinds of naturally occurring interaction.

Conversation analysis has developed a distinctive perspective on verbal communication which sets it apart from more conventional social sciences. In CA studies, interaction is viewed as a domain of activity in its own right: it is not regarded as a simple expression of psychological idiosyncrasies or personality, nor as a canvas onto which the significance of sociological factors, such as the participants' relationship, class, gender, status, and so on are projected. This means that the analyst does not begin research with a series of preestablished and theory-led questions to be explored in the data. Instead, analysis is directed towards uncovering peoples' own interpretations as they are revealed in the details of their talk. We will return to this key methodological point in a later section.

Finally, it is important to make a distinction between CA and other qualitative approaches to language, and more postmodern and social constructionist perspectives. This is because CA offers clear and formal methodological procedures which mark it out from more loosely formulated qualitative methods. Moreover, it seeks to establish formal, rigorous and cumulative knowledge claims about the linguistic structures through which social action is conducted. In this, it is set apart from approaches which assume the relative or constructed status of knowledge claims.

In the rest of this chapter I want to illustrate the application of a conversation analytic perspective. My objective is not to present a comprehensive account of CA, but rather, to illustrate the kinds of novel issues it can raise, and suggest ways in which it can address— or even transform — questions in parapsychological research.

Conversation Analysis and the Social Organization of Accounts of Spontaneous Experiences

Spontaneous experiences have always been important in parapsychological research. Reports of anomalous events motivated the earliest serious investigation of paranormal phenomena (Gurney et al. 1886). And even when parapsychology was developing into a scientific, laboratory-based discipline accounts of personal experiences were not ignored. In an editorial in the *Journal of Parapsychology,* Rhine argued that information from reports of spontaneous cases could be useful to experimental parapsychologists (Rhine 1948). In her subsequent studies of thousands of unsolicited written accounts submitted to the laboratory at Duke University, Louisa Rhine tried to identify robust aspects of the phenomena and the way they occurred in a natural environment (L. Rhine 1981). More recently, White has argued parapsychologists should develop a more experience-centered approach, as exemplified by Hufford's (1982) study of accounts of Old Hag manifestations (White 1985, 1990). She emphasizes that understanding and interpreting subjective experiences is more appropriate than laboratory experiments (White 1993).

Spontaneous experiences become known to parapsychologists because the experients report them: the experients describe what happened, either verbally or in a written form. Parapsychologists, then, use accounts as resources in the investigation of the respective phenomena. Yet there has been little consideration of the accounts themselves. This is surprising: the analyst has access to such experiences only through the experients' reports. In a real sense the experience is linguistically mediated. This surely makes it incumbent upon us to know more about the communicative practices which are used in the production of the account.

There is a more radical argument: that the experience itself always remains elusive, and that all that we have to study are the accounts and narratives. Writing of sociologists' attempts to study religious experiences, Yamane wrote

> Sociologists cannot empirically study experiencing, thus understood, for it is a wholly private, individual affair inaccessible to any currently known methods of social scientific research [Yamane 2000, p. 174].

Experiences remain inaccessible; what is available to researchers are accounts of experiences. Yamane argues therefore that scholars of religious experience need to understand that such accounts are the proper topic of their inquiries. The parallels to parapsychologists' attempts to study spontaneous paranormal experiences are clear.

It is not my intention, however, to support or criticize Yamane's radical thesis, nor to judge between competing claims about the extent to which we can be confident of our knowledge of spontaneous experiences from collections of accounts. My purpose in raising these issues is to indicate simply that there are good reasons why parapsychologists need to understand the organization of accounts when trying to investigate those events of which accounts are some kind of record. It would seem to be a necessary first step to understand how they are produced, and the communicative skills employed in their production prior to using them as research resources to make claims about the experiences which are thereby reported. To this end it is useful to consider some observations on the practice of describing from the conversation analytic literature.

It seems somehow common-sense to assume that the very properties of a state of affairs in the world somehow constrain which words or combination of words we can use when describing it. It follows from this assumption that there is only a limited number of referential items that we can use when referring to something: that is, when we have exhausted the properties of the object to which we are referring, then we can say no more. However, these assumptions rest on an incorrect understanding of the relationship between words and the worlds they describe.

The first point to consider is that no descriptive utterance can exhaust the particulars of the state of affairs to which it refers. The description of any event can be extended indefinitely. For example, with regards to the formulation of location, or "place," Schegloff has written:

> Were I now to formulate where my notes are, it would be correct to say that they are: right in front of me, next to the telephone, on the desk, in my office, in the office, in Room 213, in Lewisohn Hall, on campus, at school, at Columbia, in Morningside Heights, on the upper West Side, in Manhattan, in New York City, in New York State, in the North east, on the Eastern seaboard, in the United States, etc. Each of these terms could in some sense be correct ... were its relevance provided for [Schegloff 1972, p. 81].

The point is that any description or reference is produced from a potentially inexhaustible list of possible utterances, each of which is "logically" correct or "true" by any test of correspondence. It is important to remember that this is not a philosophical problem: it is a practical problem that people address every time they describe something. For example, in the following extract the speaker is reporting an encounter with a paranormal entity; note the variety of ways in which that entity is described.

Extract (1)   [From Wooffitt 1992, pp. 14–15] ("S" is the speaker. There is an explanation of CA transcription symbols in the Appendix.)

1	S:	[1] a man (.) pushed passed me
2		(1)
3		[2] he was spirit it (w-) or whatever you want to call it
4		[3] ur(r)h a great force
5		came rushing down
6		(.3)
7		the stairs (.) against me

Accounts of experiences are composed of descriptions: descriptions of what happened, descriptions of the experient's reactions, descriptions of the context of the experience and so on. In keeping with developments in philosophy (Austin 1962; Rorty 1979; Wittgenstein 1953), CA rejects the idea that language is a mirror of reality, and that descriptions are merely neutral reports of a world "out there," or a simple expression of a realm of inner cognitions, such as attitudes and memories. Instead it seeks to understand how descriptions are assembled and thereby identify what they have been assembled to do.

To illustrate this, consider some of the issues involved when experients describe *when* their experience happened. Parapsychologists may seek to locate precise dates and times of an experience, but in verbal accounts, experients rarely display commitment to such details. For example, the following extract comes from an interview with a person who claimed to have had a number of paranormal experiences. She has just finished discussing a particular type of clairvoyant experience, and in this extract she begins to mention a specific incident to illustrate certain claims.

Extract (2)   [From Wooffitt 1992, p. 94]:

```
1   S:   I mean>just thin(k) th- eh I mean ah-< a simple example which
2        everybody's had something similar to hhhh I was living
3        n uhm (.) inglan years ago (.) and all of a sudden I was sitting
4        in bed one night (.) getting ready to go to sleep
```

In this extract the speaker's formulation of when her experience happened is very vague: "I was living in uhm (.) inglan years ago." Note that the speaker refers to two features of when it happened: where she was living at the time, and how many years before the occasion of the telling. Both of these features of when the experience occurred are formulated in *relational* terms, in that the referent is identified in terms of its relation to an aspect of the speaker's personal biography (Pomerantz 1987). The first relational term is "living in inglan" (England), and the second is the claim that it happened "years ago." Both of these terms provide only vague characterizations of when the experience occurred. This information would not be helpful, for example, to a parapsychologist investigating a spontaneous case; indeed, it might be dismissed as an irrelevance.

But let us consider this formulation in more detail. At any one moment it would be possible to characterize a person's life in terms of a variety of such life stages. With regards to **Extract (2)** and the formulation "I was living in uhm (.) inglan years ago" we can therefore ask why is *this* characterization of *this* feature of a personal biography relevant for the speaker at *this* moment in the account? We can begin to address these questions if we take note of the experience for which the formulation "livingin uhm (.) inglan years ago" was designed as a setting.

Extract (3)   [From Wooffitt 1992, p. 95]

```
 1  S:   I mean >just thin(k) th- eh I mean ah-< a simple example which
 2        everybody's had something similar to hhhh I was living
 3        n uhm (.) inglan years ago (.) and all of a sudden I was sitting
 4        in bed one night (.) getting ready to go to sleep and I decided to
         write
 5        to a friend I hadn't seen for four years (.) in Massachusetts (.)
         a:nd
 6        I found myself congratulating her on (.) the engagement of her
 7        oldest daughter (.3) I said congratulations Marion's getti- Mar-
         ion's
 8        gotten engaged (.5) ar:hm and I sent the letter(.7) and eh (.) er:
         ah I I
 9        felt totally (r) (.) right in doing so (.5) ah mean i(t) it was just
         as
10        normal to me to know that her daughter had just gotten engaged
         as
11        to know that I've got five fingers on my ring ha:nd hhhhan' eh
12        hh she wrote back to me hhh in total chaos saying (.) how the
         Hell
13        did ↑you know she started the letter huhh ↑hah hh she said I
14        received your letter at nine o'clock in the morning (.) and you
         were
15        congratulating me on (.) Marion's getting engage:d: and I said
         what
16        the HEll is she talking about hhh at twelve o'clock that morning
         (.)
17        she walked in and announced her engagement
```

The speaker describes a precognitive experience in which she knew of an engagement before any one else, with the exception of the two people who got engaged. The authenticity of a claim to have had a precognition rests upon acquisition of information about a state of affairs *before* that state of affairs came to pass. In this extract the speaker addresses this condition by revealing that she knew of the engagement before anyone else. But there is another factor which influences the validity of precognitive claims: *could* the experient have acquired the information through the operation of the customary five senses? If the relevant information could have been obtained in this way, even perhaps subliminally, there is a warrant to question the likelihood that paranormal processes of information transmission had occurred. The design of the formulation "I was living in uhm (.) inglan" displays the speaker's orientation precisely to this issue. The precognitive knowledge concerns a family in Massachusetts, in the United States. The likelihood that the speaker was able to discover internal family secrets is minimized by the information that at the time she was resident in *England*: "living in inglan" is designed to substantiate the implicit claim that her knowledge of the engagement was paranormally acquired.

In the parapsychological literature there is an underlying suspicion about the usefulness of accounts of spontaneous experiences. Even if it is assumed that experients are not deliberately fabricating stories, there is still a sense that the value of accounts is diminished by the possibility of unconscious distortion, the vagaries of memory, the experient's emotional involvement in the experience, and so on (e.g., see West 1948, p. 265; and Pekala and Cardeña 2000). Ultimately, then, parapsychology seems skeptical towards accounts, viewing them as broadly unreliable records of "what really happened." A CA perspective begins from a different position altogether. Drawing from a range of arguments in philosophy and the social sciences, it is assumed that language does not operate like a mirror of reality: "[e]xperience does not and can not *determine* its expression in language" (Yamane 2000, p. 177; original italics). This in turn invites us to ask: if accounts are not constrained by the experience, what communicative and pragmatic concerns *do* inform the ways accounts are organized?

In recent years there has been a number of studies of how we use language to establish the factual or warrantable status of our claims or reports (Edwards and Potter 1992; Potter 1996; Pomerantz 1986). One feature of this work has been the investigation of the ways in which contentious claims can be designed to address and minimize actual or potential skeptical responses (Smith 1978; Wooffitt 1992; 2001a, 2003a). It seems clear that these kinds of matters inform the way the speaker in **Extract (2)** formulates when the experience happened. That is, the relevance of this characterization (and other aspects of the account) lies in the inferential work it is designed to do: to substantiate the claim of a paranormal event, and to defuse possible skeptical challenges.

Detailed analysis of the communicative practices through which accounts are assembled allows us to explore the range of inferential matters which are relevant when people present themselves as having experiences which are controversial and contested. It thereby affords a deeper understanding of the cultural and interpersonal consequences of paranormal experiences, their relationship to the experients' sense of self, and insight to lay standards of authority and reliability. All of this rich insight about the relationship between culture, the individual and anomalous experiences is lost if we merely treat accounts as more or less adequate mirrors of an external reality.

CA and Practitioners: The Sequential Organization of Paranormal Knowledge Claims

Although CA can be used to study accounts of spontaneous experiences, it is primarily concerned with the organization of people talking together. This means it is ideally suited to the study of interaction between psychic practitioners, such as mediums, psychics and clairvoyants, and their clients, or sitters. (From now on I will use the term "psychic" as a shorthand for all kind of psychic practitioners.)

The main task of CA studies of interaction is to analyze *sequences* of interaction: patterned exchanges with robust properties through which participants engage in particular kinds of communicative acts. To illustrate, we will look at what might be called success sequences in psychic-sitter interaction: occasions in which the sitter seems to accept or confirm a claim by the psychic. (The data used in this section come from a corpus of tape and video recordings of psychics providing readings, both from the US and the UK — see Wooffitt 2000, for a full account.)

In sittings, psychic practitioners often issue a series of utterances, usually (but not invariably) in the form of questions. These hint at or imply that they have access to knowledge about the sitter or their circumstances. If the sitter finds the psychic's utterance to be accurate, or is in some way relevant, it is receipted and accepted with a minimal turn, usually a simple "yes" or "yeah." After the sitter's minimal acceptance or confirmation the psychic practitioner moves swiftly to a turn in which the now-accepted knowledge is attributed to a paranormal source. For example: the following extract comes from the transcript of a sitting between a psychic and a young woman. During this sitting, the psychic is using tarot cards to discern aspects of the sitter's present and future life. (In this and subsequent extracts in this section, the psychic practitioner is designated by the letter "P," and the sitter by the letter "S.")

Extract (4)   (Discussing S's plans to travel after graduating.)

```
1   S:   I graduate in June I'm probably going to work until
2        about february ⌜so: jus' (.) any old j ⌜ob    ⌝y'know.
3              ⌞RIght okay        ⌞-right-⌟
4   P:   andare you going to the states,
```

```
 5        (.)
 6   S:   yeah.
 7   P:   yea:h, c'z e I can see the old ehm:
 8        (.)
 9   S:   Hh  ┌-huh Hah 'h ┌
10   P:        └-statue of    └- liberty around you,
11   S:   heh heh h ┌e 'hhh
12   P:              └there you are, there's contentment for
13        the future.
14   S:   oh go ┌od
15   P:          └who's pregnant around you?
```

The question "and are you going to the states" may be heard as displaying the psychic's special knowledge that the sitter is indeed planning to visit the US. Once this has been accepted it is retrospectively cast as having been derived from the tarot cards: the psychic's utterance "c'z e I can see the old ehm: statue of liberty around you" portrays her prior turn as a consequence of her ability to discern from the arrangement of cards a classic iconic representation of the US, and interpret its relevance to the sitter. Moreover, early in this turn, there is a contracted version of "because," thus explicitly establishing that the topic of her prior utterance was generated from the special powers claimed in her subsequent turn.

Once the attributive turn is complete, and the psychic has made a general remark about the sitter's future contentment, she initiates another topic with the question "who's pregnant around you?" which, should it be accepted by the sitter, would project the relevance of another attributive turn and further demonstration of special powers.

There is, then, a sequence of three turns in which a claim about the sitter is proposed, accepted by the sitter, and which is then characterized as originating from a paranormal source. This sequence can be described schematically as:

T1   Psychic: a question embodying a claim about, or knowledge of, the sitter, their circumstances, etc.
T2   Sitter: minimal confirmation or acceptance
T3   Psychic: demonstration that the information embodied in the question has come from a paranormal source

This is a routine organization of success sequences. For example:

Extract (5)

```
 1   P:   So spirit wants me to do a scan on your bo:dy, talk
 2        about your health, so I'm going to do that okay? I'm
 3        going to do this for your health (0.8) Let's see
 4        what's going on with you. hh number one thing
 5        is your >mother in spirit please?                    <T1
 6        (0.2)
 7   S:   Yes                                                  T2
 8   P:   >'cause I have (n-m) y'r mother standing right over  T3
 9        here,hh and she said I WANna TAlk to HEr and I want
10        to speak to her because ˙hh your mother has very
11        lou::d when she comes through. ˙h she speaks with a in
12        a very lou:d way a very uhm (.) y'understand
13        very    ┌she has to be
14   S:           └ye:s:.
15   P:   heard, ˙h and like this would not happen today
16        without her coming through for you. D'y' ┌un'erstand?
17   S:                                            └-'kay
18   S:   Ye:s.
```

Extract (5) begins with a section from the psychic practitioner's description of how the sitting will proceed. After this initial preamble, he produces a question about the sitter's mother. This has an interesting design in that it could be heard as a genuine question about the sitter's mother; that is, it may be equivalent to "has your mother passed on or is she still living?"; or it could be heard as a question which seeks confirmation of information already known to the medium. The sitter's minimal response does not disambiguate the prior turn, in that a simple "yes" could be "a telling" or "a confirmation." The medium's next turn, however, reveals that he is in contact with the spirit of the sitter's mother. Moreover, the psychic prefaces this turn with "'cause"; this establishes that his prior turn was a consequence of, or an upshot of, information or events he is about to disclose in his current turn. This retrospectively characterizes his first turn as a question seeking confirmation of information already at hand. Also, it can now be inferred that the knowledge that the sitter's mother has died came from a paranormal source: the spirit of the mother herself. There are, then, strong similarities in the structure of this sequence to that derived from analysis of **Extract (4)**.

Extract 6 provides three "latched" or adjacent examples of the sequential unit outlined above.

Extract (6)   (In this extract there are two sitters, a mother and her daughter. At this point in the sitting the medium claims to be in
contact with the spirit of their husband and father)

```
 1  P:   >'ave you 'ad< (.) bit >(o')< trouble with your
 2       back as well.                                        T1
 3       (0.2)
 4  S1:  yes a little bi ┌t                                   T2
 5  P:              └-he says ah'd best send her a bit of     T3
 6       sympathy down so you understand it,
 7       ·hh ┌-h
 8  S1:      └-ye┌-s
 9  P:            └-coz y'know ·h y'try to bottle things up   T1
10       and you don't always let people get close to you
11                   in that sense do you
12  S1:  no.                                                  T2
13  P:   he says she can be quite stubborn at times y'know    T3
14       (.)
15  P:   is that true
16  S1   :°yes°
17  P:   an'he knows cz h you are fussy about the bungalow    T1
18       aren't you ┌girl
19  S1:            └yes I am                                  T2
20  P:   bless her he says                                    T3
```

There are three questions, each of which can be heard as proposing
that the psychic has access to intimate knowledge about the sitter: that she
has a back trouble, that she can be withdrawn, and that she is house proud
("fussy"). To each of these questions the sitter provides minimal positive
responses. And in each occasion the psychic then goes on to report what
the spirit of the sitter's husband has said to him, thereby making it infer-
able that it was the spirit who provided the information about the sitter.

The display of paranormal cognition then, is sequentially ordered: it
is in the third turn of the sequence where now-accepted claims about the
sitter are attributed to a paranormal source, and thus constitute evidence
of paranormal cognitive abilities. However, I am not claiming that *all*
ostensible successful demonstrations exhibit these sequential features;
there may well be other sequentially organized practices through which
such demonstrations may be managed. But there is a certain robustness
about this particular organization. In my corpus, it occurs in the discourse
of mediums, clairvoyants, tarot readers and astrologers. It can be found
in recordings of readings by internationally known practitioners and prac-

titioners working in locally organized psychic fairs. It informs the demonstrations by men and women, by the young and the not-so-young, both in the UK and the US. It occurs in face-to-face sittings, and in demonstrations to large audiences in theaters or halls. It even informs accounts of mediums' practices in newspaper reports and in their autobiographies (Wooffitt 2001b, 2003b).

So what can be gained from analysis of the sequential organization of psychic-sitter interaction?

Most important, we can move away from a restrictive concern with trying to identify (or dispute) the relevance of cold reading practices. This is because CA is agnostic as to the truth or falsity of claims that are advanced in interaction. Think of it this way: whether a psychic practitioner gets information about a sitter from spirits, from telepathy, or by cold reading, that information still has to be reported and established as factual in the course of the exchange with the sitter. Thus whereas cold reading offers a relatively narrow analytic focus, a CA approach allows us to explore the broader communicative practices through which information is depicted as having a paranormal origin and validated in subsequent exchange; thereby, we are able to provide a more rounded account of the activities which occur in sittings.

CA offers a way of developing a rounded and sophisticated understanding of the lived experience of psychic practitioners and their clients. But it also suggests a new range of research questions. For example: Heritage (1997) has identified three criteria by which it is possible to demarcate ordinary conversational interaction from talk which occurs in institutional or work-related settings. A consideration of these criteria, and their relevance to psychic-sitter interaction, allows us to identify a range of empirically investigable issues. First, participants in institutional interaction are normally concerned with a specific set of tasks and goals which are clearly connected to the "business" of the institution; moreover, these goals are tied to identities relevant to that institution. While psychics are not necessarily perceived as working in formal institutions such as hospitals or courtrooms, we may begin to investigate how their discourse is concerned with a fairly well-defined set of goals; moreover, we can begin to explore the ways in which the verbal activities of a sitting mobilize the relevance of a strictly observed set of identities. Second, Heritage notes that in institutional talk it is understood that there are constraints on what kinds of participation are normatively appropriate. Again, there are parallels with psychic-sitter interaction, in which, for example, it is understood that only one party will be expected to provide information derived from a paranormal source. Finally, the participants' conduct in a sitting is informed by the expectation that it is a vehicle for the demonstration of paranormally acquired knowledge; and this reflects Heritage's observation that the practical tasks or business of the institution will shape the kinds of inferences about and understanding of ongoing interaction. Psychic-sitter interaction, then, can be investigated as a form of informal institutional discourse (Drew and Heritage 1992, p. 27).

An appreciation of the quasi-institutional features of psychic-sitter interaction allows comparison with interaction in other kinds of task-related settings. For example: many researchers have noted that consultations with psychic practitioners seem to parallel forms of counselling, or have a therapeutic orientation (Lester 1982; Sechrest and Bryan 1968; Tyson 1982). However, there has been little formal analysis of similarities and differences between the activities of psychic practitioners and those of counsellors and therapists. We know a great deal about interactional practices in counselling or medical settings (e.g., Heath 1986; Heritage and Sefi 1992; Maynard 1991; Wilkinson 1995), but without a detailed account of the organization of psychic-sitter interaction, comparative work is difficult. Analysis of the key sequential phases through which the tasks of a sitting are collaboratively managed is a first step towards enabling this and other kinds of comparative research.

CA and Laboratory Practice: Exploring the Dynamics of Experimenter-Subject Interaction

Parapsychology is primarily a laboratory-based experimental discipline. However, even this kind of ostensibly formal scientific environment relies on verbal interaction: researchers talk to each other and with their subjects during parapsychology experiments. The laboratory is rife with interpersonal relationships mediated through verbal interaction.

This might be significant to our understanding of the operation of anomalous communication. For example, discussions of the ganzfeld methodology suggest the importance of the rapport between experimenter and subjects, and the experimenter's "warmth," (Morris et al. 1995; Parker 2000; Schlitz and Honorton 1992; Schmeidler and Edge 1999). And more general discussions of the characteristics of psi-conducive laboratories draw attention to the effect of the experimenter's relationship with the subject (Giesler 1986; Honorton et al. 1975; Schneider et al. 2000). There are, therefore, long-standing concerns within parapsychology about the effect of the experimenter on experimental outcomes; therefore it is important to study experimenter-subject interaction in laboratory settings.

A key feature of verbal interaction is mutual coorientation: the way that a participant's conduct displays their attention to, and interpretation of the discursive activities of other co-participants. The way in which this mutual coorientation is managed may have important consequences: for example, a mutually supportive coorientation might be the basis for ascriptions or feelings of warmth or rapport.

Conversation analysis explicitly focuses on the ways that participants orient to and monitor co-participants' activities in interaction. This is because the goal of conversation analysis is not to furnish an academic or "outsider's" reading of some conversational sequence, but to describe the organized interpretations that *people themselves* employ in the moment-by-moment course of conversation. The focus of analysis is to the understanding of "what-is-going-on-right-here-right-now" which speakers themselves have, and which are revealed — and thereby, demonstrable — in the design of subsequent utterances (Sacks et al. 1974).

To explain this key methodological principle, consider the following extract, which comes from an exchange between a mother and her son about a Parent Teachers Association meeting. (The following discussion draws from observations made by Heritage 1984; Levinson 1983; and Schegloff 1988.)

Extract (7)   [Terasaki 1976, p. 45]

1	Mother:	Do you know who's going to that meeting?
2	Russ:	Who?
3	Mother:	I don't know!
4	Russ:	Oh, probably Mr Murphy and Dad said Mrs
5		Timpte an' some of the teachers

In this extract Mother's question "Do you know who's going to that meeting?" can be interpreted in two ways: as a genuine *request* for information about who is attending the meeting, or as a *preannouncement* of some news concerning the people who will be attending the meeting. In the examination of this exchange, the analyst can identify which of these interpretations Russ makes by looking at the next turn after Mother's question. He returns the floor to his mother with a question, thereby displaying that he treats her utterance as a preannouncement. Mother's next turn displays that on this occasion Russ's inference was incorrect. The kinds of interpretative and reasoning procedures that CA seeks to identify are thus displayed in the trajectory of language use which is organized on a turn-by-turn basis.

We can illustrate the parapsychological relevance of this methodological procedure by examining some properties of experimenter-subject interaction during the mentation review period. These data come from recordings of experiments conducted in the mid–1990s by researchers at the Koestler Parapsychology Unit at the University of Edinburgh (Morris et al. 1995).

The mentation review is based on the subject's verbal report of events in his consciousness during the period the target materials were being screened. During the review the experimenter goes over the images and sensations reported by the subject to remind him of key moments, or to encourage further recollections or expansion on particular images or sensations.

There are various ways in which the experimenter can introduce an item (the subject's earlier report of a sensation or an image) during the review. The main components seem to be the report of the item, the modality of perception or knowing ("saw," "sensed," "heard") and a temporal marker which connects that item to the flow of the original mentation ("next," "and then"). Another way in which a mentation item may be introduced is with a "you said" preface. For example:

Extract (8)   (KPU Ganzfeld: 01–18. In extracts 8 to 10, "E" is the experimenter; "S" is the subject)

```
 1   E:   'hh and you saw a slope with a doorway at the to:p
 2   S:   yeah
 3   E:   'hh then you mentioned that your eyes were s->beginning to
          ache a 4bit<,
 5   S:   mm
 6   E:   'h and then you saw the roof again and you were s:(l)
 7        looking straight up (.) at it.
 8        (2)
 9   S:   yeah, (.) yeah
10        (0.5)
11   E:   then you had an (.) image of a- a toothbrush h still wrapped up
          in:
12        (.) its package 'hh and it was being spun in someone's h- fingers
(0.3)
13        'hh you: er:m: (0.3) saw that on the toothbrush sai:d (0.2) i(t)it
          said
14        ↑toothbrush in big blue letters.
15   S:   yeah
16   E:   'hh and then you saw: er: an impression of mickey mouse,
17        (0.5)
```

18 E: ·hhh and then you said a drill:=the threads of a dri*ll* spi*nn*ing
19   around,
20   (1.2)
21   ((P swallowing approx. 1 second))
22 S: yeah (.) 's coming in from th- from the left (.)·h
23   >s't've (l)ika< like a like a cross section through the earth I could see
24   this huge ·hhh like a sort've er: (0.2) channel tunnel drill
25   (0.8)
26 E: okay, (.) ·hh a humming top spinning (at-) a children's toy:s
        ((continues))

In this passage the experimenter introduces a number of items, thus providing the opportunity for subjects to expand upon their earlier reports, or to correct any experimenter misunderstanding. For example, after the experimenter has introduced the drill item the subject does indeed provide more information about this topic (lines 22–24). We might say, then, that after the experimenter's report of an item, there is a "slot" in the exchange in which the subject may take a turn to add further information. However, it is noticeable that it is more common for subjects to "pass" on opportunities to expand upon items. Such "passings" display that in this instance, they are not going to use the slot available to provide more information. These are various "passing" strategies: in this extract the subject uses minimal continuers ("mm," line 5), minimal confirmation ("yeah," line 15) and silence (line 17) to pass on opportunities where expansion could occur. It is also noticeable that after each of these passing activities, the experimenter moves on to the next item. She makes no comment about the absence of further information; nor does she pursue any further information. This means that she treats these activities as legitimate passings.

Of the various ways in which experimenters can introduce items into the mentation review the "you said" preface is perhaps the most intriguing: as the subject's original mentation was a verbal report of his or her consciousness, *any* item could be introduced by the experimenter as something that the subject had said. It is noticeable though, that "you said" prefaces seem to be used selectively.

Extract (9)   (KPU Ganzfeld: 01–47)

1 E: ·hh something re:d.ehrm:: i- looks like it might be a
2   porcupine with lots of spines standing ·hhh standing up
3 S: yeah hh
4 E: and then a frog=a frog's face peering over something

```
5          (0.8)
6          ·hh a ghost? coming out of a door: or a cha:ir (0.5) like a mir-
           ror. (.)
7          in a funny house,
8    S:    yeah=
9    E:    =·hhshapes (0.3) ahr:: are in this funny house
10         and shapes look like ehm ↑bunny rabbits with weird ears
11   S:    yeah (ch)hhuh huh ·hhhh
12   E:    thenyou said sheep lots of sheep
13   S:    ·hhhh (g)oads of sheep (pf)ah didn't know what
14         it was (hi-) ·h ⌈-hhh (k)huh uh              ((smiley voice))
15   E:                 ⌊-ok(h)a(h)y                     ((smiley voice))
16         (0.5)
17   E:    huh
18         (3.5)
19   E:    okay ·hh something in the ceiling
           ((continues))
```

In this extract, the experimenter introduces a number of items: "something red"; "a porcupine"; "a frog's face"; "a ghost"; "shapes" "bunny rabbits" "sheep" and "something in the ceiling." But only the "sheep" item is introduced with a "you said" preface. The question arises, then: are "you said" prefaces used to perform particular kinds of work in the review?

Research suggests that "you said" prefaces seem to initiate the onset of a short period of clarification and expansion by the subject (Wooffitt 2003b). For example, in both **Extracts (8)** and **(9)** only the items introduced via a "you said" preface ("drill" and "sheep") elicit further contributions from the subjects.

There is also evidence that both experimenter and participant have tacit understanding that "you said" item prefaces *should* lead to some kind of further description or clarification. In the next extract, the experimenter uses a "you said" preface, but the subject remains silent. However, the subsequent turns display that the experimenter was expecting some form of clarification.

Extract (10)   (KPU Ganzfeld: 01–77)

```
1    E:    sta:rs? (0.6) things rising (0.6) kites (0.6) ·hh flashing blue, flash-
           ing
2          green. (0.5) moving (0.8) ·hh flashing white (.) in patches (0.8)
3          ↑fingers, (0.8) fairgrounds, (0.8) pavements(0.6) ·hhh and it
           sounded
```

```
 4        like you said (.) twitching: (.)bulgy
 5        (1.2)
 6   E:   does that sound ↑right
 7   S:   what was that sorry?
 8   E:   'hh it sounded like you said twitching and ↓bulgy.
 9        (0.4)
10   S:   twitching,
11        (0.2)
12   E:   yes
13   S:   'h yeah my body was twitching I could feel myself
14        twitching
15   E:   oh:, okay, (0.8) 'hh sa:nd.
```

After the experimenter's utterance, "and it sounded like you said (.) twitching: (.) bulgy" the subject does not provide clarification or expansion in the next turn. Instead, there is a gap of 1.2 seconds, and the next person to speak is the experimenter. However, she does not move on to the next item, but explicitly asks if the characterization of the previous item was correct. This reveals several features of the experimenter's ongoing monitoring of the interaction. First: it is apparent that the experimenter is not treating the absence of the subject's talk as a routine passing of the opportunity to provide more information. Second: the experimenter terminates the silence, thus indicating that she inferred that the subject was not likely to speak. Third: "does that sound ↑right" acts as a reissued invitation for the subject to speak, thus demonstrating her orientation to the relevance of a subject contribution at this point. Fourth: her subsequent turn is explicitly designed to elicit some kind of assessment from the subject on her characterization of this item, thus indicating her expectation not only that the subject *should* contribute at his point, but displaying her understanding that a *particular kind* of next activity is relevant.

The experimenter's turn is a form of repair initiation (Schegloff et al. 1977), in that it is addressed towards a perceived trouble in the interaction. But what kind of trouble is it? The way in which the repair initiation is constructed provides some clues. Had she repeated the utterance "it sounded like you said (.) twitching: (.) bulgy" we would have evidence that her interpretation was that the subject had not heard the original utterance. However, "does that sound ↑right" is not a repeat but a prompt, and is designed to show its indexical connection to the prior turn; "that" for example, only makes sense as a reference to the earlier utterance. The experimenter's post-silence turn thus exhibits the kind of interpretations she is making about the moment-by-moment unfolding of the interaction;

in this case, that the subject had heard the prior turn, but was still with-holding a response.

This is interesting. Note that the pre-silence turn was "and it sounded like you said (.) twitching: (.) bulgy." This is not an explicit request for the subject to assess this report of the item and offer clarification or confirmation. Yet the experimenter's post-silence turn suggests that she was anticipating precisely that kind of activity. In this sense, the "you said" preface seems to be used as a device to elicit clarification or confirmation.

And there is evidence that the subject also orients to the same expec-tation. After the experimenter's repair initiation, the subject says "what was that sorry?" The experimenter then simply repeats, almost word-for-word, the original item introduction. This reissued "you said" item intro-duction does now elicit some further report by the subject, during which it becomes apparent that he had said his *body* had been twitching, (for which we can now infer the experimenter had originally heard "bulgy"). Once the subject produces this short spate of clarification, the experi-menter moves on to the next item.

Let us summarize some of the main observations. "You said" pref-aces seem to be a communicative device through which the experimenter seeks clarification, confirmation or further assessment of an item without explicitly having to ask for it. Moreover, the conduct of both experimenter and subject in different ways exhibits their orientation to this property of "you said" prefaces. In **Extract (10)** the experimenter's post-silence turn displays her understanding that a particular kind of next activity *should* be forthcoming from the subject. This means that, even on an occasion in which a "you said" preface is not followed by a confirmation or clarification, the experimenter's subsequent turn exhibits her tacit under-standing that that was precisely the kind of activity it was designed to elicit. And the repeat of the "you said" preface generates some further assessment of the item from the subject. There seems, then, to be a mutual orientation to—and expectation of—the kind of sequence initiated by "you said" prefaces.

These observations are taken from the early stage of a project to inves-tigate experimenter-subject interaction in ganzfeld trials, but we can make some tentative conclusions. It is apparent that interaction in this setting displays some regular properties. Items introduced into the review via a "you said" preface seem to work as devices which manage a particular kind of communicative activity: eliciting some form of further comment from the subject on the item so introduced. Moreover, they seem to be a way of eliciting clarification without having to make an explicit request. This has a direct bearing on parapsychological concerns: one of the functions of the mentation review is to provide the subject the opportunity to reflect on the mentation. "You said" prefaces seem to be a communicative practice which facilitates precisely that kind of activity.

"You said" prefaces mark that whatever is to follow is a form of direct or indirect reported speech. This means that any satisfactory explanation of how they work in experimenter-subject interaction will necessarily take account of the broader study of reported speech in mundane and institutional settings (Holt 1996; Phillips 1986). It may be that reported speech in experimenter-subject interaction has distinctive properties, and suggests that this communicative practice is being marshalled by participants to address particular requirements of the parapsychology experiment; or it may be that we find that reported speech is used in similar ways in other contexts. Either way, to develop a satisfactory account of reported speech in parapsychological experiments it will be necessary to draw from studies of language in other settings. This in turn will facilitate links with other disciplines, and encourage further cross-fertilization of research topics and methods.

Finally: The preceding analytic observations illustrate a key methodological feature of conversation analytic research: explicating participants' own understanding of the ongoing interaction. Turns at talk unavoidably display their producer's interpretation of the immediate sequential context (the kind of activity performed by the prior utterance), and an understanding of the kind of activity which is now appropriate in-this-turn-right-now. Participants' understanding of their ongoing verbal relationship is thereby exhibited on a turn-by-turn basis as part of the routine unfolding of verbal activity.

This has an important bearing on our attempts to understand the significance of verbal relationships in the setting of a parapsychology laboratory. We do not have to speculate about the way that participants in laboratories are behaving toward each other, nor try to infer the significance of their actions. Analyzing the design of turns in the unfolding trajectory of interaction allows us to identify how experimenter and subject *themselves* interpret and make sense of the activities in which they are engaged, and the interpersonal relationships which are managed through those activities.

Conclusion

In this chapter, I have outlined one methodology for the analysis of verbal interaction in parapsychological settings, or through which anomalous claims or experiences are offered. Of course, there are other ways of analyzing interaction, and discourse more generally, and these may yield their own insights. But I believe CA offers some distinct advantages: there is a commitment to identifying highly patterned and robust regularities in verbal activities; analyses are generated from clear and formal methodological steps; and new research can be informed by, and integrated with, what is now a substantial and cumulative body of findings on the organization of interaction in a variety of settings.

There is a sense in which parapsychology and sociology are very similar. Despite the broader linguistic turn in the social sciences, the sociological study of talk in interaction has not yet emerged as one of the central core topics of the discipline along with the study of class divisions, gender relations, ethnicity, deviance, education, the family, and so on. Yet language use permeates and infuses all these aspects of society: everyday language is the medium through which society socializes young children; family life is rife with words, jokes and arguments; society's gender inequalities may resonate in patterns of conversation between women and men, and so on. It is likely that "people talking to each other" is so commonplace and taken for granted that its relationship to the "self-evidently" important issues was not explored. For the same reason, perhaps, parapsychologists have not explored its implications for their own work. But it is a relationship that needs to be investigated.

Accounts of spontaneous experiences, demonstrations of psychic abilities, and laboratory experiments are *communicative* events managed through language, specifically, talk-in-interaction. The study of anomalous communication is therefore unavoidably enmeshed in a web of more mundane, socially organized communicative practices. This may have profound implications: we can begin to see how the study of anomalous experiences—broadly defined—necessarily invites sociological analysis; and we can see how the sociological study of language offered by conversation analysis might develop as a method for parapsychological inquiry. And for both parapsychology and sociology, the subsequent blurring of disciplinary and methodological boundaries may be a significant moment.

REFERENCES

Adorno, T. 1994 *The stars down to earth and other essays on the irrational in culture*. London: Routledge.

Allison, P. D. (1979). Experimental parapsychology as a rejected science. In R. Wallis, ed., *On the margins of science: The social construction of rejected knowledge*. (pp. 271–292). University of Keele, Sociological Review Monograph, No. 27.

Atkinson, J. M., and J. Heritage, eds. (1984). *Structures of social action: Studies in conversation analysis.* Cambridge: Cambridge University Press.

Austin, J. L. (1962). *How to do things with words.* Oxford: Oxford University Press.

Boden, D., and D. Zimmerman (1992). *Talk and social structure.* Cambridge: Polity Press.

Bourque, L. B. (1969). Social correlates of transcendental experiences. *Sociological Analysis* **30**, 151–163.

Burman, E., and I. Parker eds. (1993). *Discourse analytic research: Repertoires and readings of texts in action.* London: Routledge.

Campbell, C., and S. McIver (1987). Cultural sources of support for contemporary occultism. *Social Compass* **34** (1), 41–60.

Collins, H. M., and T. J. Pinch (1979). The construction of the paranormal: Nothing unscientific is happening. In R. Wallis, ed., *On the margins of science: The social construction of rejected knowledge* (pp. 237–270). University of Keele, Sociological Review Monograph No. 27.

_____, _____. (1982). *Frames of meaning: The social construction of extraordinary science.* London: Routledge & Kegan Paul.

Coulter, J. (1979). *The social construction of mind: Studies in ethnomethodology and linguistic philosophy.* London: Macmillan.

Dalton, K. S., R. L. Morris, D. L. Delanoy, D. I. Radin, R. Taylor, and R. Wiseman (1996). Security measures in an automated ganzfeld system. *Journal of Parapsychology* **60**, 129–147.

Drew, P., and J. Heritage (1992). *Talk at work: Interaction in institutional settings.* Cambridge: Cambridge University Press.

Edwards, D., and J. Potter (1992). *Discursive psychology.* London: Sage.

Fairclough, N. (1995). *Critical discourse analysis: The critical study of language.* London: Longman.

Fox, J. W. (1992). The structure, stability and social antecedents of reported paranormal experiences. *Sociological Analysis* **53**, 417–431.

Giesler, P. V. (1986). Sociolinguistics and the psi conducive context of laboratory and field setting: a speculative commentary. In D. H. Weiner and R. D. Radin, eds., *Research in parapsychology 1985* (pp. 111–115). Metuchen, N.J., & London: Scarecrow Press.

Gilbert, G. N., and M. J. Mulkay (1984). *Opening Pandora's box: A Sociological analysis of scientists' discourse.* Cambridge: Cambridge University Press.

Greeley, A. (1991). The paranormal is normal: A sociologist looks at parapsychology. *Journal of the American Society for Psychical Research* **85**, 367–374.

Gurney, E., F. W. H. Myers, and F. Podmore (1886). *Phantasms of the living.* (2 vols.) London: Trubner.

Hansen, G. P. (2001). *The trickster and the paranormal.* Philadelphia: Xlibris.

Hartman, P. (1976). Social dimensions of occult participation: the "gnostica study." *British Journal of Sociology* **27**, 169–183.

Hay, D. and A. Morisy (1978). Reports of ecstatic paranormal, or religious experience in Great Britain and the United States — A comparison of trends. *Journal for the Scientific Study of Religion* **17**, 255–268.

Heath. C. (1986). *Body movement and speech in medical interaction.* Cambridge: Cambridge University Press.

Heritage, J. (1984). *Garfinkel and ethnomethodology.* Cambridge: Polity Press.

Heritage, J., and S. Sefi (1992). Dilemmas of advice: aspects of the delivery and reception of advice in interactions between health visitors and first time mothers. In P. Drew and J. Heritage, eds., *Talk at work: Interaction in institutional settings* (pp. 359–418). Cambridge: Cambridge University Press.

_____, _____. (1997). Conversation analysis and institutional talk: analyzing data. In D. Silverman, ed., *Qualitative research: Theory, method and practice* (pp. 161–182). London: Sage.

Hess, D. J. (1994). *Science in the new age: The paranormal, its defenders and debunkers, and American culture.* Madison: University of Wisconsin Press.

Holt, E. (1996). Reporting on talk: The use of direct reported speech in conversation. *Research on Language and Social Interaction* 29, 219–245.

Honorton, C., M. Ramsey, and C. Cabibbo (1975). Experimenter effects in extrasensory perception. *Journal of the American Society for Psychical Research* 69, 135–139.

Hufford, D. (1982). *The terror that comes in the night: An experience-centered study of supernatural assault traditions.* Philadelphia: University of Pennsylvania Press.

Hutchby, I., and R. Wooffitt (1998). *Conversation analysis: Principles, practices and applications.* Oxford: Polity Press.

Hyman, R. (1981). Cold reading: How to convince strangers that you know all about them. In K. Frazier, ed., *Paranormal borderlands of science* (pp. 79–96). New York: Prometheus Books.

Keen, M., A. Ellison, and D. Fontana (1999). The Scole report. *Proceedings of the Society for Psychical Research* 58, 151–392.

Lester, D. (1982). Astrologers and psychics as therapists. *American Journal of Psychotherapy* 36, 56–66.

Levinson, S. (1983). *Pragmatics.* Cambridge: Cambridge University Press.

Lynch, F. R. (1975). Sociology and parapsychology. *Journal of Parapsychology* 39, 297–305.

McClenon, J. (1990). Chinese and American anomalous experiences: The role of religiosity. *Sociological Analysis* 51, 1 53–67.

_____. (1991) Social science and anomalous experience: Paradigms for investigating sporadic social phenomena. *Journal of the American Society for Psychical Research* 85, 25–41.

_____. (1994). *Wondrous events: Foundations of religious belief.* Philadelphia: University of Philadelphia Press.

Markovsky, B., and S. R. Thye (2001). Social influence on paranormal beliefs. *Sociological Perspectives* 44, 21–44.

Maynard, D. W. (1991). Interaction and asymmetry in clinical discourse. *American Journal of Sociology* 97, 448–495.

Moody, E. J. (1974). Urban witches. In E. A Tiryakin, ed., *On the margins of the visible* (pp. 223–234). New York: John Wiley.

Morris, R. L., K. Dalton, D. Delanoy, and C. Watt (1995). Comparison of the sender/no sender condition in the ganzfeld. In N. L. Zingrone, ed., *Proceedings of presented papers, 38th Annual Parapsychological Association Convention* (pp. 244–259). Fairhaven, MA: Parapsychological Association.

Nelson. G. K. (1975). Toward a sociology of the psychic. *Review of Religious Research* 1, 166–173.

Parker, A. (2000). A review of the ganzfeld work at Gothenburg University. *Journal of the Society for Psychical Research* 64, 1–15.

Pekala, R. J., and E. Cardena (2000). Methodological issues in the study of altered states of consciousness and anomalous experience. In E. Cardena, S. J. Lynn, and S. Krippner, eds., *Varieties of anomalous experience: Examining the scientific evidence* (pp. 47–82). Washington: American Psychological Association.

Phillips, S. U. (1986). Reported speech as evidence in an American trial. In D. Tannen and J. E. Alatis, eds., Languages and linguistics: The interdependence of theory, data and application. In *Georgetown University Round Table on Languages and Linguistics 1985* (pp. 154–170). Washington: Georgetown University Press.

Plummer, K. (1995). *Telling sexual stories: Power, change and social worlds.* London: Routledge.

Pomerantz, A. M. (1986). Extreme case formulations: a way of legitimizing claims. *Human Studies* 9, 219–229.

_____. (1987). Descriptions in legal settings. In G. Button and J. R. E. Lee, eds., *Talk and social organization* (pp. 226–243). Clevedon: Multilingual Matter.

Potter, J. (1996). *Representing reality: Discourse, rhetoric and social construction.* London: Sage.

Potter, J., and M. Wetherell (1987). *Discourse and social psychology: Beyond attitudes and behaviour.* London: Sage.

Randi, J. (1981). Cold reading revisited. In K. Frazier, ed., *Paranormal borderlands of science* (pp. 106–110). New York: Prometheus.

Rhine, J. B. (1948). The value of reports of spontaneous psi phenomena. *Journal of Parapsychology* 12, 231–235.

Rhine, L. E. (1981). *The invisible picture: A study of psychic experiences.* Jefferson, NC: McFarland.

Roe, C. A. (1995). Pseudopsychics and the Barnum effect. *European Journal of Parapsychology* 11, 76–91.

Rorty, R. (1979). *Philosophy and the mirror of nature.* Princeton, NJ: Princeton University Press.

Sacks, H. (1992). *Lectures on conversation.* In G. Jefferson and E. A. Schegloff, eds. Oxford and Cambridge, MA: Basil Blackwell.

Sacks, H., E. A. Schegloff, and G. Jefferson (1974). A simplest systematics for the organization of turn-taking for conversation. *Language* 50, 696–735.

Schegloff, E. A. (1972). Notes on a conversational practice: Formulating place. In D. Sudnow, ed., *Studies in social interaction* (pp. 75–119). New York: The Free Press.

_____. (1988). Presequences and indirection: Applying speech act theory to ordinary conversation. *Journal of Pragmatics* 12, 55–62.

Schegloff, E. A., G. Jefferson, and H. Sacks (1977). The preference for self-correction in the organization of repair in conversation. *Language* 53, 361–382.

Schlitz. M. J., and C. Honorton (1992). Ganzfeld psi performance within an artistically gifted population. *Journal of the American Society for Psychical Research* 86, 83–98.

Schmiedler, G. R., and H. Edge (1999). Should ganzfeld research continue to be crucial in the search for a replicable psi effect? II: Edited ganzfeld debate. *Journal of Parapsychology* 63, 335–388.

Schneider, R., M. Binder, and H. Walach (2000). Examining the role of neutral versus personal experimenter-participant interactions: An EDA-DMILS experiment. *Journal of Parapsychology* 64, 181–194.

Sechrest, S., and D. Bryan (1968). Astrologers as useful marriage counsellors. *Transaction* 6, 34.

Smith, D. E. (1978). K is mentally ill: the anatomy of a factual account. *Sociology* 12, 23–53.

Stanford R. G., S. Frank, G. Kass, and S. Skoll (1989a). Ganzfeld as an ESP-favorable setting: I. Assessment of spontaneity, arousal, and internal attention state through verbal transcript analysis. *Journal of Parapsychology* 53, 1–42.

_____, _____, _____, _____. (1989b). Ganzfeld as an ESP-favorable setting: II. Prediction of ESP-task performance through verbal-transcript measures of spontaneity, suboptimal arousal and internal attention state. *Journal of Parapsychology* 53, 95–124.

Terasaki, A. (1976). Pre announcement sequences in conversation. *Social Science Working Paper 99*, University of California, Irvine.

Truzzi, M. (1974a). Witchcraft and Satanism. In E. A. Tiryakin, ed., *On the margin of the visible* (pp. 215–222). New York and London: John Wiley.

_____. (1974b). Toward a sociology of the occult: Notes on modern witchcraft. In I. Zaretsky and M. P. Leone, eds., *Religious movements in contemporary America*. (pp. 628–645). Princeton: Princeton University Press.

Tyson, G. A. (1982). People who consult astrologers: A profile. *Personality and Individual Differences* 3, 119–126.

Warren, D. I. (1970). Status inconsistency theory and flying saucer sightings. *Science*, 170, 599–603.

West, D. J. (1948). The investigation of spontaneous cases. *Proceedings of the Society for Psychical Research* 48, 264–300.

Wetherell, M., and J. Potter (1992). *Mapping the Language of Racism: Discourse and the Legitimization of Exploitation*. Hemel Hempstead: Harvester Wheatsheaf.

Wilkinson, R. (1995). Aphasia: Conversation analysis of a non-fluent aphasic. In M. Perkins and S. Howard, eds., Case studies in clinical linguistics. (pp. 72–96). London: Whurr.

Wiseman, R., and R. L. Morris (1995). *Guidelines for testing psychic claimants*. Buffalo, NY: Prometheus.

Wittgenstein, L. (1953). *Philosophical investigations*. Oxford: Basil Blackwell. (Edited by. G. Anscombe.)

White, R. A. (1985). The spontaneous, the imaginal, and psi: Foundations for a depth psychology. In R. A. White and J. Solfvin, eds., *Research in parapsychology 1984* (pp. 166–190). Metchuen NJ: Scarecrow.

_____. (1990). An experience-centered approach to parapsychology. *Exceptional Human Experience* 8, 7–36.

_____. (1993). A dynamic view of psi experience: By their fruits shall ye know them. *Proceedings of the Parapsychological Association 36th Annual Convention* (pp. 285–297). Parapsychological Association.

Wooffitt, R. (1992). *Telling tales of the unexpected: The organisation of Factual Discourse.* Hemel Hempstead: Harvester Wheatsheaf.

_____. (2000). Some properties of the interactional organization of displays of paranormal cognition in psychic-sitter interaction. *Sociology* 43, 457–479.

_____. (2001a). Analyzing factual accounts. In G. N. Gilbert, ed., *Researching social life* (2nd ed.) (pp. 324–342). London: Sage.

_____. (2001b). Raising the dead: Reported speech in medium-sitter interaction. *Discourse Studies* 3, 351–374.

_____. (2003a). The organization of demonstrations of paranormal cognition in psychic-sitter interaction. *Proceedings of the 46th Annual Convention of the Parapsychological Association* (pp. 329–346). New York: Parapsychological Association.

_____. (2003b). Conversation analysis and parapsychology: experimenter-subject interaction in ganzfeld experiments. *Proceedings of the 46th Annual Convention of the Parapsychological Association* (pp. 305–328). New York: Parapsychological Association.

Wuthnow, R. (1976). Astrology and marginality. *Journal of the Scientific Study of Religion* 15, 157–168.

Yamane, D. (2000). Narrative and religious experience. *Sociology of Religion* 61, 171–190.

Zimmer, T. A. (1984). Social psychological correlates of possible UFO sightings. *Journal of Social Psychology* 123, 199–206.

Zingrone, N. L. (2002). Controversy and the problems of parapsychology. *Journal of Parapsychology* 66, 3–30.

Appendix: Transcription Symbols

The transcription symbols used here are common to conversation analytic research, and were developed by Gail Jefferson. The following symbols are used in the data.

(.5)	The number in brackets indicates a time gap in tenths of a second.
(.)	A dot enclosed in a bracket indicates pause in the talk less than two-tenths of a second.
·hh	A dot before an "h" indicates speaker inbreath. The more h's, the longer the inbreath.

hh	An "h" indicates an out-breath. The more h's the longer the breath.
(( ))	A description enclosed in a double bracket indicates a non-verbal activity. For example *((banging sound))*
-	A dash indicates the sharp cut-off of the prior word or sound.
:::	Colons indicate that the speaker has stretched the preceding sound or letter. The more colons the greater the extent of the stretching.
( )	Empty parentheses indicate the presence of an unclear fragment on the tape.
(guess)	The words within a single bracket indicate the transcriber's best guess at an unclear fragment.
.	A full stop indicates a stopping fall in tone. It does not necessarily indicate the end of a sentence.
Under	Underlined fragments indicate speaker emphasis.
↑↓	Pointed arrows indicate a marked falling or rising intonational shift. They are placed immediately before the onset of the shift.
CAPITALS	With the exception of proper nouns, capital letters indicate a section of speech noticeably louder than that surrounding it.
° °	Degree signs are used to indicate that the talk they encompass is spoken noticeably quieter than the surrounding talk.
Thaght	A "gh" indicates that word in which it is placed had a guttural pronunciation.
> <	"More than" and "less than" signs indicate that the talk they encompass was produced noticeably quicker than the surrounding talk.
=	The "equals" sign indicates contiguous utterances. For example:

S2   yeah September ⌐seventy six=
S1   └-September
S2   =it would be
S2   yeah that's right

[	Square brackets between adjacent lines of concurrent speech indicate
]	the onset and end of a spate of overlapping talk.

A more detailed description of these transcription symbols can be found in Atkinson and Heritage (1984: pp. *ix–xvi*).

The Ritual Healing Theory: Hypotheses for Psychical Research

James McClenon

Dr. James McClenon argues that rituals for healing were involved in the shaping of certain dissociative capacities in our species—this process took place as an evolutionary process going back some 30,000 years. Anomalous experiences (such as psi, OBEs, etc.), trance, and religiosity emerged out of this process. McClenon's ritual healing theory explains the presence of shamanism among all hunter-gatherer societies. By way of his theory, Dr. McClenon makes a strong case for research in the future in the areas of psychology, parapsychology, anthropology, and medicine. (Editors)

The ritual healing theory provides scenarios describing the origin of religion. It specifies hypotheses pertaining to anomalous experience that are particularly suitable for testing by psychical researchers. As opposed to *psi*, a concept requiring experimental verification, *anomalous experiences* can be viewed as unusual perceptions associated with brain processes. Such incidents have physiological bases since, like dreaming, they have occurred in similar forms in every society throughout history. The ritual healing theory argues that the physiological bases for these processes developed within an evolutionary context.

The ritual healing theory offers an alternative to the present parapsychological paradigm. Much evidence suggests that parapsychological theories are not likely to be accepted within mainstream science in the near-term future. Most innovative scientific fields grow exponentially during their decade of origin, during which they either resolve basic research issues or cease to exist. Parapsychology does not fit this pattern. Membership in the field's major professional organization, the Parapsychology Association, has not increased exponentially. Membership was 205 in 1970; 279 in 1980; 306 in 1983; 275 in 1986; 246 in 1992; 251 in 1999; and 254 in 2001 (McClenon 1994: 200; Varvoglis 1999; Utts 2001). Many introductory psychology texts dismiss major parapsychological arguments, stating that the field has not generated a replicable experiment (McClenon, Roig, Smith, and Ferrier, in press; Roig, Icochea, and Cuzzucoli 1991). Parapsychology's longevity, nonscientific financial support, and stagnant growth illustrate a "deviant science" (McClenon 1984). The field's deviant status suggests that future claims of replicability will be treated skeptically and that parapsychology will not gain acceptance in the near-term future.

The ritual healing theory provides an alternative paradigm. It specifies replicable hypotheses based on Darwin's evolutionary theory. Unlike parapsychology, evolutionary psychology has had profound impacts on psychology and anthropology. Introductory psychology textbooks discuss a wide range of findings pertaining to evolutionary topics ranging from mating strategies to altruism. Some introductory texts are devoted specifically to this paradigm (Buss 1998; Gaulin and McBurney 2001; Palmer and Palmer 2002).

The ritual healing theory argues that genes related to dissociation increased in frequency among ancient hominids since dissociation alleviated negative impacts of trauma. Hominids devised therapeutic rituals based on these dissociative capacities and practiced these rituals for many millennia, further increasing the frequency of dissociative genotypes (McClenon 1997a, 2002a). At some stage, homo sapiens linked rituals with language, coupling suggestions with altered states of consciousness. As a result, rituals shaped human hypnotizability, a genetically based trait correlated with the incidence of anomalous experience. Over the millennia, anomalous experiences such as apparitions, extrasensory perceptions (ESP), psychokinesis (PK), and out-of-body experiences (OBE) generated beliefs in spirits, souls, life after death, and magical abilities. As a result, similar folk religious traditions related to shamanism exist in all societies (McClenon 1997a, 2002a).

The ritual healing theory views psychic phenomena (psi) as experiences rather than events requiring verification. Researchers evaluating the ritual healing theory need not "prove" that psi is real; they seek to demonstrate that certain anomalous experiences have universal features reflecting physiological bases. The propensity to experience any specific form of anomalous perception is a phenotype (a physiologically based manifestation) associated with a genotype (the collection of genes causing the propensity). This argument could be evaluated through twin studies.

Dawkins (1999) explains the evolutionary orientation by noting that genes are like oarsmen in a racing boat. After a number of races, the winning oarsmen (genes) are randomly assigned to new boats (bodies) and the races continue. All boats contain incompetent oarsmen but there is a tendency for skillful teams to win. Genotypes— groups of genes with specific purposes— are like oarsmen teams fulfilling complex functions. Such teams are often effective only in certain environments. The ritual healing theory argues that oarsmen allowing dissociation and hypnotizability proved valuable during humankind's era of evolutionary adaptation. Resulting teams contained members facilitating trance, ESP, PK, OBE, apparitions, and other anomalous experiences sustaining shamanism. Ultimately, oarsmen teams were shaped to allow the modern propensity for religiosity.

Evolutionary theories are subject to evaluation and modification. Modern Darwinian theory portrays genes changing in frequency over time through mutation and selection. Most evolutionists ignore nature-versus-nurture controversies because they acknowledge that genes are not directly linked to behaviors; genotypes trigger physiological effects when exposed to certain environments, resulting in specific phenotypes. Although culture shapes phenotypes, culture is shaped and made possible by genotypes.

Irwin (1992, 1993) provides a testable model portraying relationships between cultural variables and topics important within psychical research. He specifies relationships between childhood trauma, fantasy proneness, paranormal experience, and paranormal belief. He argues that "traumatic childhood experiences" and "encouragement of fantasy in childhood" contribute to "fantasy proneness" and a "need for absorbing experiences." These variables, shaped by culture, lead to paranormal belief and experience.

Irwin's theory can be reformulated so that it coincides with the ritual healing theory. Fantasy proneness is correlated with both hypnotizability and dissociation, variables shown to have genetic basis. Figure 14.1 portrays how "encouragement of childhood fantasy" and "childhood trauma" affect "dissociative ability." Paleolithic children with dissociative ability had greater survival advantages when exposed to trauma than those lacking this ability. Over time, genotypes associated with dissociation

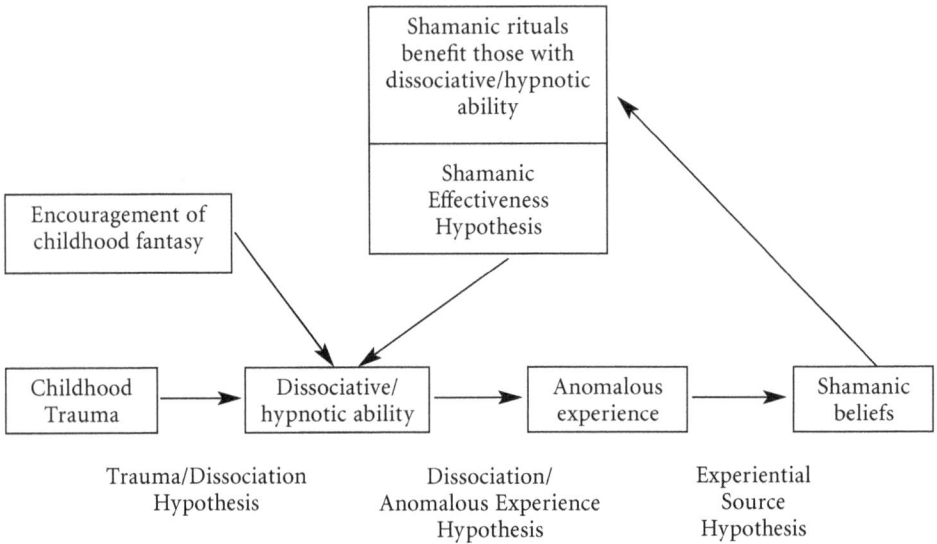

Figure 14.1. Ritual Healing Theory

increased. Much evidence indicates that these genotypes are linked to various anomalous experiences— and these cognitive events generated beliefs providing the foundation for shamanism (McClenon 1997a, 2002a). Shamanism involved rituals that provided greater benefits to those with dissociative capacities. As a result, the frequency of dissociative genotypes continued to increase.

Using Dawkin's (1999) metaphor, dissociation genotypes contain oarsmen who allowed anomalous experiences. Over time, the composition of these teams was shaped by ritual suggestion, and genes related to dissociation and hypnotizability increased due to their contributions to survival. Because oarsmen on these teams facilitated trance and other anomalous experiences, shamanism developed in all hunter-gatherer societies and, over time, the genetic basis for modern forms of religiosity evolved.

Dissociative and hypnotic capacities could not increase infinitely because these traits had negative consequences. Highly dissociative people are prone to fantasy and tend to suffer from psychosomatic disorders. Not all recover when treated by shamans. The ritual healing theory portrays a process where those with moderate levels of dissociative and hypnotic capacity have optimal survival advantage. This situation corresponds with modern observations; those with extremely high levels of religiosity and hypnotizability have less reproductive success. Genotypes associated with religiosity and hypnotizability are hypothesized to have become more frequent as symbolizing ability increased since symbolization allowed linking rituals with suggestion (McClenon 2002a).

The ritual healing theory is open to evaluation and modification. Evidence supports four broad hypotheses, all replicable using various strategies: (1) *The Trauma/Dissociation Hypothesis:* Although excessive dissociation leads to identity disorders, moderate levels protect against psychological trauma. As humans gained the capacity to symbolize, the frequency of genes associated with dissociation increased due to survival advantages provided by this trait. (2) *The Dissociation/Anomalous Experience Hypothesis:* Dissociation is correlated with hypnotizability, fantasy proneness, and the capacity for anomalous experiences. As genes related to dissociation increased, human propensities for anomalous and trance experience also increased. (3) *The Experiential Source Hypothesis:* Certain anomalous and trance experiences induce beliefs in spirits, souls, life after death, and magical abilities— notions central to shamanism. (4) *The Shamanic Effectiveness Hypothesis:* Shamanism, and other forms of spiritual healing, are effective, in part, due to hypnotic and placebo processes. As a result, some people achieve greater benefit from shamanic healing than do others, a differential effect that can be verified empirically.

The Trauma/Dissociation Hypothesis

Dissociation is defined as "experiences and behaviors that exist apart from, or have been disconnected from, the mainstream of one's conscious awareness, behavioral repertoire, and/or self-concept" (Krippner 1994, p. 357). Trance states, central to shamanism, indicate dissociative processes. Dissociation can also refer to the "absence of conscious awareness of impinging stimuli or ongoing behaviors" (Cardeña 1994, p. 17); "the coexistence of separate mental systems that should be integrated in the person's consciousness, memory, or identity" (p. 19); or "ongoing behavior or perception inconsistent with a person's introspective verbal report" (p. 21). Hypnosis is "a psychophysiological condition in which attention is so focused that there occurs a relative reduction of both peripheral awareness and critical analytic mentation, leading to distortions in perception, mood, and memory which in turn produce significant behavioral and biological changes" (Wickramasekera 1987, p. 12).

Although scholars argue regarding precise definitions, dissociative and hypnotic processes have been found to have physiological correlates (Graffin, Ray, & Lundy 1995) and twin studies demonstrate the genetic basis of hypnotizability (Morgan 1973). Physiological processes involving dissociation and hypnosis govern the ability to focus attention (Spiegel & Vermutten 1994). As knowledge of these mechanisms increases, dissociation and hypnosis can be defined more precisely.

The ritual healing theory describes three processes by which dissociative genotypes were selected. Dissociative capacities evolved due to survival benefits derived from (1) cognitive multitasking, (2) defense mechanisms reducing the negative effects of trauma, and (3) ritual suggestions made possible by increased ability to symbolize.

Cognitive Multitasking

Hominids who could perform multiple tasks simultaneously had survival advantages. Coordinating different tasks with each hand while speaking requires multitasking and a form of dissociation. Human evolutionary processes created an increasingly bilateral brain, one in which modules became "disassociated" from each other. As a result, consciousness evolved, allowing self-monitoring and modification of behavior following feedback. Because not all performance requires conscious self-regulation, well-learned behaviors often occur outside of consciousness. Learned tasks requiring quick response often involve dissociation.

Survival threats to animals can trigger automatic responses, such as the Totstell reflex. The Totstell phenomenon is often called "animal hypnosis" since its appearance parallels that of hypnosis in humans (Hoskovec and Svorad 1969). Many animals "play dead" when in danger in order to avoid predators' attacks. Such startle responses include rapid changes in consciousness, paralysis, and the "sleepy" appearance often associated with human hypnotic response. Much observational evidence links human and animal hypnosis. Repetitive, nonverbal rituals function as hypnotic inductions for both primates and humans, creating similar behavioral responses (Völgyesi 1966).

Dissociation as an Effective Defense Mechanism

It is almost axiomatic within the therapy literature that traumatic events cause some children to develop dissociative capacities (Albini and Pease 1989; Fink 1988; Putnam 1985; Spiegel 1986). Although excessive use of dissociation results in identity disorders (Ross 1997), dissociation is not intrinsically pathological but is related to fantasy and imaginative ability (Putnam 1991). The "dissociation benefit" argument, used within the ritual healing theory, is based on two assumptions: (1) Dissociation can protect against negative effects of stress; (2) Humans used this mechanism for sufficient time that frequencies of related genes increased.

Much evidence supports these assertions. It is easy to find people who used dissociative strategies to avoid psychological and physical pain during childhood. Their descriptions of stressful events often contain phrases suggesting dissociative defense mechanisms. For example, a North Carolina informant described her childhood trauma:

> He would be yelling so loud that the window pains would rattle. He was trying to hurt me both psychologically and physically ... but I would look at a little spot in the wallpaper and I would pretend I was there. I would concentrate on it so that I wasn't really present. I was away — so he couldn't get me. ... When he hit me, I was away [McClenon 2000a, p. 3].

Dissociative identity disorders (or multiple personality disorders) are culturally specific reactions to childhood trauma, particularly sexual abuse (Ross 1997). Dissociative pathologies include psychosomatic disorders, sometimes labeled hysteria. Ancient medical texts from many societies describe hysterical symptoms treated through ritual suggestion (Veith 1965, 1977). Dissociative phenomena include hysteria, conversion disorders, dissociative identity disorder, depersonalization, dissociative amnesia, hypnosis, out-of-body experience, trance possession, shamanic trance, and automatisms (Cardeña 1994, p. 28). Although reactions to childhood abuse are culturally shaped, physiologically based dissociative processes create recurring features in people's accounts.

The Prevalence of Generational Conflict

Conflict, inherent within human child rearing, has had evolutionary impacts (Daly and Wilson 1998; Trivers 1974). It is in the evolutionary interest of mothers to wean infants earlier than infants wish, contributing to conflict. Parents are required to discipline their children and punishment severity, affected by environmental stress, varies widely. Infanticide, the most extreme form of child abuse, is not unusual among nontechnological peoples (Eisenberg, Muckenhirn, and Rudran 1978, p. 127). The Yanomana, for example, kill between 15 to 20 percent of all live births (Neel 1978, p. 352). Anthropologists describe "discriminative parental solicitude" as a reaction to resource scarcity (Haustater and Hrdy 1984). Women in a Brazilian shantytown, for example, withhold food from some children due to high infant death rates (46 percent die before the age of five; Scheper-Hughes 1992). Children who can dissociate, transcending the effects of physical and psychological trauma, have survival advantages.

Although conflicts occur during all phases of the life cycle, adolescent primates face special dangers. Many leave their troop, seeking mates, and are more vulnerable to competitors' attacks than experienced adults. The human capacity for dissociation and hypnosis peaks during adolescence, providing a psychological defense mechanism during this critical phase.

Psychical Research and Dissociation

The ritual healing theory generates hypotheses regarding anomalous experience, childhood trauma, and dissociation. Shamans, mediums, and other psychic practitioners often use dissociative processes to facilitate ESP and PK performances. Psychical researchers could extend existing research. Standardized scales allow evaluation of childhood trauma, neglect, and frequency of anomalous experience (McClenon 1994; Kent and Waller 1998; Sanders and Becker-Lausen 1995). The ritual healing theory specifies that: (1) Frequency of anomalous experience should be positively correlated with childhood trauma and neglect. (2) Groups claiming higher levels of anomalous experience should report higher rates of childhood trauma and neglect. (3) Samples of psychic practitioners and spiritual healers should report more childhood trauma and neglect than general populations.

The Dissociation/Anomalous Experience Hypothesis

Research indicates that the propensity for anomalous experience, hypnosis, dissociation, fantasy proneness, temporal lobe lability, and thinness of cognitive boundaries are intercorrelated (McClenon 1994, 2002a; Targ, Schlitz, and Irwin 2000). This literature supports the argument that a "shamanic syndrome" governs the nature and incidence of shamanism. As evolutionary processes brought about increasing dissociative and symbolizing capacities, the human tendency for anomalous experience was shaped.

Dissociation and Paranormal Experience

Various studies report positive significant correlations between dissociativity and frequency of paranormal and anomalous experience (Pekala et al. 1995; Ross and Joshi 1992; Ross et al. 1991; Richards 1991). Richards (1991) presents typical findings. He concluded that the dissociation was most correlated with waking clairvoyance, precognition, apparitions, psychokinesis, and volitional telepathy and that out-of-body experiences, trance channeling, and spirit guides imply dissociative processes (as indicated by high significant correlations). This evidence links psychic and other anomalous experiences with dissociative capacities.

Hypnotizability and Paranormal Experience

Kumar and Pekala (2001) summarize the literature regarding hypnotizability and paranormal experience: "A total of 23 correlations were reported in 11 different studies" (pp. 275–276). Nineteen correlations were significant and ranged from weak to moderate in terms of effect size strength. Kumar and Pekala (2001) added: "Studies … examining group differences in experiences also support a relationship [except for one study] in the sense that participants with high hypnotizability tend to report a greater number of experiences than those with low hypnotizability" (pp. 275–276).

Shamanic Syndrome

Various other variables, correlated with each other, hypnosis, and dissociation, have been linked to anomalous experience. Thalbourne and Delin (1994, 1999) conducted a principal components analysis of variables such as belief in paranormal phenomena, magical ideation, manic and depressive experiences, and scores on a creative personality scale. They found that a single factor accounted for 52.5 percent of the variance in one study and 54.2 percent in a replication. They labeled this factor "transliminality," the degree to which there is a gap in the barrier or gating mechanism between the unconscious (subliminal) and conscious mind (Thalbourne et al. 1997). Transliminality was highly correlated with a measure of mysticism, and people who are high in transliminality are more susceptible to incursions of ideational and affective input from subliminal regions (Thalbourne and Delin 1999).

Hartmann (1991) conducted parallel studies, linking cognitive processes with anomalous experience. He hypothesized positive correlations between a measure of "thinness" of cognitive boundaries and factors equivalent to transliminality. He defines cognitive boundaries as physiologically based and culturally socialized barriers to the spontaneous flow of images and information within the brain. People with thin boundaries have the sense of merging with their perceptions. They reveal greater fluidity of thought and feelings since they have fewer barriers or walls separating them cognitively from the world. Thin cognitive boundaries allow hypnotic suggestions to affect unconscious processes, a characteristic associated with certain pathologies. Thinness facilitates the flow of anomalous perceptions into conscious awareness; as a result those displaying thin boundaries on Hartmann's scale tend to report more frequent anomalous experiences and to be more hypnotizable (Hartmann 1991).

Persinger and his associates conducted a series of studies indicating that responses to questionnaire items related to temporal lobe epilepsy (temporal lobe signs) are related to specific EEG patterns indicating temporal lobe lability (Makarec and Persinger 1990). These responses are correlated with the propensity to report anomalous and religious experiences (Persinger 1984a, 1984b, Persinger and Makarec 1987, 1993; Persinger and Valliant 1985). This body of evidence supports the argument that the propensity for anomalous experience has a physiological basis and is linked to other cognitive processes.

Studies linking frequency of anomalous experience with other parameters support arguments regarding the existence of a shamanic syndrome (McClenon 1994, 2002a). Anthropologists observe that people with a propensity for anomalous experience often suffer from psychologically based disorders and culturally specific pathologies (often attributed to spiritual forces). Such people may be healed by spiritual practitioners and, as part of this process, become spiritual practitioners themselves (Lewis 1971). In northern Sudan, for example, a woman, caught within a stressful life situation, may find herself possessed by a spirit that affects her health. She regains wholeness through ritual healing ceremonies that provide a new, healthy identity as a cult member and healer (Broddy 1988). This process requires the troubled person to be cognitively open, to have had anomalous experiences, to be responsive to ritual suggestion, to be capable of further anomalous experience, and to be suitable for becoming a healer. Sick people who are not cognitively open and responsive to suggestion are less likely to be healed within this system.

Dissociation/Anomalous Experience Hypotheses and Psychical Research

Psychical researchers can replicate and extend hypotheses tested previously. Studies should find significant correlations between frequency of anomalous experience, dissociative experience, temporal lobe signs, transliminality (see, Thalbourne, Crawley, and Houran submitted), and cognitive openness. Anthropologists can observe universal features within spiritual healing related to these variables. Ethnographers can note that those who display elements related to the shamanic syndrome gain greater benefit from healing rituals and have greater potential to become spiritual healers themselves.

Experiential Source Hypotheses

Hufford's (1992) research indicates that sleep paralysis experiences are not merely cultural products but have the capacity to generate folk belief. He seeks to refute what he refers to as the *cultural source theory*, a set of arguments implying that anomalous experiences have no other source than culture. His *experiential source theory* states that various forms of anomalous experience generate and shape folk religious traditions. McClenon's (1994) analyses of apparitions, waking ESP, paranormal dreams, out-of-body experiences, psychokinesis, synchronicity, and other anomalous episodes support the experiential source theory. These forms of anomalous experience display similar defining elements in all societies, bringing about parallel beliefs in spirits, souls, life after death, and magical abilities (McClenon 1994, 2002a). It is natural that people recognizing the apparition of a deceased person or experiencing psychokinesis linked to a death should come to believe in an afterlife. People who perceive that they have left their bodies (out-of-body experience) tend to accept the existence of souls. Those who perceive that they have gained information through extrasensory perception are more likely to believe in magical abilities.

A wide variety of research strategies supports these arguments. Analyses of survey response from Japan, China, Europe, and the USA reveal that all groups report ESP and contacts with the dead (McClenon 1994). Collections of narrative accounts from Finland, Germany, Great Britain, and the USA indicate that people from all these cultures report similar forms of apparitions, waking ESP, paranormal dreams, psychokinesis, out-of-body experience, and synchronicity (McClenon 1994). Anomalous stories can be classified into clearly defined categories associated with reliable coding systems (McClenon 1994, 1997b, 2000b). This evidence implies that these forms of anomalous experience have a physiological basis, just as do dreams and trance perceptions. Dominant social scientific positions arguing that anomalous experiences are totally *produced* by culture are clearly false.

Studies also indicate that waking extrasensory perceptions, paranormal dreams, and apparitions have inherent structural features, consistent among cultures (McClenon 2000b). This evidence implies physiological bases for these cognitive events. Analysis of collections from Finland, Germany, China, and the USA reveal that: (1) ESP tends to pertain to family members, etc.; (2) Death is often an important theme within ESP accounts; (3) Paranormal dreams tend to pertain to future events while waking ESP tends to pertain to present events; (4) Waking ESP tends to generate greater conviction, indicated by the respondent taking action, than do paranormal dreams; (5) Paranormal dreams tend to provide more information than do waking ESP episodes; (6) There is a tendency for "quality of information" to be negatively correlated with "severity of event" within paranormal dreams. Paranormal dreams often fail to reveal the identity of a person who later dies while providing more complete information for events not associated with death; and (7) Apparitions contain similar "abnormal features of perception" in all societies. These features include disappearance of image, insubstantial image, glowing image, white or black clothes, sickly or deformed image, partial body, abnormal walking or floating, and abnormal sound (Emmons 1982; McClenon 1994).

Those who argue that similarities within anomalous experiences are due to common cultural features fail to understand the relationship between culture and physiology. Human culture became possible as a result of natural selection. All universal features within culture (procreation, food preparation, diet, etc.) are linked with physiological processes derived from genotypes. Correlational studies verify links between anomalous experience and belief (Pekala, Kumar, and Cummings 1992; Targ, Schlitz, and Irwin 2000) and qualitative studies indicate that many people report that anomalous experiences changed their beliefs (McClenon 1994). Although a dominant paradigm within religious studies portrays anomalous experiences as products of belief, tests of this argument consistently demonstrate it to be false (Hufford 1982; McClenon 1994). For example, historical analysis of Icelandic mediumship reveals that psychic experiences and performances transformed Icelandic religious traditions in an innovative direction (Swatos and Gissurarson 1997).

Social-psychological research indicates that attitudes formed by direct experience are stronger than those gained through other means and that experience-based attitudes are better predictors of later behavior (Millar and Millar 1996). People reporting frequent anomalous experiences reveal particularly robust belief systems which we would expect to affect their behavior. Researchers have found that anomalous experiences are not distributed normally — that the majority of experiences are reported by a small segment of any population; such people tend to hold powerful convictions associated with folk beliefs (Palmer 1979; Greeley 1995, 1987).

Experiential Source Hypotheses and Psychical Research

Experiential source hypotheses are particularly amenable to evaluation by psychical researchers. Psychical researchers could replicate previous findings regarding anomalous experience: (1) Collections of anomalous accounts from any society should include stories regarding apparitions, waking ESP, paranormal dreams, psychokinesis, out-of-body experience, sleep paralysis, synchronicity, and spiritual healing. These experiential forms can be differentiated, based on seemingly universal elements that imply a physiological basis. (2) Apparitions, waking ESP, and paranormal dreams have structural features related to recurring elements and states of consciousness associated with family, death, temporal factors, and conviction. (3) People reporting anomalous experiences tend to have unique characteristics associated with dissociation, hypnotizability, transliminality, cognitive openness, and temporal lobe lability. (4) Those who report one experience are more likely to report multiple experiences and to reveal particular beliefs and behaviors as a result.

Psychical researchers can engage in participant observation studies, designed to monitor creation of belief through experience. Some methods allow semicontrolled conditions. "Sitter groups" investigate PK through table-tipping experiments (Batcheldor 1966, 1979, 1984; Owen with Sparrow 1976). These groups sit regularly, often once a week, for an hour or more, with their hands on a table, seeking to generate psychokinetic effects. Groups often report table movements and auditory "rapping" thought by some to be generated by spirits. Although observational results have a bearing on parapsychological theories, it is often impossible to verify psi within these settings. Whether authentic or not, people report that "sitter group" psi affected their beliefs.

Observers should find that psi phenomena experienced by shamanic, spiritualist, and sitter groups have similar forms even though cultures vary (McClenon in press). Participants report seeing spirit lights, perceiving objects moving magically, hearing unexplained sounds and voices, and even feeling the whole room shake as during an earthquake. Psychical researchers could contribute to the anthropological literature regarding shamanism, anomalous experience, and belief (Young and Goulet 1994). Such evidence tends to refute cultural source hypotheses and support experiential source hypotheses.

Ethnographers could conduct haunting and poltergeist investigations within this paradigm. They should find that haunting and poltergeist experiences occur more often among those reporting previous anomalous experiences, that haunting accounts contain culturally universal features, and that resulting stories generate specific folk religious traditions (McClenon 2001).

The Shamanic Effectiveness Hypothesis

Anthropologists note that some clients derive benefits from spiritual healers. It is almost axiomatic within these studies that spiritual healing can be effective due to psychological processes (Bergman 1973; de Montellano 1975; Finkler 1985; Garrison 1977; Harner 1973; Kapferer 1983; Kleinman and Sung 1979; Kleinman 1980; Laderman 1987, 1991; Lambo 1974; Moerman 1979; Sharon 1978; Vogel 1970). This argument coincides with findings from the emerging fields of psychoneuroimmunology and mind-body medicine: health is influenced by psychological states affected by suggestion (Benson 1996; Friedman, Klein, and Friedman 1996).

Much evidence implies that spiritual healing effectiveness is due, in part, to hypnotic and placebo effects (McClenon 1997a,b, 2002a). Rituals can induce hypnotic, suggestive states. Spiritual healing symptoms, procedures, and outcomes are parallel to those associated with hypnotic processes. Rituals may include sensory restriction or overload, fasting, ingesting drugs, repetitive movements, dancing, drumming, chanting, prayer, and prolonged postures—features inducing altered states of consciousness. When coupled with suggestion, this entails hypnosis. Cognitive states associated with shamanism are linked to hypnosis: alterations in thinking, changes in sense of time and body image, loss of control, changes in emotional expression, perceptual distortions, changes in meaning and significance, sense of ineffability, feelings of rejuvenation, and hypersuggestivity (Ludwig 1966).

Paleoanthropological evidence implies a link between ritual and altered states of consciousness. This should be expected since repetitive rituals tend to induce altered states. Paleolithic cave paintings indicate that shamanic rituals involved altered states of consciousness as early as 30,000 year ago (Lewis-Williams and Dowson 1988). Paleolithic people cared for their sick and engaged in symbolic actions seemingly for their benefit. Shamanism, having a physiological basis, provided the foundation for all later religious forms (Winkelman 1992, 2000). With the invention of writing, humans left evidence connecting ritual healing and hypnosis. Ancient texts provide "abundant evidence which shows that hypnosis or a similar induced altered state of consciousness was used in ancient Greece, Egypt, India, China, Africa, and pre–Columbian America" (MacHovec 1975, p. 215).

Clinical studies indicate that hypnosis is particularly effective for pain, asthma, warts, headache, burns, bleeding, gastrointestinal disorders, skin disorders, insomnia, allergies, psychosomatic disorders, and minor psychological problems (Bowers and LeBaron 1983; Brown 1992). Folk healing

methods also effectively deal with these problems, often through suggestion. Researchers note that hypnotic suggestion does not require trance
induction to be effective. Hypnosis can change the response of human skin
to heat, probably through reducing edema and fluid retention following
thermal injury (Margolis, Domangue, Ehleben, and Shrier 1983). It can
also accelerate healing — perhaps through mechanisms involving hypnotic
control of blood flow (Barber 1984; Chapman, Goodell, and Wolff 1959;
Moore and Kaplan 1983; Ullman 1947). This process may explain some of
the extremely anomalous healing stories found in all societies (McClenon
2002a). For example, patients may cut off blood flow to cancerous tumors
as a result of hypnotic suggestion, causing cancerous growths to wither
away.

The Shamanic Effectiveness Hypotheses and Psychical Research

Psychic researchers have investigated many phenomena associated
with shamanism and spiritual healing: alleged extrasensory perception,
psychokinesis, and firewalking. Observers could document the effects of
these performances on people's belief. People witnessing and accepting
psychic performances should have greater probability of being healed than
those not exposed or skeptical. Healed people should display more dissociativity, hypnotizability, frequency of anomalous experience, temporal
lobe lability, and thinner cognitive boundaries than those not healed.

Previous research indicates relationships between dissociation and
healing. Krippner (1994) reviews studies of patients with dissociative identity disorders who benefited from ritual treatments and portrays dissociative processes within spiritual healing. Krippner and Colodzin (1989)
note the use of Native American and Oriental healing methods to treat
combat veterans with posttraumatic stress disorders. Goodwin, Hill, and
Attias (1990) encourage psychotherapists to familiarize themselves with
historical and folk techniques of exorcism since these techniques might
be adapted to treat dissociative disorders.

Anthropologists have also described processes within spiritual healing
coinciding with hypnosis and dissociation (McClenon 2002a). Csordas
(1997), for example, links successful spiritual healing among charismatic
Christians with transformations of identity. The processes he describes
seem related to the shamanic syndrome. A person suffering from psychosomatic symptoms may be healed through gaining a healthy identity. Psychical researchers could contribute to this literature by specifying which

individuals are more likely to respond to magical performances, achieving this transformation.

Applied Research: An Example Case

Duncan and Kang (1985) provide an example case illustrating how theories can be tested in field settings. They monitored a mental health program designed to facilitate the resettlement of Khmer refugee children who had survived the Pol Pot atrocities in Cambodia. These children had experienced extremely stressful life events, often forcibly separated from family and friends. All reported sleep disturbances, frequently characterized by dreams or nightmares of lost family members. Many reported disturbing visits by spirits, including deceased parents and grandparents (Williams and Berry 1991, p. 636).

As would be predicted by the ritual healing theory, the Cambodian children reported many contacts with the dead. Researchers should find that any sample of traumatized people reveal greater frequency of anomalous experience, the result of increased dissociative and hypnotic capacity. Wickramasekera (1988) argues that both high and low hypnotic susceptibility creates major risk factors for development of psychophysiological disorders. Highly hypnotizable people more often report problems linked to the shamanic syndrome while unhypnotizable people describe alternate symptoms. Wickramasekera (1988, p. 8) found that hypnotizable clients often benefited from talking about their psi experiences. Psychical researchers could devise parallel studies demonstrating that frequency of anomalous experience is an important variable for identifying (1) those with a propensity for psychologically based disorders and (2) those more likely to benefit from spiritual healing.

Resettlement program workers sought to reduce the children's symptoms by organizing three Theravada Buddhist ceremonies conducted by Khmer Buddhist spiritual leaders:

> A list of the family members, prepared in advance by the child, was burned and its ashes slowly doused with water in a ceremony symbolic of cremation. This was particularly meaningful for those children who witnessed family members' bodies left to rot in mass graves or who were fearful of such a fate for their loved ones. ... Rituals like these have been hypothesized to serve protective function ... in times of loss and grief. ... Duncan and Kang (1985) provided anecdotal reports from 47 Khmer children who participated in this program. During the Ban Skol ceremony, many of the children withdrew or were overcome

with grief. ... There were some reports after the ceremony of grief resolution, decreased sleep disturbances and spirit visits, and increased
bonding with the foster family [Williams and Berry 1991, pp.
636–637].

These results coincide with anthropologists' observations all over the world
that ritual treatments can be effective.

Psychical researchers could help specify elements within ceremonies
that contribute to success. Shamanic healers sometimes demonstrate
sleight-of-hand magic, pain defiance, heat immunity, and resistance to the
cutting action of blades (McClenon 1994, 2002a). Researchers could investigate the ways that such performances facilitate spiritual healing. Preliminary evidence indicates specific relationships between anomalous
experience and healing: spontaneous healings are more often linked with
unusual perceptions (visions, apparitions, etc.) while group ritual healings tend to involve body movements and sensations (shaking, feelings of
warmth, coldness, paralysis; McClenon 1997b, 2002).

The ritual healing theory argues that greater evolutionary benefits are
derived from hypnotic and placebo effects rather than psychokinesis. A
parapsychological "direct benefit" theory suggests that ESP and PK provide direct evolutionary benefits (Stanford 1974a,b; 1977, 1990; Broughton
1988). People are thought to use psychic ability to increase their chances
for survival and procreation. As a result, the frequency of genotypes related
to psychic ability increased. The direct benefit and ritual healing theories
are not mutually exclusive since they can operate simultaneously.

A previous study evaluates hypotheses derived from these theories
(McClenon 2002b). Evolutionists find that, in general, negative emotions
are linked to evolutionary costs and positive emotions are connected to
benefits. By evaluating the emotions associated with any specific cognitive
event we can evaluate its previous evolutionary impact. Snakes and heights
often stimulate fear, for example, while food and sex tend to stimulate positive emotions. We can also note the frequency with which people mention benefits associated with particular experiences. A collection of 1,215
anomalous experience narratives gathered in northeastern North Carolina
provides data for evaluating hypotheses derived from the ritual healing and
direct benefit theories. The ritual healing theory specifies that spiritual
healing should be coupled with positive emotions and benefits while the
direct benefit theory emphasizes ESP and PK as generating positive emotions and benefits. Findings were very conclusive. The data support ritual
healing hypotheses and fail to support direct benefit hypotheses (McClenon
2002b).

These theories remain open to further evaluation and revision. Palmer (personal communication, January 3, 2001) hypothesizes that psi was used by ancient hominids but proved less valuable than other faculties. He suggests that the original psi process was connected to emotions, explaining the modern linkage. As with all direct benefit theories, this argument is open to empirical evaluation. If the direct benefit theory is correct, different species should have differing frequencies of genotypes allowing psi capacities; differences in psi abilities should be detectable through laboratory experiments.

These hypotheses portray how the evolutionary paradigm encourages psychical research hypotheses. This line of research transcends fruitless conflicts between skeptics and believers regarding the authenticity of psi. Psychical research, conducted within the framework of evolutionary psychology, can contribute to the scientific study of religion. It can also lead to more effective treatment of psychologically based disorders.

Conclusion

The ritual healing theory provides replicable hypotheses regarding anomalous experience. The theory specifies that hominids developed dissociative capacities as a mechanism for reducing effects of stress. Hominid rituals capitalized on these capacities, providing survival advantages to those more responsive to suggestion. Much evidence supports this theory. Studies indicate that dissociation is correlated with child abuse, hypnotic suggestibility, spiritual healing, fantasy proneness, and anomalous experience. Controlled studies also indicate that hypnotic rituals effectively treat hemorrhage, pain, and minor psychopathologies.

These studies support the argument that evolutionary processes involving healing rituals shaped dissociative capacities, creating modern propensities for anomalous experience, trance, and religiosity. As frequencies of dissociative genotypes increased, anomalous experiences became more prevalent, generating the ideological foundations for shamanism. Trance, apparitions, extrasensory perceptions, psychokinesis, out-of-body experiences, and other unusual episodes created belief in spirits, souls, life after death, and magical abilities. The ritual healing theory explains why shamanism emerged among all hunter-gatherer societies. It provides hypotheses testable within the fields of psychical research, anthropology, social psychology of religion, folklore, history, physiology, and medicine.

References

Albini, T. K. and T. E. Pease (1989). Normal and pathological dissociations of early childhood. *Dissociation* 2, 144–150.

Barber, J. (1984). Changing "unchangeable" bodily processes by (hypnotic) suggestions: A new look at hypnosis, cognitions, imagining and the mind-body problem. In A. A. Sheikh, eds., *Imagery and healing* (pp. 69–128). Farmingdale, NY: Baywood Publishing Co.

Batcheldor, K. J. (1966). Report on the case of table levitation and associated phenomena. *Journal of the Society for Psychical Research* 43, 339–356.

_____. (1979). PK in sitter groups. *Psychoenergetic Systems* 3, 77–93.

_____. (1984). Contributions to the theory of PK induction from sitter-group work, *Journal of the American Society for Psychical Research* 78, 105–132.

Benson, H., with M. Stark (1996). *Timeless healing: The power and biology of belief.* New York: Scribner.

Bergman, R. L. (1973). A school for medicine men. *American Journal of Psychiatry* 130, 663–66.

Bowers, K.S. and S. LeBaron (1986). Hypnosis and hypnotizability: Implications for clinical intervention. *Hospital and Community Psychiatry* 37, 457–467.

Broddy, J. (1988). Spirits and selves in Northern Sudan: The cultural therapies of possession and trance. *American Ethnologist* 15, 4–27.

Broughton, R. (1988). If you want to know how it works, first find out what it's for (Presidential Address). In D. H. Weiner and R. L. Morris, eds., *Research in parapsychology 1987* (pp. 187–202). Metuchen, NJ: Scarecrow Press.

Brown, D. P. (1992). Clinical hypnosis research since 1986, In E. Fromm and M. R. Nash, eds., *Contemporary hypnosis research* (pp. 427–458). New York: Guilford Press.

Buss, D. M. (1998). *Evolutionary psychology: The new science of the mind.* Boston: Allyn and Bacon.

Cardeña, E. (1994). The domain of dissociation. In S. J. Lynn and J. W. Rhue, eds., *Dissociation: Clinical and theoretical perspectives* (pp. 15–31). New York: Guilford Press.

Chapman L., H. Goodell, and H. Wolff (1959). Increased inflammatory reaction induced by central nervous system activity. *Transactions of the Association of American Physicians* 72, 84–110.

Csordas, T.J. (1997). *The sacred self: A cultural phenomenology of charismatic healing.* Berkeley, CA: University of California Press.

Daly, M. and M. Wilson (1998). The evolutionary social psychology of family violence. In C. B. Crawford and D. L. Kribs, eds., *Handbook of evolutionary psychology: Ideas, issues, and applications* (pp. 431–456). Mahwah, NJ: Erlbaum.

Dawkins, R. (1999). *The selfish gene.* New York: Oxford University Press.

de Montellano, B. O. (1975). Empirical Aztec medicine. *Science* 188, 215–20.

Duncan, J., and S. Kang (1985). Using Buddhist ritual activities as a foundation for a mental health program for Cambodian children in foster care. Unpublished manuscript (as cited by Williams and Berry 1991).

Eisenberg, J. F., N. A. Muckenhirn, and R. Rudran (1978). The relation between ecology and social structure in primates. In N. Korn, ed., *Human evolution: Readings for physical anthropology* (pp. 114–139). New York: Holt, Rinehart and Winston.

Emmons, C. F. (1982). *Chinese ghosts and ESP: A study of paranormal beliefs and experiences.* Metuchen, NJ: Scarecrow Press.

Fink, D. L. (1988). The core self: A developmental perspective on the dissociative disorders. *Dissociation* 1, 43–47.

Finkler, K. (1985). *Spiritualist healers in Mexico: Successes and failures of alternative therapeutics.* New York: Bergin & Garvey.

Friedman, H., T. W. Klein, and A. L. Friedman, eds. (1996). *Psychoneuroimmunology, stress, and infection,* Boca Raton, FL: CRC Press.

Garrison, V. (1977). The "Puerto Rican syndrome" in psychiatry and Expiritismo. In V. Crapanzano and V. Garrison, eds., *Case studies in spirit possession* (pp. 383–449). New York: John Wiley and Sons.

Gaulin, S. J. C. and D. H. McBurney (2001). Psychology: An evolutionary approach. Upper Saddle River, NJ: Prentice Hall.

Goodwin, J., S. Hill, and R. Attias (1990). Historical and folk techniques of exorcism: Applications to the treatment of dissociative disorders. *Dissociation* 3, 94–101.

Graffin, N. F., W. J. Ray, and R. Lundy (1995). EEG concomitants of hypnosis and hypnotic susceptibility. *Journal of Abnormal Psychology* 104, 123–131.

Greeley, A. M. (1975). *Sociology of the paranormal: A reconnaissance.* Beverly Hills, CA: Sage Publications.

_____. (1987). Mysticism goes mainstream. *American Health* 6, 47–49.

Harner, M. J. (1973). *Hallucinogens and shamanism.* London: Oxford University Press.

Hartmann, E. (1991). *Boundaries in the mind: A new psychology of personality.* New York: Basic.

Haustater, G., and S. B. Hrdy (1984). *Infanticide: Comparative and evolutionary perspectives.* New York: Aldine.

Hoskovec, J., and D. Svorad (1969). The relationship between human and animal hypnosis, *American Journal of Clinical Hypnosis* 11, 180–182.

Hufford, D. J. (1982). *The terror that comes in the night: An experience-centered study of supernatural assault traditions.* Philadelphia: University of Pennsylvania Press.

Irwin, H. J. (1992). Origins and functions of paranormal belief: The role of childhood trauma and interpersonal control. *Journal of the American Society for Psychical Research* 86, 199–208.

_____. (1993). Belief in the paranormal: A review of the empirical literature. *Journal of the American Society for Psychical Research* 87, 1–39.

_____. (1994) Proneness to dissociation and traumatic childhood events. *Journal of Nervous and Mental Disease* 182, 456–460.

Kapferer, B. (1983). *A celebration of demons: Exorcism and the aesthetics of healing in Sri Lanka.* Bloomington: Indiana University Press.

Kent, A., and G. Waller (1998). The impact of emotional abuse: An extension of the Child Abuse and Trauma Scale. *Child Abuse and Neglect* 22, 393–399.

Kleinman, A., and L. H. Sung (1979). Why do indigenous practitioners successfully heal? A follow-up study of indigenous practice in Taiwan. *Social Science and Medicine* 13B, 7–26.

Kleinman, A. (1980). *Patients and healers in the context of culture: An exploration of the borderland between anthropology, medicine, and psychiatry.* Berkeley, CA: University of California Press.

Krippner, S. (1994). Cross-cultural treatment perspectives on dissociation disorders, In S. J. Lynn and J. W. Rhue, eds., *Dissociation: Clinical and theoretical perspectives* (pp. 338–361). New York: Guilford Press.

Krippner, S., and B. Colodzin (1989). Multi-cultural methods of treating Vietnam veterans with post-traumatic stress disorder. *International Journal of Psychosomatics* 36, 79–85.

Krippner, S., and P. Welch (1992). *Spiritual dimensions of healing: From native shamanism to contemporary health care.* New York: Irvington.

Kakarec, K., and M. A. Persinger (1990). Electroencephalographic validation of a temporal lobe signs inventory in a normal population. *Journal of Research in Personality* 24, 323–337.

Kumar, V. K., and R. J. Pekala (2001). Relation of hypnosis-specific attitudes and behaviors to paranormal beliefs and experiences: A technical review, in J. Houran and R. Lange, eds., *Hauntings and poltergeists: Multidisciplinary perspectives* (pp. 260–279). Jefferson, NC: McFarland.

Laderman, C. (1991). *Taming the wind of desire: Psychology, medicine, and aesthetics in Malay shamanistic performance.* Berkeley, CA: University of California Press.

_____. (1987). The ambiguity of symbols in the structure of healing. *Social Science and Medicine* 24, 293–301.

Lambo, T. A. (1974). Psychotherapy in Africa. *Psychotherapy and Psychosomatics* 24, 311–326.

Lewis, I. M. (1971). *Ecstatic religion: An anthropological study of spirit possession and shamanism.* Middlesex, UK: Penguin.

Lewis-Williams, J. D., and T. A. Dowson (1988). The signs of all times: Entoptic phenomena in Upper Paleolithic art. *Current Anthropology* 29, 201–245.

Ludwig, A. (1966). Altered states of consciousness. *Achieves of General Psychiatry* 15, 225–234.

Mac Hovec, F. J. (1975). Hypnosis before Mesmer. *American Journal of Clinical Hypnosis* 17, 215–220.

Margolis, C. G., B. B. Domangue, C. Ehleben, and L. Shrier (1983). Hypnosis in the early treatment of burns: A pilot study. *American Journal of Clinical Hypnosis* 26, 9–15.

McClenon, J. (1984). *Deviant science: The case of parapsychology.* Philadelphia: University of Pennsylvania Press.

_____. (1994). *Wondrous events: Foundations of religious belief.* Philadelphia: University of Pennsylvania Press.

_____. (1997a). Shamanic healing, human evolution, and the origin of religion, *Journal for the Scientific Study of Religion* 36, 345–354.

_____. (1997b). Spiritual healing and folklore research: Evaluating the hypnosis/placebo theory. *Alternative Therapies in Health and Medicine* 3, 61–66.

_____. (2000a). Narrative collection — experiences of family violence. Unpublished collections of narrative accounts of family violence, Elizabeth City State University, Elizabeth City, NC.

_____. (2000b). Content analysis of an anomalous memorate collection: Testing hypotheses regarding universal features. *Sociology of Religion* **61**, 155–169.

_____. (2001). The sociological investigation of haunting cases. In J. Houran and R. Lange, eds., *Hauntings and poltergeists: Multidisciplinary perspectives* (pp. 62–81). Jefferson, NC: McFarland.

_____. (2002a). *Wondrous healing: Shamanism, human evolution and the origin of religion*. DeKalb, IL: Northern Illinois University Press.

_____. (2002b). Content analysis of an anomalous experience collection: Evaluating evolutionary perspectives. *Journal of Parapsychology* **66**, 291–316.

_____. (in press). How shamanism began: Human evolution, dissociation, and anomalous experience. In J. Houran and R. Lange, eds., *From shamans to scientists: Humanity's search for spirits*.

McClenon, J., M. Roig, M.D. Smith, and G. Ferrier (in press). The coverage of parapsychology in introductory psychology textbooks: 1990–2002. *Journal of Parapsychology*.

Millar, M. G., and K. U. Millar (1996). The effects of direct and indirect experience on affective and cognitive responses and the attitude-behavior relation. *Journal of Experimental Social Psychology* **32**, 561–579.

Moerman, D. E. (1979). Anthropology of Symbolic Healing. *Current Anthropology* **20**, 59–80.

Moore, L. E., and J. Z. Kaplan (1983). Hypnotically accelerated wound healing. *American Journal of Clinical Hypnosis* **26**, 16–19.

Morgan, A. H. (1973). The heritability of hypnotic susceptibility in twins. *Journal of Abnormal and Social Psychology* **82**, 55–61.

Neel, J. V. (1978). Lessons from a primitive people, In N. Korn, ed., *Human evolution: Readings for physical anthropology* (pp. 346–364). New York: Holt, Rinehart & Winston.

Owen, I. M., with M. Sparrow (1976). *Conjuring up Philip: An adventure in psychokinesis*. New York: Harper & Row.

Palmer, J[ack] A., and L. K. Palmer (2002). Evolutionary psychology: The ultimate origins of human behavior. Boston: Allyn & Bacon.

Palmer, J[ohn]. A. (1979). A community mail survey of psychic experiences. *Journal of the American Society for Psychical Research* **73**, 221–251.

Pekala, R. J., V. K. Kumar, and G. Marcano (1995). Anomalous/paranormal experience, hypnotic susceptibility, and dissociation. *Journal of the American Society for Psychical Research* **89**, 313–332.

Pekala, R. J., V. K. Kumar, and J. Cummings (1992). Types of high hypnotically-susceptible individuals and reported attitudes and experiences of the paranormal and anomalous. *Journal of the American Society for Psychical Research* **86**, 135–150.

Persinger, M. A. (1984a). People who report religious experiences may display enhanced temporal lobe signs. *Perceptual and Motor Skills* **58**, 963–975.

_____. (1984b). Propensity to report paranormal experiences is correlated with temporal lobe signs. *Perceptual and Motor Skills* **59**, 583–586.

Persinger, M. A., and K. Makarec (1987). Temporal lobe epileptic signs and correlative behaviors displayed by normal populations, *Journal of General Psychology* **114**, 179–195.

_____, _____. (1993). Complex partial epileptic signs as a continuum from normals to epileptics: Normative data and clinical populations. *Journal of Clinical Psychology* **49**, 33–45.

Persinger, M. A., and P. M. Valliant (1985). Temporal lobe signs and reports of subjective paranormal experiences in normal population: A replication. *Perceptual and Motor Skills* **60**, 903–909.

Putnam, F. W. (1985) Dissociation as a response to extreme trauma. In R. P. Kluft, ed., *Childhood antecedents of multiple personality* (pp. 66–97). Washington: American Psychiatric Press.

_____. (1991). Dissociative disorders in children and adolescents: A developmental perspective. *Psychiatric Clinics of North America* **14**, 519–531.

Richards, D. (1991). A study of the correlations between subjective psychic experiences and dissociative experiences. *Dissociation* **4**, 83–91.

Roig, M., H. Icochea, and A. Cuzzucoli (1991). Coverage of parapsychology in introductory psychology textbooks. *Teaching of Psychology* **18**, 157–160.

Ross, C. A. (1997). *Dissociative identity disorder: Diagnosis, clinical features, and treatment of multiple personality*. New York: John Wiley & Sons.

Ross, C. A., L. Ryan, H. Voight, and L. Eide (1991). High and low dissociators in a college student population. *Dissociation* **4**, 147–151.

Ross, C. A., and S. Joshi (1992). Paranormal experiences in the general population. *Journal of Nervous and Mental Disease* **180**, 357–361.

Sanders, B., and E. Becker-Lausen (1995). The measurement of psychological maltreatment: Early data on the Child Abuse and Trauma Scale. *Child Abuse and Neglect* **19**, 315–323.

Scheper-Hughes, N. (1992). *Death without weeping: The violence of everyday life in Brazil*. Berkeley, CA: University of California Press.

Sharon, D. (1978). *Wizard of the four winds: A shaman's story*. New York: The Free Press.

Spiegel, D. (1986). Dissociating damage. *American Journal of Clinical Hypnosis* **29**, 123–131.

Spiegel, D., and E. Vermutten (1994). Physiological correlates of hypnosis and dissociation, In David Spiegel, ed., *Dissociation: Culture, mind, and body* (pp. 185–209). Washington: American Psychiatric Press.

Stanford, R. G. (1974a). An experimentally testable model for spontaneous psi events I. Extrasensory events. *Journal of the American Society for Psychical Research* **68**, 34–57.

_____. (1974b). An experimentally testable model for spontaneous psi events II. Psychokinetic events. *Journal of the American Society for Psychical Research* **68**, 321–356.

_____. (1977). Conceptual frameworks of contemporary psi research. In B. B. Wolman, ed., *Handbook of parapsychology* (pp. 823–858). New York: Van Nostrand Reinhold.

_____. (1990). An experimentally testable model for spontaneous psi events: A review of related evidence and concepts from parapsychology and other sciences. In S. Krippner, ed., *Advances in parapsychological research 6* (pp. 54–167). Jefferson, NC: McFarland.

Swatos, W. H. Jr., and L. R. Gissurarson (1997). *Icelandic spiritualism: Mediumship and modernity in Iceland*. New Brunswick, NJ: Transaction.

Targ, E., M. Schlitz, and H. J. Irwin (2000). In E. Cardeña, S. J. Lynn, and S. Krippner, eds., *Varieties of anomalous experience: Examining the scientific evidence* (pp. 219–252). Washington: American Psychological Association.

Thalbourne, M. A., L. Bartemucci, P. S. Delin, B. Fox, and O. Nofi (1997). Transliminality: Its nature and correlates. *Journal of the American Society for Psychical Research* **91**, 305–331.

Thalbourne, M. A., and P. S. Delin (1994). A common thread underlying belief in the paranormal, creative personality, mystical experience and psychopathology. *Journal of Parapsychology* **58**, 3–38.

_____, _____. (1999). Transliminality: Its relation to dream life, religiosity, and mystical experience. *International Journal for the Psychology of Religion* **9**, 35–43.

Thalbourne, M. A., J. Houran, and S. E. Crawley (2003). Childhood trauma as a possible antecedent of transliminality. *Psychological Reports* **93** 687–674.

Trivers, R. L. (1974). Parent-offsping conflict. *American Zoologist* **14**, 249–264.

Ullman, M. (1947). Herpes simplex and second degree burn induced under hypnosis. *American Journal of Psychiatry* **103**, 823–830.

Utts, J. (2001). Annual Report for 2001, Durham, NC: Parapsychological Association.

Varvoglis, M. P. (1999). Annual Report for 1999, Durham, NC: Parapsychological Association.

Veith, I. (1965). *Hysteria: The history of a disease*. Chicago: University of Chicago Press.

_____. (1977). Four thousand years of hysteria. In M. J. Horowitz, ed., *Hysterical personality* (pp. 7–93). New York: Jason Aronson.

Vogel, V. (1970). *American Indian medicine*. New York: Ballantine.

Völgyesi, F. A. (1966). *Hypnosis on man and animals*, (2nd ed.), revised in collaboration with G. Klumbies. Baltimore: Williams & Wilkins.

Williams, C. L., and J. W. Berry (1991) Primary prevention of acculturative stress among refugees: Application of psychological theory and practice. *American Psychologist* **46**, 632–641.

Wickramasekera, I. E. (1987). Risk factors leading to chronic stress-related symptoms. *Advances: Journal of the Institute for the Advancement of Health* **4**, 9–35.

_____. (1988). *Clinical behavioral medicine: Some concepts and procedures*. New York: Plenum.

Winkelman, M. (1992). *Shamans, priests and witches: A cross-cultural study of magico-religious practitioners*. Tempe, AZ: Arizona State University Anthropological Research Papers No. 44.

_____. (2000). *Shamanism: The neural ecology of consciousness and healing*. Westport, CT: Bergin & Garvey.

Young, D., and J. Goulet, eds. (1994). *Being changed by cross-cultural experience: The anthropology of extraordinary experience*. Peterborough, Ontario: Broadview.

Experiential Research: Unveiling Psi Through Phenomenological Enquiry

Pamela Rae Heath

This chapter describes a phenomenological approach to psi, and an effort is made to show how the subjective component (the personal experience) of the paranormal is as important as the objective component. Dr. Pamela Heath explains the origins of phenomenology and its contribution to parapsychology. She then outlines a procedure for undertaking a phenomenological investigation of psi, and gives examples whereby general meanings attached to psi by the psi experient have been uncovered, such as feelings of connection and unity, peak emotions, and "knowing." Dr Heath concludes that ESP and PK do not seem to be described all that differently by psi experients—they may be the same process. By using phenomenological enquiry we may discover what it is that inhibits ESP and PK performance, and discern the key differences between beginners and adepts of paranormal experience. (Editors)

Schmeidler (1988) was one of the first to point out that parapsychology has long held the unspoken theory that "psi is a psychological function" (p. 6). The idea that psi could be a general, if often latent, human ability would seem to be supported by a number of facts. First, similar forms of activity appear across a wide range of cultures and times (Gauld and Cornell 1979; Robinson 1981). Second, the psychological nature of psi is consistent with experimental findings showing that it responds similarly to other human abilities, and appears to be influenced by normal psychological variables, such as mood, emotion, motivation, and belief (Schmeidler 1988; Stanford 1986). Third, the average college student or person off the street can often successfully perform psi. It would therefore appear to exist commonly, even if it is often weak in nature.

One might ask why psychic phenomena have often been described as elusive if they are normal in people. This perception may in part be due to the fact that psi is, in large part, subjective in nature. Quantitative experimental research is the only way of determining proof and cause and effect relationships, but it is best suited towards dealing with objective phenomena. Phenomenology, on the other hand, is a relatively new technique that was developed specifically for studying subjective phenomena (Polkinghorne 1989). It can be thought of as a rigorous form of content analysis that is both qualitative and descriptive. It is important to note that phenomenology considers every experience to be valid in and of itself. Proof is not an issue. Instead, this method is concerned only with exploring the underlying meaning of what was felt and capturing its true essence in words. This can in turn lead to new insights not only about the experience itself, but also how one might better approach the topic using qualitative and quantitative methods.

Background to Phenomenology

In order better to understand the value and significance of phenomenology, it is worthwhile to take a moment to review its history and how the technique is actually performed. German philosopher Edmund Husserl (1859–1938) is considered to be the founder of this form of inquiry (Eckartsberg 1998a). He developed the idea that the individual cannot be considered separately from his or her own world. Instead, the two are an indissoluble unity. Husserl proposed that the meaning of things could thus only be grasped through the exploration of human consciousness.

Phenomenology was later enriched by the work of Martin Heidegger (Alessi 1994; Eckartsberg 1998a). He expanded on the idea that the Cartesian subject-object split is a false one, proposing that people are deeply involved in a complex dynamic network of interdependent ongoing relationships that demand response and participation. It is through this participation that our world comes into existence. Thus, Heidegger believed that we are both the illuminator, and the creator, of our own world(s).

The existential-phenomenological approach in psychology assumes that identically named experiences refer to the same reality (Eckartsberg 1998a). This is to say that the basic essence of something, such as loneliness, would be the same from one person to the next. An investigation can either focus on the general structure of a phenomenon (such as loneliness itself), or on a process structure that describes the unfolding of the phenomenon in terms of sequentially aligned essential stages (e.g., development and manifestation of loneliness). Afterward, anyone who reads the resulting description should be able to understand exactly what that experience feels like.

The first step in performing a phenomenological investigation is to formulate a question, such as, "what is the experience of ..." (Eckartsberg 1998a). The investigator then gathers a number of naïve descriptions from people who either are having, or have had, the experience being investigated (Polkinghorne 1989). There are three kinds of sources that can be used to generate descriptions of the experience: 1) from the researcher's own personal experiences and self-reflections; 2) from the written material or words of study participants; and 3) from depictions of the experience in research, fictional literature, art, dance, poetry, etc. (Eckartsberg 1998b). The richer, more detailed, and more dramatic the experiential descriptions are, the better will be the researcher's chances of drawing meaningful conclusions from the data. Once this is done, the investigator (who is considered a participant observer) follows a set of explicit steps to analyze the descriptions.

Studying consciousness is inherently problematic in that it is an activity (not an object), involves complex integrated modes of presentation and levels, and assumes that we do not have direct access to anyone's consciousness but our own (Polkinghorne 1989). Bias is always a hazard that must be guarded against. Thus, to understand a given phenomenon, the investigator must first suspend his or her preconceptions and presuppositions (Valle, King, and Halling 1989). This is done by "bracketing," or laying those preconceived thoughts and beliefs about the experience out in as clear and complete a form as possible. Only then can the researcher have a chance of accurately representing the experience from the participant's own frame of reference. Remaining detached and distanced from the phenomenon is impossible because the researcher is intimately connected to the experience (Polkinghorne 1989). Bracketing is one of the key features of phenomenological methodology. It should be noted that bracketing is not simply done before the interviews are performed, but should occur repeatedly throughout the data analysis.

The second method of preventing bias is the use of imaginative variation. This involves playing games with the sentences to see if they could have more than one possible meaning. Where a sentence is found which could have more than one possible meaning, the descriptions are checked to see whether other sentences can clarify it. If the import remains in doubt, the participant is asked to please explain what they meant, or "say more about that."

There are four stages to the data analysis (Giorgi 1985). First, the entire description is read from beginning to end as many times as are necessary to get a sense of the whole. These meaning units are constituents, rather than elements, because they are context-dependent. Reflection and imaginative variation allow the researcher to elucidate the psychological aspects that are involved. Second, the same descriptions are read more slowly, delineating each time that a transition in meaning is perceived, to obtain a series of meaning units or constituents. Third, all of the units are reviewed for their underlying psychological insights. Finally, the previously achieved insights are synthesized and integrated into a consistent statement or description of the experience. In the final synthesis, individual themes can be clustered into general themes, while trying to ensure that no important aspects of the experience have been overlooked or left out (Polkinghorne 1989). The last step is necessary because this research is usually conducted with more than one participant, and each one will vary from the others.

Phenomenology differs from many other forms of data analysis in that to be done well, the investigator must alternate back and forth between what has traditionally been thought of as left- and right-brain functioning. Giorgi (1985) stated:

> What differentiates the phenomenologically inspired method is the fact that a disciplined spontaneity is allowed to function whereby one first discovers the relevant meaning unit, or its category, and only later, based upon a subsequent analysis, explicates its actual full import.
>
> In a certain sense the procedure being outlined here is the practice of science within the "context of discovery" rather than in the "context of verification" [p. 14].

The end product of the study should be a report that gives an accurate, clear, and articulate description of the experience (Eckartsberg 1998a). The idea is to communicate the experience to the readers in a way that gives them a better understanding of it. Thus, phenomenology uses reflective analysis to translate the everyday level of life-text narrative language into structural conceptual language reflective of the universally valid meaning of a given experience. Having once read the end description, it should be possible to have a real sense of the essence of that experience — to know on a gut level what it must have been like for the experiencer.

Phenomenology and the Paranormal

As noted previously, the ubiquitous nature of psi reports, their consistent patterns transtemporally and transculturally, and the experimental findings indicative of the notion that most (if not all) individuals have some psychic ability, and that this talent is affected by the same psychological factors that affect other normal human abilities, suggests that it is appropriate to look at this area of question as we would any other human experience. Indeed, considering the subjective, personal nature of psychic experiences, phenomenology would seem to be an ideal technique for this form of research. However, there have been few such studies to date. Hanson and Klimo (1998) looked at synchronicity, Barrett (1996) analyzed channeling, West (1998) described near-death experiences, Reed (1996a, 1996b) studied apparent ESP experiences, Murphy and White (1978, 1995) investigated exceptional human functioning in sports, and Heath (1999, 2000) examined PK experiences. These studies vary somewhat in how rigorously phenomenological technique was applied and to what level the experience was broken down. Nonetheless, it is worth looking at what each of them reveals about transcendent phenomena.

Synchronicity

Hanson and Klimo (1998) investigated the experience of synchronicity, which they described as, "coincidence that is acausal, wherein certain events do not seem to be connected by normal causal means, and that is also particularly meaningful to the experiencer" (p. 281). They stated that synchronicity "appears to be nonordinary or paranormal in nature" (p. 306). Considering that synchronicity has also been proposed as an acausal theory of psi, it is appropriate to consider this study as looking at a form of psi.

Hanson and Klimo (1998) analyzed the descriptions of 28 participants who had experienced being carried along by a series or flow of unforeseen circumstances or events which ended in a right and desired outcome. They found a total of 16 constituent themes. All of the subjects had the following constituents: 1) there was a point of embarkation; 2) a desire, need, or goal was identified; 3) there was a period of gathering information, both factual and intuitive; 4) action was taken toward the desire, need, or goal; 5) a change occurred; 6) there was assignment of meaning; and 7) circumstances or events led to a desired outcome. Another nine constituents were not universally experienced. These included: 1) 70 percent of the subjects had resistance, either by self or others, to the change; 2) 45 percent surrendered control; 3) 22 percent had a time lapse before the change; 4) 61 percent experienced inner, or intuitive, promptings; 5) 56 percent had a synchronistic occurrence, either singular or as a chain of events; 6) 96 percent felt they took a risk; 7) 46 percent had a peak experience, spiritual experience, or transpersonal state of consciousness; 8) 43 percent felt faith or trust; and 9) 57 percent speculated on the future.

In their integration and analysis, Hanson and Klimo (1998) suggested that individuals co-create their own lives, and that synchronistic teleology "includes a dynamic pattern of directional, purposeful movement with synchronistic aspects, and with less or no presence of efficacy of conscious intention" (p. 302). They pointed out that this kind of experience is compatible with both ancient Eastern philosophy and contemporary physics, including such models as Bohm's holomovement.

The fact that these events were intensely meaningful would seem to be an important one. Irwin (1994) noted that personal meaning was a key element in Louisa Rhine's compilation of case studies, saying:

> The PK experiences in Rhine's case collection were marked by personal significance. Indeed, Rhine (1963b) appears to have assumed this to be a necessary or even defining feature: she refers to the PK cases as "unexplained physical effects seeming to have personal meaning" [Irwin 1994, p. 30].

This factor of personal meaning is one which appears to be important to the manifestation of spontaneous PK (or ESP), whether it occurs as an isolated episode or recurrently. The other, less common, constituents of surrender, sense of intuition or "knowing," altered states of consciousness (ASC), and trust also appear as factors in other psi studies. Furthermore, there is the implication that these events often had a positive impact on the experiencers.

Channeling

Barrett (1996) used phenomenological technique to study nine mediums who felt they were receiving, or channeling, information from paranormal sources. For fairly obvious reasons she only used subjects who were conscious of their trance experience. Moreover, Barrett interviewed not only the mediums, but their sources as well. Ten essential themes emerged. These can be summarized as the medium: (1) perceived the source as in a close relationship to them, but as a separate, nonphysical or nonhuman being; (2) felt in control of staging the transmission; (3) received and expressed information from the source; (4) felt a sense of cooperating with the source in a working partnership; (5) had a mental and emotional detachment from the channeled information; (6) experienced physical sensations related to the transmission; and (7) had positive feelings about the experience.

The sources, as interviewed through the channels, reported very similar experiences (Barrett 1996). However, they differed in describing: (1) a sense of adjusting their vibrational frequency to communicate with the channel; (2) monitoring and protecting the channel's body and mind; (3) fulfilling a previous commitment; and (4) viewing channeling as a learning experience.

It is difficult to say how much the sense of having a close connection and feeling positive emotions, including love, were a cause, or a byproduct of, these apparent channel-source relationships. It is interesting to note that several mediums stated that "channeling helped them to balance their logical, left-brain activity in a constructive way" (Barrett 1996, p. 164). This implies that the mediums saw paranormal communication as a form of right-brain activity. It is not currently known whether there is an actual shift in brain activity during psi activity.

Elements that appeared in Barrett's study which appear to be common to other psi constituents uncovered phenomenologically include the sense of connection (to the entity being channeled), sense of obtaining information intuitively, being detached, having physical sensations, and that the experience had a positive impact on the channeler. It is also possible, based on their statements about balancing their logical left brain, that the mediums were suspending their intellects during the experience. The constituents of the entities being channeled would appear to be less similar to those of other psi phenomena, perhaps in part because the process is seen as more of a normal job from their viewpoint. Nonetheless, there may be some sense of energy, guiding the process, and focusing awareness on the task.

Near-Death Experiences

West (1998) performed a phenomenological study of 10 individuals (six men and four women) who claimed to have encountered a divine presence during their near-death experiences (NDE). This study would seem to tie in to psychical research on the topic of whether there could be survival of bodily death, as NDEs suggest that the mind may not be limited to the physical body. West found seven comprehensive constituent themes. These were: (1) leaving the body, traveling, and returning to the body; (2) experiencing infinity with a surrender to or merger with a higher power; (3) experiencing divine refuge or homecoming with feelings of love, acceptance, peace, and joy; (4) experiencing absolute truth and divine knowledge; (5) recognizing the experience as ineffable; (6) perceiving a personal message; (7) seeing the experience as transformative (West 1998).

Common themes between the NDE and other psi experiences include what would appear to be an ASC, the sense of surrender, merger (connection), feeling peak emotions, having a sense of "knowing"—in this case of higher truth. Furthermore, there was an intrinsic meaningfulness to the event, which related to it having a positive impact. West (1998) made the valuable observation that:

> Mere words and the normal avenues of human communication are found to be quite limiting. ... If, indeed, we use language to help ourselves make sense of our experiences, the fact that this experience is largely ineffable for those who undergo it may account for the difficulty and extended time period required in integrating the encounter into one's personality and belief system [pp. 399–400].

Although the ASC may itself be hard to describe, the difficulty of verbally capturing an experience may also be in part due to current limits in our everyday language. We have relatively little in the way of terminology that can be used to express spiritual occurrences and ASC. This point is a significant one, as it has the potential to impact all phenomenological studies on experiences involving ASC—which would certainly include psi.

ESP Experiences

Several nonrigorous studies have looked at the experience of what might be ESP. Reed (1996a, 1996b) investigated ordinary individuals who felt they were in psychic contact with another person during workshops where they were paired up and asked to imagine being in contact with the other person. He then obtained descriptions of this experience from participants, and, based on that material and his own experiences, boiled the material down to three phases.

First, there was a contact phase, which could involve images of light, warmth (often in the hands), wind, or other energetic images suggestive of merger. Some participants also felt a barrier during this phase which then disappeared.

Second, there was a period of mild dissociation, or a lapse of attention or consciousness, which he considered to be a creative time.

Third, there was a narrative fantasy, or experience of the "couple." Some subjects reported feeling their mind simply wandering during the exercise, which Reed (1996a) interpreted as a defensive reaction to the potential intimacy of contact.

Reed felt that real ESP occurred because the subjective feedback on the "psychic readings" performed during these imaginal dyadic couplings is that accurate information is being transmitted by virtual strangers. One of the more interesting findings of these studies, was that people felt a sense of satisfaction, in addition to a sense of greater closeness to their partner.

Reed (1996b) also looked at pairs who practiced imaginal encounters separately from their homes every day for a month, and found their diaries displayed apparent synchronicity, though he was unable to figure out a statistical way to analyze the data. Reed believed that this experience had transformative power. However, he admitted that it may not be a case of psychic material being transmitted, so much as a case of "one person's experience synchronistically 'reminds' the other person of something similar" (p. 224). These experiences are interesting, however, because their description implies that there may be a shift in the state of consciousness during the second phase which is significant for being able to proceed to making a connection, whether it be called synchronistic sympathetic vibration or ESP.

PK and Exceptional Human Functioning in Sport

Heath (2003) informally reviewed the ESP experiences casually mentioned by the participants in her PK study. This came about because two of Heath's (1999) participants stated that they felt PK and ESP were identical experiences. She went back to her original data to analyze the ESP experiences that, although unsolicited, had been reported to her. She found that all of the constituents of the PK experience also appeared in the ESP experiences. These included: 1) an ASC; 2) connection; 3) dissociation; 4) suspension of the intellect; 5) feeling emotion; 6) having a sense of energy; 7) physical sensations; 8) focused awareness; 9) trust in the process; 10) openness to the experience; 11) knowing; 12) guiding the process; and 13) impact.

It should be noted that this study looked at a limited number of descriptions and may have missed some unique aspects that could occur in ESP experiences. However, should the two experiences be the same, it would explain why RNG/REG experiences— thought by some to represent ESP — were identical to macro-PK ones. Although this is by no means a definitive or adequate phenomenological study of ESP, it does support the idea that there could indeed be one fundamental process going on.

There have been several phenomenological studies of the "zone," or that state where the athlete may be capable of exceptional performance, in sports. Alessi (1994) performed a phenomenological study on the experience of "breakaway into the zone." She interviewed 16 athletes and found that the experiences tended to have a strong impact on the individual's life. Alessi (1994) found:

> The core themes derived from the participant interviews include: (1) sensation of moving in a flowing, effortless manner with no pain or discomfort; (2) total immersion and clarity of focus; (3) athlete overcomes all fears, inhibitions, and negative thinking; (4) experience is marked by extraordinary strength and endurance, heightened energy, and an increased ability to function; (5) fusion of the mind-body dichotomy; (6) alterations in temporal and visual perception; (7) transcendent dimension involving changes in spatial and auditory perception; (8) premonition, tacit awareness, intuitive sense; (9) experience was unplanned and occurred in stages; and (10) joyful, euphoric, and personally satisfying [p. 164–165].

Although this study was not oriented towards psychic experiences in sports, it seems nonetheless significant that intuitive knowing appeared. It may not be surprising then that constituents such as an ASC, connection, sense of energy and peak emotions also appeared.

Murphy and White (1978, 1995) used in-depth interviews to look at the qualitative state that an athlete experiences as the "zone" where he or she is capable of extraordinary feats—which frequently sound as if they involved PK. They noted the same core themes as reported by Alessi. Interviewees frequently reported feelings of well-being, calm, peace, stillness, detachment, freedom, weightlessness, floating, ecstasy, power, control, being in the present, instinctive action, a sense of mystery, awe, immortality, and unity. Occasionally, athletes also noted that time appeared to have slowed down or stopped. Many of these descriptions overlap with the self-reported qualitative experience of PK performers, in particular the calm, detachment, experience of peak emotions, and sense of connection or unity.

Sports training shares similarities with martial arts training, in developing relaxation, concentration, the use of breathing, mental emptying, and rhythm (Murphy and White 1995). There are numerous reports of sports figures being able to successfully predict scores, plays, and outcomes, though it is hard to say how much this represents self-fulfilling prophecy rather than precognition. Nonetheless, there seem to be more reports of accurate premonitions, seeing and communicating with nonphysical beings, and other events suggestive of enhanced psi functioning in solitary sports such as solo flights or sea voyages, mountain climbing, and expeditions to the poles of the Earth. One might postulate that the isolation and sensory deprivation in these pursuits could create a ganzfeld-like effect which enhances psi functioning by reducing extraneous sensory "noise."

Heath (1999, 2000, 2003) studied the spontaneous and intentional PK experiences of eight individuals. Despite the wide range of experiences, targets, and settings, 13 core constituents (14 for intentional PK) appeared repeatedly across descriptions regardless of target type. These included having: (1) an ASC that often involved an altered sense of time; (2) a sense of connection to the target or other people, which often involved a transcendent level of interconnectedness; (3) dissociation or detachment from the individual ego identity; (4) suspension of the intellect; (5) feelings of playfulness or peak levels of emotion; (6) a sense of energy; (7) awareness that the body, or physical state, could contribute to, and reflect, PK energy; (8) focused attention; (9) trust in the process (sometimes seen as a release of effort, effortlessness, not trying too hard, and surrender to the experience); (10) investment in the outcome; (11) openness to the experience; (12) a sense of "knowing" or intuitive knowledge; and (13) a positive impact. One additional constituent, that of guiding the process (typically done in an interactive, or reactive, manner), separated intentional PK experiences from spontaneous ones. Furthermore, spontaneous experiences seemed to emphasize emotion more, and ASC less. However, whether spontaneous or intentional, these experiences sometimes had a profound effect on the people who are involved.

Many of the descriptions that resulted from Heath's (1999) interviews—such as a sense of detachment, being in the present, having an altered sense of time, and feelings of unity or connection—were the same as reported by Murphy and White (1978, 1995) and Alessi (1994) for transcendent experiences in sport. Indeed, Murphy and White (1995) documented all of the same factors except for openness to the experience in their book on transcendent experience in sports. Considering that athletes are willing to endure hours of training and ordeals of pain to excel in their sports, it seems likely that they are open to the very experience that may result in their success. Thus, it would appear that PK and transcendent experience in sports have a similar, if not identical, fundamental structure.

Several other interesting findings came out of Heath's (1999, 2003) study. First, the constituents appear to be both highly interactive and interrelated. In fact, a key finding was that the PK experience is an extremely fluid one, without the static qualities of fixed boundaries, discrete elements, or a linear configuration as is associated with normal experience. Furthermore, PK seemed to involve participating in an active process, reacting to feedback to stay in harmony with the experience. To affect something, you must first become a part of it, involving openness and connection. Likewise, trust in the process appeared to be a crucial constituent of this experience, and often appears as release of effort and attention (although it seemed of less importance when there was detached attention), although it may also be seen as, "not trying too hard," effortlessness, or surrender. Dissociation from the individual ego identity and suspending the intellect may be key aspects of trusting the process, or simply may be byproducts of accessing a transcendent level of reality where everything is interconnected. Emotion may similarly aid in letting go of the intellect (which is the prime defender or bastion of the self) and enhancing the sense of connection. Impact seemed to be a natural outcome of exposure to things that our materialist upbringing tells us cannot occur. Also, the events themselves can have intense personal meaning to those who are involved with them.

Many participants openly discussed what seemed to inhibit their ability to perform PK (Heath 1999, 2003). Because of this, Heath decided to review what factors appeared to block performance. Most often, they appeared to be those things that are the natural opposites of the constituents, such as emotional distance from the target, awareness of individual ego identity, an active intellect, seriousness, lack of trust in the process, inability to focus awareness, lack of openness, and a negative impact. Bystander hostility showed up as a new factor, and probably due to performer defensiveness and the activation of normal defense mechanisms. Investment was the only constituent that seemed capable of both helping and hindering the experience. Too much investment seemed to block trust in the process, while too little led to difficulty connecting with the target.

There is a large body of literature already that studies psi phenomena using quantitative methods, much of it of excellent quality. However, perhaps because of the long-standing emphasis on the need for proof-oriented research, there has been much less qualitative research, much of it involving the informal reports of study participants (Heath 1999). This represents a gap in our knowledge. To truly understand a phenomenon, like psi, it is important to learn its fundamental nature. In some ways, traditional research has been like the problem of the blind men feeling different parts of an elephant. Without the whole picture, it is harder to make sense of each piece that is discovered. By giving us an overview of psi, phenomenological research can provide important clues about its functioning that cannot only enhance our general understanding of the field, but also allow us to design better future research.

Looking back on the phenomenological studies that have been performed, we can see common themes emerging. Psi appears to be extremely meaningful to the experiencer, and can have a significant impact on their life. Furthermore, an ASC and feelings of connection or unity, dissociation or detachment, peak emotions, "knowing," and trust appear to be extremely important. Each of these investigations helps shed light not only on the individual experiences themselves, but on transcendent experiences (of which psi is a part) in general. Unfortunately, phenomenological studies can be difficult to perform and time intensive. Compounding the problems, there are currently not many individuals trained in using the technique who are working in this area.

The Future

The future of phenomenological inquiry in psi would seem to be a bright one, with a number of promising topics as yet untouched. Many individual manifestations of psi — such as remote viewing, premonitions, out-of-body experiences, teleportation, bilocation, RSPK, and materialization, to name just a few — have never been studied at all phenomenologically. Furthermore, future phenomenological studies on ESP could help answer one of the questions currently debated in the literature — whether or not ESP and PK are truly different, or in fact one single process. Should they indeed turn out to be the same, not only could their respective literatures be combined, meaning that what has already been "proven" for ESP could perhaps automatically be applied for PK and vice versa, but it could perhaps drastically change our experimental approach. No longer would researchers need to worry about separating out one process from the other.

Another way in which this phenomenological research could greatly benefit us is by allowing us to better understand ESP and PK inhibition. Knowing what diminishes success would allow us to design experiments that obtain greater or more consistent effect sizes. Likewise, looking at how psi experiences vary between beginners and adept performers could shed light on how this ability develops and changes over time. The possibilities for research seem endless, and hold the potential for yielding a great deal of valuable information.

REFERENCES

Alessi, L. E. (1994). Breakaway into the zone: A phenomenological investigation from the athlete's perspective. *Dissertation Abstracts International, 5602B.* (University Microfilms No. DAI9518256)

Barrett, K. (1996). A phenomenological study of channeling: The experience of transmitting information from a source perceived as paranormal. *Dissertation Abstracts International,* RA12106. (University Microfilms No. LD03475).

Eckartsberg, R. von (1998a). Introducing existential-phenomenological psychology. In R. S. Valle, ed., *Phenomenological inquiry in psychology* (pp. 3–20). New York: Plenum.

_____. (1998b). Existential-phenomenological research. In R. S. Valle, ed., *Phenomenological inquiry in psychology* (pp. 21–61). New York: Plenum.

Gauld, Alan, and A. D. Cornell (1970). *Poltergeists.* London, Boston, and Henley: Routledge & Kegan Paul.

Giorgi, Amedeo, ed. (1985). *Phenomenology and Psychological Research: Edited and with an Introduction by Amedeo Giorgi.* Pittsburgh: Duquesne University Press.

Hanson, D., and J. Klimo (1998). Toward a phenomenology of synchronicity. In R. S. Valle, ed., *Phenomenological inquiry in psychology* (pp. 281–307). New York: Plenum Press.

Heath, Pamela (1999). Into the Psychokinetic Zone: A Phenomenological Study of the Experience of Performing Psychokinesis (PK). Dissertation Abstracts International, 60-07B (University Microfilms No. 9940063).

_____. (2000). The PK zone: A phenomenological study. *Journal of Parapsychology* 64, 53–72.

_____. (2003). *The Psychokinetic Zone: A Cross-Cultural Review of Psychokinesis (PK).* New York, Lincoln, and Shanghai: iUniverse.

Irwin, H. J. (1994). The phenomenology of parapsychological experiences. In S. Krippner, ed., *Advances in parapsychological research 7* (pp. 10–76). Jefferson, NC: McFarland.

Murphy, M., and R. White (1978). *The psychic side of sports.* Reading, MA: Addison-Wesley.

_____, _____. (1995). *In the zone: Transcendent experience in sports.* New York: Penguin/Arkana.

Polkinghorne, D. E. (1989). Phenomenological research methods. In R. S. Valle and S. Halling, eds., *Existential-phenomenological perspectives in psychology* (pp. 41–60). New York: Plenum.

Reed, H. (1996a). Close encounters in the liminal zone: Experiments in imaginal communication. Part I. *Journal of Analytical Psychology* 41, 81–116.

_____. (1996b). Close encounters in the liminal zone: experiments in imaginal communication. Part II. *Journal of Analytical Psychology* 41, 203–226.

Rhine, L.E. (1963b). Auditory psi experience: Hallucinatory or physical? *Journal of Parapsychology* 27, 182–198.

Robinson, D. (1981). *To stretch a plank.* Chicago: Nelson-Hall.

Schmeidler, G. R. (1988). *Parapsychology and psychology: Matches and mismatches.* Jefferson, NC: McFarland.

Stanford, R. G. (1986). Experimental psychokinesis: A review from diverse perspectives. In B. B. Wolman, L. Dale, G. Schmeidler, and M. Ullman, eds., *Handbook of parapsychology* (pp. 324–381). Jefferson, NC: McFarland. Original work published New York: Van Nostrand Reinhold, 1977.

Valle, R. S., M. King, and S. Halling (1989). An introduction to existential-phenomenological thought in psychology. In R. S. Valle and S. Halling, eds., *Existential-phenomenological perspectives in psychology* (pp. 3–16). New York: Plenum Press.

West, T. (1998). On the encounter with a divine presence during a near-death experience: a phenomenological inquiry. In R. Valle, ed., *Phenomenological inquiry in psychology: Existential and transpersonal dimensions* (pp. 387–405). New York: Plenum.

About the Contributors

William Braud earned his Ph.D. in experimental psychology at the University of Iowa in 1967. At the University of Houston, he taught and conducted research in learning, memory, motivation, psychophysiology, and the biochemistry of memory. At the Mind Science Foundation in San Antonio, Texas, he directed research in parapsychology; health and well-being influences of relaxation, imagery, positive emotions, and intention; and psychoneuroimmunology. Currently, he is professor and research director at the Institute of Transpersonal Psychology in Palo Alto, California, where he directs doctoral dissertation research, and continues research, teaching, and writing in areas of exceptional human experiences, consciousness studies, transpersonal studies, spirituality, and expanded research methods.

Suitbert Ertel is professor emeritus of psychology at Göttingen University, Germany. He sees himself as imprinted, 1951–1957 at Münster University, by Köhler's/Metzger's Gestalt theory, one of the forerunners of systems theory and synergetics. He has added anomalistic topics to his conventional (psycholinguistic, psychometric) fields of research and obtained negative results with Sheldrake's concept of morphic fields and with the postulated Maharishi field effect. He obtained confirming results when testing Chizhevsky's heliobiological model, Gauquelin's planetary claims, and, recently, J. B. Rhine's ESP theory.

Christine Hardy is a psychological anthropologist who has conducted cross-cultural investigations into states of consciousness and techniques of mental self-control over a period of several years, during her travels in the Far East, the Middle East, and Africa. While developing her doctoral thesis for Paris University, Jussieu, she worked as research assistant at Princeton's Psychophysical Research Laboratories (PRL). She was president of Interface Psi (LRIP), a research association investigating extended psychophysical interactions and latent human potentials, for more than

10 years. To date, she has published 10 books, mainly on progressive scientific research and her own theoretical research, which she regularly presents through articles in scientific journals as well as in international conferences. In recent years, Dr. Hardy has developed a cognitive theory (semantic fields theory) based on a merging of neural nets, chaos theory and systems theory, as outlined in her book *Networks of Meaning*. She is currently president of Centre ECO-Mind, a research association, exploring mind and consciousness within a theoretical framework and through personal development techniques.

Pamela Rae Heath received her medical degree from the University of Texas Medical Branch at Galveston in 1980 and is board certified in anesthesiology. She practiced at multiple locations, including twice serving as the chief of anesthesia and spending two years working on a Navaho reservation before returning to school to receive her doctorate in psychology specializing in parapsychology in 1999 from the American School of Professional Psychology, Rosebridge campus. She is an associate member of the Parapsychological Association and on the board of directors for the California Society for Psychical Research. Dr. Heath continues to practice medicine part time, in addition to working with the Office of Paranormal Investigations and writing. Her publications include the book *Into the Psychokinetic (PK) Zone: A Phenomenological Study of the Experience of Performing Psychokinesis*, and essays in the *Journal of Parapsychology*.

Gerd H. Hövelmann studied philosophy of science at Marburg University, Germany, where he gained his M.A. in 1984. From 1984 to 1993, he was a senior research associate in the Department of Philosophy at Marburg University. Hövelmann has published over 150 articles in six languages covering a wide range of topics including the philosophy and history of science, the philosophy of language, psychology, and parapsychology. Hövelmann is founder, owner, and managing director of several firms, including a public-relations agency, a translations office, and an auction company. He is an active free-lance writer with more than 1,150 popular articles (about 18,000 manuscript pages) on matters other than science.

Stanley Krippner is the Alan W. Watts Professor of Psychology at Saybrook Graduate School, San Francisco. He is a fellow in three APA divisions, and former president of two divisions. Formerly, he was director of the Kent State University Child Study Center, Kent, Ohio, and the Maimonides

Medical Center Dream Research Laboratory, Brooklyn, New York. He is co-author of *Extraordinary Dreams* and co-editor of *Varieties of Anomalous Experience: Examining the Scientific Evidence*. Dr. Krippner has conducted workshops and seminars on dreams, hypnosis, and anomalous phenomena in 24 countries and at the last four congresses of the Interamerican Psychological Association. He has given invited addresses for the Chinese Academy of Sciences and the Russian Academy of Pedagogical Sciences. In 2002, he was awarded the American Psychological Association's Award for Contributions to International Psychology.

James McClenon is a professor of sociology at Elizabeth City State University, North Carolina. He is the author of many journal articles pertaining to the sociology of unusual experiences and the author of three books: *Deviant Science: The Case of Parapsychology, Wondrous Events: Foundations of Religious Belief*, and *Wondrous Healing: Shamanism, Human Evolution, and the Origin of Religion*. He has studied shamanism in Okinawa, Taiwan, Korea, Thailand, Sri Lanka, and the Philippines. His research areas include anomalous experience, shamanism, the sociology of the paranormal, and spiritual healing.

Robert L. Morris received an undergraduate degree in psychology from the University of Pittsburgh in 1963, and a Ph.D. in psychology from Duke University in 1969. He performed research and taught at several universities, including four years at the University of California, Santa Barbara; two years at the University of California, Irvine; four years at Syracuse University; and 16 years at the University of Edinburgh as holder of the Koestler Chair of Parapsychology. He was twice president of the Parapsychological Association, and once president of the Psychology Section of the British Association of the Advancement of Science. To our sorrow, and before this book was published, Robert Morris died suddenly in Edinburgh.

Vernon M. Neppe is the director of the Pacific Neuropsychiatric Institute in Seattle, Washington. He is also adjunct professor of psychiatry and human behavior, St. Louis University School of Medicine, St. Louis, Missouri; and clinical faculty (and formerly director, Division of Neuropsychiatry), University of Washington, Seattle, Washington. He has acted as a referee for more than a dozen scientific journals, and has over 200 publications. His published books include *Cry the Beloved Mind, Innovative Psychopharmacotherapy*, and *The Psychology of Déjà Vu*. He has served as guest editor of the *Journal of Clinical Psychiatry* and founding editor of a

South African scientific journal and on the editorial boards of several others. His major research areas include developing neuropsychiatric instruments and inventories, evaluating anomalistic psychology and pharmacological areas.

John Palmer graduated from Duke University with a B.A. in psychology and received his Ph.D. in psychology from the University of Texas at Austin. After spending two years on the psychology faculty at McGill University, he entered parapsychology on a full-time basis. He headed the graduate program in parapsychology at John F. Kennedy University, and has held research positions at the University of Virginia, University of California at Davis, and the University of Utrecht in the Netherlands. He has served twice as president of the Parapsychological Association, and is presently the director of research at the Rhine Research Center in Durham, North Carolina, where he also edits the *Journal of Parapsychology*. Dr. Palmer has published over 100 scientific articles and book chapters, and he is co-author of the book *Foundations of Parapsychology: Exploring the Boundaries of Human Capability*. His primary research interest is discovering the psychological and neurological processes associated with extrasensory perception and psychokinesis as manifested both inside and outside the laboratory.

Adrian Parker holds both a doctoral and master's degree in psychology from the University of Edinburgh, qualifying in clinical psychology in 1974 from the Tavistock Clinic, London, and obtaining his doctorate at Edinburgh in 1977. Along with Charles Honorton and William Braud, he was the first to use the ganzfeld technique as a means of producing an experimental analog of paranormal experiences in a laboratory setting. Dr. Parker and his co-workers in Stockholm and Freiburg are developing the new digital real-time ganzfeld as a means of "catching" psi-imagery exactly as it enters consciousness. He has published extensively in the area of clinical psychology and parapsychology including the book *States of Mind*. He is currently senior lecturer (associate professor) in psychology at the University of Gothenburg, Sweden, and formerly edited the *European Journal of Parapsychology*.

Dean Radin has an M.S. in electrical engineering and a Ph.D. (1979) in educational psychology, both from the University of Illinois, Champaign-Urbana. For 16 years, he has conducted experimental studies of psi phenomena in academia and industry, including appointments at Princeton University, University of Edinburgh, University of Nevada, and SRI

International. Prior to becoming president of the Boundary Institute, he was in charge of a psi research program at Interval Research Corporation in Palo Alto, California. Dr. Radin was elected president of the Parapsychological Association, an affiliate of the American Association for the Advancement of Science (AAAS), in 1988, 1993, and 1998. His research awards include the Parapsychological Association's 1996 Outstanding Achievement Award and the Rhine Research Center's Alexander Imich Award for advances in experimental parapsychology, also presented in 1996. He has appeared in dozens of television programs, most recently PBS's *Closer to Truth*. Radin is author of the award-winning book *The Conscious Universe*, and is author or co-author of over 175 journal articles and technical reports. He is currently senior scientist at the Institute of Noetic Sciences in Petaluma, California.

Fiona Steinkamp gained her Ph.D. in Continental philosophy from the University of Dundee in 1991. In 1995, she joined the Koestler Parapsychology Unit as a contract research worker focusing on precognition. From 1999 to 2001, she was invited to the Institut für Grenzgebiete der Psychologie und Psychohygiene in Freiburg (Germany) to work with Holger Boesch and Emil Boller in the area of meta-analysis. Her work has also been funded by the Bial Foundation and the Perrott-Warwick Fund. She has been published in the areas of parapsychology and philosophy, and her major credits include editing the book *Parapsychology, Philosophy and the Mind*, and her translation of the book *Clara, or, On Nature's Connection to the Spirit World*. She has a keen interest in Continental philosophy.

Lance Storm earned a B.A. (Honors) in psychology (1998) and a Ph.D. in parapsychology (2001) at University of Adelaide, South Australia. He has published in *Psychological Bulletin*, the *Journal of Parapsychology* and the Jungian journal *Quadrant*. He is on the editorial board of the *Australian Journal of Parapsychology*, and is a member of the Parapsychological Association. He is also a professional photographer and has been consulted to analyze and assess alleged paranormal photographs. He has written an introductory book on photography, and a book on the psychology and symbolism of numbers from a Jungian perspective. He is co-recipient with Dr. Michael Thalbourne of the D. Scott Rogo Award for literature (2002). In 2003, he was awarded the Gertrude R. Schmeidler Student of the Year Award for work in parapsychology. Currently, as a visiting research fellow, he is conducting parapsychological and psychophysiological research in the Department of Psychology, University of Adelaide, where he assisted Dr. Thalbourne in establishing an Anomalistic Psychology Research Unit.

Michael A. Thalbourne obtained his B.A. (Honors) degree at the University of Adelaide, South Australia, in 1976, and his Ph.D. in parapsychology at Edinburgh University in 1981. He has been published in all the major English-speaking parapsychological journals, and has written the widely used book *A Glossary of Terms Used in Parapsychology*. He is a member of the American and British Societies for Psychical Research, the Parapsychological Association, and the Australian Institute of Parapsychological Research of whose journal, the *Australian Journal of Parapsychology*, he is editor. His most recent publications are the second edition of the above-mentioned *Glossary* and the parapsychological monograph *The Common Thread Between ESP and PK*. He is currently visiting research fellow at University of Adelaide, where he is also the director of the Anomalistic Psychology Research Unit.

Robin Wooffitt is a senior lecturer in the Department of Sociology at the University of Surrey, UK. His research interests are conversation analysis and discourse analysis, and social science responses to anomalous human experiences. He is currently a Perrott Warwick Researcher with the Koestler Parapsychology Unit at the University of Edinburgh, where he is examining verbal interaction between experimenter and subject in the ganzfeld procedure.

Index

www.ingramcontent.com/pod-product-compliance
Lightning Source LLC
Chambersburg PA
CBHW030900270326
41929CB00008B/504